D1212772

Standard Catalogue of British Coins

COINS OF ENGLAND

AND
THE UNITED KINGDOM

31st Edition

Edited by
Stephen Mitchell and Brian Reeds

adapted, with additional material, from catalogues originally compiled by H. A. *and* P. J. Seaby

Seaby

An imprint of B.T. Batsford Ltd.
London

A Catalogue of the Coins of Great Britain
and Ireland
first published 1929

Standard Catalogue of British Coins
Coins of England and the United Kingdom
31st edition, 1996

4 Fitzhardinge Street
London W1H 0AH

Typeset by Data Layout Ltd, 136 Tooley Street, London
Printed and bound in the EC.
The Cromwell Press
Broughton Gifford
Melksham
Wiltshire

ISBN 0 7134 7677 X

Jacket illustration

Silver halfcrown of 1696, struck at the Chester Mint.
1996 marks the 300th anniversary of the start of the Great Recoinage, which saw the withdrawal between 1696 and 1698 of the old hammered silver coins that remained in circulation. The recoinage was undertaken by the Tower Mint with the assistance of provincial mints at Bristol, Chester, Exeter, Norwich and York.
By courtesy of the Royal Mint.

CONTENTS

PREFACE

Over twenty years ago we prepared the text for the first issue of *Coins of England and the United Kingdom* as the first volume of Seaby's *Standard Catalogue of British Coins*, which itself had been an adaptation and improvement upon our *Standard Catalogue of the Coins of Great Britain and Ireland,* first published in 1945. Over the years the text has been subject to considerable change, the most important being in 1978 when the first of the current series of revised editions was published in a format consistent with our other catalogues on Greek, Roman and Byzantine coins.

For the collector the principal improvements may be seen in the steady increase of detailed information; in values being stated in more than one grade of preservation; in the constant improvement and revision of the text to take into account new coins found each year, and to keep abreast of current numismatic research.

The Standard Catalogue is edited by dealers active in the trade and closely in touch with the market. In their role as editors they also keep up to date with the latest research into their series and incorporate the results into the text.

We do not try to lead the market or consciously to anticipate demand for any particular series of coins; we try to reflect the market, taking note of fixed and auction prices during the year. As only few of the coins herein actually turn up in any one year, our aim, as far as possible, is to present to the collector our opinion of what he may reasonably expect to pay for a particular coin.

The catalogue, then, is primarily intended for the collector, but it will also be found to be a compact general handbook for the archaeologist, museum curator and amateur coin finder and, for that matter, any person who has a coin to identify and who wishes to know its approximate value. This is not a catalogue of coins held for sale. It is a guide to the current values of all the coins of the realm.

We would like to acknowledge the help we receive from a number of collectors and specialists. These include David Fletcher, for his work on the Decimal Coinage section, Graham Dyer of the Royal Mint, who continues to help us by providing coin photographs and Eric McFadden of Seaby Coins, who has updated the prices of coins in the Roman section. We value the comments and suggestions of those who use this catalogue and we would particularly like to thank all those who have contributed in the past.

INTRODUCTION

Arrangement

The arrangement of this catalogue is not completely uniform, but generally it is divided into metals (gold, silver, copper, etc) under each reign, then into coinages, denominations and varieties. In the Celtic section the uninscribed coins are listed before the dynastic coins; under Charles II all the hammered coins precede the milled coinage; the reign of George III is divided into coins issued up to 1816 and the new coinage from 1816 to the end of the reign; and under Elizabeth II the decimal issues are separated from the *£.s.d.* coinages.

Every major coin type is listed though not every variety. We have endeavoured to give rather more coverage to the varieties of relatively common coins, such as the pence of Edward I, II and III, than to the very much rarer coins of, for instance, King Offa of Mercia.

Values

The values given represent the range of retail prices at which coins are being offered for sale at the time of going to press and **not** the price which a dealer will pay for those coins. These prices are based on our knowledge of the numismatic market, the current demand for particular coins, recent auction sale prices and, in those cases where certain coins have not appeared for sale for some years, our estimation of what they would be likely to sell at today, bearing in mind their rarity and appeal in relation to somewhat similar coins where a current value is known. Values are given for two grades of preservation from the Celtic period onwards and three to four grades of preservation for coins of the 17th to the 20th century.

Collectors normally require coins in the best condition they can afford and, except in the case of a really rare coin, a piece that is considerably worn is not wanted and has little value. The values given in the catalogue are for the exact state of preservation stated at the head of each column; and bearing in mind that a score of identical coins in varying states of wear could be lined up in descending order from mint condition (FDC, *fleur de coin*), through very fine (VF) to *poor* state, it will be realized that only in certain instances will the values given apply to particular coins. A 'fine' (F) coin may be worth anything between one quarter and a half of the price quoted for a 'very fine' (VF), on the other hand a piece in really mint condition will be valued substantially higher than the price quoted for 'extremely fine' (EF). The designation BV has been adopted for coins whose value on the market has yet to exceed its bullion value. Purchasing sovereigns, catalogued as BV, will attract a dealers' premium.

We emphasize again that the purpose of this catalogue is to give a general value for a particular class of coin in a specified state of preservation, and also to give the collector an idea of the range and value of coins in the English series. The value of any particular piece depends on three things:

Its exact design, legend, mintmark or date.

Its exact state of preservation; this is of prime importance.

The demand for it in the market at any given time.

Some minor varieties are much scarcer than others, and, as the number of coins issued varies considerably from year to year, coins of certain dates and mintmarks are rarer and of more value than other pieces of similar type. The prices given for any type are for the commonest variety, mintmark or date of that type.

A BEGINNER'S GUIDE TO COIN COLLECTING

The Scope

Coin collecting is a fascinating recreation. It requires little physical exertion and only as much mental effort as one wishes to give at any time. Numismatics has vast scope and boundless ramifications and byways. It encompasses not only things historical and geographical, but also touches on economics, metallurgy, heraldry, literature, the fine arts, politics, military history and many other disciplines. This catalogue is solely concerned with British coinage, but from the start the beginner should appreciate that the coinage of our own nation may be seen as a small but important part of the whole gamut of world currency.

The first coins, made of electrum, a natural alloy of gold and silver, were issued in western Asia Minor about the middle of the seventh century B.C. Over the next century or so coinage of gold and silver spread across the Aegean to mainland Greece, southwards to the eastern Mediterranean lands and eventually westward to the Adriatic cities and the Greek colonies in southern Italy, Sicily and beyond. The coins of the Greeks are noted for their beautiful, sometimes exquisite craftsmanship, with many of the coin types depicting the patron deities of their cities. Coins of Philip II of Macedon (359-336 B.C.), father of Alexander the Great, circulated amongst the Celtic peoples of the Danubian basin and were widely copied through central Europe and by the Gauls in France. Gold Gaulish staters were reaching Britain around the beginning of the first century B.C. and the earliest gold to be struck in the island must have been produced shortly afterwards.

The coins of the Romans cover some seven centuries and comprise an enormous number of different types current throughout a major part of the civilized world from Spain to Syria and from the Rhine in the north to the Sudan in the south. The Roman province of Britain was part of this vast empire for four hundred years and innumerable Roman coins have been recovered from sites in this country, most being made of brass or bronze. Many are quite inexpensive.

Following the revival of commerce after the Dark Ages, coinage in Western Europe was virtually restricted to silver until the thirteenth century, though gold was still being minted at Byzantium and in the Islamic world. In the Middle Ages many European cities had their own distinctive coinage,and money was issued not only by the kings but also by many lesser nobles, bishops and abbots. From the time of the later Crusades gold returned to the west, and the artistic developments of the Renaissance brought improved portraiture and new minting techniques.

Large silver crown-size thalers were first minted at Joachimsthal in Bohemia early in the sixteenth century. With substantial shipments of silver coming to Europe from the mines of Spanish America over the next couple of centuries a fine series of larger coins was issued by the European states and cities.

Both Germany and Italy became unified nation states during the nineteenth century but balancing the reduction in European minting authorities were the new coins of the independent states of South and Central America. Over the past quarter century many new nations have established their independence and their coinage provides a large field for the collector of modern coins.

It can be seen that the scope for the collector is truly vast, but besides the general run of official coinage there is also the large series of token coins—small change unofficially produced to supplement the inadequate supply of authorized currency. These tokens were issued by merchants, innkeepers and manufacturers in many towns and villages in the 17th, 18th and 19th centuries and many collectors specialize in their local issues.

Some coins have designs of a commemorative nature; an example being the Royal Wedding crown, but there are also large numbers of commemorative medals which, though never intended for use as coinage, are sometimes confused with coins, being metal objects of a similar shape and sometimes a similar size to coins. This is another interesting field for collectors as these medals may have excellent portraits of famous men or women, or they may commemorate important events or scientific discoveries. Other metallic objects of coin-like appearance may be reckoning counters, advertising tickets, various other tickets and passes, and items such as brass coin weights.

Minting processes

From the time of the earliest Greek coins to about the middle of the 16th century coins were made by hand. The method of manufacture was simple. The obverse and reverse designs were engraved or punched into the prepared ends of two bars of iron, shaped or tapered to the diameter of the required coin. The obverse die, known as the *pile,* was usually spiked to facilitate its being anchored firmly into a block of wood or metal. The reverse die, the *trussel,* was held by hand or grasped by tongs.

The coin was struck by placing a metal blank between the two dies and striking the trussel with a hammer. Thus, all coinage struck by this method is known as 'hammered money'. Some dies are known to have been hinged to ensure exact register between the upper and lower die. Usually a 'pair of dies' consisted of one obverse die (normally the more difficult to make) and two reverse dies. This was because the shaft of iron bearing the reverse design eventually split under the constant hammering; two reverse dies usually being needed to last out the life of the obverse die.

Some time toward the middle of the 16th century, experiments, first in Germany and later in France, resulted in the manufacture of coins by machinery.

The term 'milled' which is applied to all machine-made coins comes from the type of machinery used, the mill and screw press. With this machinery the obverse die was fixed and the reverse die brought into contact with the blank by heavy vertical pressure applied by a screw or worm-drive connected to a cross bar with heavy weights at each end. These weights usually had long leather thongs attached which allowed a more powerful force to be applied by the operators who revolved the arms of the press. New blanks were placed on the lower die and struck coins were removed by hand. The screw press brought more pressure to bear on the blanks and this pressure was evenly applied.

Various attempts were made during the reigns of Elizabeth I and Charles I to introduce this type of machinery with its vastly superior products. Unfortunately problems associated with the manufacture of blanks to a uniform weight greatly reduced the rate of striking and the hand manufacture of coins continued until the Restoration, when Charles II brought to London from Holland the Roettiers brothers and their improved screw press.

The first English coins made for circulation by this new method were the silver crowns of 1662, which bore an inscription on the edge, DECVS ET TVTAMEN, 'an ornament and a safeguard', a reference to the fact that the new coins could not be clipped, a crime made easier by the thin and often badly struck hammered coins.

The mill and screw press was used until new steam powered machinery made by Boulton and Watt was installed in the new mint on Tower Hill. This machinery had been used most successfully by Boulton to strike the 'cartwheel' two- and one- penny pieces of 1797 and other coins, including 'overstriking' Spanish eight real pieces into Bank of England 'dollars', since the old Mint presses were not able to exert sufficient power to do this. This new machinery was first used at the Mint to strike the 'new coinage' halfcrowns of 1816, and it operated at a far greater speed than the old type of mill and screw presses and achieved a greater sharpness of design.

The modern coining presses by Horden, Mason and Edwards, now operating at the new mint at Llantrisant, are capable of striking at a rate of up to 300 coins a minute.

Condition

One of the more difficult problems for the beginner is to assess accurately the condition of a coin. A common fault among collectors is to overgrade and, consequently, overvalue their coins.

Most dealers will gladly spare a few minutes to help new collectors. Many dealers issue price lists with illustrations, enabling collectors to see exactly what the coins look like and how they have been graded.

Coins cannot always be graded according to precise rules. Hammered coins often look weak or worn on the high parts of the portrait and the tops of the letters; this can be due to weak striking or worn dies and is not always attributable to wear through long use in circulation. Milled coins usually leave the mint sharply struck so that genuine wear is easier to detect. However a x 5 or x 10 magnifying glass is essential, especially when grading coins of Edward VII and George V where the relief is very low on the portraits and some skill is required to distinguish between an uncirculated coin and one in EF condition.

The condition or grade of preservation of a coin is usually of greater importance than its rarity. By this we mean that a common coin in superb condition is often more desirable and more highly priced than a rarity in poor condition. Few coins that have been pierced or mounted as a piece of jewellery have any interest to collectors.

One must also be on the lookout for coins that have been 'plugged', i.e. that have been pierced at some time and have had the hole filled in, sometimes with the missing design or letters re-engraved.

Badly cleaned coins will often display a complexity of fine interlaced lines and such coins have a greatly reduced value. It is also known for coins to be tooled or re-engraved on the high parts of the hair, in order to 'increase' the grade of coin and its value. In general it is better to have a slightly more worn coin than a better example with such damage.

Cleaning coins

Speaking generally, *don't* clean coins. More coins are ruined by injudicious cleaning than through any other cause, and a badly cleaned coin loses much of its value. A nicely toned piece is usually considered desirable. Really dirty gold and silver can, however, be carefully washed in soap and water. Copper coins should never be cleaned or washed, they may be lightly brushed with a brush that is not too harsh.

Buying and selling coins

Exchanging coins with other collectors, searching around the antique shops, telling your relatives and friends that you are interested in coins, or even trying to find your own with a metal detector, are all ways of adding to your collection. However, the time will come for the serious collector to acquire specific coins or requires advice on the authenticity or value of a coin.

At this point an expert is needed, and the services of a reputable coin dealer are necessary. There are now a large number of coin dealers in the U.K., many of whom belong to the B.N.T.A. or the I.A.P.N. (the national and international trade associations) and a glance through the 'yellow pages' under 'coin dealer' or 'numismatist' will often provide local information. Many dealers publish their own lists of coins. Studying these lists is a good way for a collector to learn about coins and to classify and catalogue their own collections.

We have been publishing the Standard Catalogue of Coins of England and the UK since 1929. It serves as a price guide for all coin collectors. We also publish books on many aspects of English, Greek, Roman and Byzantine coins and on British tokens. These books serve as a valuable source of information for coin collectors. Our books are available from B.T. Batsford Ltd, 4 Fitzhardinge Street, W1H 0AH or your local bookseller. W. H. Smith stock the Seaby Standard Catalogue.

Numismatic Clubs and Societies

There are well over one hundred societies and clubs in the British Isles, a number of which form a part of the social and cultural activities of scholastic or commercial industrial concerns. For details and addresses see Appendix II.

Useful suggestions

Security and insurance. The careful collector should not keep valuable coins at home unless they are insured and have adequate protection. Local police and insurance companies will give advice on what precautions may be necessary.

Most insurance companies will accept a valuation based on the Standard Catalogue. It is usually possible to have the amount added to a householder's contents policy. A 'Fire, Burglary and Theft' policy will cover loss only from the assured's address, but an 'All Risks' policy will usually cover accidental damage and loss anywhere within the U.K.

Coins deposited with a bank or placed in a safe-deposit box will usually attract a lower insurance premium.

Keeping a record. All collectors are advised to have an up-to-date record of their collection, and, if possible, photographs of the more important and more easily identifiable coins. This should be kept in a separate place from the collection, so that a list and photographs can be given to the police should loss occur. Note the price paid, from whom purchased, the date of acquisition and the condition.

Storage and handling. New collectors should get into the habit of handling coins by the edge. This is especially important as far as highly polished proof coins are concerned.

Collectors may initially keep their coins in paper or plastic envelopes housed in boxes, albums or special containers. Many collectors will eventually wish to own a hardwood coin cabinet in which the collection can be properly arranged and displayed. If a home-made cabinet is being constructed avoid oak and cedar wood; mahogany, walnut and rosewood are ideal. It is important that coins are not kept in a humid atmosphere; especial care must be taken with copper and bronze coins which are very susceptible to damp or condensation which may result in a green verdigris forming on them.

From beginner to numismatist

The new collector can best advance to becoming an experienced numismatist by examining as many coins as possible, noting their distinctive features and by learning to use the many books of reference that are available. It will be an advantage to join a local numismatic society, as this will provide an opportunity for meeting other enthusiasts and obtaining advice from more knowledge able collectors. Most societies have a varied programme of lectures, exhibitions and occasional auctions of members' duplicates.

Those who become members of one or both of the national societies, the Royal Numismatic Society and the British Numismatic Society, can be sure of receiving an annual journal containing authoritative papers.

Many museums have coin collections available for study and a number of museum curators are qualified numismatists.

SOME COIN DENOMINATIONS

Gold

Angel	Eighty pence (6s. 8d.) from 1464; later 7s. 6d., 8s., 10s. and 11s.
Angelet or 1/2 Angel	Forty pence (3s. 4d.) from 1464, later 3s. 9d., 4s., 5s., 5s. 6d.
Aureus	Roman currency unit (originally 1/60th lb), discontinued A.D. 324.
Britain Crown	Five shillings, 1604-12; 5s. 6d. (66d.) 1612-19.
Broad	Twenty shillings, Cromwell, 1656.
Crown	Five shillings, from 1544 (and see below and Britain crown above).
Crown of the Rose	Four shillings and 6 pence, 1526.
Crown of the Double Rose	Five shillings, 1526-44.
Florin (Double Leopard)	Six shillings, Edward III.
George Noble	Eighty pence (6s. 8d.) 1526.
Gold 'Penny'	Twenty to twenty-four pence, Henry III.
Guinea	Pound (20s.) in 1663, then rising to 30s. in 1694 before falling to 21s. 6d., 1698-1717; 21s., 1717-1813.
Halfcrown	Thirty pence, 1526 intermittently to 1612; 2s. 9d. (33d.), 1612 19.
Helm (Quarter Florin)	Eighteen pence, Edward III.
Laurel	Twenty shillings, 1619-25.
Leopard (Half florin)	Three shillings, Edward III.
Noble	Eighty pence (6s. 8d., or half mark), 1344-1464.
Pound	Twenty shillings, 1592-1600 (see also Unite, Laurel, Broad, Guinea and Sovereign).
Quarter Angel	Two shillings, 1544-7 and later 2s. 6d.
Rose Noble (Ryal)	Ten shillings, 1464-70.
Rose-Ryal	Thirty shillings, 1604-24.
Ryal	Ten shillings, Edward IV and Henry VII; fifteen shillings under Mary and Elizabeth I (see also Spur Ryal).
Solidus	Roman currency unit (1/72nd lb) from A.D. 312; the 's' of the *£.s.d.*

Sovereign	Twenty shillings or pound, 1489-1526 (22s. 6d., 1526-44), 1544-53, 1603 -04 and from 1817 (see also Pound, Unite, Laurel, Broad and Guinea, and Fine Sovereign below).
'Fine' Sovereign	Thirty shillings, 1550-96 (see also Rose-Ryal).
Spur-Ryal	Fifteen shillings, 1605-12; 16s. 6d., 1612-25.
Stater	Name commonly given to the standard Celtic gold coin.
Third guinea	Seven shillings, 1797-1813.
Thistle Crown	Four shillings, 1604-12; 4s. 5d., 1612-19.
Thrymsa	Early Anglo-Saxon version of the late Roman tremissis (one-third solidus).
Triple Unite	Three pounds, Charles I (Shrewsbury and Oxford only, 1642-4).
Unite	Twenty shillings, 1604-12 and 1625-62; 22s., 1612-19.

Silver (and Cupro-Nickel)

Antoninianus	Roman, originally 1 1/2 denarii in A.D. 214 (later debased to bronze).
Argenteus	Roman, a revived denarius.
Crown	Five shillings, 1551-1965.
Denarius	Roman, originally 10 then 16 asses (25 to the aureus), later debased: the 'd' of the *£.s.d.*
Farthing	Quarter penny, 1279-1553.
Florin	Two shillings, from 1849-1967.
Groat	Four pence, 1279 - *c. 1300 and 1351-1662 (Halfgroat from 1351).* 'Britannia' groat, 1836-55 (and 1888 for Colonial use only). See also Maundy.
Halfcrown	Thirty pence (2s. 6d.), 1551-1967.
Halfpenny	Intermittently, *c. 890-c. 970, c. 1108, short cross and, more* generally, 1279-1660.
Maundy money	Four, three, two and one penny, from 1660.
New pence	Decimal coinage: 50p from 1969, 25p. (crown) 1972 and 1977, 80, 81, 10p. and 5p. from 1968. 'New' removed in 1982.
Quinarius	Roman, half denarius or 8 asses; later debased.
Penny *(pl. pence)*	Standard unit of currency from c. 775/780 A.D.
Sceat	Early Anglo-Saxon, small, thick penny.
Shilling	Twelve pence, 1548-1966.
Siliqua	Roman, 1/24th solidus.
Sixpence	From 1551-1967.
Testern (Portcullis money)	One, two, four and eight testerns for use in the Indies (and equal to the Spanish 1, 2, 4 and 8 reales); 1600 only.
Testoon	Shilling, Henry VII and VIII.
Threefarthings	Elizabeth I, 1561-82.
Threehalfpence	Elizabeth I, 1561-82, and for Colonial use, 1834-62.
Threepence	From 1551-1944 (then see Maundy).
Twenty pence	Decimal coinage from 1982.

Copper, Bronze, Tin, Nickel-Brass, etc.

As	Roman, an early unit of currency; reduced in size and equal to 1/16th denarius in Imperial times.
Centenionalis	Roman, replaced the depleted follis in A.D. 346.
Dupondius	Roman, brass two asses or one-eighth of a denarius.
Farthing	Quarter penny: Harrington, Lennox, Richmond, Maltravers and 'rose' farthings, 1613-49; regal issues, 1672-1956 (tin, 1684-92).
Follis	Roman, silver-washed bronze coin, 1/5th argenteus, introduced *c. A.D. 290, later debased.*
Half Farthing	Victoria, 1842-56 (and for Colonial use 1828-39).
Halfpenny	From 1672 to 1967 (tin, 1685-92).
New Pence	Decimal coinage; 2p., 1p. and 1/2p. from 1971. 'New' removed from 1982.
Penny	From 1797 to 1967 (previously a silver coin).
Pound	Decimal coin from 1983.
Quadrans	Roman, quarter as or 1/64th denarius.
Quarter Farthing	For Colonial use only, 1839-53.
Semis	Roman, half as or 1/32nd denarius.
Sestertius	Roman, brass four asses or quarter denarius.
Third Farthing	For Colonial use only, 1827-1913.
Threepence	Nickelbrass, 1937-67.
Twopence	George III, 'Cartwheel' issue, 1797 only. From 1971 Decimal only.
Mark	Various denominations have been used as moneys of account for which no actual coin existed e.g. the 'mark' was 160 pennies or two thirds of a pound.

SOME NUMISMATIC TERMS EXPLAINED

Obverse	That side of the coin which normally shows the monarch's head or name.
Reverse	The side opposite to the obverse.
Blank	The coin as a blank piece of metal, i.e. before it is struck.
Flan	The whole piece of metal after striking.
Type	The main, central design.
Legend	The inscription. Coins lacking a legend are called 'mute'.
Field	That flat part of the coin between the main design and the inscription or edge.
Exergue	That part of the coin below the main design, usually separated by a horizontal line, and normally occupied *by the date.*
Die	The block of metal, with design cut into it, which actually impresses the coin blank with the design.
Die variety	Coin showing slight variation of design.
Mule	A coin with the current type on one side and the previous (and usually obsolete) type on the other side, or a piece struck from two dies that are not normally used together.
Graining or reeding	The crenellations around the edge of the coin, commonly known as 'milling'.

Proof	Carefully struck coin from special dies with a mirror-like or matt surface. (In this country 'Proof' is *not* a term used to describe the state of preservation, but the method of striking.)
Hammered	Refers to the old craft method of striking a coin between dies hammered by hand.
Milled	Coins struck by dies worked in a coining press. The presses were hand powered from 1560-1800, powered by steam from 1790 and by electricity from 1895.

ABBREVIATIONS

Archb.	Archbishop	*mm.*	*mintmark*
Bp.	Bishop	mon.	monogram
cuir.	cuirassed	*O., obv.*	obverse
d.	penny, pence	p.	new penny, pence
diad.	diademed	pl	plume
dr.	draped	quat.	quatrefoil
ex.	exergue	qtr.	quarter
grs.	grains	rad.	radiate
hd.	head	℞., *rev.*	reverse
i.c.	inner circle	r.	right
illus.	illustration	s.	shillings
l.	left	var.	variety
laur.	laureate	wt.	weight

CONDITIONS OF A COIN

The grade of preservation in order of merit as generally used in England.

Proof	Carefully struck coin from special dies with a mirror - like or matt surface.
FDC	*Fleur-de-coin.* Flawless, unused, without any wear, scratches or marks. Usually only applied to proofs.
Unc.	*Uncirculated.* A coin in new condition as issued by the Mint but, owing to modern mass-production methods of manufacture and storage, not necessarily perfect.
EF	*Extremely Fine.* A coin that shows little sign of having been in circulation, but which may exhibit slight surface marks or faint wear on very close inspection.
VF	*Very Fine.* Some wear on the raised surfaces; a coin that has had only limited circulation.
F	*Fine.* Considerable signs of wear on the raised surfaces, or design weak through faulty striking.
Fair	*Fair.* A coin that is worn, but which has the inscriptions and main features of the design still distinguishable, or a piece that is very weakly struck.
Poor	*Poor.* A very worn coin, of no value as a collector's piece unless extremely rare.

EXAMPLES OF CONDITION GRADING

EXTREMELY FINE

VERY FINE

FINE

FAIR

Edward III groat *George II halfcrown* *Victoria halfcrown*

BRITISH MINTS

LEGEND

Anglo Saxon and Norman, including Angevin mints. (to 1279) ●

Edwardian and later mints. (after 1279) ○

Mints operating in both periods. ◉

Charles 1 and Civil War mints. *

CELTIC COINAGE

PERIOD OF BELGIC MIGRATION

The earliest uninscribed coins found in Britain were made in Gaul and brought to this country by trade and by the migration of Belgic peoples from the continent (Gallo-Belgic issues A to F). The earliest may date from some time late in the second century B.C., coinciding with Germanic tribes pushing westward across the Rhine and ending with refugees fleeing from the Roman legions of Julius Caesar. Certain of these coins became the prototypes for the first gold staters struck in Britain, their designs being ultimately derived from the gold staters (M) of Philip II, King of Macedonia (359-336 B.C.).

The following list is based on the 1975 edition of R. P. Mack, *The Coinage of Ancient Britain,* which now incorporates the classification for the coins published by D. F. Allen, *The Origins of Coinage in Britain: A Reappraisal*, and from information kindly supplied by H. R. Mossop, Esq.

The new 'V' reference in this series equates to R. D. Van Arsdell, *Celtic Coinage of Britain*, in which are listed many more varieties and sub-varieties than are included here.

M 1 3 5 7

		F	*VF*
	Gold Gallo-Belgic Issues	£	£
1	Gallo-Belgic A. (Ambiani), *c.* 125-100 B.C. *Stater.* Good copy of Macedo-nian stater, large flan. Laureate hd. of Apollo to l. or r. ℞. Horse to l. or r. *M. 1, 3; V. 10, 12*	500	1650
2	— — *Quarter stater.* As last. *M. 2, 4; V. 15, 20*	225	500
3	— B. (Ambiani), *c.* 115 B.C. *Stater.* Somewhat similar to 1, but small flan and 'defaced' *obv.* die, some with lyre shape between horse's legs on *rev. M. 5, 7; V. 30, 33*	200	450
4	— — *Quarter stater.* As last. *M. 6, 8; V. 35, 37*	125	200
5	— C. (Ambiani), *c.* 100-70 B.C. *Stater.* Disintegrated face and horse. *M. 26; V. 44*	175	325
6	— D. *c.* 80 B.C. *Quarter stater.* Portions of Apollo head. ℞. A mixture of stars, crescents, pellets, zig-zag lines; often referred to as 'Geometric' types. (See also British 'O', *S. 49.*) *M. 37, 39, 41, 41a, 42; V. 65/7/9/146*	75	125
7	— E. (Ambiani), *c.* 57-45 B.C. *Stater.* Blank obv. ℞. Disjointed curved horse, pellet below. *M. 27; V. 52, 54*	125	225
8	— F. (Suessiones), *c.* 50 B.C. *Stater.* Disintegrated head and horse to r. *M. 34a; V. 85*	150	275

		F £	VF £
9	— Xc. *c.* 80 B.C. *Stater.* Blank except for VE monogram at edge of coin, ℞. S below horse to r. *M. 82; V. 87-1*	200	375
10	— *Quarter stater.* Similar, but horse to l. *M. 83; V. 355*	150	250
11	— — Xd. *c.* 50 B.C. Head l. of good style, horned serpent behind ear. ℞. Horse l. *M. 79; V. 78*	225	400

12 13

Billon Issues

Armorican (Channel Isles and N.W. Gaul), *c.* 75-50 B.C.

		F £	VF £
12	*Stater* Class I. Head r. ℞. Horse, boar below, remains of driver with Victory above, lash ends in one or two loops, or 'gate'	35	70
13	— Class II. Head r. ℞. Horse, boar below, remains of Victory only, lash ends in small cross of four pellets	30	65
14	— Class III. Head r., anchor-shaped nose. ℞. Somewhat similar to Class I	35	70
15	— Class IV. Head r. ℞. Horse with reins, lyre shape below, driver holds vertical pole, lash ends in three prongs	35	65
16	— Class V. Head r. ℞. Similar to last, lash ends in long cross with four pellets	35	65
17	— Class VI. Head r. ℞. Horse, boar below, lash ends in 'ladder'	40	80

18

		F £	VF £
18	*Quarter stater* Similar types to above	45	100

Celtic Coins Struck In Britain
Uninscribed gold staters

19 20 21 22

		F £	VF £
19	A. Westerham type, *c.* 95-65 B.C. As 5, but horse more disjointed. *M. 28, 29; V. 200, 202*	160	325
20	B. Chute type, *c.* 85-55 B.C. Similar but crab-like figure below horse. *M. 32; V. 1205*	125	200
21	C. Yarmouth (I.O.W.) type, *c.* 80-70 B.C. Crude variety of 5. *M. 31; V.* 1220	300	500
22	D. Cheriton type, *c.* 80-70 B.C. Variety of 20 with large crescent face. *M. 33; V. 1215*	225	375
23	E. Waldingfield type, *c.* 90-70 B.C. Annulet and pellet below horse. *M.48, V. 1462*	*Extremely rare*	
24	F. Clacton type 1, *c.* 90-70 B.C. Similar to Westerham type but rosette below horse to l. *M. 47; V. 1458*	250	450

24 25 26 28

		F £	VF £
25	G. Clacton type 2. Similar, but horse r., with pellet, or pellet with two curved lines below. *M. 46, 46a; V. 30, 1455*	200	330
26	H. North East Coast type, *c.* 75-30 B.C. Variety of 5, pellet or rosette below horse to r. *M. 50, 50a, 51, 51a; V. 800*	175	275
27	I. — — Similar, horse l., pellet, rosette or star with curved rays below. *M. 52-57; V. 804, 805, 807*	150	250
28	J. Norfolk wolf type, *c.* 65-45 B.C. R. Crude wolf to r. or l. *M. 49, V. 610-11*	250	475
28A	— — Similar, but wolf to l. usually base gold. *M 49a, 49b; V 610-2, 612/3.*	135	475

30 30A

		F £	VF £
29	Ka. Coritani, South Ferriby type, *c.* 30 B.C.-A.D. 10. Crude wreath. ℞. Disjointed horse l., rectangular compartment enclosing four pellets above. *M. 447-448; V. 825, 829*	175	325
30	Kb. — — Similar, but star or rosette below horse. *M. 449-450a; V. 809, 811, 815, 817*	150	250
30A	— — — Trefoil with central rosette of seven pellets. ℞. Similar to last. *M. 450a; V. 821.* In auction 1985 $5500. (this coin)	*Extremely rare*	

31 34 35

		F £	VF £
31	L. Whaddon Chase type, *c.* 45-20 B.C. ℞. Spirited horse r. of new style, various symbols below. *M. 133-138a, 139a; V. 1470-6, 1485/7/91/93* .	210	260
32	— — — Plain. ℞. Horse r., with ring ornament below or behind. *M. 140-143; V. 1498-1505*	200	330
33	Lx. North Thames group, *c.* 40-20 B.C. Blank apart from reversed SS. ℞. Similar to last. *M. 146; V. 1509*	*Extremely rare*	
34	Ly. North Kent group, *c.* 45-20 B.C. Blank. ℞. Horse l. or r., numerous ring ornaments in field. *M. 293, 294; V. 14 2, 157*	275	500
35	Lz. Weald group, *c.* 35-20 B.C. Blank. ℞. Horse l., panel below. *M. 84, 292; V. 150, 144*	350	650
36	— — Blank with some traces of Apollo head. ℞. Horse r., large wheel ornament below. *M. 144-145; V. 1507*	300	525

37 38 39

		F £	VF £
37	M. Wonersh type. *c.* 35-20 B.C. Crossed wreath design with crescents back to back in centre. ℞. Spiral above horse, wheel below. *M. 148; V. 1520.*	225	500
38	Na. Iceni, *c.* 30 B.C.-A.D. 10. Double crescent design. ℞. Horse r. *M. 397, 399; V. 620*	150	350
39	Nb. — Trefoil on cross design. ℞. Similar to last. *M. 401-403a; V. 626*	175	400

		F £	VF £
40	Nc. — Cross of pellets. R. Similar to last. *M. 400; V. 624*	200	425

41 42

41	Qa. British 'Remic' type, *c.* 45-25 B.C. Crude laureate head. R. Triple-tailed horse, wheel below. *M. 58, 60, 61; V. 210-14*	175	350
42	Qb. — Similar, but *obv.* blank. *M. 59, 62; V. 216, 1526*	125	250
43	R. Dobunni, *c.* 30 B.C.-A.D. 10. Similar, but branch emblem or ear of corn on *obv. M. 374; V. 1005*	275	450

Uninscribed gold quarter Staters

43A	F. Clacton type. Plain, traces of pattern. R. Ornamental cross with pellets. *M. 35; V. 1460*	200	350

44 45 46

44	Lx. N. Thames group, *c.* 40-20 B.C. Floral pattern on wreath. R. horse l. or r. *M. 76, 151, 270-271; V. 234, 1608, 1623, 1688*	120	200
45	Ly. N. Kent group, *c.* 45-20 B.C. Blank. R. Horse r. *M. 78, 284-285;* V. 158/163/170	100	175
46	Lz. Weald group, *c* . 35-20 B.C. Spiral design on wreath. R. Horse l. or r. *M. 77, 80-81; V. 250, 254, 366*	100	185
47	— — Blank. R. Horse l., panel below. *M. 85; V. 151*	120	200
48	N. Iceni, *c.* 30 B.C.-A.D. 10. Floral pattern. R. Horse r . *M. 404; V. 628*	120	200

49 50 51

49	O. Geometric type, Sussex group, *c.* 80-60 B.C. Unintelligible patterns (some blank on *obv.*). *M. 40, 43-45; V. 143, 1425/27/29*	75	120
50	P. Kentish group, *c.* 65- 45 B.C. Blank. R. Trophy design. *M. 36, 38; V. 145-7*	100	65
51	Qc. British 'Remic' type, *c.* 40-20 B.C. Head or wreath pattern, R. Triple-tailed horse, l. or r. *M. 63-67, 69-75; V. 220-32, 36, 42-6, 56, 1015*	135	225
52	R. Dobunni, *c.* 30 B.C.-A.D. 10. *O.* Blank. R. Somewhat as last. *M. 68; V. 1010*	150	250

Uninscribed silver units (except where stated)

53 55

56 58

		F £	VF £
53	L x N. Thames group Head l. or r. ℞. Horse l. or r. *M. 280, 435, 436, 438, 441; V. 80, 1546, 1549, 1555*	35	90
54	— — Head l. ℞. Goat r., with long horns. *M. 437; V. 1552*	65	150
55	— — Two horses or two beasts. *M. 442, 443, 445; V. 474, 1626, 1948*	70	160
56	— — Star of four rays or wreath pattern. ℞. Horse or uncertain animal r. *M. 272a, 414, 439; V. 164, 679, 1543*	60	125
56A	— — Hd. r. with corded hair and headband. ℞. Horse l., leaf (?) below, ornaments in field. (Somewhat similar to *S.* 77).) *M.* —	*Extremely rare*	
56B	— — *Half unit.* Cruciform pattern with ornaments in angles. ℞. Horse l., ear of corn between legs, crescent and pellets above. *M.* —	80	175
56C	— — *Quarter unit* (minim). Cross pattern. ℞. Two-tailed horse *VA 482*	50	110
57	L z . South Thames group. Wreath or head left. ℞. Horse *M.* 446B (*Allen L 28-10*) *VA 355*	35	95
58	— — Helmeted head r. ℞. Horse. *M. 89; V. 264*	80	175
59	— — *Quarter unit* . Similar to 58. *M. 90-91; V. 268-70*	50	110

60

61

61A

		F £	VF £
60	Durotriges, *c.* 60 B.C.-A.D. 20. Size and type of Westerham staters (nos. 19 and 81). *M. 317; V. 1235* Quality of Æ varies, price for good Æ	40	85
61	— Size and type of Sussex Geometric type (no. 49 above). *M. 319; V. 1242/ 49*	35	75
61A	— 'Starfish' design. ℞. 'Geometric' pattern. *M. 320; V. 1270*	40	90
62	— Very thin flans, *c.* 55 B.C. Crude hd. of lines and pellets. ℞. Horse similar. *M. 321; V. 1280*	45	100

63 64 66

		F £	*VF* £
63	Dobunni, *c.* 30 B.C.-A.D. 10. Head r., with recognisable face. ℞. Triple-tailed horse l. or r. *M. 374a, b, 375, 376, 378; V. 1558, 1020, 1042*	40	90
64	— Very crude head. ℞. Similar to last. *M. 378a-384d; V. 1035, 37, 45, 49, 74, 75, 78, 85, 95*	30	65
65	— *Quarter unit.* As last. *M. 384c; V. 1080*	*Extremely rare*	
66	Coritani, *c.* 50 B.C.-A.D. 10. I. Prototype issue of good style and execution. Boar r., with rosette and ring ornaments. ℞. Horse. *M. 405, 405a, b, 406, 451; V. 855, 57, 60, 64*	65	150
67	— — *Half unit.* Similar. *M. 406a, 451a; V. 862/6*	50	110
68	— II. South Ferriby type. Vestiges of boar on *obv.* ℞. Horse. *M. 410, 452, 453; V. 875/7*	50	110

69 72

		F £	*VF* £
69	— — Plain. ℞. Horse. *M. 453a, 454; V. 884/7*	30	75
70	— — *Half unit.* Similar. *M. 455-456; V. 879/89*	25	55
71	— — *Quarter unit.* Similar. *M. 456a; V. 881*	25	55
72	Iceni, *c.* 10 B.C.-A.D. 60. Boar r. ℞. Horse r. *M. 407-409; V. 655/7/9*	25	45
73	— *Half unit.* Similar. *M. 411; V. 661*	30	65

74 77 82

		F £	*VF* £
74	— Head r. ℞. Horse. *M. 412-413e; V. 665, 790, 792, 794*	40	90
74A	— Similar, but inverted ear of corn between legs of horse on *rev. M. — (413 variety)*	70	150
75	— Double crescent and wreath pattern. ℞. Horse. *M. 414-415, 440; V. 675/79/1611*	20	45
76	— *Half unit.* Similar. *M. 417a; V. 683*	30	60
76A	— — Three crescents back to back. ℞. Horse r. *M. 417; V. 681*	35	75

Uninscribed bronze

		F £	*VF* £
77	Lx. North Thames group. Head l. with braided hair. ℞. Horse l. *M. 273, 274,* see also *M. 281; V. 1615, 1646*	40	85
78	— — Horned pegasus l. ℞. Pegasus l. *M. 446; V. 1629*	85	175
80	Ly. North Kent group. Boar. ℞. Horse. *M. 295-296; V. 154*	70	140
81	Durotriges, *c.* A.D. 20-50. Debased form of Æ stater (no. 60). *M. 318; V. 1290*	20	45
82	— Cast coins, *c.* A.D. 50-70. As illustration. *M. 322-370; V. 1322-70*	30	75

Potin (bronze with very high tin content)

83

84

83	Thames and South, *c.* 1st century B.C. Cast. Class I. Crude head. ℞. Lines representing bull. (Allen, types A-L.) *M. 9-22a; V. 104, 106, 108, 112, 114, 115, 117, 119, 120, 122, 123, 125, 127, 129, 131, 133*.	25	50
84	Kent and N. Thames, *c.* mid. 1st century A.D. Cast. Class II. Smaller flan, large central pellet. (*Allen* types M-P.) *M. 23-25; V. 135-9*..........	35	75
84A	Thurrock (Essex) 100-90 B.C. Cast, better style Apollo head L. ℞ Charging bull r. *V.A. 1402-42*	30	70

CELTIC DYNASTIC ISSUES

The Celtic dynastic issues are among the most interesting and varied of all British coins. Something is known about some of the issuers from Julius Caesar's *Commentaries* and other sources—chiefly the kings of the Atrebates, Regni and Catuvellauni—while many are issues of kings quite unknown to history bearing legends which defy interpretation.

Roman influence in coinage design is particularly noticeable in the reign of Cunobelin, but the Icenian revolt of A.D. 61, in which Colchester and London were sacked with the massacre of over 70,000 Romans, resulted in the termination of British Celtic coinage which previously had been allowed to circulate along with Roman coins. The dates given for the various rulers are, in most cases, very approximate. **Staters and quarter staters are gold coins of varying quality.** Bronze coins in poor condition are worth very much less than the values given. All coins, even good specimens, are worth less if they lack clear legends, are struck off-centre or have striking cracks.

SOUTHERN BRITAIN

	F	VF
	£	£
Atrebates and Regni. *Berks., Hants., Surrey and Sussex*		
85 **Commius** *c.* 35-20 B.C. *Stater.* Portions of laureate hd. r. ℞. COMMIOS around triple tailed hor se r. *M. 92; V. 350*	800	1850
Copied from the 'Remic' type QA *(no. 41), this is the first inscribed British coin.*		

85 86 88 89

	F	VF
86 **Tincommius,** *c.* 20 B.C.-A.D. 5. Celtic style. *Stater.* Similar, but TINC COMMI F, or TIN DV around horse. *M. 93, 94; V. 362, 363*	300	800
87 *Quarter stater.* TINCOM, zig-zag ornament below. ℞. Horse l. *M. 95; V. 365*	175	425
88 Classical style. *Stater.* TINC or COM F on tablet. ℞. Horseman with javelin. *M. 96, 98, 100; V. 375, 376, 385*	300	650
89 *Quarter stater.* TINC on a tablet, C above, A or B below. ℞. Medusa hd. facing. *M. 97; V. 378*	225	425

No.	Description	*F* £	*VF* £
90	— As 88. ℞. Horse l. or r. *M. 99, 101-104; V. 379, 387-90*	125	225
91	*Silver.* Head r., TINCOM. ℞. Eagle facing. *M. 105; V. 397*	75	200
91A	— Head l. ℞. Bull charging l., TINC. *M. 106; V. 396*	70	175
92	— Facing hd. with ornate hair. ℞. As last. *M. —; V. 370*	65	125
92A	— Laureate head l. ℞. Boar charging l., pentagram, TINCO in field. *V. 396*	75	165
92B	— but head r., C (?) behind. ℞. Bull charging r. *M. —; V. 381*	60	150
92C	— TINCOMMIVS. ℞. Horse l. *M. 131b; V. 473.* (Listed in Mack under Verica.)	75	175
93	— TINC. ℞. Animal prancing l. *M. 106a; V. 382*	75	175
93A	— Victory r., TIN. ℞. CO.F. within wreath. *M. —*	70	165
93B	— TINC in angles of four rays, pellets in centre. ℞. Lion on hippocamp l. *M. —; V. 372*	60	135
93C	— Five pointed star, pellet in centre. ℞. Boy on a dolphin r., TIN below. *M. —; V. 371*	45	85
94	*Silver quarter unit.* C F within two interlinked squares. ℞. Dog to r., TINC. *M. 118; V. 383*	120	240
94A	— Tablet contains CoF. ℞. Medusa hd	135	275

95 96

No.	Description	*F* £	*VF* £
95	**Eppillus,** *c.* A.D. 5-1 0 (see also under Cantii). *Quarter stater.* Stars above and below CALLEV *(Silchester).* ℞. EPPI over hound r. *M. 107; V.407*	100	175
95A	— EPPILLV ·. COMM ·. F ·. around crescent. ℞. Horse r., star above and below. *M. —; V. 409*	135	250
96	*Silver.* EPP over eagle. ℞. REX crescent CALLE. *M. 108; V. 415*	30	65
96A	— Bearded hd. r. in wreath, no legend. ℞. Boar r., EPPI COM or EPPI F CO. *M. —; V. 416*	45	100
96C	*Quarter unit.* Crook-ended cross, pellets in angles. ℞. Horse r., EPP; *V. 421*	80	175
96D	— Bull's hd. facing. ℞. Ram (?)r., dividing EPPI CO. *M. —; V. 422*	70	150
96E	*Bronze* Floral design of 8 petals surrounded by 4 crescents and 4 annulets. R . Hound r., EPPI above, COM F below	*Extremely rare*	
97	**Verica,** *c.* A.D. 10-40. *Stater.* Group I. COM .· F on tablet. ℞. VIR below horseman r. *M. 109, 110; V. 460/1*	200	400

98

99

No.	Description	*F* £	*VF* £
98	— II. Similar but title REX added. *M. 121; V. 500*	175	350
99	— III. Vineleaf between VI-RI. ℞. Horseman r. *M. 125; V. 520*	225	450

		F £	VF £
100	*Quarter stater* I. COM · F etc. ℞. Horse VIR etc. *M. 111-114; V. 465-8*	110	175
101	— II. VERIC COM ·. F in two lines. ℞. Horse r., REX below. *M. 122; V. 501*	135	225
102	— III. Vineleaf, VERI below. ℞. Horseman as no. 97. *M. 124; V. 525*	225	400
103	— — Head or seated figure. ℞. Horseman r. *M. 126-127; V. 526/7*	250	450
104	*Silver* I. Crescents, COM ·. F. ℞. Boar. *M. 115; V. 470*	35	75
104A	— — — ℞. Eagle l. VIR. *M. —; V. 471*	35	75
104B	— — VIRIC across field, ornaments above and below. ℞. Pegasus r., star design below (12.2 grs)	125	225

105 107 110

105	— II. Name around circles. ℞. Lion r. *M. 123; V. 505*	45	100
106	— III. Horseman with spear. ℞. Horseman with shield. *M. 128; V. 530*	50	110
107	— — Seated figure. ℞. Two cornucopiae. *M. 129; V. 531*	40	90
108	— — Head r. ℞. Seated or standing figure. *M. 130-131; V. 532/3*	45	100
108A	— — Head r. ℞. Eagle. *M. 131a; V. 534*	65	140
108B	— — Bull dividing VERICA REX. ℞. Stg. fig. with head on a standard, COMM F. *M.* — ; *V.* 506	40	90
109	*Silver quarter unit* I. *O.* Various. ℞. Animal. *M. 116-117; 119-120e; V. 480/2/4, 510/11, 552*	35	85
109A	— — VIR in box. ℞. Boar's hd. r., *M. —; cf. V. 564*	40	95
109B	— — Sphinx C.F. ℞. Dog or wolf curled head to tail. VERI; *V. 557*	40	95
109C	— — Eagle r. VERCA COMMI F. ℞. Wine krater. *M. —; V. 563*	45	100
110	— III. C ·. F in wreath. ℞. Head r., VERI. *M. 132; V. 551*	45	100
111A	— IV. VIR/VAR on tablet. ℞. Pegasus r., CO below. *M. —; V. 551*	45	100
111B	— — VERICA around bucranium. ℞. Tomb, or altar, C.F. *M. —; V. 552*	60	125
111C	— — 'Maltese cross' design, pellets in angles. ℞. Hand grasping trident, VER REX; *V. 487* (now attributed to Eppillus)	75	175
111D	— Two cornucopiae. ℞. Eagle. *M.; V. 555*	40	90
111E	— Acorn pattern r. ℞. RVER CA, hippocamp; *V. 556*	50	110
111F	— Interlinked C's or crescents, standard between dividing CR at top. ℞. Hippocamp, VERICA. *M. —*	60	125
111G	— Sphinx, VERIC. ℞. Hd. r., SCF(?). *M. —*	60	125
111H	— Helmeted bust r. in Roman style. ℞. Horse r., CF between legs. *M. —, V. 558*	50	110

112

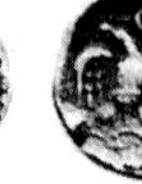

113

No.		F £	VF £
112	**Epaticcus**, *c.* A.D. 25-35. *Stater.* TASCI ·. F, ear of wheat. ℞. EPATICCV, horseman r. *M. 262; V. 575*	700	1500
113	*Silver* Head of Hercules r., EPATI. ℞. Eagle stg. on snake. *M. 263; V. 580*	25	55
114	— Victory seated r. ℞. Boar. *M. 263a; V. 581*	30	70
114A	— EPATI in panel. ℞. Lion r. *M. —; V. 583*	140	175
115	*Silver quarter unit.* EPATI. ℞. Boar's head (?), TA below. *M. 264; V. 585*	45	100
116	— Lion (?) r., EPA. ℞. TA in centre of double lozenge. *M. —*	60	125

117

117A

No.		F £	VF £
117	**Caratacus,** *c.* A.D. 35-40. *Silver.* As 113, CARA. *M. 265; V. 593*	120	200
	The above two rulers were brother and son of Cunobelin (see Catuvellauni), but their coins appear in the same area as Verica's.		
117A	*Silver quarter unit* CARA around pellet in circle. ℞. Pegasus r., no legend. *M. —; V. 595*	85	150

Cantii *Kent*

118

No.		F £	VF £
118	**Dubnovellaunus** *c.* 15-1 B.C. *(See also under Trinovantes.) Stater.* Blank. ℞. Horse r., DVBNOVELLAVNOS or DVBNOVI. *M. 282-283; V. 169/76*	300	550
119	*Silver.* Griffin r. or horned animal. ℞. Horse l. or seated figure. *M. 286-287; V. 171/8*	130	250
119A	— Triangular or cruciform design. ℞. Horse r.; *cf. V. 164*	135	260
120	— Head l. ℞. Pegasus. *M. 288; V. 165*	135	260
121	*Bronze.* Boar. ℞. Eagle, horseman or horse. *M. 289, 291, 291a, V. 173, 180/1*	80	175
122	— Animal. ℞. Horse or lion l., DVBN on tablet below. *M. 290; V. 166*	80	175
123	**Vosenos**, *c.* A.D. 5. *Stater.* Blank. ℞. Serpent below horse. *M. 297; V. 184*	*Extremely rare*	

124

128

		F £	*VF* £
124	*Quarter stater.* Similar. VOSII below horse. *M. 298; V. 185*	275	475
125	*Silver.* Griffin and horse. ℞. Horse, retrograde legend. *M. 299a; V. 186*	175	350
126	*Bronze.* Boar l. ℞. Horse l., SA below. *M. 299; V. 187*.....................	125	275
127	**Eppillus**, *c.* A.D. 10-25. *(See also under Atrebates.) Stater.*COM ·. F in wreath. ℞. Horseman l., EPPILLVS. *M. 300; V. 430*.......................	525	1100
128	— Victory in wreath. ℞. Horseman r. Illustrated above. *M. 301; V. 431*	800	1650
129	*Quarter stater.* EPPIL/COM ·. F. ℞. Pegasus. *M. 302; V. 435*	125	225

130 131 136

130	— EPPI a round wreath, or COM ·. F. ℞. Horse. *M. 303-304; V. 436/7*	140	265
131	*Silver.* Head r. or l. ℞. Lion or horseman. *M. 305-306; V. 417/41*	55	115
132	— Diademed head l. or r., IOVIR. ℞. Victory or capricorn. *M. 307-308a; V. 442/3*..	125	200
133	*Bronze.* Head l. ℞. Victory holding wreath. *M. 311; V. 452*	70	150
134	— Cruciform ornament or bull. ℞. Eagle. *M. 309-310; V. 450/1*.......	70	150
135	— Bearded head l. ℞. Horse r. *M. 312; V. 453*................................	70	150
136	**Amminus,** *c.* A.D. 15? *Silver.* Plant. ℞. Pegasus r. *M. 313; V. 192*...	175	350
136A	— Bust r. AMMI in front. ℞ Biga facing, S below *M —, V. —*.........	225	475
137	— A within wreath. ℞. Capricorn r. *M. 314; V. 194*	165	300
138	*Silver quarter unit.* A within curved lines. ℞. Bird. *M. 316; V. 561* ..	90	180
139	*Bronze.* Head r. ℞. Capricorn r. *M. 315; V. 195*	110	225
139A	– 'B' within octagonal pattern. ℞. Bird. *M.*—....................................	125	250

Unattributed coins of the Cantii

140	*Silver quarter unit* Horseman. ℞. Seated figure wearing belt and holding spear or staff. *M. 316e; V. 153*..	125	225
141	*Bronze.* Boar or head. ℞. Lion to r. or l. *M. 316a, c; V. 154*	60	140
143	— *Obv.* uncertain. ℞. Ring ornaments. *M. 316d; V. 154*....................	70	165
144	*Bronze quarter unit.* Quatrefoil pattern. ℞. Horse r. *M. 316f; V. 154*	60	140

145

Durotriges *W. Hants., Dorset, Somerset and S. Wilts*

145	**Crab.** *Silver.* CRAB in angles of cross. ℞. Eagle. *M. 371; V. 1285*...	250	450
146	*Silver quarter unit.* CRAB on tablet. ℞. Star shape. *M. 372; V. 1286*	175	350

NORTH THAMES

Trinovantes *Essex and counties to the West*

148

150

		F £	VF £
148	**Addedomaros**, *c.* 15-1 B.C. *Stater.* Crossed wreath or spiral. ℞. Horse, wheel or cornucopiae below. *M. 266-267; V. 1605/20*	200	375
149	— Double crescent ornament. ℞. Horse, branch below. *M. 268; V. 1635*	225	500
150	*Quarter stater.* Similar, but rectangle or wheel below horse. *M. 269; V. 1638*	220	450

[Note. For uninscribed bronze, sometimes attributed to Addedomaros, see S. 77 (M. 273/274; V. 1646).]

152

154

		F £	VF £
151	**Diras?**, *c.* A.D. 1? *Stater. O.*Blank. ℞. DIRAS and snake (?) over horse, wheel below. *M. 279; V. 162*	*Extremely rare*	
152	**Dubnovellaunus** *c.* A.D. 1-10. *(See also under Cantii.) Stater.* Wreath design. ℞. Horse l., branch below. *M. 275; V. 1650*	200	450
153	*Quarter stater.* Similar. *M. 276; V. 1660*	160	250
154	*Bronze.* Head r. or l. ℞. Horse l. or r. *M. 277-278*, see also *M. 281; V. 1665, 1667, 1669*	35	90
155	— Without legend but associated with the Trinovantes. Head or boar. ℞. Horse or horseman. *M. 280a, b, d*	60	125

Catuvellauni *N. Thames, Herts., Beds., spreading East and South*

157

Tasciovanus, *c.* 20 B.C.-A.D. 10, and associated coins

		F £	VF £
157	*Stater.* Crescents in wreath. ℞. TASCIAV and bucranium over horse. *M. 149-150; V. 1680/2*	250	525
158	— Similar, sometimes with VER *(Verulamium).* ℞. Horseman r., TASC. *M. 154-156; V. 1730/2/4*	240	475
159	— Similar, but T, or V and T. ℞. Similar to last. *M. 157; V. 1736*	275	550

		F £	VF £
160	— As 157. ℞. Horse, CAMV monogram *(Camulodunum). M. 186; V. 1684*	375	800
161	— TASCIOV / RICON in panel. ℞. Horseman l. *M. 184; V. 1780*	500	950
162	— TASCIO in panel. ℞. Horseman r., SEGO. *M. 194; V. 1845*	550	1000
163	*Quarter stater.* Wreath, TASCI or VERO. ℞. Horse, TAS or TASC. *M. 152-153; V. 1690/2*	130	250
164	— As 160. ℞. CAMVL mon. over horse. *M. 187; V. 1694*	140	270
165	— As 161, omitting RICON. ℞. Pegasus l. *M. 185; V. 1786*	125	225
166	— As 162. ℞. Horse l. omitting SEGO. *M. 195; V. 1848*	140	270
167	*Silver.* Bearded head l. ℞. Horseman r., TASCIO . *M. 158; V. 1745*	75	200
168	— Pegasus l., TAS . ℞. Griffin r., within circle of pellets. *M. 159; V. 1790*	75	200
169	— Eagle stg. l., TASCIA. ℞. Griffin r., *M. 160; V. 1792*	75	200
170	—VER in beaded circle. ℞. Horse r., TASCIA. *M. 161; V. 1699*	70	175
171	— — ℞. Naked horseman, no legend. *M. 162; V. 1747*	70	175

172 175 178

172	— Laureate hd. r., TASCIA. ℞. Bull butting l. *M. 163; V. 1794*	75	185
173	— Cruciform ornament, VERL. ℞. Boar, r. TAS *M. 164; V. 1796*	75	185
173A	— Saltire over cross within square, serpentine design around. ℞. Boar r. DIAS below. *M—*	150	325
174	— TASC in panel. ℞. Pegasus l. *M. 165; V. 1798*	65	150
175	— — ℞. Horseman l. carrying a long shield. *M. 166; V. 1800*	50	135
176	— SEGO on panel. ℞. Horseman. *M. 196; V. 1851*	140	325
177	— DIAS / C / O. ℞. Horse, VIR (?) below. *M. 188; V. 1877*	140	325
178	*Bronze.* Two heads in profile, one bearded. ℞. Ram l., TASC . *M. 167; V. 1705*	55	150
179	— Bearded head r. ℞. Horse l., VIIR, VER or TAS. *M. 168-169; V. 1707-9*	55	150
180	— Head r., TASC. ℞. Pegasus l., VER. *M. 170; V. 1711*	55	150
181	— — TAS ANDO. ℞. Horse r. *M. 170a; V. 1873a*		*Unique*
182	— — TAS. ℞. Horseman r., VER. *M. 171; V. 1750*	55	150
183	— VERLAMIO between rays of star-shaped ornament. ℞. Bull l. *M. 172; V. 1808*	55	150
184	— Similar, without legend. ℞. Sphinx l., legend SEGO? *M. 173; V. 1855*	55	150

185

185	— Similar. ℞. Bull r. *M. 174; V. 1810*	55	150

		F	VF
		£	£
186	— Similar. ℞. Horse l., TASCI. *M. 175; V. 1812*	55	150
187	— Head r., TASC. . . ℞. Horse r. in double circle. *M. 175a; V. 1873*	100	175
188	— Laureate hd. r., TASCIO. ℞. Lion r., TASCIO. *M. 176; V. 1814*	55	150
189	— Head r. ℞. Figure std. l., VER below. *M. 177; V. 1816*	60	160

190 191

190	— — TASCIAVA. ℞. Pegasus l., TAS. *M. 178; V. 1818 (double bronze denomination*	100	200
191	— Cruciform ornament of crescents and scrolls. ℞. Boar r., VER. *M. 179; V. 1713*	65	160
192	— Laureate head r. ℞. Horse l., VIR. *M. 180; V. 1820*	55	150
193	— Raised band across centre, VER or VERL below, uncertain objects above. ℞. Horse grazing r. *M. 183a; V. 1717*	70	170
194	— RVII above lion r. within wide beaded circle. ℞. Eagle looking l., sometimes reading RVE. *M. 189; V. 1890*	80	185
195	— Bearded head r., RVIIS. ℞. Horseman r., VIR. *M. 190; V. 1892*	70	170

196 202

196	— RVIIS on panel. ℞. Animal l. *M. 191; V. 1895*	65	160
197	— Head r., TASC DIAS. ℞. Centaur r. playing double pipe, or sometimes horses. *M. 192; V. 1882*	75	175
198	*Bronze half denomination.* Lion? r. ℞. Sphinx l. *M. 181; V. 1824*	65	160
199	— Bearded head l. or r., VER. ℞. Goat or boar r. *M. 182-183; V. 1715, 1826*	60	155
200	— Head l. ℞. Animal l. with curved tail. *M. 183b, c; V. 1822*	60	150
201	— Annulet within square with curved sides. ℞. Eagle l., RVII. *M. 193; V. 1903*	60	145
202	**Andoco**, *c.* A.D . 5-15. *Stater.* Crossed wreath design. ℞. Horse r., AND. *M. 197; V. 1860*	525	1100

203

205

		F £	VF £
203	*Quarter stater.* Crossed wreaths, ANDO. R. Horse l. *M. 198; V. 1863*	175	325
204	*Silver.* Bearded head l. in looped circle. R. Pegasus l., ANDOC. *M. 199; V. 1868*............	140	300
205	*Bronze.* Head r., ANDOCO. R. Horse r., AND. *M. 200; V. 1871*......	80	200
206	*Bronze half denomination.* Head l. R. Horse r., A between legs, branch in exergue. *M. —*............	65	175

207

208

207	**Cunobelin** *(Shakespeare's Cymbeline). c.* A.D. 10-40. 207. *Stater.* CAMVL on panel. R. Leaf above two horses galloping l., CVNOBELIN on curved panel below. *M. 201; V. 1910*............	650	1200
208	— Ear of corn dividing CA MV. R. Horse prancing r., CVNO below. *M. 203, 206, 210-213. V. 2010/25/1925/31/33/2020* Varying in style, from—............	210	425
209	— Similar, but horse l. *M. 208; V. 2029*............	425	800
210	*Quarter stater.* Similar to 207. *M. 202; V. 1913*	250	450
211	— Similar to 208. *M. 204, 209; V. 1927, 2015*	125	215

212

212	— Similar to 208 but CAM CVN on *obv. M. 205; V. 2017*............	150	275
213	*Silver.* Two bull headed snakes inter twined. R. Horse l. , CVNO. *M. 214; V. 1947*	80	200
214	— Head l., CAMVL before. R. CVNO beneath Victory std. r. *M. 215; V. 2045*	60	140
215	— CVNO BELI in two panels. R. CVN below horseman galloping r. (legends sometimes retrograde). *M. 216, 217; V. 1951/3*............	60	140
216	— Two leaves dividing CVN. R. CAM below horseman galloping r. *M. 218; V. 2047*............	70	160
217	— Flower dividing CA MV. R. CVNO below horse r. *M. 219; V. 2049*	70	160

		F £	VF £
218	— CVNO on panel. ℞. CAMV on panel below griffin. *M. 234; V. 2051*	60	125
219	— CAMVL on panel. ℞. CVNO below centaur l. carrying palm. *M. 234a; V. 1918*	60	125
219A	— CAMVL on panel. ℞. Figure seated l. holding wine amphora, CVNOBE. *M. —*	70	160
219B	— Plant, CVNOBELINVS (see no. 136 Amminus). ℞. Hercules stg. r. holding club and thunderbolt, dividing CA MV. *M. —*	100	225
219C	— Laur. hd. r., CVNOBELINVS. ℞. Pegasus springing l., CAMV below. *M. —*	90	210
220	— CVNO on panel. ℞. TASC F below Pegasus r. *M. 235; V. 2053* ..	90	210

221 225

221	— Head r., CVNOBELINI. ℞. TASCIO below horse r. *M. 236; V. 2055*	100	225
222	— Winged bust r., CVNO. ℞. Sphinx std. l., TASCIO. *M. 237; V. 2057*	60	125
223	— Draped female figure r., TASCIIOVAN. ℞. Figure std. r. playing lyre, tree behind. *M. 238; V. 2059*	75	175
224	— Male figure stg. dividing CV NO. ℞. Female std. side saddle on animal, TASCIIOVA. *M. 239; V. 2061*	75	175
224A	— Laur. hd. r., CVNOBELINVS. ℞. Victory r., TASCIO[VAN . . .]	75	175
225	— Figure r. carrying dead animal, CVNOBELINVS. ℞. Figure stg. holding bow, dog at side, TASCIIOVANI. *M. 240; V. 2063*	90	200
226	— CVNO on panel, horn above, two dolphins below. ℞. Figure stg. r., altar behind. *M. 241a; V. 2065*	100	225
227	— CVNO on panel. ℞. Fig. walking r., CV N. *M. 254; V. 2067*	85	190
228	— — ℞. Animal springing l. *M. 255; V. 1949*	95	225
229	— CVN in centre of wreath. ℞. CAM below dog or she-wolf stg. r. *M. 256; V. 2069*	110	250
230	— CVNO, animal l. ℞. CA below figure std. r. holding caduceus. *M. 258; V. 2071*	125	275
231	— SOLIDV in centre of looped circle. ℞. Standing figure l., CVNO. *M. 259; V. 2073*	175	400
232	*Bronze.* Head l., CVNO. ℞. Boar l., branch above. *M. 220; V. 1969*.	50	125
233	— CVNOB ELINI in two panels. ℞. Victory std. l., TASC ·. F. *M. 221; V. 1971*	50	125
234	— Winged animal l., CAM below. ℞. CVN before Victory stg. 1. *M. 222a; V. 1973*	50	125
235	— Bearded head facing. ℞. Similar to no. 232. *M. 223; V. 1963*	70	170
236	— Ram-headed animal coiled up within double ornamental circle. ℞. CAM below animal. *M. 224; V. 1965*	80	200
237	— Winged animal r., CAMV. ℞. CVN below horse galloping r. *M. 225; V. 2081*	55	150
238	— Bearded head l., CAMV. ℞. CVN or CVNO below horse l. *M. 226, 229, V. 2085/2131*	55	140

No.	Description	F £	VF £
239	— Laureate head r., CVNO. ℞. CVN below bull butting l. *M. 227; V. 2083*	80	200
240	— Crude head r., CVN. ℞. Figure stg. l., CVN. *M. 228; V. 2135*	55	140
241	— CAMVL / ODVNO in two panels. ℞. CVNO beneath sphinx crouching l. *M. 230; V. 1977*	55	150

242 245 251

No.	Description	F £	VF £
242	— Winged beast springing l., CAMV. ℞. Victory stg. r. divides CV NO. *M. 231; V. 1979*	60	125
243	— Victory walking r. ℞. CVN below, horseman r. *M. 232; V. 1981*	60	125
244	— Beardless head l., CAM. ℞. CVNO below eagle. *M. 233; V. 2087*	60	125
245	— Laureate he ad l., CVNOBELINI. ℞. Centaur r., TASCIOVANI ·F. *M. 242; V. 2089*	50	125
246	— Helmeted bust r. ℞. TASCIIOVANII above, sow stg. r., F below. *M. 243; V. 2091*	50	125
247	— Horseman galloping r. holding dart and shield, CVNOB. ℞. Warrior stg. l., TASCIIOVANTIS. *M. 244; V. 2093*	45	110
248	— Helmeted bust l., CVNOBII. ℞. TASC . FIL below boar l. std. on haunches. *M. 245; V. 1983*	85	200
249	— Bare head r., CVNOBELINVS REX. ℞. TASC below bull butting r. *M. 246; V. 2095*	55	140
250	Bare head l., CVNO. ℞. TASC below bull stg. r. *M. 247; V. 1985*	80	200
251	— Winged head l., CVNOBELIN. ℞. Metal worker std. r. holding hammer, working on a vase, TASCIO behind. *M. 248; V. 2097*	45	120
252	— Pegasus springing r., CVNO. ℞. Victory r., sacrificing bull, TASCI. *M. 249; V. 2099*	45	110
253	— CVNO on panel within wreath. ℞. CAMV below horse, full faced, prancing r. *M. 250; V. 2101*	70	190

254 255

No.	Description	F £	VF £
254	— Bearded head of Jupiter Ammon l., CVNOBELIN. ℞. CAM below horseman galloping r. *M. 251; V. 2103*	70	175
255	— Janus head, CVNO below. ℞. CAMV on panel below, sow std. r. beneath a tree. *M. 252; V. 2105*	80	200

	F	*VF*
	£	£
256 — Bearded head of Jupiter Ammon r., CVNOB. ℞. CAM on panel below lion crouched r. *M. 253; V. 2107*	75	185
257 — Sphinx r., CVNO. ℞. Fig. stg. l. divides CA M. *M. 260; V. 2109*	80	200
258 — Animal stg. r. ℞. CVN below horseman r. *M. 261; V. 1987*	90	200
259 *Bronze half denomination.* Animal l. looking back. ℞. CVN below horse l. *M. 233a; V. 1967*	95	200

S.W. MIDLANDS

Dobunni *Glos., Here., Mon., Som., Wilts. and Worcs.*

No.	Description		
260	**Anted.** *Stater.* Ear of corn. R. ANTED or ANTEDRIG over triple-tailed horse r. *M. 385-386; V. 1062/6*	350	650
261	*Silver.* Crude head r., as 64. R. ANTED over horse l. *M. 387; V. 1082*	110	200
262	**Eisu.** *Stater.* Similar to 260 but EISV or EISVRIG. *M. 388; V. 1105*	600	1100
263	*Silver.* Similar to 261 but EISV. *M. 389; V. 1110*	65	130
264	**Inam.** (or Inara). *Stater.* Similar to 260 but INAM (or INARA). *M. 390; V. 1140*	*Extremely rare*	

265 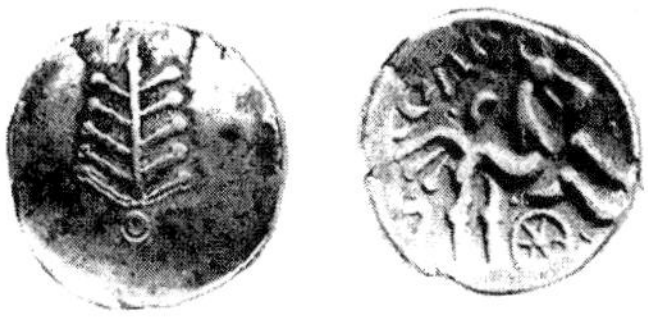 267

No.	Description		
265	**Catti.** *Stater.* Similar to 260 but CATTI. *M. 391; V. 1130*	375	725
266	**Comux.** *Stater.* Similar to 260 but COMVX outwardly. *M. 392; V. 1092*	525	1000
267	**Corio.** *Stater.* Similar to 260 but CORIO. *M. 393; V. 1035*	400	750
268	*Quarter stater.* COR in centre. R. Horse r. without legend. *M. 394; V. 1039*	500	1000

269  270

No.	Description		
269	**Bodvoc.** *Stater.* BODVOC across field. R. As last. *M. 395; V. 1052*	650	1250
270	*Silver.* Head l., BODVOC. R. As last. *M. 396; V. 1057*	125	225

EASTERN ENGLAND

Iceni *Cambs., Norfolk and Suffolk* *c.*A.D. 10-61

272  273

No.	Description		
271	**Duro.** *Silver.* Boar. R. Horse r., CAN(s) above, DVRO below. *M. 434; V. 663*	200	375
272	**Anted.** *Stater.* Triple crescent design. R. ANTED in two monograms below horse. *M. 418; V. 705*	425	950
273	*Silver.* Two crescents back to back. R. ANTED as last. *M. 419-421; V. 710/11/15*	20	45
274	*Silver half unit.* Similar to last. *M. 422; V. 720*	25	50

		F £	VF £
275	**Ecen.** *Silver.* As 273. ℞. Open headed horse r., ECEN below. *M. 424 V. 730*	30	50
276	*Silver half unit.* Similar, but legends read ECE, EC, or ECN. *M. 431; V. 736*	35	55
277	**Ed.** *Silver.* Similar to 275 but ED (also, E, EI and EDN) below horse. *M. 423, 425b; V. 734/40*	35	65
278	**Ece.** *Silver.* As 273. ℞. Stepping horse r., ECE below. *M. 425a; V. 761*	30	55

279 283

		F £	VF £
279	— Similar, but 'Y' headed horse r., ECE below. *M. 426-427; V. 762/4*	25	50
280	— Similar, but horse l. *M. 428; V. 766*	25	50
281	**Saenu.** *Silver.* As 273. ℞. 'Y' headed horse r., SAENV below. *M. 433; V. 770*	55	125
282	**Aesu.** *Silver.* As 273. ℞. As last, AESV. *M. 432; V. 775*	65	150
283	**Prasutagus,** Client King of the Iceni under Claudius; husband of Boudicca. *Silver.* Head of good style l. SUB RII PRASTO. ℞. Rearing horse r., ESICO FECIT. *M. 434a; V. 780*	475	1100

The attribution by H. Mossop of these rare coins to King Prasutagus has been made after a study of the legends on the ten known specimens and is published in 'Britannia', X. 1979.

Coritani (usually known as 'Corieltauvi') *Lincs., Yorks. and E. Midlands c.* A.D. 10-61

		F £	VF £
284	**Iat Iso.** *Silver.* IAT ISO (retrograde) on tablet, rosettes above and below. ℞. Horse r., E above. *M. 416; V. 998*	200	375
285	**Ale Sca.** *Silver.* Boar r., ALE below. ℞. Hor se, SCA below. *M. 469; V. 996*	175	325
286	**Aun Cost.** *Stater.* Crude wreath type. ℞. Disjointed horse l., AVN COST. *M. 457; V. 910*	425	750
287	*Silver. O.* Blank or crude wreath design. ℞. AVN above horse l. *M. 458; V. 914*	75	140
288	*Silver half unit.* Similar. *Vide M. p. 166; V. 918*	65	125
289	**Esup Asu.** *Stater.* As 286 but IISVP ASV. *M. 456b; V. 920*	425	750
290	*Silver.* Similar. *M. 456c; V. 924*	125	225

291 294

		F £	VF £
291	**Vep Corf.** *Stater.* As 286. ℞. Disjointed horse, VEP CORF. *M. 459, 460; V. 930*	300	525
292	*Silver.* Similar. *M. 460b, 464; V. 934, 50*	75	140
293	*Silver half unit.* Similar. *M. 464a; V. 938*	55	100
294	— Similar but VEPOC (M)ES, pellets below horse. *M. —; V. 955*	65	125
295	*Silver half unit.* Similar. *M. —; V. 958*	75	140

		F £	*VF* £
296	**Vep.** *Stater. O.* Blank. R. VEP.*M. 460a; V. 905*	500	900

297 299

297	*Silver.* As 286 or blank. R. VEP only. *M. —; V. 965*	80	150
298	*Silver half unit.* Similar. *M. 464b; V. 967*	65	125
298A	*Silver quarter unit.* Wreath pattern with two 'eyes'. R. Horse r. with VE above	85	160
299	**Dumno Tigir Seno.** *Stater.* DVMN (OC)? across wreath. R. Horse l., TIGIR SENO. *M. 461; V. 972*	550	950
300	*Silver. O.* DVMNO(C)? R. Horse r., legend as last. *M. 462; V. 974*	145	275

300 301

301	**Volisios Dumnocoveros.** *Stater.* VOLI / SIOS in two lines. R. Horse, DVMNOCOVEROS across crude wreath. *M. 463; V. 978*	350	650
302	*Silver.* As last. *M. 463a; V. 978 or 80*	145	275
303	*Silver half unit.* As last but DVMNOCO. *M. 465; V. 984*	110	200
304	**Volisios Dumnovellaunos.** *Stater.* As 301. R. Horse, DVMNOVELAV NOS. *M. 466; V. 988*	475	900

305

305	*Silver half unit.* As last but DVMNOVE. *M. 467; V. 992*	120	200
306	**Volisios Cartivel.** *Silver half unit.* As 301. R. Horse, CARTIVEL. *M. 468; V. 994*	150	225

ROMAN BRITAIN

From the middle of the first century A.D. until the early part of the fifth century, Britannia was a province of the vast Roman Empire—a single state encompassing the whole of the Mediterranean basin. In common with other western provinces, no local coinage was officially produced in Britain during this period (unlike the Eastern part of the Empire where hundreds of towns were permitted to issue muncipal currency) until the latter part of the third century. It was, therefore, the regular Imperial coinage produced mainly at Rome until the mid-third century, that supplied the currency requirements of the province, and no representative collection of British coins is complete without some examples of these important issues.

Although Britain was on the fringe of the Roman World, and never entirely subdued by the legions, a surprisingly large number of coin types allude to events in the province—usually frontier wars in the north. In the closing years of the third century, the usurper Carausius established two mints in Britain; one in London, the other not yet certainly identified (either Camulodunum: Colchester or Clausentum: Bitterne, Southampton). After the defeat of the rebellion London became an official Roman mint, with a substantial output of billon coinage until its closure, by Constantine the Great, in A.D. 325. Other coins were produced unofficially in Britain at various times: soon after the conquest (copies of bronze coins of Claudius, etc.), in the troubled times of the early 270s (copies of Claudius II and the Tetrici, i.e., 'Barbarous radiates') and the final years of the occupation (mostly imitated from the bronze coinage of Constantius II—'soldier spearing fallen horseman' type).'

The Roman legions were withdrawn to the Continent by Honorius in A.D. 411, and this date can be taken to be the formal end of Roman Britain, although a Romano-British civil administration continued to operate for some time afterward until disrupted by the Teutonic invasions.

For more detailed information on Roman coinage including a more comprehensive list of types see *Roman Coins and their Values* by D. R. Sear and *Roman Coins* by J. P. C. Kent, *Roman Imperial Coinage,* the British Museum Catalogues of Roman coins, *Roman Silver Coins* (5 vols.), and *The Coinage of Roman Britain* by G. Askew (2nd edition).

Invaluable companion volumes for anyone studying Roman coinage are J. Melville Jones, *A Dictionary of Ancient Roman Coins*, and R. Reece, *Coinage in Roman Britain.*

THE REPUBLIC

Only a few representative examples are listed. Many Republican coins circulated well into the Imperial period and found their way to Britain where they are often found in many early hoards.

		F £	*VF* £
451	C. Naevius Balbus, moneyer, 79 B.C. Æ *denarius.* Diad. hd. of Venus r. ℞. Victory in triga r.	20	50
452	C. Calpurnius Piso, moneyer, 67 B.C. Æ *denarius.* Head of Apollo r. ℞. Horseman galloping r.	20	60

452

454

		F £	*VF* £
453	**Julius Caesar,** dictator, †44 B.C. Made two expeditions to Britain in 55 and 54 B.C. Æ *denarius.* Laur. head r. ℞. Venus stg. l.	200	700
454	Æ *denarius.* Elephant stg. r. ℞. Sacrifical implements	90	200
455	**Mark Antony,** triumvir, †30 B.C. Æ *denarius.* Galley r. ℞. Legionary eagle between two standards	35	100

Known for all Legions from I (PRI*mus) to XXIII, though only the following are known to have served in Britain during the Roman occupation—II Augusta, VI Victrix, IX Hispania, XIV Gemina Martia Victrix and XX Valeria Victrix.*

THE EMPIRE

456

461

		F £	VF £
456	**Augustus,** 27 B.C.-A.D. 14. Æ *denarius.* ℞. Caius and Lucius Caesars	40	125
457	**Æ.** as ℞. The altar of Lugdunum	50	125
458	**Divus Augustus Pater,** commemorative issue. Æ *as.* ℞. PROVIDENT S . C. Altar	40	150
459	**Livia,** wife of Augustus. Æ *dupondius.* ℞. Legend around S. C	80	300
460	**Agrippa,** general and statesman, †12 B.C. Æ *as.* ℞. Neptune stg. l.	35	125
461	**Tiberius,** A.D. 14-37. Æ *denarius.* ℞. Livia seated r. *This coin is often referred to as the 'Tribute Penny' of the Bible.*	60	125
462	**Drusus,** son of Tiberius, †A.D. 23. Æ *as.* ℞. Legend around S. C.	45	110
463	**Nero Claudius Drusus,** father of Claudius, †9 B.C. Æ *sestertius.* ℞. Claudius seated amidst arms	110	350
464	**Antonia,** mother of Claudius, †A.D. 37. Æ *dupondius.* ℞. Claudius stg.l.	65	150
465	**Germanicus,** father of Caligula, †A.D. 19. Æ *as.* ℞. Legend around S. C.	45	150
466	**Agrippina Senior,** wife of Germanicus, †A.D. 33. Æ *sestertius.* ℞. Two mules drawing covered carriage	150	750
467	**Caligula,** 37-41. Æ *as.* ℞. VESTA. Vesta seated l.	65	250

468

473

		F £	VF £
468	**Claudius,** 41-54. Invaded Britain A.D. 43. AV *aureus.* ℞. DE BRITANN on triumphal arch.	800	3500
469	Æ *denarius.* Similar	400	1000
470	Æ *didrachm* of Caesarea. ℞. DE BRITANNIS below Emperor in quadriga r.	110	500
471	Æ *sestertius.* ℞. SPES AVGVSTA S. C. Spes walking l., of barbarous style, struck in Britain	100	300
472	Æ *dupondius.* ℞. CERES AVGVSTA S. C. Ceres seated l., of barbarous style, struck in Britain	45	95
473	Æ *as.* ℞. S . C. Minerva brandishing javelin r., of barbarous style, struck in Britain	35	85
474	**Nero,** 54-68. Æ *denarius.* ℞. SALVS. Salus seated l.	65	250
475	Æ *as.* ℞. S . C. Victory flying l.	35	125
476	**Galba,** 68-69. Æ *denarius.* ℞. DIVA AVGVSTA. Livia stg. l.	100	300

		F £	VF £
477	**Otho,** 69. *Æ denarius.* ℞. SECVRITAS P . R. Securitas stg. l.	200	500
478	**Vitellius,** 69. *Æ denarius.* ℞. XV. VIR SACR. FAC. Tripod with dolphin	100	300

479

482

479	**Vespasian,** 69-79. Commanded one of the legions in the Claudian invasion of Britain. *Æ denarius.* ℞. ANNONA AVG. Annona seated l.	25	75
480	Æ *as.* ℞. PROVIDENT. S. C. Large altar	35	75
481	**Titus,** 79-81. *Æ denarius.* ℞. FORTVNA AVGVST. Fortuna stg. l.	45	100
482	**Domitian,** 81-96. *Æ denarius.* ℞. IMP . XI. COS . XI . CENS . P . P . P. Minerva fighting	35	50
483	Æ *dupondius.* ℞. VIRTVTI AVGVSTI. S . C. Virtus stg. r.	20	50
484	**Nerva,** 96-98. *Æ denarius.* ℞. CONCORDIA EXERCITVVM. Clasped hands	35	100

485

489

485	**Trajan,** 98-117. *Æ denarius.* ℞. P . M . TR . P . COS . III . P . P. Victory standing r. on prow	35	65
486	Æ *sestertius.* ℞. S . P . Q . R . OPTIMO PRINCIPI. S . C. Fortuna stg l.	40	150
487	**Hadrian,** 117-138. Visited Britain *c.* A.D. 122 and constructed his famous wall from the Tyne to the Solway. *Æ denarius.* ℞. FIDES PVBLICA. Fides stg. r.	25	65
488	Æ *sestertius.* ℞. ADVENTVI AVG . BRITANNIAE. S . C. Emperor and Britannia sacrificing over altar	*Extremely rare*	
489	— ℞. BRITANNIA. S . C. Britannia seated l.	*Extremely rare*	
490	— ℞. EXERC. BRITANNI. S. C. Emperor on horseback addressing soldiers	*Extremely rare*	

491

		F £	VF £
491	Æ *as*. R. PONT. MAX . TR . POT . COS . III . BRITANNIA. S . C. Britannia seated l.	120	330
492	**Sabina,** wife of Hadrian, AR *denarius*. R. CONCORDIA AVG. Concordia seated l.	35	100
493	**Aelius Caesar,** 136-138. Æ *as*. R. TR . POT . COS . II . S . C. Fortuna stg. l.	40	125
494	**Antoninus Pius,** 138-161. His generals in Britain pushed the Roman frontier forward to the Forth-Clyde line (the Antonine Wall). AV *aureus*. R. IMPERATOR II . BRITAN. Victory stg. on globe	550	2000
495	AR *denarius*. R. AEQVITAS AVG. Aequitas stg. l.	20	50

496

		F £	VF £
496	Æ *sestertius*. R. BRITANNIA. S . C. Britannia seated l. on rocks	350	1000
497	— R. IMPERATOR II . BRITAN. S . C. Victory stg. on globe	150	450
498	Æ *as*. R. Victory l. holding shield inscribed BRI. TAN	75	225
499	— R. BRITANNIA COS . III . S . C. Britannia seated l. *This coin was very possibly struck at a temporary travelling mint in Britain.*	45	135
500	**Faustina Senior,** wife of Antoninus Pius, AR *denarius*. R. AVGVSTA. Ceres stg. r.	20	50
501	Æ *sestertius*. R. IVNO S . C. Juno stg. l.	35	85
502	**Marcus Aurelius,** 161-180. AR *denarius*. R. COS III. Jupiter seated l.	25	65
503	Æ *sestertius*. R. IMP . VI . COS . III. S . C. Roma seated l.	85	200

504

		F £	VF £
504	**Faustina Junior,** wife of Marcus Aurelius. Æ *denarius.* ℞. IVNONI REGINAE. Juno and peacock	20	45
505	Æ *as.* ℞. DIANA LVCIF . S . C. Diana stg. l.	20	60
506	**Lucius Verus,** 161-169. Æ *denarius.* ℞. CONCORD . AVG . COS . II. Concordia seated l.	20	50
507	**Lucilla,** wife of Lucius Verus. Æ *dupondius.* ℞. SALVS S . C. Salus stg. l.	20	55
508	**Commodus,** 177-192. There was considerable military activity in northern Britain in the early part of his reign. Æ *denarius.* ℞. MARTI VLTORI AVG. Mars stg. l.	20	50
509	Æ *sestertius.* ℞. BRITT . etc. Britannia stg., holding sword and wreath	*Extremely*	*rare*

510

510	— ℞. VICT . BRIT . etc. Victory seated r., inscribing shield	75	225
511	**Crispina,** wife of Commodus, Æ *as.* ℞. IVNO LVCINA S . C. Juno stg. l	20	55
512	**Pertinax,** 193. One time governor of Britain, under Commodus. Æ *denarius.* ℞. LAETITIA TEMPOR COS . II. Laetitia stg. l	300	700
513	**Didius Julianus,** 193. Æ *sestertius.* ℞. CONCORD MILITS . C. Concordia stg. l.	250	600
514	**Clodius Albinus,** 195-197. Proclaimed emperor while governor of Britain. Æ *denarius.* ℞. MINER . PACIF . COS . II. Minerva stg. l. ...	55	150

515

515	**Septimius Severus,** 193-211. Campaigned in Britain with his sons Caracalla and Geta; died at York. *AV aureus.* ℞. VICTORIAE BRIT. Victory l., holding wreath and palm	1000	4000

		F £	VF £
516	*Æ denarius.* ℞. Similar	40	80
517	— ℞. Similar, but Victory seated l.	40	80
518	— ℞. Similar, but Victory stg. beside palm tree	40	85
519	— ℞. VIRT . AVG. Roma stg. l.	15	40

520

520	*Æ sestertius.* ℞. VICTORIAE BRITTANNICAE S.C. Two Victories affixing shield to palm tree, two captives below	450	1200
521	*Æ dupondius.* ℞. Similar, but Victory inscribing shield on palm tree	85	250
522	*Æ as.* ℞. Similar, Victory stg. r. holding vexillum	85	250
524	**Julia Domna,** wife of Septimius Severus. *Æ denarius.* ℞. PIETAS PVBLICA. Pietas stg. l.	20	50
525	**Caracalla,** 198-217. Personally led the campaign of A.D. 210. *AV aureus.* ℞. VICTORIAE BRIT. Victory seated l., holding shield	850	3000
526	*AV quinarius.* ℞. VICTORIAE BRIT. Victory advancing l., holding wreath and palm	1100	3000
527	*Æ denarius.* ℞. MARTI PACATORI. Mars stg. l.	15	30

528

528	— ℞. VICTORIAE BRIT. Victory advancing l., holding wreath and palm.	40	80
529	— ℞. VICTORIAE BRIT. Victory advancing r., holding trophy	40	80
530	*Æ sestertius.* ℞. VICT . BRIT . P . M . TR . P . XIII . COS . III . P . P . S . C. Victory stg. r., erecting trophy	200	450
531	— ℞. VICT . BRIT . etc. Victory inscribing shield on tree	200	450
532	— ℞. VICTORIAE BRITTANNICAE. S . C. Two Victories erecting shield on tree	250	500
533	*Æ dupondius.* ℞. VICTORIAE BRITTANNICAE. S . C. Victory seated l., on shields	75	200
534	**Plautilla,** wife of Caracalla. *Æ denarius.* ℞. PIETAS AVGG. Pietas stg. r.	20	50
535	**Geta,** 209-212. *Æ denarius.* ℞. PONTIF . COS . II. Genius stg. l.	20	50
536	— ℞. VICTORIAE BRIT. Victory advancing r., holding wreath and palm	35	80

537

		F £	VF £
537	Æ *sestertius.* ℞. VICTORIAE BRITTANNICAE. S . C. Victory seated r., inscribing shield	250	500
538	— ℞. VICTORIAE BRITTANNICAE. S . C. Victory standing r., erecting trophy; Britannia stg. facing with hands tied	250	500
538A	Billon tetradrachm of Alexandria, Egypt. ℞. NEIKH . KATA . BPET . Victory flying l.	300	700
539	**Macrinus,** 217-218. Æ *denarius.* ℞. SALVS PVBLICA. Salus seated l., feeding snake	30	75
540	**Diadumenian Caesar**, 217-218. Æ *denarius.* ℞. PRINC IVVENTVTIS. Diadumenian holding sceptre	80	200

541 546

		F £	VF £
541	**Elagabalus,** 218-222. Æ *denarius.* ℞. FIDES MIL ITVM. Fides stg. l., head r., holding standards	15	35
542	**Julia Paula,** wife of Elagabalus. Æ *denarius.* ℞. CONCORDIA. Concordia seated l.	40	90
543	**Aquilia Severa,** wife of Elagabalus. Æ *denarius.* ℞. CONCORDIA. Concordia stg. l.	65	140
544	**Julia Soaemias,** mother of Elagabalus. Æ *denarius.* ℞. VENVS CAELESTIS. Venus stg. l.	30	65
545	**Julia Maesa,** grandmother of Elagabalus. Æ *denarius.* ℞. IVNO. Juno stg. l.	20	40
546	**Severus Alexander,** 222-235. Æ *denarius.* ℞. PAX AVG. Pax advancing l.	15	35
547	Æ *sestertius.* ℞. FIDES MILITVM. S . C. Fides stg l.	15	45
548	**Orbiana,** wife of Severus Alexander. Æ *denarius.* ℞. CONCORDIA AVGG. Concordia seated l.	65	150
549	**Julia Mamaea,** mother of Severus Alexander. Æ *denarius.* ℞. VENVS VICTRIX. Venus stg. l.	20	45

550

		F	VF
		£	£
550	**Maximinus I,** 235-238. Æ *denarius.* ℞. PAX AVGVSTI. Pax stg. l...	20	45
551	Æ *sestertius.* ℞. VICTORIA AVG. S . C. Victory advancing r.	30	85
552	**Maximus Caesar,** 235-238. Æ *sestertius.* ℞. PRINCIPI IVVENTVTIS. S . C. Maximus stg. l.	45	120
553	**Balbinus,** 238. Æ *denarius.* ℞. VICTORIA AVGG. Victory stg. l.	90	200
554	**Pupienus,** 238. Æ *denarius.* ℞. PAX PVBLICA. Pax seated l.	90	200
555	**Gordian III** 238-244. Æ *denarius.* ℞. SALVS AVGVSTI. Salus stg. r. feeding serpent	15	25
556	Æ *antoninianus.* ℞. ORIENS AVG . Sol stg. l.	15	25
557	Æ *sestertius.* ℞. AEQVITAS AVG. S . C. Aequitas stg. l.	20	60

558

563

		F	VF
558	**Philip I,** 244-249. Æ *antoninianus.* ℞. ROMAE AETERNAE. Roma seated l.	12	25
559	Æ *sestertius.* ℞. SECVRIT. ORBIS S . C. Securitas seated l.	25	60
560	**Otacilia Severa,** wife of Philip I. Æ *antoninianus.* ℞. PIETAS AVGVSTAE. Pietas stg. l.	15	35
561	**Philip II,** 247-249. Æ *antoninianus.* ℞. AETERNIT . IMPER. Sol advancing l.	20	45
562	**Trajan Decius,** 249-251. Æ *antoninianus.* ℞. DACIA. Dacia stg. l. ...	15	45
563	**Herennia Etruscilla,** wife of Trajan Decius. Æ *antoninianus.* ℞. PVDICITIA AVG. Pudicitia stg. l.	10	25
564	**Herennius Etruscus Caesar,** 251. Æ *antoninianus.* ℞. SPES PVBLICA. Spes advancing l.	30	65
565	**Hostilian Caesar,** 251. Æ *antoninianus.* ℞. PIETAS AVGVSTORVM. Sacrificial implements	35	80
566	**Trebonianus Gallus,** 251-253. Æ *antoninianus.* ℞. LIBERTAS AVGG. Libertas stg. l.	12	30
567	**Volusian,** 251-253. Æ *antoninianus.* ℞. CONCORDIA AVGG. Concordia seated l.	10	25
568	**Aemilian,** 252-253. Æ *antoninianus.* ℞. PACI AVG. Pax stg. l.	45	95
569	**Valerian I,** 253-260. Billon *antoninianus.* ℞. VICTORIA AVGG. Victory stg. l.	8	20

570

576

No.		F £	VF £
570	**Gallienus,** 253-268. Æ *antoninianus.* ℞. DIANAE CONS . AVG. Antelope	10	20
571	**Salonina,** wife of Gallienus. Æ *antoninianus.* ℞. PIETAS AVG. Pietas stg. l.	6	18
572	**Valerian II Caesar**, 253-255. Billon antoninianus. ℞. PIETAS AVGG. Sacrificial implements	12	30
573	**Saloninus Caesar,** 259. Billon *antoninianus.* ℞. SPES PVBLICA. Spes advancing l.	7	20
574	**Macrianus,** usurper in the East, 260-261. Billon *antoninianus.* ℞. SOL. INVICTO. Sol stg. l.	30	80
575	**Quietus,** usurper in the East, 260-261. Billon *antoninianus.* ℞. ROMAE AETERNAE. Roma seated l.	30	80
576	**Postumus,** usurper in the West, 259-268. Æ *antoninianus.* ℞. MONETA AVG. Moneta stg. l.	15	40
577	**Laelianus,** usurper in the West, 268. Æ *antoninianus.* ℞. VICTORIA AVG. Victory advancing r.	100	300
578	**Marius,** usurper in the West, 268. Æ *antoninianus.* ℞. VICTORIA AVG. Victory advancing r.	30	70
579	**Victorinus,** usurper in the West, 268-270. AV *aureus.* ℞. LEG . XX . VAL . VICTRIX. Boar l	3500	10000
580	Æ *antoninianus.* ℞. SALVS AVG. Salus stg. l.	8	20
581	**Claudius II Gothicus,** 268-270. Æ *antoninianus.* ℞. MARTI PACIF. Mars advancing l.	8	20
582	**Tetricus I,** usurper in the West, 270-273. Æ *antoninianus.* LAETITIA AVG. Laetitia stg. l.	8	20
583	**Tetricus II Caesar,** usurper in the West, 270-273. Æ *antoninianus.* ℞. SPES AVGG. Spes advancing l.	8	20

584A

584B

584C

No.		F £	VF £
584	**Barbarous radiates.** British and Continental copies of Æ *antoniniani*, mostly of Claudius II (A), Tetricus I (B) and Tetricus II (C)	5	10
585	**Quintillus,** 270. Æ *antoninianus.* ℞. FIDES MILIT. Fides stg. l.	18	50
586	**Aurelian,** 270-275. Æ *antoninianus.* ℞. SECVRIT . AVG. Securitas stg. l.	8	25

587

596

		F £	*VF* £
587	**Severina,** wife of Aurelian. Æ *antoninianus.* ℞. PROVIDEN . DEOR. Fides and Sol stg.	15	45
588	**Tacitus,** 275-276. Æ *antoninianus.* ℞. CLEMENTIA TEMP. Clementia stg. l.	15	45
589	**Florianus,** 276. Æ *antoninianus.* ℞. SALVS AVG. Salus stg. l.	30	100
590	**Probus,** 276-282. Æ *antoninianus.* ℞. ABVNDANTIA AVG. Abundantia stg. r.	10	25
591	**Carus,** 282-283. Æ *antoninianus.* ℞. PAX EXERCITI. Pax stg. l.	12	35
592	**Numerian,** 283-284. Æ *antoninianus.* ℞. ORIENS AVG. Sol advancing l.	12	35
593	**Carinus,** 283-285. Æ *antoninianus.* ℞. AETERNIT. AVG. Aeternitas stg. l.	10	30
594	**Diocletian,** 284-305, London mint reopened *c.* 297. AR *argenteus.* ℞. VIRTVS MILITVM. Tetrarchs sacrificing before camp gate	80	300
595	Æ *antoninianus.* ℞. CLEMENTIA TEMP. Diocletian and Jupiter stg.	8	25
596	Æ *follis.* ℞. GENIO POPVLI ROMANI. Genius stg. l., LON (London) mm.	15	45

597

600

		F £	*VF* £
597	Æ *follis.* ℞. Similar, no *mm.* (London)	12	40
598	— ℞. Similar, other *mms.*	10	35
599	**Maximianus,** 286-310. AR *argenteus.* ℞. VIRTVS MILITVM. Tetrarchs sacrificing before camp gate	80	250
600	Æ *antoninianus.* ℞. SALVS AVGG. Salus stg. l.	8	20
601	Æ *follis.* ℞. GENIO POPVLI ROMANI. Genius stg. l., LON. *mm.*	10	30
602	— ℞. Similar, no *mm.*	7	24
603	**Carausius,** commander of the Roman Channel fleet, who took power in Britain and Northern Gaul, 287-293. *London mint.* AV *aureus.* ℞. PAX AVG. Pax stg. l., no *mm.*	7500	17500

604

623

		F	VF
		£	£
604	Æ *denarius.* R. RENOVAT ROMANO. Wolf and Twins.	500	1500
605	Æ *antoninianus.* R. ADVENTVS AVG. Emperor riding l.	55	160
606	— R . COHR . PRAEF. Four standards	70	200
607	— R . COMES AVG. Victory stg. l.	40	100
608	— R. CONCORD . EXERCI. Four standards	40	120
609	— R. CONCORDIA MILITVM. Clasped hands	40	120
610	— R. CONSERVAT . AVG. Sol stg. l.	55	160
611	— R. FELICIT . TEMP. Felicitas stg. l.	25	70
612	— R. FIDES MILITVM. Fides stg. l.	55	160
613	— R. FORTVNA AVG. Fortuna stg. l.	20	55
614	— R. GENIVS AVG. Genius stg. l.	55	160
615	— R. GERMANICVS MAX . V. Trophy between captives	130	360
616	— R. LAETITIA AVG. Laetitia stg. l.	20	55
617	— R. LEG . II . AVG. Capricorn l.	55	160
618	— R. LEG XX . V . V. Boar r.	65	175
619	— R. MARS VLTOR. Mars walking r.	55	160
620	— R. MONETA AVG. Moneta stg. l.	20	55
621	— R. ORIENS AVG. Sol walking r.	25	70
622	— R. PACATOR ORBIS. Bust of Sol r.	95	280
623	— R. PAX AVG. Pax stg. l.	15	50
624	— R. PIETAS AVG. Pietas sacrificing at altar	25	70
625	— R. SALVS AVG. Salus feeding serpent	20	55
626	— R. SECVRIT . PERP. Securitas stg. l.	25	70
627	— R. VICTORIA AVG. Victory walking r.	25	70

628

		F	VF
628	Æ *antoninianus.* Struck in the name of Diocletian. R. PAX AVGGG. Pax stg. l.	20	60
629	Æ *antoninianus.* Struck in the name of Maximianus. R. PROVIDENTIA AVG. Providentia stg. l.	20	60
630	*Colchester or Clausentum (C) mint. Æ denarius.* R. CONCORDIA MILITVM. Clasped hands	350	1000
631	Æ *antoninianus.* R. ABVNDANTIA AVG. Abundantia stg. l.	25	70
632	— R. APOLINI CON . AV. Griffin walking r.	90	240

		F £	VF £
633	— R. CONCORDIA AVGGG. Two emperors stg.	110	320
634	— R. CONSTANT. AVG. Nude male stg. r.	55	160
635	— R. EXPECTATE VENI. Britannia stg. r.	90	240
636	— R. FELICITAS AVG. Galley	70	200
637	— R. GENIO BRITANNI. Genius stg. l.	120	340
638	— R. HILARITAS AVG. Hilaritas stg. l.	20	55
639	— R. IOVI CONSERV. Jupiter stg. l.	25	70
640	— R. LEG. I. MIN. Ram stg. r.	55	160
641	— R. LIBERALITAS AVG. Carausius seated with subordinates	70	200
642	— R. PAX AVG. Pax stg. l.	20	55

643 653

		F £	VF £
643	— R. PROVID . AVG. Providentia stg. l.	20	60
644	— R. RENOVAT . ROMA. She-wolf suckling Romulus and Remus	65	175
645	— R. RESTIT . SAECVL. Carausius and Victory stg.	65	175
646	— R. ROMAE AETER. Roma seated l.	40	100
647	— R. SAECVLARES AVG. Lion walking r.	70	200
648	— R. SOLI INVICTE. Sol in quadriga	55	160
649	— R. SPES PVBLICA. Spes walking r.	20	60
650	— R. TEMP . FELICIT. Felicitas stg. l.	20	60
651	— R. VIRTVS AVG. Mars stg. r.	20	55
651A	Æ *antoninianus.* Struck in the name of Diocletian. R. PAX AVGGG. Pax stg. l.	20	60
652	Æ *antoninianus.* Struck in the name of Maximianus. R. PAX AVGGG. Pax stg. l.	20	60
653	**Carausius, Diocletian and Maximianus.** Æ *antoninianus.* Struck by Carausius. CARAVSIVS ET FRATRES SVI. Jugate busts of three emperors l. R. PAX AVGGG. Pax stg. l.	600	1750
654	**Allectus,** chief minister and murderer of Carausius, 293-296. *London mint.* AV *aureus.* R. PAX AVG. Pax stg. l.	7500	20000
655	Æ *antoninianus.* R. AEQVITAS AVG. Aequitas stg. l.	25	65
656	— R. COMES AVG. Minerva stg. l.	25	65
657	— R. FORTVNA AVG. Fortuna seated l.	55	160
658	— R. HILARITAS AVG. Hilaritas stg. l.	20	60
659	— R. LAETITIA AVG. Laetitia stg. l.	25	65
660	— R. LEG . II. Lion walking l.	150	400
661	— R. ORIENS AVG. Sol stg. l.	60	175

662 678

No.	Description	F £	VF £
662	— ℞. PAX AVG. Pax stg. l.	30	70
663	— ℞. PIETAS AVG. Pietas stg. l.	25	65
664	— ℞. PROVIDENTIA AVG. Providentia stg. l.	40	80
665	— ℞. SAECVLI FELICITAS. Emperor stg. r.	65	150
666	— ℞. SALVS AVG. Salus feeding serpent	25	65
667	— ℞. SPES PVPLICA. Spes holding flower	25	60
668	— ℞. TEMPORVM FELICI. Felicitas stg. l.	25	60
669	— ℞. VICTORIA AVG. Victory stg. r.	25	60
670	— ℞. VIRTVS AVG. Mars stg. r.	25	65
671	Æ *quinarius.* ℞. VIRTVS AVG. Galley	25	65
672	*Colchester or Clausentum (C) mint. Æ antoninianus.* ℞. ABVND . AVG. Abundantia stg. l.	30	70
673	— ℞. ADVENTVS AVG. Emperor riding l.	90	220
674	— ℞. DIANAE REDVCI. Diana leading stag	70	180
675	— ℞. FELICITAS SAECVLI. Felicitas stg. l.	70	180
676	— ℞. FIDES EXERCITVS. Four standards	65	150
677	— ℞. IOVI CONSERVATORI. Jupiter stg. l.	70	180
678	— ℞. MONETA AVG. Moneta stg. l.	30	85
679	— ℞. PAX AVG. Pax stg. l.	28	70
680	— ℞. ROMAE AETERN. Roma in temple	75	200

681 683

No.	Description	F £	VF £
681	Æ *quinarius.* ℞. LAETITIA AVG. Galley	30	70
682	— ℞. VIRTVS AVG. Galley	40	80
683	**Constantius I, Chlorus, Caesar** 293-305. Augustus 305-306, campaigned in Britain and died at York. Æ follis. ℞. GENIO POPVLI ROMANI. Genius stg. l., no *mm.*	10	30
684	Æ *follis.* ℞. MEMORIA FELIX. Eagles beside altar. PLN. *mm.*	15	50
685	Æ *radiate.* ℞. CONCORDIA MILITVM. Constantius and Jupiter stg.	7	20
686	**Galerius,** Caesar 293-305, Augustus 305-311. Æ *follis.* ℞. GENIO IMPERATORIS. Genius stg. l.	5	15
687	— ℞. GENIO POPVLI ROMANI. Genius stg. l., no *mm.*	10	25
688	**Galeria Valeria,** wife of Galerius. Æ *follis.* ℞. VENERI VICTRICI. Venus stg. l.	40	80

		F	VF
		£	£
689	**Severus II,** 306-307. Æ *follis.* ℞. FIDES MILITVM. Fides seated l.	40	80
690	Æ *follis.* ℞. GENIO POPVLI ROMANI. Genius stg. l., no *mm.*	40	100
691	Æ *radiate.* ℞. CONCORDIA MILITVM. Severus and Jupiter stg.	20	55
692	**Maximinus II,** 309-313. Æ *follis.* ℞. GENIO AVGVSTI. Genius stg. l.	8	25
693	— ℞. GENIO POP . ROM. Genius stg. l., PLN. *mm.*	10	30
694	**Maxentius,** 306-312, Æ *follis.* ℞. CONSERV . VRB SVAE. Roma in temple	12	35
695	**Licinius I,** 308-324. Æ *follis.* ℞. GENIO POP . ROM. Genius stg. l., PLN . *mm.*	10	30
696	Æ 3. ℞. SOLI INVICTO COMITI . Sol stg. l.	5	15
697	**Licinius II Caesar,** 317-324. Æ 3. ℞. PROVIDENTIAE CAESS. Camp gate	8	20

698 701

698	**Constantine I, the Great,** 307-337. Came to power in Britain following his father's death at York. London mint closed 325. Æ *follis.* ℞. COMITI AVGG NN Sol stg. l., PLN *mm.*	15	35
699	Æ 3. ℞. BEATA TRANQVILLITAS. Altar. PLON *mm.*	10	20
700	Æ 3. ℞. VOT . XX. in wreath	5	10
701	**Commemorative issues,** Æ 3/4, commencing A.D. 330. Bust of Roma. ℞. She-wolf suckling Romulus and Remus	5	15

702 707

702	Æ 3/4. Bust of Constantinopolis. ℞. Victory stg. l.	5	12
703	**Fausta,** wife of Constantine. Æ 3. ℞. SPES REIPVBLICAE. Fausta stg.	18	50
704	— ℞. Similar. PLON *mm.*	55	135
705	**Helena,** mother of Constantine. Æ 3. ℞. SECVRITAS REIPVBLICE. Helena st g. l.	10	25
706	— ℞. Similar. PLON *mm.*	55	135
707	**Theodora,** second wife of Constantius I, struck after her death. Æ 4. ℞. PIETAS ROMANA. Pietas holding child	8	30
708	**Crispus Caesar,** 317-326. Æ 3. ℞. CAESARVM NOSTRORVM VOT . V. Wreath	6	20
709	— ℞. PROVIDENTIAE CAESS. Camp gate. PLON *mm.*	8	22
710	**Delmatius Caesar,** 335-337. Æ 3. ℞. GLORIA EXERCITVS. Two soldiers stg.	15	40
711	**Hanniballianus Rex,** 335-337. Æ 4. ℞. SECVRITAS PVBLICA. Euphrates reclining	100	250

		F £	VF £
712	**Constantine II Caesar,** 317-337. Æ 3. ℞. BEAT . TRANQLITAS. Altar. PLON *mm.*	10	25
713	Æ 3/4. ℞. GLORIA EXERCITVS. Two soldiers stg.	7	20

714 715

		F £	VF £
714	**Constans,** 337-350. Visited Britain in 343. Æ *centenionalis.* ℞. FEL . TEMP . REPARATIO. Constans stg. on galley	8	30
715	**Constantius II,** 337-361. Æ *centenionalis.* ℞. FEL . TEMP . REPARATIO. Soldier spearing fallen horseman	8	30
716	Æ 3. ℞. PROVIDENTIAE CAESS. Camp gate. PLON *mm.*	30	60
717	**Magnentius,** usurper in the West, 350-353. Æ *centenionalis.* ℞. VICTOR IAE DD . NN. AVG . ET CAE. Two Victories	30	80
718	**Decentius Caesar,** usurper in the West, 351-353. Æ *centenionalis.* ℞. VICTORIAE DD . NN . AVG . ET . CAE . Two Victories	20	50
719	**Constantius Gallus Caesar,** 351-354. Æ *centenionalis.* ℞. FEL . TEMP REPARATIO. Soldier spearing fallen horseman	8	22
720	**Julian II,** 360-363. AR *siliqua.* ℞. VOT . X . MVLT . XX with wreath	25	55
721	Æ 3. ℞ Similar	10	20
722	**Jovian,** 363-364. Æ 3. ℞. VOT . V . within wreath	20	50

723 733

		F £	VF £
723	**Valentinian I,** 364-375. Æ 3. ℞. SECVRITAS REIPVBLICAE. Victory advancing l.	5	15
724	**Valens,** 364-378. AR *siliqua.* ℞. VRBS ROMA. Roma seated l.	20	45
725	Æ 3. ℞. GLORIA ROMANORVM. Valens dragging captive	5	15
726	**Gratian,** 367-383. AR *siliqua.* ℞. VRBS ROMA. Roma seated l.	25	55
727	Æ 3. ℞. CONCORDIA AVGGG. Constantinopolis seated l.	7	18
728	**Valentinian II,** 375-392. AR *siliqua.* ℞. VICTORIA AVGGG. Victory advancing l.	30	65
729	Æ 2. ℞. GLORIA ROMANORVM. Valentinian stg. on galley	10	30
730	Æ 4. ℞. SALVS REIPVBLICAE. Victory advancing l.	5	15
731	**Theodosius I,** 379-395. Æ 2. ℞. GLORIA ROMANORVM. Theodosius stg. on galley	10	30
732	Æ 4. ℞. SALVS REIPVBLICAE. Victory advancing l.	5	15
733	**Magnus Maximus,** usurper in the West, 383-388, proclaimed emperor by the Roman army in Britain, AV *solidus.* ℞. VICTORIA AVGG. Two emperors seated. Victory between them; AVGO B *mm.* (London)	3000	10000

		F £	*VF* £
734	Ꭱ *siliqua.* ℞. VICTORIA AVGG. Victory advancing l. AVGPS *mm.* (London)	400	1000
735	— ℞. VIRTVS ROMANORVM. Roma seated l.	25	60
736	**Flavius Victor,** usurper in the West, 387-388. Æ 4. ℞. SPES ROMANORVM. Camp gate	40	80
737	**Eugenius,** usurper in the West, 392-394. Ꭱ *siliqua.* ℞. VIRTVS ROMANORVM. Roma seated l.	90	250
738	**Arcadius,** 383-408. Æ 2. ℞. GLORIA ROMANORVM. Arcadius stg. r.	10	30
739	**Honorius,** 393-423, during whose reign the so-called 'Roman withdrawal' from Britain took place. Ꭱ *siliqua.* ℞. VIRTVS ROMANORVM. Roma seated l.	25	65
740	Æ 3. ℞. VIRTVS EXERCITI. Honorius stg. r.	7	20

741

741	**Constantine III,** usurper in the West, proclaimed emperor in Britain, 407-411. Ꭱ *siliqua.* ℞. VICTORIA AVGGGG. Roma seated l.	100	300
742	**Valentinian III,** 425-455, Æ 4. ℞. VOT . PVB. Camp gate	20	60

ANGLO-SAXON EARLY PERIOD, *c.* 600-*c.* 775

The withdrawal of Roman forces from Britain early in the 5th century A.D. and the gradual decline of central administration resulted in a rapid deterioration of the money supply. The arrival of Teutonic raiders and settlers hastened the decay of urban commercial life and it was probably not until late in the 6th century that renewed political, cultural and commercial links with the kingdom of the Merovingian Franks led to the appearance of small quantities of Merovingian gold *tremisses* (one-third solidus) in England. A purse containing such pieces was found in the Sutton Hoo ship-burial. Native Anglo-Saxon gold *thrymsas* were minted from about the 630s, initially in the style of their continental prototypes or copied from obsolete Roman coinage and later being made in pure Anglo-Saxon style. By the middle of the 7th century the gold coinage was being increasingly debased with silver, and gold had been superseded entirely by about 675.

These silver coins, contemporary with the *deniers or denarii* of the Merovingian Franks, are the first English pennies, though they are commonly known today as *sceattas* (a term more correctly translated as 'treasure' or 'wealth'). They provide important material for the student of Anglo-Saxon art.

Though the earliest sceattas are a transition from the gold thrymsa coinage, coins of new style were soon developed which were also copied by the Frisians of the Low Countries. Early coins appear to have a standard weight of 20 grains (1.29 gms) and are of good silver content, though the quality deteriorates early in the 8th century. These coins exist in a large number of varied types, and as well as the official issues there are mules and other varieties which are probably contemporary imitations. Many of the sceattas were issued during the reign of Aethelbald of Mercia, but as few bear inscriptions it is only in recent years that research has permitted their correct dating and the attribution of certain types to specific areas. Some silver sceats of groups II and III and most types of groups IV to X were issued during the period (A.D. 716-757) when Aethelbald, King of Mercia, was overlord of the southern English. In Northumbria very debased sceattas or *stycas* continued to be issued until the middle of the ninth century. Though a definitive classification has not yet been developed, the arrangement given below follows the latest work on the series: this list is not exhaustive.

This section has ben catalogued in line with research published by Dr D. M. Metcalf. Wherever possible the Seaby number previously in use has been retained. Where it has been necessary to allocate a new and different number, the 'old' S. number is listed, in brackets, at the end of the entry. New entries are given a new number. The primary sceattas are followed by the secondary sceattas and, finally, the continental sceattas. This is not chronologically correct but has been adopted for ease of reference and identification. The reference '*B.M.C.*' is to the type given in *British Museum Catalogue: Anglo-Saxon Coins*. Other works of reference include:

North, J. J. *English Hammered Coinage*, Vol. 1, *c.* 650-1272 (1980).
Metcalf, D.M. *Thrymsas and Sceattas in the Ashmolean Museum,* Vols I-III.
Rigold, S. E. 'The two primary series of sceattas', *B.N.J.*, xxx (1960).
Sutherland, C. H. V. *Anglo-Saxon Gold Coinage in the light of the Crondall Hoard* (1948).

ᚠ ᚢ ᚦ ᚩ ᚱ ᚳ · ᚷ ᚹ ᚻ ᚾ ᛁ ᛄ ᛇ ᛈ ᛉ ᛋ ᛏ ᛒ ᛖ ᛗ ᛚ ᛝ ᛞ ᛟ ᚪ ᚫ ᛠ ᚣ

f u th o r k . z w h n i j ih p x s t b e m l ng d œ a Æ ea y

Early Anglo-Saxon Runes

GOLD

		F £	*VF* £
A.	**Early pieces, of uncertain monetary status**		
751	Thrymsa. Name and portrait of Bishop Leudard (chaplain to Queen Bertha of Kent). ℞. Cross. *(S.751)*	*Unique*	
752	Solidus. Imitating solidi of Roman rulers. Blundered legends, some with runes. *(S.757)*	*Extremely rare*	

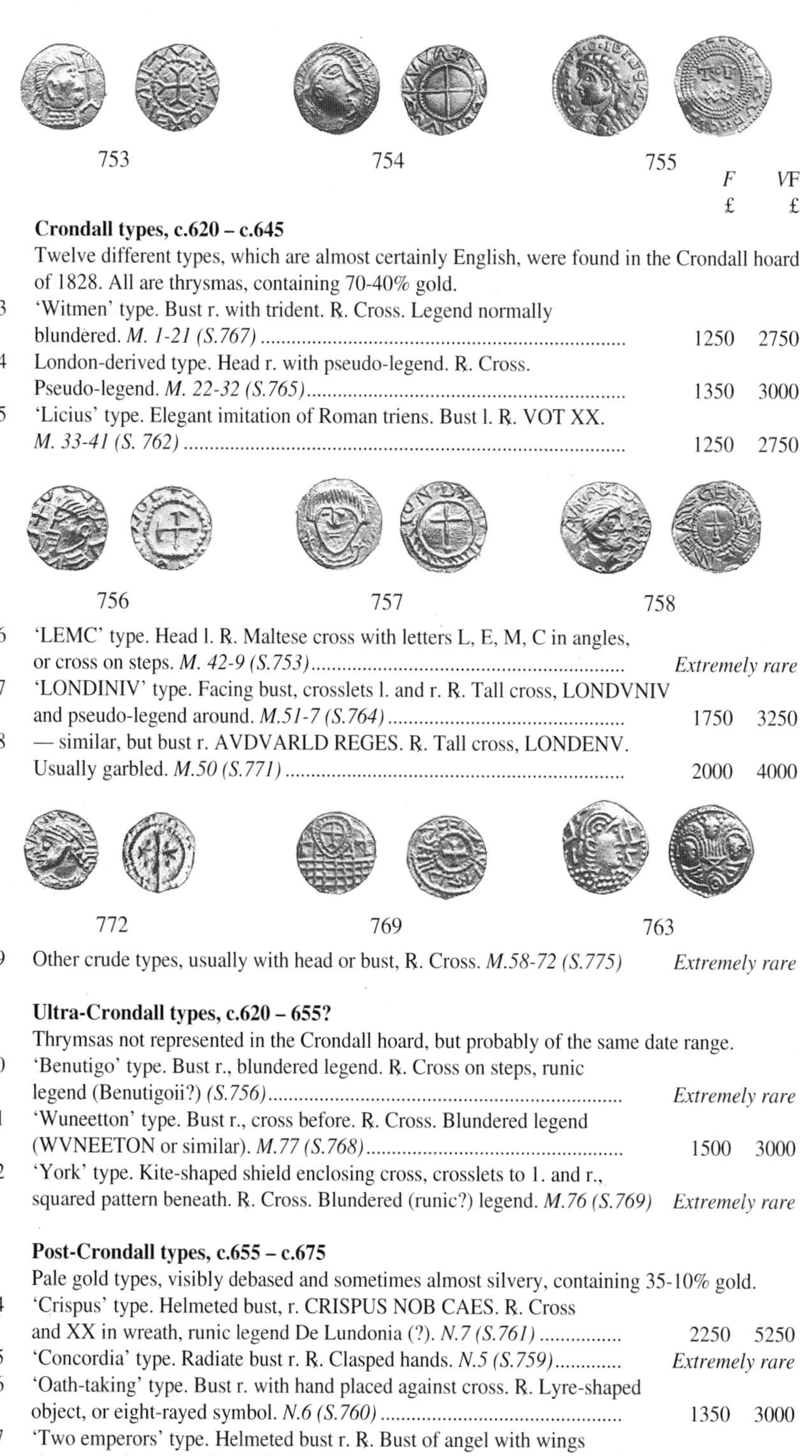

753 754 755

		F £	*VF* £
B.	**Crondall types, c.620 – c.645**		
	Twelve different types, which are almost certainly English, were found in the Crondall hoard of 1828. All are thrysmas, containing 70-40% gold.		
753	'Witmen' type. Bust r. with trident. ℞. Cross. Legend normally blundered. *M. 1-21 (S.767)*	1250	2750
754	London-derived type. Head r. with pseudo-legend. ℞. Cross. Pseudo-legend. *M. 22-32 (S.765)*	1350	3000
755	'Licius' type. Elegant imitation of Roman triens. Bust l. ℞. VOT XX. *M. 33-41 (S. 762)*	1250	2750

756 757 758

756	'LEMC' type. Head l. ℞. Maltese cross with letters L, E, M, C in angles, or cross on steps. *M. 42-9 (S.753)*	*Extremely rare*	
757	'LONDINIV' type. Facing bust, crosslets l. and r. ℞. Tall cross, LONDVNIV and pseudo-legend around. *M.51-7 (S.764)*	1750	3250
758	— similar, but bust r. AVDVARLD REGES. ℞. Tall cross, LONDENV. Usually garbled. *M.50 (S.771)*	2000	4000

772 769 763

759	Other crude types, usually with head or bust, ℞. Cross. *M.58-72 (S.775)*	*Extremely rare*	
C.	**Ultra-Crondall types, c.620 – 655?**		
	Thrymsas not represented in the Crondall hoard, but probably of the same date range.		
760	'Benutigo' type. Bust r., blundered legend. ℞. Cross on steps, runic legend (Benutigoii?) *(S.756)*	*Extremely rare*	
761	'Wuneetton' type. Bust r., cross before. ℞. Cross. Blundered legend (WVNEETON or similar). *M.77 (S.768)*	1500	3000
762	'York' type. Kite-shaped shield enclosing cross, crosslets to l. and r., squared pattern beneath. ℞. Cross. Blundered (runic?) legend. *M.76 (S.769)*	*Extremely rare*	
D.	**Post-Crondall types, c.655 – c.675**		
	Pale gold types, visibly debased and sometimes almost silvery, containing 35-10% gold.		
764	'Crispus' type. Helmeted bust, r. CRISPUS NOB CAES. ℞. Cross and XX in wreath, runic legend De Lundonia (?). *N.7 (S.761)*	2250	5250
765	'Concordia' type. Radiate bust r. ℞. Clasped hands. *N.5 (S.759)*	*Extremely rare*	
766	'Oath-taking' type. Bust r. with hand placed against cross. ℞. Lyre-shaped object, or eight-rayed symbol. *N.6 (S.760)*	1350	3000
767	'Two emperors' type. Helmeted bust r. ℞. Bust of angel with wings above two facing heads. *M.79-80 (S.763)*	1100	2250

768 'Pada', Type Ia Helmeted bust r. ℞. Runic Pada on panel. *M.p.73. (S.777)* 600 1250
768A — Type Ib. Similar. ℞. Standard TTXX, Pada in runes in legend. *M.81*. 600 1250
769 — Type IIa. Diademed bust r. ℞. Pada in runes in field, blundered legend around, *M.p.73. (S.773)* 1000 2250

770/3 771/4 775

770 — Type III. Diademed bust r. ℞. Cross with annulet in angles. ℞. Runic Pada in legend. *M.p.73. (S.779)* 700 1400
771 'Varimundus', Type A. Diademed bust r. holding sceptre. ℞. Cross, with CA in lower angles. VARIMVNDVS MONE. *M.p.82 (S.780)*........ 850 1750
772 — Type B. Similar. ℞. Small cross in double circle of dots. *M.84*........ 750 1500

SILVER

A. Early transitional types by thrymsa moneyers, c.675-685

773 'Pada', Type III. As 770, but silver. *M.82. (S.779)*........ 450 1000
774 'Varimundus', Type B. As 772, but silver. *M.85-7. (S.780)*........ 550 1100

B. Primary Sceattas, c.680 – c.710

Minted in various regions of England.

775 Series A, Radiate bust r., TIC. ℞. Standard, TOTII. *B.M.C.2a M.89-94. (S.781)* 70 150

776 777 778

776 Series BX. Diad. bust r., VANTAVMA or similar. ℞. Bird r. above cross on steps. *B.M.C.26. M.97-9.(S.782)*........ 100 225
777 — BI. Similar but diad. head r. within serpent circle. ℞. Bird r. on cross. *B.M.C. 27a.. M.100-106. (S.783)*........ 70 135
777A — BII. Similar but simplified legend VAVAVA. ℞. Crosslet beside bird. *M.113-6. (S.784)* 75 175
778 — BZ. Crude facing head. ℞. Crude bird on cross (imitation of 776). *M.138-9. (S.784A)*........ 110 225

779 780 782A

779 Series C. Radiate bust r., similar to 775 but runic aepa replaces TIC. ℞. Standard, TOTII. *B.M.C. 2b. M.117-125. (S.785)* 60 105
780 King Aethelred of Mercia? (674-704). 'Porcupine'. ℞. Aethiliraed on runes in two lines. *M134-5. (S.837)*........ 275 525
781 Series F. Bust r., with broad-rimmed hat, blundered legend. ℞. Small cross on steps, annulets around. *M.136-7. (S.839A)* 75 150
782 Series Z. Facing head with moustaches. ℞. Long-legged dog r. with head lowered. *M.140-2. (S.817)* 250 625
782A Series Z-related. Crude animal r., perhaps copy of 782. ℞. Crude cross-crosslet design *M.143-4.* 150 350

783 784 791

No.	Description	F	VF
783	'Vernus' type. Porcupine-related head r., VERNVS before. ℞. Standard. *M.146-8.*	125	225
784	'Saroaldo' type. Unusual bust r. ℞. Saltire and pellets in square, SAROALDO legend around. *M.151-3.*	200	450
785	Series W. Half or full-length facing figure holding two crosses. ℞. Cross crosslet on saltire. *M.155. (S.807A)*	275	550

C. Secondary Sceattas, c.710-760

Minted in all the main regions of southern and eastern England, but especially in the south-east and the Thames basin.

No.	Description	F	VF
791	Series J, Type 85. Large head r. ℞. Bird on cross. *M.293-5.*	75	150
791A	— Type 36. Bust r., cross in front. ℞. One large and one small bird r. *M.301-2. (S.801)*	200	425

792 793 797

No.	Description	F	VF
792	— Type 37. Two heads face-to-face. ℞. Four birds clockwise round cross. *M.296-300.*	110	250
792A	— Type 72. Similar. ℞. Bird r., looking back. *M.303.*	175	350
793	Series U, Type 23b. Standing figure r. holds two crosses. ℞. Pecking bird. *M.445-51.*	125	275
794	Series K, Type 42. Bust r. with bird, cross or flower. ℞. Hound 1., plant behind. *M 311-3*	150	375
795	— Type 20. Bust r. with chalice. ℞. Standing figure holds cross and hawk. *M.314-18.*	100	250
796	— Type 32a. Bust r. with cross. ℞. Wolf curled head to tail. *M.309.*	150	350
797	— — Similar. ℞. Wolf-headed serpent. *M.310*	135	300
798	— Type 32b. Similar. but ℞. Wolf-serpent within torque. *M.307-8.*	135	300
799	— Type 33. Bust r., cross in front. ℞. Wolf's head with long tongue, l. or r. *M.306.*	150	375

800 801 803

No.	Description	F	VF
800	'Archer' type. Kneeling archer r. ℞. Bird on branch r., head turned back. *M.349. (S.800A)*	*Extremely rare*	
801	'Carip' group. Bust r., CARIP. ℞. Pecking bird, wolf-serpent, or standing figure. *M 336-40.*	175	400
802	Series O, Type 38. Bust r. in cable border. ℞. Bird r. in torque. *M.373-5.*	150	350
803	— Type 21. Similar, but bust l. ℞. Standing figure with two crosses. *M.376*	200	400

804 805 806

804	'Triquetras' eclectric group. Facing bust, man and crosses, winged figure, or bird and branch. ℞. Interlace pattern. *M.p.425.*	275	600
805	Series H, Type 39. Pecking bird. ℞. Round shield with bosses. *M.283-4.*	120	210
806	— Type 49. 'Wodan' head, annulets around. ℞. Pecking bird. *M.285-8.*	125	220
807	— Type 48. Whorl of 3 wolf heads. ℞. Round shield with bosses. *M.289-92.*	130	250

808 809A 810

808	Series G. Bust r., cross before. R. Standard with 3 or 4 X's. *(Minted in Northern France?) M.267-70.*	125	240
809	— crude copies, some with bird or bird on cross. *M.271-4.*	80	135
809A	Series M. Prancing dog l. or r. ℞. Spiral branch. *M.363-6. (S.836c.)*	135	275
810	Series N. Two standing figures. ℞. Monster looking back r. or l. *M.368-72.*	110	250

811 813 815

811	Series O, Type 40. Standing figure holds two crosses. ℞. As last. *M.379-81.*	125	275
812	— Type 43. Interlace shield. ℞. As last. *M.p.482.*	175	350
813	— Type 57. Bust r. in cable border. ℞. Monster looking back l. *M.377...*	175	350
814	'Animal mask' group. Facing animal (lion?) mask. ℞. Bird, figure, monster or cross. *M.354-6. (S.814v).*	300	650
815	Series V. Wolf and twins. ℞. Bird in vine. *M.453.*	275	625

816 818 822

816	Series T. Diad. bust r., +LEL. ℞. 'Porcupine' l. *M.442-4.*	175	400
818	Series L, Type 12. Bust r., LVNDONIA. ℞. Standing figure holds two crosses. *M.319-22.*	215	500
820	— Type 13. Similar. ℞. Seated figure holds hawk and cross. *M.p.409.* ...	300	750
821	— Type 14. Similar, but bust l. ℞. Celtic cross. *M.p.427.*	200	500
822	— Type 15. Bust r. with cross, no legend. ℞. Standing figure holds two crosses. *M.323-6.*	150	300
825	— Type 16. Bust r. with floral scroll. ℞. Standing figure holds branch and cross, or two branches. *M.329-30.*	135	300
827	— Type 18. Bust r. with cross. ℞. Standing figure holds cross and bird. *M.331-3.*	150	300
828	— Type 19. Similar, but bust l. *M.335.*	140	325
828A	— Type 34. Bust r. with cross or sceptre. ℞. Celtic cross. *M.345-6. (S.800)*	145	350

828B	Series L-related. Bust r. rosetes in field. ℞. Standing figure holds two crosses. *M.347.*	200	450

829 831 832

829	Type 22. Victory standing with wreath. ℞. Winged figure, or standing figure holding two crosses. *M.350-1.*	250	600
830	Type 23e. Standing figure holds two crosses. ℞. Whorl of 3 wolf heads. *M.359-62.*	110	225
831	Series S. Female centaur. ℞. Whorl of 4 wolf heads. *M.438-41.*	125	250
832	Series ℞. Bust r. or l. Epa, Wigraed, Spi, etc in runes. ℞. Standard. *M.391-428.*	70	135

832v 833 836

832B	Series Q(R), Type 73. Crude radiate bust r. or l. ℞. Quadruped r. *M.388.*	175	400
833	'Saltire Standard' types. Bust l. or r. with cross, two standing figures, or double croix ancree. ℞. Saltire and pellets in square. *M.432-5.*	125	250
834	'Monita Scorum' type. Small bird looking back, MONITA SCORUM. ℞. Standard with saltire of annulets. *M.p.436.*	350	750
834A	— Bust r., MONITA SCORUM. ℞. 'porcupine' l., figure with two crosses, or triquetra. *M.348.*	450	950
835	Type 70. Saltire-standard. ℞. Standard. *M.436-7.*	80	150
836	Series Q, Types QII-IVD Bird l. or r. ℞. Quadruped l. or r. *M.386-7.*	140	300
836A	— Type QIVE Quadruped both sides. *M.p.501*	140	300
836B	— Type QIE Bust r. with cross. ℞. Walking bird l. *M.383.*	175	425
836C	— Type QIF Standing figure with two crosses. ℞. Walking bird l. *M.384.*	275	600
836D	— Type QIG Facing head. ℞. Long-legged quadruped looking back. *M.p.492.*	265	550

844 790A

844	Type 30. Facing 'Wodan' head. ℞. Two standing figures, or standard. *M.429-31.*	150	300
790A	— Type 53. 'Porcupine', similar to 787. ℞. Steppd cross, annulet at centre. *Mint? M.258-62.*	100	225

C. Continental Sceattas, c.695-c.740

Most are from the Rhine mouths area, or Fisia

786

786 Series E. Porcupine-like figure, body with annulet at one end, triangle at other. ℞. 'Standard' with four pellets around central annulet. *Dorestad. M.209-11.* 60 100

787 789 790

787 — Similar, with triangular fore-leg. ℞. 'Standard' with four lines and central annulet. *M.200-5.* 50 90

788 — Similar, with parallel lines in cruve of body. ℞. 'Standard' with VICO. *M.194-8.* 45 85

789 — Figure developed into plumed bird. ℞. Standard. *M.190-3.* 65 125

790 Later issues. ℞. 'Standard' 'Porcupine'. Innumerable varieties. *M.214-53.* 35 70

832A Type 10. Bust r., AEPA or APA. ℞. Porcupine modified into profile face. *Mint? M.p.248.* 175 350

838 'Porcupine' ℞. Small cross, S E D E in angles. *Mint? M.263.* .... *Extremely rare*

839 840 843

839 Series D, Type 2c. Bust r., pseudo-runes. ℞. Plain cross with pellets in angles. *Domburg? M.158-80.* 45 85

840 — Type 8. Standard. ℞. As 839. *M.183-6.* 50 100

841 'Maastricht' Type. Crude head l. ℞. Quatrefoil interlace. *M.265-6* 175 350

843 Series X. Facing 'Wodan' head. ℞. Monster l. *Ribe, Jutland, M.275-81.* 125 250

843A — cruder copies. *English, M.282.* 150 325

KINGS OF NORTHUMBRIA

In the North a series of silver sceats was struck with the king's name on the obverse and a fantastic animal on the reverse. Towards the end of the eighth century the coinage degenerated to one of base silver and finally to copper or brass; from the second reign of Aethelred I the design becomes standardised with the king's name retained on the obverse but with the moneyer's name on the reverse and in the centre of both sides a cross, pellet or rosette., etc. A parallel series of ecclesiastical coins was struck by the Archbishops of York.

The coinage continued until the conquest of Northumbria by the Danes and the defeat of Osbert in 867, almost a century after introduction of the broad silver penny in Southern England.

		F £	*VF* £
846	**Aldfrith** (685-705). *AR sceat.* Pellet in annulet. R. Fantastic animal l. with trifid tail	475	1050
852	**Eadberht** (737-758). *AR sceat.* Small cross. R. Fantastic quadruped to l. or r.	150	335
	Aethelwald Moll (759-765). See Archbishop Ecgberht of York		

853 859 861

853	**Alcred** (765-774). *AR sceat.* As 852	350	800
854	**Aethelred I,** first reign (774-779). *AR sceat.* As last	400	900
855	**Aelfwald I** (779-788). *AR sceat.* As last	425	950
856	— — Small cross. R. With name of moneyer CVDBEVRT	375	900
857	**Aethelred I,** second reign (789-796). *AR sceat.* Similar. R. SCT CVD (St. Cuthbert), shrine	*Extremely rare*	
858	— Small cross. R. With moneyer's name	165	350

The last and the rest of the sceats, except where otherwise stated, have on the obv. *the king's name,and on the* rev. *the moneyer's name: in the centre on both sides is a cross, a pellet, a rosette, etc. During the following reign the silver sceat becomes debased and later issues are only brass or copper.*

859	**Eanred** (810-*c.* 854). Base *AR sceat*	40	85
859A	— *AR penny.* Bust r. R. Cross, part moline part crosslet	*Unique*	
860	— *Æ sceat*	20	45
861	**Aethelred II,** first reign (*c.* 854-858). *Æ sceat*	20	45
862	— R. Quadruped	250	550
863	**Redwulf** (*c.* 858). *Æ sceat.*	40	90
864	**Aethelred II,** second reign (*c.* 858-*c.* 862). *Æ sceat,* mainly of the moneyer EARDWVLF	20	45
865	**Osbert** (*c.* 862-867). *Æ sceat*	60	130

Coins with blundered legends are worth less than those with normal readings, and to this series have been relegated those coins previously attributed to Eardwulf and Aelfwald II.

ARCHBISHOPS OF YORK

866 868

		F £	VF £
866	**Ecgberht** (732 or 734-766). Ʀ *sceat*, with king Eadberht. As illustration, or holds cross and crozier	350	750
866A	— — with Aethelwald Moll. Cross each side	450	950
867	— — with Alchred. Cross each side.	450	950
868	Eanbald II (796-c. 830). A sceat. R. With name of moneyer	75	175
869	— Æ *sceat,* as last	50	125

870 871

		F £	VF £
870	**Wigmund** (837-854). Gold *solidus.* Facing bust. ℞. Cross in wreath	*Unique*	
871	— Æ *sceat,* various	30	60
872	**Wulfhere** (854-900). Æ *sceat*	85	150

ANGLO-SAXON MIDDLE PERIOD, C.780-973

In the kingdom of the Franks a reformed coinage of good quality *deniers* struck on broad flans had been introduced by Pepin in 755 and continued by his son Charlemagne and his descendants. A new coinage of *pennies* of similar size and weighing about 20 grains (1.3 gms) was introduced into England, probably by Offa, the powerful king of Mercia, about 755/780, though early pennies also exist of two little known kings of Kent, Heaberht and Ecgberht, of about the same period.

The silver penny (*Lat.* 'denarius', hence the *d.* of our *£ s. d.*) remained virtually the sole denomination of English coinage for almost five centuries, with the rare exception of occasional gold coins and somewhat less rare silver halfpence. The penny reached a weight of 24 grains, i.e., a 'pennyweight' during the reign of Aelfred the Great. Silver pennies of this period normally bear the ruler's name, though not always his portrait, and the name of the moneyer responsible for their manufacture.

Pennies were issued by various rulers of the Heptarchy for the kingdoms of Kent, Mercia, East Anglia and Wessex (and possibly Anglian Northumbria), by the Danish settlers in the Danelaw and the Hiberno-Norse kings of York, and also by the Archbishops of Canterbury and a Bishop of London. Under Eadgar, who became the sole ruler of England, a uniform coinage was instituted throughout the country, and it was he who set the pattern for the 'reformed' coinage of the later Anglo-Saxon and Norman period.

Halfpence were issued by most rulers from Alfred to Eadgar between 871-973 for S. England, and although all are rare today, it is probable that reasonable quantities were made.

Nos. 873-1387 are all silver pennies except where stated.

NB. Many pennies of the early part of this period have chipped flans and prices should be reduced accordingly.

KINGS OF KENT

		F £	*VF* £
873	**Heaberht** (*c.* 765). Monogram for REX. ℞. Five annulets, each containing a pellet, joined to form a cross		*Unique*
874	**Ecgberht** (*c.* 780). Similar. ℞. Varied *from*	1350	3500

875 877

875	**Eadberht Praen** (796-798). As illustration. ℞. Varied	1350	3500
876	**Cuthred** (798-807). *Canterbury.* Various types without portrait ...*from*	425	1000
877	— As illustration	475	1250

878 879

878	**Anonymous** (*c.* 822-823). *Canterbury.* As illustration	650	1650
879	**Baldred** (*c.* 823-825). *Canterbury.* Head or bust r. ℞. Varied	1000	2500

		F £	*VF* £
880	— Cross each side	750	2250
881	*Rochester*. Diademed bust r. ℞. Varied	1000	2500

ARCHBISHOPS OF CANTERBURY

882

		F £	*VF* £
882	**Jaenberht** (765-792). His name around central ornament or cross and wedges. ℞. OFFA REX in two lines	1250	2750
883	— His name in three lines. ℞. OFFA REX between the limbs of Celtic cross	1650	3500
884	**Aethelheard** (el. 792, cons. 793, d. 805). With Offa as overlord. First issue (792-793), with title *Pontifex*	1250	3250

885

887

		F £	*VF* £
885	— Second issue (793-796), with title *Archiepiscopus*	1200	3000
886	— With Coenwulf as overlord. Third issue (796-805)	1150	2500
886a	— Alone, as last. ℞. Moneyer, cross with pellets etc.	—	3000
887	**Wulfred** (805-832). group I (805-*c.* 810). As illustration. ℞. Crosslet, alpha-omega	600	2000
888	— Group II (*c.* 810). As last. ℞. DOROVERNIA C monogram	550	1450
889	— Group III (pre- 823). Bust extends to edge of coin. ℞. As last	500	1350
890	— Groups IV and V (*c.* 822-823). Anonymous under Ecgberht. Moneyer's name in place of the Archbishop's. ℞. DOROBERNIA CIVITAS in three or five lines	525	1400
891	— Group VI (*c.* 823-825). Baldred type. Crude portrait. ℞. DRVR CITS in two lines	550	2100
892	— Group VII (*c.* 832). Second monogram (Ecgberht) type. Crude portrait r., PLFRED. ℞. DORIB C. Monogram as 1035	550	2100

893

894

No.	Description	F £	VF £
893	**Ceolnoth** (833-870). Group I with name CIALNOD. Tonsured bust facing. ℞. Varied .... *from*	350	800
894	— Group II. Similar but CEOLNOD. ℞. Types of Aethelwulf of Wessex	325	700
895	— Group III. Diad. bust r. ℞. Moneyer's name in and between lunettes ..	400	950

896

898

No.	Description	F £	VF £
896	**Aethered** (870-889). Bust r. ℞. As illustration or with long cross with lozenge panel	1750	4500
897	— Cross pattee. ℞. ELF / STAN		*Unique*
898	**Plegmund** (890-914). DORO in circle. ℞. As illustration above, various moneyers .... *from*	350	850
899	— Similar, but title EPISC, and XDF in centre	550	1300
900	— Small cross pattee. ℞. Somewhat as last	300	750
901	— Crosses moline and pommee on *obv.*	550	1300

KINGS OF MERCIA

Until 825 Canterbury was the principal mint of the Kings of Mercia and some moneyers also struck coins for the Kings of Kent and Archbishops of Canterbury.

GOLD

902

903

No.	Description	F £	VF £
902	**Offa** (757-796). Gold *dinar.* Copy of Arabic dinar of Caliph Al Mansur, dated 157 A.H. (A.D. 774), with OFFA REX added on *rev.*		*Unique*
903	Gold *penny.* Bust r., moneyer's name. ℞. Standing figure, moneyer's name		*Unique*

SILVER

904 905v. 905v.

		F £	VF £
904	*Canterbury.* Group I (*c.* 784-*c.* 787). Early coins without portraits, small flans. Various types ... *from*	450	900
905	— Group II (*c* 787-*c.* 792). Various types with portrait, small flans ... *from*	650	1500
906	— — — Various types without portraits, small flans ... *from*	350	750

907

909

		F £	VF £
907	*Canterbury.* Group III (*c.* 792-796). Various types without portrait, large flans ... *from*	450	900
908	*East Anglia.* Copies of Group II and III, possibly struck *c.* 790. Ornate, crude, and sometimes with runic letters ...	600	1250
908A	— — with portrait. ℞. Similar ...	750	1600
909	**Cynethryth** (wife of Offa). Coins as Group II of Offa. As illustration.....	2500	5000
910	— *O.* As *rev.* of last. ℞. EOBA on leaves of quatrefoil ...	2000	4000
911	**Eadberht** (Bishop of London, died 787/789). EADBERHT EP in three lines. ℞. Name of Offa ... *The attribution to this particular cleric is uncertain.*	1500	3000
912	**Coenwulf** (796-821). Group I (796-805). *Canterbury and London.* Without portrait. His name in three lines. ℞. Varied ...	450	1100
913	— *Canterbury.* Name around m as illus. below. ℞. Moneyer's name in two lines ...	*Unique*	

914

915

		F £	VF £
914	— *Both mints.* Tribrach type as illustration ...	300	600
915	— Group II (*c.* 805-810). *Canterbury.* With portrait. Small flans. ℞. Varied but usually cross and wedges ...	400	900

		F £	VF £
916	— Groups III and IV (*c.* 810-820). *Canterbury.* Similar but larger flans. ℞. Varied	350	800
917	— *Rochester.* Large diad. bust of coarse style. ℞. Varied. (Moneyers: Dun, Ealhstan)	475	1100
918	— *London.* With portrait generally of Roman style. ℞. Crosslet	450	1000
919	— *E. Anglia.* Crude diad. bust r. ℞. Moneyer's name LVL on leaves in arms of cross	450	950
920	— — *O.* as last. ℞. Various types *from*	400	900

921

929

		F £	VF £
921	**Ceolwulf I** (821-823). *Canterbury.* Group I. Bust r. ℞. Varied. (Moneyers: Oba, Sigestef)	575	1350
922	— — Group II. Crosslet. ℞. Varied	500	1250
923	— — Group III. Tall cross with MERCIORŪ. ℞. Crosslet. SIGESTEF DOROBERNIA	*Unique*	
924	— *Rochester.* Group I. Bust r. ℞. Varied	500	1250
925	— — Group IIA. As last but head r.	550	1350
926	— — Group IIB. Ecclesiastical issue by Bp. of Rochester. With mint name, DOROBREBIA, but no moneyer	*Extremely rare*	
927	— *East Anglia.* Crude style and lettering with barbarous portrait. ℞. Varied	500	1150
928	**Beornwulf** (823-825). Bust r. ℞. Moneyer's name in three lines	1100	2500
929	— ℞. Cross crosslet in centre	900	2300
930	Crude copy of 928 but moneyer's name in two lines with crosses between	*Extremely rare*	
931	**Ludica** (825-827). Bust r. ℞. Moneyer's name in three lines as 928	–	7500

932

933

		F £	VF £
932	— Similar. ℞. Moneyer's name around cross crosslet in centre, as 929	*Extremely rare*	
933	**Wiglaf,** first reign (827-829). Crude head r. ℞. Crosslet	1750	4500

934

935

		F £	VF £
934	Second reign (830-840). Cross and pellets. ℞. Moneyer's name in and between lunettes of pellets	1350	3500
935	**Berhtwulf** (840-852). Various types with bust *from*	650	1500
936	— Cross potent over saltire. ℞. Cross potent	750	1850
937	Berhtwulf with Aethelwulf of Wessex. As before. ℞. IAETHELWLF REX. cross pommee over cross pattee		*Unique*

938 939 940 941

938	**Burgred** (852-874). *B.M.C. type A.* Bust r. ℞. Moneyer's name in and between lunettes	90	150
939	— — B. Similar but lunettes broken in centre of curve	125	250
940	— — C. Similar but lunettes broken in angles	110	190
941	— — D. Similar but legend divided by two lines with a crook at each end	95	160
942	— — E. As last, but m above and below	350	900
943	**Ceolwulf II** (874-*c.* 880). Bust r. ℞. Two emperors seated. Victory above.		*Unique*

944

944	— ℞. Moneyer's name in angles of long cross with lozenge centre	3000	7500

VIKING COINAGES

945

946

		F £	VF £
945	**Beonna,** King of East Anglia, *c.* 758. AR sceat. Pellet in centre, Runic inscription. ℞. EFE in Roman characters around saltire cross	350	750
945A	— Similar. ℞. Name in Runic	600	1100
945B	— Similar. ℞. Interlace pattern (large flans)	*Extremely rare*	
946	**Aethelberht** (d. 794). As illustration	*Only 3 known*	
947	**Eadwald** (*c.* 798). King's name in three lines. ℞. Moneyer's name in quatrefoil or around cross	900	2000

948

950

		F £	VF £
948	**Aethelstan I** (*c.* 825-840). Bust r. or l. ℞. Crosslet or star	750	2000
949	Bust r. ℞. Moneyer's name in three or four lines	750	2000
950	Alpha or A. ℞. Varied	335	750
951	*O.* and *rev.* Cross with or without wedges or pellets in angles	350	825
952	— Similar, with king's name both sides	500	1250
952A	Name around ship in centre. ℞. Moneyer Eadgar, pellets in centre. (Possibly the earliest of his coins.)	*Extremely rare*	

953

954

		F £	VF £
953	**Aethelweard** (*c.* 840-*c.* 855), A. Omega or cross and crescents. ℞. Cross with pellets or wedges	550	1250
954	**Edmund** (855-870). Alpha or A. ℞. Cross with pellets or wedges	225	450
955	— *O.* Varied. ℞. Similar	225	450

For the St. Edmund coins and the Danish issues struck in East Anglia bearing the name of Aethelred I of Wessex, see Danish East Anglia.

Danish East Anglia, *c.* **885-915**

956 957

		F £	*VF* £
956	**Aethelstan II** (878-890), originally named Guthrum? Cross pattee. ℞. Moneyer's name in two lines	1000	2500
957	**Oswald** (unknown except from his coins). Alpha or A. ℞. Cross pattee...		*rare*
958	— Copy of Carolinigian 'temple' type. ℞ Cross and pellets	*Unique fragment*	
959	**Aethelred I.** As last, with name of Aethelred I of Wessex. ℞. As last, or cross-crosslet	*Extremely rare*	
960	**St. Edmund,** memorial coinage, Æ *penny,* type as illus. below, various legends of good style	85	150

961 963

		F	*VF*
961	— Similar, but barbarous or semi-barbarous legends	80	135
962	*Halfpenny.* Similar	400	850
963	**St. Martin of Lincoln.** As illustration	1500	3750
964	**Alfred.** (Viking imitations, usually of very barbarous workmanship.) Bust r. ℞. *Londonia* monogram	550	1500
965	— Similar, but *Lincolla* monogram	*Extremely rare*	

966 970

		F	*VF*
966	— Small cross, as Alfred group II (*Br. 6*), various legends, some read REX DORO ... *from*	200	425
967	— Similar. ℞. 'St. Edmund type' A in centre	500	1500
968	— Two emperors seated. ℞. As 964. (Previously attributed to Halfdene.)		*Unique*
969	*Halfpenny.* As 964 and 965 ... *from*	500	1500
970	— As 966	450	1350

Danelaw, *c.* 898-915

971 975

No.		*F* £	*VF* £
971	**Alfred** (Imitations). ELFRED between ORSNA and FORDA. ℞. Moneyer's name in two lines (occasionally divided by horizontal long cross)	250	650
972	— *Halfpenny.* Similar, of very crude appearance	*Extremely rare*	
973	**Alfred/Plegmund.** *Obv.* ELFRED REX PLEGN	*Extremely rare*	
974	**Plegmund.** Danish copy of 900	300	750
975	**Earl Sihtric.** Type as 971. SCELDFOR between GVNDI BERTVS. ℞ SITRIC COMES in two lines	*Extremely rare*	

Viking Coinage of York?

References are to 'The Classification of Northumbrian Viking Coins in the Cuerdale hoard', by C. S. S. Lyon and B. H. I. H. Stewart, in Numismatic Chronicle, 1964, p. 281 ff.

No.		*F* £	*VF* £
976	**Siefred.** C. SIEFRE DIIS REX in two lines. ℞. EBRAICE CIVITAS (or contractions), small cross. *L. & S. Ia, Ie, Ii*	200	550
977	— Cross on steps between. ℞. As last. *L. & S. If, Ij*	275	750
978	— Long cross. ℞. As last. *L. & S. Ik*	*Extremely rare*	
979	SIEFREDVS REX, cross crosslet within legend. ℞. As last. *L. & S. Ih*	150	350

980 984

No.		*F* £	*VF* £
980	SIEVERT REX, cross crosslet to edge of coin. ℞. As last. *L. & S. Ic, Ig, Im*	150	350
981	— Cross on steps between. ℞. As last. *L. & S. Il*	240	650
982	— Patriarchal cross. ℞. DNS DS REX, small cross. *L. & S. Va*	175	425
983	— — ℞. MIRABILIA FECIT, small cross. *L. & S. VIb*	185	500
984	REX, at ends of cross crosslet. ℞. SIEFREDVS, small cross. *L. & S. IIIa, b*	165	400
985	— Long cross. ℞. As last. *L. & S. IIIc*	150	350
986	*Halfpenny.* Types as 977, *L. & S. Ib;* 980, *Ic;* and 983, *VIb*	*Extremely rare*	
987	**Cnut.** CNVT REX, cross crosslet to edge of coin. ℞. EBRAICE CIVITAS, small cross. *L. & S. Io, Iq*	100	200
988	— — ℞. CVNNETTI, small cross. *L. & S. IIc*	100	225

		F	VF
		£	£
989	— Long cross. ℞. EBRAICE CIVITAS, small cross. *L. & S. Id, In, Ir*	85	170
990	— — ℞. CVNNETTI, small cross. *L. & S. IIa, IId*	85	160
991	— Patriarchal cross. ℞. EBRAICE CIVITAS, small cross. *L. & S. Ip, Is*	80	150
992	— — ℞.—*Karolus* monogram in centre. *L. & S. It*	400	1000
993	— — ℞. CVNNETTI, small cross. *L. & S. IIb, IIe*	75	140
994	*Halfpenny*. Types as 987, *L. & S. Iq*; 989, *Id;* 991, *Is;* 992, *Iu;* 993, *IIb and e* ... *from*	400	850

993

995

995	As 992, but CVNNETTI around *Karolus* monogram. *L. & S. IIf*	400	875
996	**Cnut and/or Siefred.** CNVT REX, patriarchal cross. ℞. SIEFREDVS, small cross. *L. & S. IIId*	130	240
997	— — ℞. DNS DS REX, small cross. *L. & S. Vc*	160	350

998

998	— — ℞. MIRABILIA FECIT. *L. & S. VId*	150	275
999	EBRAICE C, patriarchal cross. ℞. DNS DS REX, small cross. *L. & S. Vb*	140	260

1000

1002

1000	— — ℞. MIRABILIA FECIT. *L. & S. VIc*	150	280
1001	DNS DS REX in two lines. ℞. ALVALDVS, small cross. *L. & S. IVa*	—	1500
1002	DNS DS O REX, similar. ℞. MIRABILIA FECIT. *L. & S. VIa*	250	550
1003	*Halfpenny*. As last. *L. & S. VIa*	*Extremely rare*	
1004	**'Cnut'.** Name blundered around cross pattée with extended limbs. ℞. QVENTOVICI around small cross. *L. & S. VII*	300	600
1005	*Halfpenny*. Similar. *L. & S. VII*	450	1000

Possibly not Northumbrian; the reverse copied from the Carolingian coins of Quentovic, N. France.

1006 1009

York, early tenth century issues

		F £	VF £
1006	**St. Peter coinage.** Early issues. SCI PETRI MO in two lines. ℞. Cross pattee	175	400
1007	— similar. ℞. 'Karolus' monogram	*Extremely rare*	
1008	*Halfpenny.* Similar. ℞. Cross pattee	1000	2250
1009	**Regnald** (blundered types). RAIENALT, head to l. or r. ℞. EARICE CT, 'Karolus' monogram	1400	3500
1010	— Open hand. ℞. Similar	1000	2500
1011	— Hammer. ℞. Bow and arrow	1250	3000
1012	— Similar. ℞. Sword	*Extremely rare*	

English Coins of the Hiberno-Norse Vikings

Early period, *c.* **919-925**

		F £	VF £
1013	**Sihtric** (921-927). SITRIC REX, sword. ℞. Cross or T	1500	3750
1014	**St. Peter coinage.** Late issues SCI PETRI MO, sword and hammer. ℞. EBORACEI, cross and pellets	350	850

1015 1016

		F £	VF £
1015	— Similar. ℞. Voided hammer	450	1000
1016	— Similar. ℞. Solid hammer	700	1600

St. Peter coins with blundered legends are rather cheaper.

NB. *Modern coins of this type are sold at the Jorvic Centre, York . They have a larger flan.*

Later period, 939-954 (after the battle of Brunanburh). Mostly struck at York.

		F £	VF £
1017	**Anlaf Guthfrithsson,** 939-941. Flower type. Small cross, ANLAF REX TO D. ℞. Flower above moneyer's name	2500	6000
1018	**Olaf Guthfrithsson.** Circumscription type, with small cross each side, ANLAF CVNVNC, M in field on reverse (*Derby*)	2500	6000
1018A	— Two line type. ONLAF REX. Large letter both sides (*Lincoln?*)	2000	5000

1019

1020

		F £	VF £
1019	— Raven type. As illustration, ANLAF CVNVNC	2000	5000
1020	**Olaf Sihtricsson,** first reign, 941-944. Triquetra type. As illus., CVNVNC. ℞. Danish standard	2000	5000
1021	— Circumscription type (a). Small cross each side, CVNVNC	2000	5000
1022	— Cross moline type, CVNVN C. ℞. Small cross	*Extremely rare*	
1023	— Two line type. Small cross. ℞. ONLAF REX. ℞. Name in two lines	2000	5000
1024	**Regnald Guthfrithsson,** 943-944. Triquetra type. As 1020. REGNALD CVNVNC	3000	7500

1025

1030

		F £	VF £
1025	— Cross moline type. As 1022, but REGNALD CVNVNC	2500	6000
1026	**Sihtric Sihtricsson,** *c.* 942. Triquetra type. As 1020, SITRIC CVNVNC	*Unique*	
1027	— Circumscription type. Small cross each side	*Unique*	
1028	**Eric Blood-axe,** first reign, 948. Two line type. Small cross, ERICVC REX A; ERIC REX AL; or ERIC REX EFOR. ℞. Name in two lines	2500	6000
1029	**Olaf Sihtricsson,** second reign, 948-952. Circumscription type (b). Small cross each side. ONLAF REX	2750	6500
1029A	— Flower type. small cross ANLAF REX ℞. Flower above moneyer's name	2500	6000
1029B	— Two line type. Small cross, ONLAF REX. ℞. Moneyer's name in two lines	2000	5000
1030	**Eric Blood-axe,** second reign, 952-954. Sword type. ERIC REX in two lines, sword between. ℞. Small cross	2750	6500

KINGS OF WESSEX

Later, KINGS OF ALL ENGLAND

All are silver pennies unless otherwise stated

BEORHTRIC, 786—802

Beorhtric was dependent on Offa of Mercia and married a daughter of Offa.

1031

		F £	*VF* £
1031	As illustration	*Extremely rare*	
1032	Alpha and omega in centre. ℞. Omega in centre	*Extremely rare*	

ECGBERHT, 802—839

King of Wessex only, 802-825; then also of Kent, Sussex, Surrey, Essex and East Anglia, 825—839, and of Mercia also, 829-830.

1033	*Canterbury.* Group I. Diad. hd. r. within inner circle. ℞. Various *from*	1450	3500
1034	— II. Non-portrait types. ℞. Various *from*	750	2250

1035

1035	— III. Bust r. breaking inner circle. ℞. DORIB C	1000	2250
1036	*London.* Cross potent. ℞. LVN / DONIA / CIVIT	*Unique*	
1037	— — ℞. REDMVND MONE around TA	1500	4250
1038	*Rochester,* royal mint. Non-portrait types with king's name ECGBEO RHT *from*	1150	3000
1039	— — Portrait types, ECGBEORHT *from*	1250	3000
1040	*Rochester,* bishop's mint. Bust r. ℞. SCS ANDREAS (APOSTOLVS)	1450	4600
1041	*Winchester.* SAXON monogram or SAXONIORVM in three lines. ℞. Cross	1150	3000

AETHELWULF, 839—858

Son of Ecgberht; sub-King of Essex, Kent, Surrey and Sussex, 825-839; King of all southern England, 839-855; King of Essex, Kent and Sussex only, 855-858. No coins are known of his son Aethelbald who ruled over Wessex proper, 855-860.

1042 1044

		F	*VF*
		£	£
1042	*Canterbury.* Phase I (839-*c.* 843). Head within inner circle. ℞. Various. *Br. 3*	235	600
1043	— — Larger bust breaking inner circle. ℞. A. *Br. 1 and 2*	235	600
1044	— — Cross and wedges. ℞. SAXONIORVM in three lines in centre. *Br. 10*	220	550
1045	— — Similar, but OCCINDENTALIVM in place of moneyer. *Br. 11*	245	650
1046	— Phase II (*c.* 843-848?). Cross and wedges. ℞. Various, but chiefly a form of cross or a large A. *Br. 4*	235	550
1047	— — New portrait, somewhat as 1043. ℞. As last. *Br. 7*	235	550
1048	— — Smaller portrait. ℞. As last, with *Chi/Rho* monogram. *Br. 7*	265	600

1049 1051

1049	— Phase III (*c.* 848/851-*c.* 855). DORIB in centre. ℞. CANT mon. *Br. 5*	235	550
1050	— — CANT mon. ℞. CAN M in angles of cross. *Br. 6*	265	600
1051	— Phase IV (*c.* 855-859). Type as Aethelberht. New neat style bust ℞. Large voided long cross. *Br. 8*	240	450
1052	*Winchester.* SAXON mon. ℞. Cross and wedges. *Br. 9*	350	750

AETHELBERHT, 858-865/866

Son of Aethelwulf; sub-King of Kent, Essex and Sussex, 858-860; King of all southern England, 860-865/6.

1053

		F	*VF*
		£	£
1053	As illustration below	250	435
1054	*O*. Similar, ℞. Cross fleury over quatrefoil	700	1500

AETHELRED I, 865/866-871

Son of Aethelwulf; succeeded his brother Aethelberht.

1055

1055	As illustration	250	700
1056	Similar, but moneyer's name in four lines	600	1500

For another coin with the name Aethelred see 959 under Viking coinages.

ALFRED THE GREAT, 871—899

Brother and successor to Aethelred, Alfred had to contend with invading Danish armies for much of his reign. In 878 he and Guthrum the Dane divided the country, with Alfred holding all England south and west of Watling Street. Alfred occupied London in 886.

Types with portraits

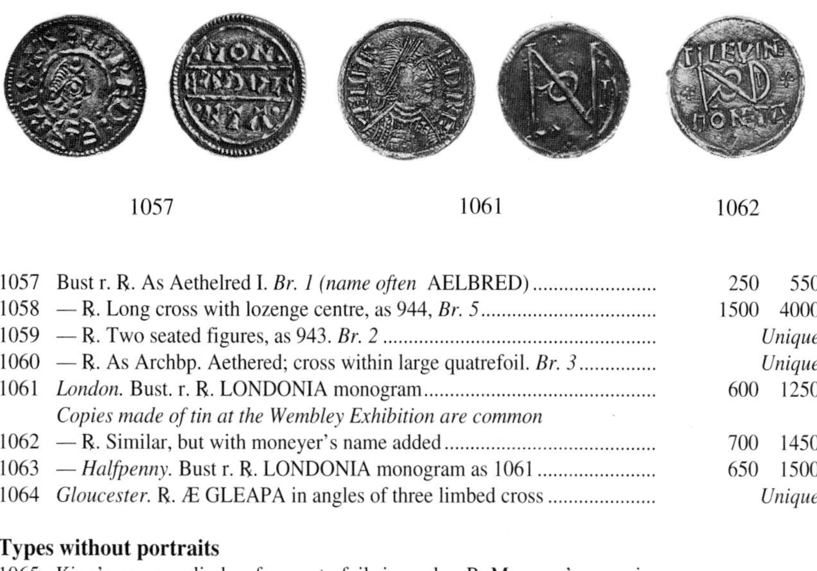

1057 1061 1062

1057	Bust r. ℞. As Aethelred I. *Br. 1 (name often* AELBRED)	250	550
1058	— ℞. Long cross with lozenge centre, as 944, *Br. 5*	1500	4000
1059	— ℞. Two seated figures, as 943. *Br. 2*		*Unique*
1060	— ℞. As Archbp. Aethered; cross within large quatrefoil. *Br. 3*		*Unique*
1061	*London.* Bust. r. ℞. LONDONIA monogram	600	1250
	Copies made of tin at the Wembley Exhibition are common		
1062	— ℞. Similar, but with moneyer's name added	700	1450
1063	— *Halfpenny.* Bust r. ℞. LONDONIA monogram as 1061	650	1500
1064	*Gloucester.* ℞. Æ GLEAPA in angles of three limbed cross		*Unique*

Types without portraits

1065	King's name on limbs of cross, trefoils in angles. ℞. Moneyer's name in quatrefoil. *Br. 4.*		*Unique*

1066 1069

1066	Cross pattée. ℞. Moneyer's name in two lines. *Br. 6*	200	415
1067	— As last, but neater style, as Edw, the Elder	215	425
1068	— *Halfpenny.* As 1066	625	1400
1069	*Canterbury.* As last but DORO added on *obv. Br. 6a*	225	500

For other pieces bearing the name of Alfred see under the Viking coinages.

1070	*Exeter?* King name in four lines. ℞. EXA vertical	—	5000
1071	*Winchester?* Similar to last, but PIN		*Extremely rare*
1072	'Offering penny'. Very large and heavy. AELFRED REX SAXORVM in four lines. ℞. ELIMO in two lines i.e. (*Elimosina,* alms)		*Extremely rare*

Edward, the son of Alfred, aided by his sister Aethelflaed 'Lady of the Mericians', annexed all England south of the Humber and built many new fortified boroughs to protect the kingdom.

1074

		F £	*VF* £
Rare types			
1073	*Br. 1. Bath?* ℞. BA	*Extremely rare*	
1074	— *2. Canterbury.* Cross moline in pommee. ℞. Moneyer's name	800	2000
1075	— *3. Chester?* Small cross. ℞. Minster	825	2500
1076	— *4.* — Small cross. ℞. Moneyer's name in single line	700	1800
1077	— *5.* — ℞. Two stars	950	2250

1078 1082

1078	— *6.* — ℞. Flower above central line, name below	900	2500
1079	— *7.* — ℞. Floral design with name across field	900	2400
1080	— *8.* — ℞. Bird holding twig	*Extremely rare*	
1081	— *9.* — ℞. Hand of Providence	1500	3000
1082	— *10.* — ℞. City gate of Roman style	*Extremely rare*	
1083	— *11.* — ℞. Anglo-Saxon burg	900	2250

Ordinary types

1084 1087

1084	*Br. 12.* Bust l. ℞. Moneyer's name in two lines *from*	400	950
1085	— — As last, but in *gold*	*Unique*	
1086	— *12a.* Similar, but bust r. of crude style	350	1250
1087	— *13.* Small cross. ℞. Similar (to 1084)	130	240
1088	*Halfpenny.* Similar to last	700	1600

Aethelstan, the eldest son of Eadward, decreed that money should be coined only in a borough, that every borough should have one moneyer and that some of the more important boroughs should have more than one moneyer.

1089

		F	*VF*
		£	£
1089	**Main issues.** Small cross. ℞. Moneyer's name in two lines	200	385
1090	Diad. bust r. ℞. As last	650	1500
1091	— ℞. Small cross	550	1350
1092	Small cross both sides	225	450

1093 1094

1093	— Similar, but mint name added	225	425
1094	Crowned bust r. As illustration. ℞. Small cross	450	900
1095	— Similar, but mint name added	400	850
1096	**Local Issues.** *N. Mercian mints.* Star between two pellets. ℞. As 1089	550	1250
1097	— Small cross. ℞. Floral ornaments above and below moneyer's name	550	1250
1098	— Rosette of pellets each side	275	550
1099	— Small cross one side, rosette on the other side	300	650

1100 1104

1100	*N.E. mints.* Small cross. ℞. Tower over moneyer's name	650	1750
1101	Similar, but mint name added	800	2000
1102	— Bust in high relief r. or l. ℞. Small cross	500	1150
1103	— Bust r. in high relief. ℞. Cross-crosslet	500	1150
1104	'Helmeted' bust r. ℞. As last	600	1500
1104A	Halfpenny, small cross. ℞. Moneyer's name in two lines	*Extremely rare*	

Eadmund, the brother of Aethelstan, extended his realm over the Norse kingdom of York.

1105

1107

		F £	VF £
1105	Small cross or rosette. ℞. Moneyer's name in two lines with crosses or rosettes between	150	300
1106	Crowned bust r. ℞. Small cross	300	750
1107	Similar, but with mint name	400	950
1108	Small cross either side, or rosette on one side	200	425
1109	Cross of five pellets. ℞. Moneyers' name in two lines	225	475
1110	Small cross. ℞. Flower above name	900	2000
1111	'Helmeted' bust r. ℞. Cross-crosslet	750	1750

1112

1112	*Halfpenny.* As 1105	700	1600

EADRED, 946-955

Eadred was another of the sons of Eadward. He lost the kingdom of York to Eric Bloodaxe.

1113

1115

1113	As illustration. ℞. Moneyer's name in two lines	135	250
1114	— Similar, but mint name after REX	300	750
1115	Crowned bust r. As illustration	350	700
1116	— ℞. Similar, with mint name added	400	950

		F	VF
		£	£
1117	Rosette. ℞. As 1113	150	325
1118	Small cross. ℞. Rosette	175	375
1119	— ℞. Flower enclosing moneyer's name. *B.M.C. II*	*Extremely rare*	
1120	*Halfpenny.* Similar to 1113	700	1500

HOWEL DDA, d. 949/950

Grandson of Rhodri Mawr, Howel succeeded to the kingdom of Dyfed *c.* 904, to Seisyllog *c.* 920 and became King of Gwynedd and all Wales, 942.

1121

1121 HOPÆL REX, small cross or rosette. ℞. Moneyer's name in two lines... *Unique*

EADWIG, 955-959

Elder son of Eadmund, Eadwig lost Mercia and Northumbria to his brother Eadgar in 957.

1122

1123

		F	VF
1122	*Br. 1.* Type as illustration	185	375
1123	— — Similar, but mint name in place of crosses	300	850
1123A	— Similar to 1122,but star in place of cross on *obv.*	*Unique*	
1124	— *2.* As 1122, but moneyer's name in one line	700	2100
1125	— *3.* Similar. ℞. Floral design	850	2250
1126	— *4.* Similar. ℞. Rosette or small cross	250	550
1127	— *5.* Bust r. ℞. Small cross	*Extremely rare*	

1128

		F	VF
1128	*Halfpenny.* Small cross. ℞. Flower above moneyer's name	*Unique*	
1128A	— Similar. ℞. PIN (Winchester) across field	*Extremely rare*	

EADGAR, 959-957

King in Mercia and Northumbria from 957; King of all England 959-975.

It is now possible on the basis of the lettering to divide up the majority of Eadgar's coins into issues from the following regions: N.E. England, N.W. England, York, East Anglia, Midlands, S.E. England, Southern England, and S.W. England. (*See* 'Anglo-Saxon Coins', ed. R. H. M. Dolley.)

1129

1135

		F	*VF*
		£	£
1129	*Br I.* Small cross. ℞. Moneyer's name in two lines, crosses between, trefoils top and bottom	110	210
1130	— — ℞. Similar, but rosettes top and bottom (a N.W. variety)	125	225
1131	— — ℞. Similar, but annulets between	150	300
1132	— — ℞. Similar, but mint name between (a late N.W. type)	125	325
1133	— *2.* — ℞. Floral design	750	2000
1134	— *4.* Small cross either side	130	225
1135	— — Similar, with mint name	225	475
1136	— — Rosette either side	150	275
1137	— — Similar, with mint name	225	475
1138	— *5.* Large bust to r. ℞. Small cross	400	1000
1139	— — Similar, with mint name	600	1300
1140	*Halfpenny.* (8.5 grains.) *Br. 3.* Small cross. ℞. Flower above name	*Extremely rare*	
1140A	— — ℞. Mint name around cross (Chichester)		*Unique*
1140B	— Bust r. ℞. `Londonia' monogram		4500

For Eadgar 'reform' issues see overleaf

In 973 Eadgar introduced a new coinage. A royal portrait now became a regular feature and the reverses normally have a cruciform pattern with the name of the mint in addition to that of the moneyer. Most fortified towns of burghal status were allowed a mint, the number of moneyers varying according to their size and importance: some royal manors also had a mint and some moneyers were allowed to certain ecclesiastical authorities. In all some seventy mints were active about the middle of the 11th century (see list of mints pp. 73-5).

The control of the currency was retained firmly in the hands of the central government, unlike the situation in France and the Empire where feudal barons and bishops controlled their own coinage. Coinage types were changed at intervals to enable the Exchequer to raise revenue from new dies and periodic demonetization of old coin types helped to maintain the currency in a good state. No halfpence were minted during this period. During the latter part of this era, full pennies were sheared into 'halfpennies' and 'farthings'. They are far rarer than later 'cut' coins.

Eadgar, 959-975 *continued*

1141

		F	*VF*
		£	£
1141	**Penny**. Type 6. Small bust l. ℞. Small cross, name of moneyer and mint.	500	950

EDWARD THE MARTYR, 975-978

Son of Eadgar and Aethelflaed, Eadward was murdered at Corfe castle, reputedly on the orders of his stepmother Aelfthryth.

1142

1142	Type as illustration above	600	1100

AETHELRED II, 978–1016

He was the son of Eadgar and Aelfthryth. His reign was greatly disturbed by incursions of Danish fleets and armies which massive payments of money failed to curb. He was known as 'The Unready', from UNREDE, meaning 'without counsel', ie. he was without good advice.

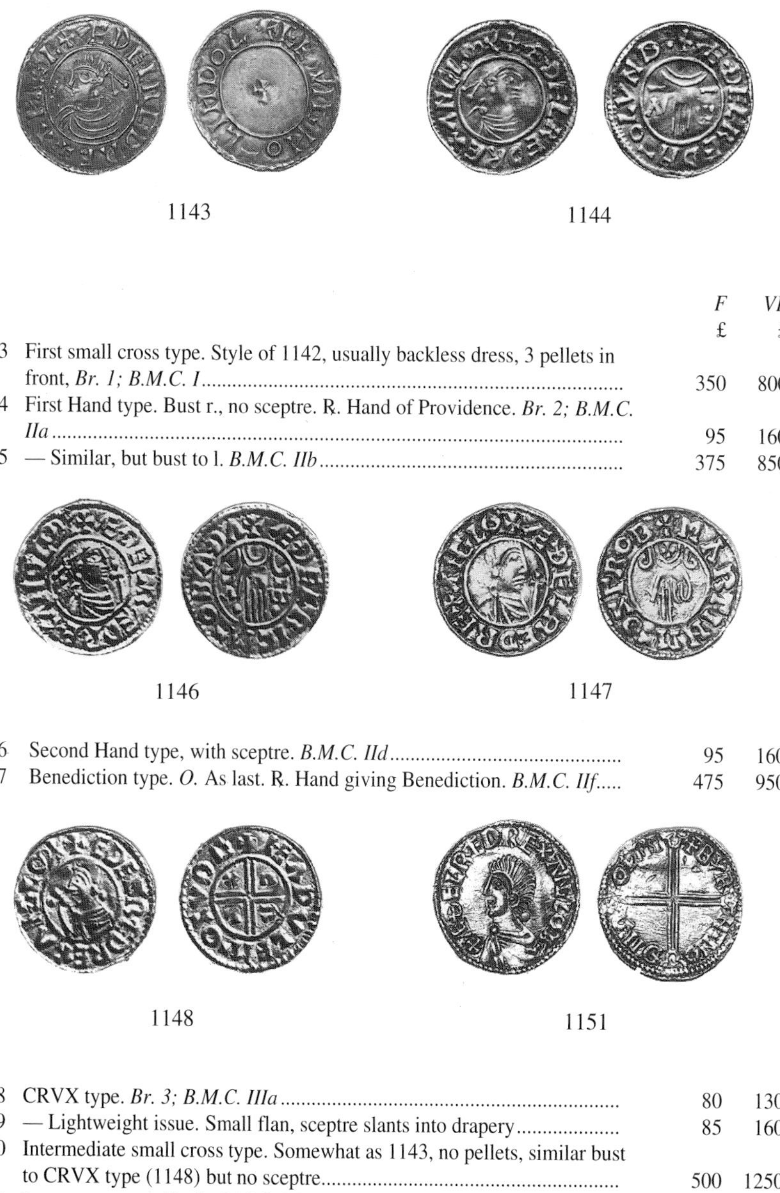

1143 1144

		F £	VF £
1143	First small cross type. Style of 1142, usually backless dress, 3 pellets in front, *Br. 1; B.M.C. I*	350	800
1144	First Hand type. Bust r., no sceptre. ℞. Hand of Providence. *Br. 2; B.M.C. IIa*	95	160
1145	— Similar, but bust to l. *B.M.C. IIb*	375	850
	1146 1147		
1146	Second Hand type, with sceptre. *B.M.C. IId*	95	160
1147	Benediction type. *O.* As last. ℞. Hand giving Benediction. *B.M.C. IIf*	475	950
	1148 1151		
1148	CRVX type. *Br. 3; B.M.C. IIIa*	80	130
1149	— Lightweight issue. Small flan, sceptre slants into drapery	85	160
1150	Intermediate small cross type. Somewhat as 1143, no pellets, similar bust to CRVX type (1148) but no sceptre	500	1250
1151	Long cross type. *Br. 5; B.M.C. IVa*	80	125

1152

		F	VF
		£	£
1152	Helmet type. *Br. 4; B.M.C. VIII*	90	145
1153	— — Similar, but struck in **gold**	*Unique*	

1154

1156

1154	Last small cross type. As 1143, but different style	75	120
1154A	Similar, but bust r.	175	400
1155	— Similar, but bust to edge of coin. *B.M.C. Id*	250	550
1156	Agnus Dei type. c. 1009. *Br. 6; B.M.C. X*	*Extremely rare*	

CNUT, 1016-1035

Son of Swegn Forkbeard, King of Denmark, Cnut was acclaimed King by the Danish fleet in England in 1014 but was forced to leave. He returned in 1015 and in 1016 agreed on a division of the country with Eadmund Ironsides, the son of Aethelred. No coins of Eadmund are known and on his death in November 1016 Cnut secured all England, marrying Emma of Normandy, widow of Aethelred.

Main types

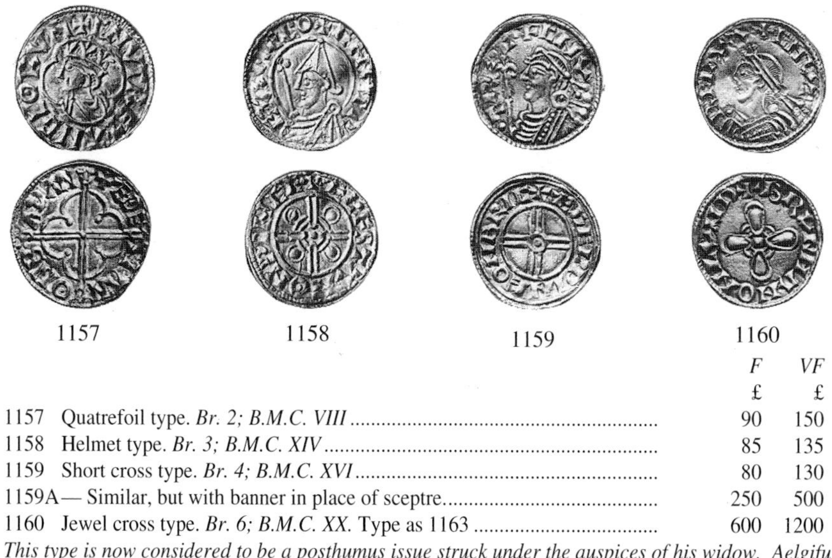

1157 1158 1159 1160

		F £	VF £
1157	Quatrefoil type. *Br. 2; B.M.C. VIII*	90	150
1158	Helmet type. *Br. 3; B.M.C. XIV*	85	135
1159	Short cross type. *Br. 4; B.M.C. XVI*	80	130
1159A	— Similar, but with banner in place of sceptre	250	500
1160	Jewel cross type. *Br. 6; B.M.C. XX.* Type as 1163	600	1200

This type is now considered to be a posthumus issue struck under the auspices of his widow, Aelgifu Emma.

HAROLD I, 1035-1040

Harold, the son of Cnut and Aelgifu of Northampton, initially acted as regent for his half-brother Harthacnut on Cnut's death, was then recognised as King in Mercia and the north, and King throughout England in 1037.

1163 1165

		F £	VF £
1163	Jewel cross type, as illustration. *Br. 1; B.M.C. 1*	165	360
1164	Long cross and trefoils type. *Br. 2; B.M.C. V*	175	385
1165	— Similar, but fleur de lis in place of trefoils. *B.M.C. Vc*	160	350

HARTHACNUT, 1035-1042

He was heir to Cnut but lost the throne to his half-brother Harold owing to his absence in Denmark. On Harold's death he recovered his English realm.

		F	*VF*
		£	£
1166	**Early period, 1036.** Jewel cross type, as 1163; bust l. *Br. 1; B.M.C. I*.....	750	1600

1167

1168

1167	— Similar, but bust r. *B.M.C. Ia*	700	1500
1168	**Restoration, 1040-1042.** Arm and sceptre type, with name Harthacnut. *Br. 2; B.M.C. II*	700	1500

1169

1170

1169	— Similar, but with name 'Cnut'	400	800
1170	**Danish types,** of various designs, some of English type mostly struck at Lund, Denmark (now Sweden) ....*from*	180	380

EDWARD THE CONFESSOR, 1042-1066

Edward was the son of Aethelred II and Emma of Normandy. A number of new mints were opened during his reign.

1171

1173

1171	PACX type, cross extends to edge of coin. *Br. 4; B.M.C. IVa*	150	300
1172	— Similar, but cross ends at legend. *B.M.C. IV*..	160	325
1173	Radiate type. *Br. 2; B.M.C. I*..	85	140

1174

1175

		F	VF
		£	£
1174	Trefoil quadrilateral type. *Br. 1; B.M.C. III*	80	135
1175	Short cross type, small flans. *Br. 3; B.M.C. II*	70	120

1176

1179

1176	Expanding cross type; light issue (18 grs.). *Br. 5; B.M.C. V*	85	140
1177	— — Heavy issue (27 grs.)	90	150
1178	— — Similar, but struck in **gold**	*Unique*	
1179	Helmet type. *Br. 6; B.M.C. VII*	80	135
1180	— — Similar but bust l.	350	900

1181

1182

1181	Sovereign type. *Br. 7; B.M.C. IX*	100	175
1182	Hammer cross type. *Br. 8; B.M.C. XI*	80	135

1183

1184

1183	Facing bust type. *Br. 9; B.M.C. XIII*	80	130
1184	Pyramids type. *Br. 10; B.M.C. XV*	100	160

1185

		F	VF
		£	£
1185	Large facing bust with sceptre. ℞. Similar	950	2000

Most York coins of this reign have an annulet in one quarter of the reverse.

HAROLD II, 1066

Harold was the son of Godwin Earl of Wessex. He was the brother-in-law of Edward the Confessor and was recognised as King on Edward's death. He defeated and killed Harald of Norway who invaded the north, but was himself defeated and killed at the Battle of Hastings by William of Normandy.

1186

1187

		F	VF
1186	Bust l. with sceptre. ℞. PAX across centre of *rev. B.M.C. I*	350	600
1187	Similar, but without sceptre. *B.M.C. Ia*	375	700
1188	Bust r. with sceptre	600	1250

ANGLO-SAXON, NORMAN AND EARLY PLANTAGENET MINTS

In Anglo-Saxon times coins were struck at a large number of towns. The place of mintage is normally given on all coins from the last quarter of the 10th century onwards, and generally the name of the person responsible (e.g. BRVNIC ON LVND). Below we give a list of the mints, showing the reigns (Baronial of Stephen's reign omitted), of which coins have been found. After the town names we give one or two of the spellings as found on the coins, although often they appear in an abbreviated or extended form. On the coins the Anglo-Saxon and Norman *w* is like a P or Γ and the *th* is Ð. We have abbreviated the kings' names, etc.:

Alf	—	Alfred the Great	Wi	—	William I
EE	—	Edward the Elder	Wii	—	William II
A'stan	—	Aethelstan	He	—	Henry I
EM	—	Edward the Martyr	St	—	Stephen (regular issues)
Ae	—	Aethelred II	M	—	Matilda
Cn	—	Cnut	HA	—	Henry of Anjou
Hi	—	Harold I	WG	—	William of Gloucester
Ht	—	Harthacnut	T	—	'Tealby' coinage
ECfr	—	Edward the Confessor	SC	—	Short cross coinage
Hii	—	Harold II	LC	—	Long cross coinage

Abergavenny (FANI), Wi.
Aylesbury (AEGEL) Ae, Cn, ECfr.
Bath (BADAN) EE-Edmund, Edwig-ECfr, Wi, He, St.
Bedford (BEDANF, BEDEF) Edwig-T.
Berkeley (BEORC) ECfr, Wi.
Bridport (BRIPVT, BRIDI) A'stan, Ae, Cn, Ht, ECfr, Wi.
Bruton (BRIVT) Ae-Cn, ECfr.
Bury St. Edmunds (EDMVN, SEDM, SANTEA) A'stan?, ECfr, Wi, He-LC.
Cambridge (GRANTE) Edgar-Wii.
Cardiff (CAIRDI, CARDI, CARITI) Wi, He, St, M.
Carlisle (CAR, CARDI, EDEN) He-LC.
Castle Rising (RISINGE) St.
Chichester (CISSAN CIV, CICES, CICST) A'stan, Edgar-St, SC
Christchurch, see Twynham.
Colchester (COLEAC, COLECES) Ae-Hi, ECfr-T.
Cricklade (CROCGL, CRIC, CREC) Ae-Wii.
Dorchester (DORCE, DORECES) Ae-ECfr, Wi-He, WG.
Dover (DOFER) A'stan, Edgar-St.
Dunwich (DVNE) St.
Exeter (EAXANC, EXEC, XECST) Alf, A'stan, Edwig-LC.
Frome ? (FRO) Cn-ECfr.
Guildford (GILDEF) EM-Cn, Ht-Wii.
Hastings (HAESTIN) Ae-St.
Hereford (HEREFOR) A'stan, Ae-St, HA, T, LC.
Horncastle ? (HORN) EM, Ae.
Huntingdon (HVNTEN) Edwig-St.
Ilchester (IVELCE, GIFELCST, GIVELC) Edgar, E M-He, T, LC.
Langport (LANCPOR) A'stan, Cn, Hi, ECfr.
Leicester (LIGER, LIHER, LEHRE) A'stan, Edgar-T.
Lewes (LAEPES) A'stan, Edgar-T.
Lincoln (LINCOLNE, NICOLE) Edgar-LC.
Louth ? (LVD) Ae.
Lympne (LIMEN) A'stan, Edgar-Cn.
Malmesbury (MALD, MEALDMES) Ae-Wii, HA.
Milbourne Port (MYLE) Ae, Cn.
Newcastle (NEWEC, NIVCA) St, T, LC.
Northampton (HAMTVN, NORHANT) Edwig, Edgar-Wi, He-LC.

Axbridge (ACXEPO, AGEPOR) Ae, Cn, Ht.
Barnstaple (BEARDA, BARDI), Edwig, Ae-Hi, ECfr, Wi, He.
Bedwyn (BEDE CIN) ECfr, Wi.
Bramber ? (BRAN) St.
Bristol (BRICSTO) Ae-T, M. HA, LC.
Buckingham (BVCIN) EM-Hi, ECfr.
Cadbury CADANB) Ae, Cn.
Caistor (CASTR) EM, Ae, Cn.
Canterbury (DORO, CAENT, CANTOR, CANT CAR) Alf, A'stan, Edgar-LC.
Castle Gotha ? (GEOÐA, IOÐA) Ae-Ht.
Chester (LEIGECES, LEGECE, CESTRE) A'stan, Edgar-T.
Chippenham ? (CIPEN) St.
Cissbury (SIÐEST) Ae, Cn.
Crewkerne (CRVCERN) Ae, Cn.
Derby (DEOR, DIORBI, DERBI) A'stan, Edgar-ECfr, Wi-St.
Droitwich (PICC, PICNEH) ECfr. Hii.
Durham (DVRE, DVRHAN) Wi, St-LC.
Eye (EI, EIE) St.
Gloucester (GLEA C EC, GLE C , G C) Alf, A'stan, Edgar-St, HA, T, LC.
Hedon, near Hull (HEDVN) St.
Hertford (HEORTF) A'stan, Edwig-Hi, ECfr, Wi, Wii.
Horndon ? (HORNIDVNE) ECfr.
Hythe (HIÐEN) ECfr, Wi, Wii.
Ipswich (GIPES C IC) Edgar-SC.
Kings Lynn (LENN, LENE) SC.
Launceston (LANSTF, SANCTI STEFANI) Ae, Wi, Wii, St. T.
Lichfield (LIHFL) SC.
London (LVNDENE) Alf-LC.
Lydford (LYDAN) EM-Hi, ECfr.
Maldon (MAELDVN, MAELI) A'stan, Ae-Hi, ECfr, Wii.
Marlborough (MAERLEB) Wi, Wii.
Newark (NEPIR, NIPOR) Edwig, Eadgar, Ae, Cn.
Newport (NIPAN, NIPEP) Edgar, ECfr.
Norwich (NORPIC) A'stan-LC.
Nottingham (SŊOTINC) A'stan, Ae-St.

Oxford (OXNAFOR, OXENEF) A'stan, Edmund, Edred, Edgar-St, M, T-LC.
Peterborough (MEDE, BVR) Ae, Cn, Wi.
Pevensey (PEFNESE, PEVEN) Wi, Wii, St.
Rhuddlan (RVDILI, RVLA) Wi, SC.
Romney (RVME, RVMNE) Ae-Hi, ECfr-He.
Salisbury (SAEREB, SALEB) Ae-ECfr, Wi- T.
Shaftesbury (SCEFTESB, SCEFITI) A'stan, Ae-St.
Southampton (HAMWIC, HAMTVN) A'stan, Edwig-Cn.
Stafford (STAFF, STAEF) A'stan, Ae-Hi, ECfr, Wi, Wii, St, T.
Steyning (STAENIG) Cn-Wii.
Swansea (SWENSEI) HA?
Taunton (TANTVNE) Ae, Cn, Ht-St.
Thetford (ĐEOTFOR,, TETFOR) Edgar-T.
Totnes (DARENT VRB, TOTANES, TOTNESE) A'stan, Edwig-Cn, Wii.
Wareham (PERHAM) A'stan, Ae, Cn, Ht-St, M, WG.
Warminster (PORIME) Ae-Hi, ECfr.
Watchet (PECEDPORT, PICEDI) Ae-ECfr, Wi-St.
Winchcombe (PINCELE, PINCL) Edgar-Cn, Ht-Wi.
Worcester (PIHRAC, PIHREC) Ae-Hi, ECfr-Sc.
Pembroke (PAN, PAIN) He-T.
Pershore (PERESC) ECfr.
Petherton (PEDĐR) ECfr.
Reading (READIN) ECfr.
Rochester (ROFEC) A'stan, Edgar-He, SC.
Rye (RIE) St.
Sandwich (SANPIC) ECfr, Wi-St.
Shrewsbury (SCROBES, SALOP) A'stan, Edgar-LC.
Southwark (SVDGE, SVD C EEORC) Ae-St.
Stamford (STANFOR) Edgar-St.
Sudbury (SVDBI, SVB) Ae, Cn, ECfr, Wi- St.
Tamworth (TOMPEARĐGE, TAMPRĐ) A'stan, Edwig-Hi, ECfr, Wi-St.
Torksey (TORC, TVRC) EM-Cn.
Twynham, now Christchurch (TPIN, TVEHAM) Wi, He.
Wallingford (PELING, PALLIG) A'stan, Edgar-He, T, LC.
Warwick (PAERING, PERPIC) A'stan, Edgar-St.
Wilton (PILTVNE) Edgar-LC.
Winchester (PINTONIA, PINCEST) Alf-A'stan, Edwig -LC.
York (EBORACI, EOFERPIC) A'stan, Edmund, Edgar-LC.

The location of the following is uncertain.
AESTHE *(? Hastings)* Ae.
DERNE, DYR *(E. Anglian mint East Dereham?)* ECfr.
DEVITVN *(? Welsh Marches* or *St. Davids)* Wi.
MAINT, Wi.
WEARDBYRIG *(? Warborough)* A'stan, Edgar.
BRYGIN *(? Bridgnorth*, but die-links with NIPAN and with *Shaftesbury)* Ae.
EANBYRIG, Cn.
ORSNAFORDA *(? Horsforth or Orford)* Alf.

EDWARDIAN AND LATER MINTS

London, Tower: Edw. I-Geo. III.
London, Durham House: Hen. VIII (posth.)-Edw. VI.
Aberystwyth: Chas. I.
Bridgnorth: Chas. I.
Birmingham, Heaton: Vic., Geo. V.
Birmingham, Soho: Geo. III.
Bristol: Edw. I, Edw. IV, Hen. VI rest., Hen. VIII-Edw. VI, Chas. I, Wm. III.
Canterbury: Edw. I-Edw. III, Edw. IV, Hen. VII-Edw. VI.
Chester: Edw. I, Chas. I, Wm. III.
Coventry: Edw. IV.
Exeter: Edw. I, Chas. I, Wm. III.
Hereford: Chas. I.
Lincoln: Edw. I.
Melbourne, Australia (branch mint): Vic.-Geo. V.
Newcastle-upon-Tyne: Edw. I.
Ottowa, Canada (branch mint): Edw. VII-Geo. V.
Perth, Australia (branch mint): Vic.-Geo. V.
Pretoria, South Africa (branch mint): Geo. V.
Scarborough: Chas. I.
Southwark: Hen. VIII-Edw. VI.
Tournai, Belgium: Hen. VIII.
Welsh Marches: Chas I
York: Edw. I, Edw. III-Edw. IV, Rich. III-Edw. VI, Chas. I, Wm. III.
London, Tower Hill: Geo. III-Eliz. II.
Ashby de la Zouche: Chas. I.
Aberystwyth: -Furnace: Chas. I.
Berwick-on-Tweed: Edw. I-Edw. III.
Birmingham, King's Norton: Geo. V.
Bombay, India (branch mint): Geo. V.
Bury St. Edmunds: Edw. I-Edw. III.
Calais: Edw. III-Hen. IV, Hen. VI.
Carlisle: Chas. I.
Colchester: Chas. I.
Durham: Edw. I-Edw. IV, Rich. III-Hen. VIII.
Hartlebury Castle, Worcs.: Chas. I.
Kingston-upon-Hull: Edw. I.
Llantrisant: Eliz. II (decimal coinage).
Newark: Chas. I.
Norwich: Edw. IV, Wm. III.
Oxford: Chas I.
Pontefract: Chas. I.
Reading: Edw. III.
Shrewsbury: Chas. I.
Sydney, Australia (branch mint): Vic.-Geo. V.
Truro: Chas. I.
Worcester: Chas I.

NORMAN KINGS

There were no major changes in the coinages following the Norman conquest. The controls and periodic changes of the type made in the previous reigns were continued. Nearly seventy mints were operating during the reign of William I; these had been reduced to about fifty-five by the middle of the 12th century and, under Henry II, first to thirty and later to eleven. By the second half of the 13th century the issue of coinage had been centralized at London and Canterbury, with the exception of two ecclesiastical mints. Of the thirteen types with the name PILLEMVS, PILLELM, etc. (William), the first eight have been attributed to the Conqueror and the remaining five to his son William Rufus. Cut 'halfpennies' and 'farthings' were still made in this period and are scarce until the later issues of Henry I and Stephen.

From William I to Edward II inclusive all are silver pennies unless otherwise stated.

WILLIAM I, 1066-1087

William Duke of Normandy was the cousin of Edward the Confessor. After securing the throne of England he had to suppress several rebellions.

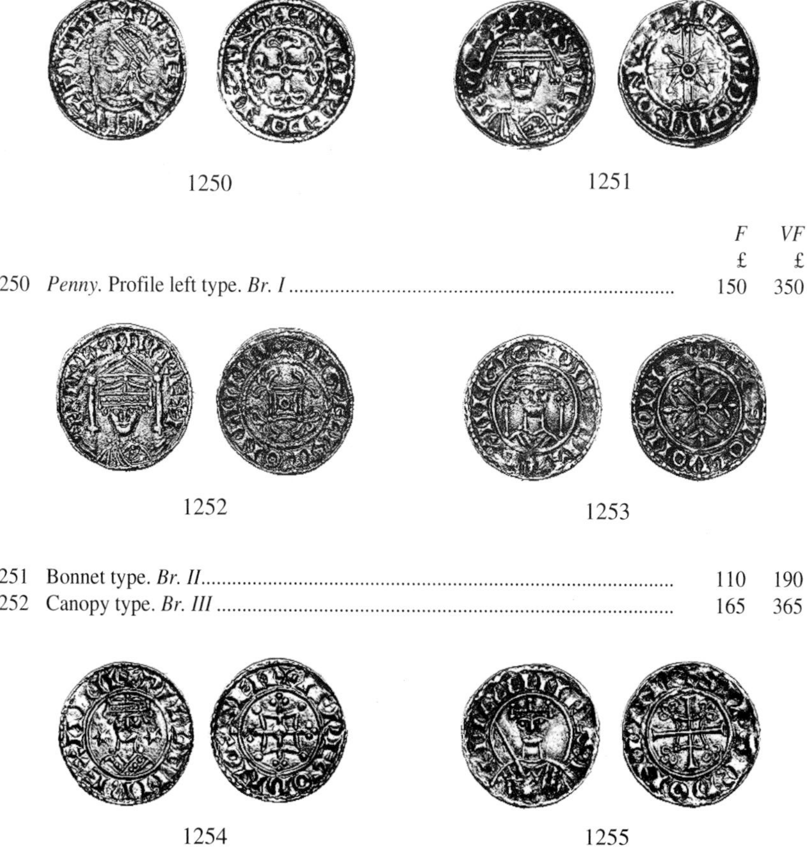

1250 1251

		F £	*VF* £
1250	*Penny*. Profile left type. *Br. I*	150	350

1252 1253

1251	Bonnet type. *Br. II*	110	190
1252	Canopy type. *Br. III*	165	365

1254 1255

1253	Two sceptres type. *Br. IV*	140	280
1254	Two stars type. *Br. V*	110	190
1255	Sword type. *Br. VI*	150	350

1256

1257

	F	VF
	£	£
1256 Profile right type. *Br VII*	225	500
1257 PAXS type. *Br. VIII*	100	145

WILLIAM II, 1087-1100

William Rufus was the second son of William I, his elder brother Robert succeeded to the Dukedom of Normandy. He was killed while hunting in the New Forest.

1258

1259

1258 *Penny.* Profile type. *Br. 1*	225	500
1259 Cross in quatrefoil type. *Br. 2*	225	425

1260

1261

1260 Cross voided type. *Br. 3*	225	425
1261 Cross pattée and fleury type. *Br. 4*	250	500

1262

1262 Cross fleury and piles type. *Br. 5*	300	550

HENRY I, 1100-1135

Fifteen types were minted during this reign. In 1106-7 provision was made for minting round halfpence again, none having been struck since the time of Eadgar, but relatively few can have been made. The standard of coinage manufacture was now beginning to deteriorate badly. Many genuine coins were being cut to see if they were plated counterfeits and there was a reluctance by the public to accept such damaged pieces. About 1107-8 an extraordinary decision was taken to order the official mutilation of all new coins by snicking the edges, thus ensuring that cut coins had to be accepted. Pennies of types VII to XII (Nos. 1268-1273) usually have a cut in the flan that sometimes penetrated over a third of the way across the coin.

At Christmas 1124 the famous 'Assize of the Moneyers' was held at Winchester when all the moneyers in England were called to account for their activities and a number are said to have been mutilated for issuing coins of inferior quality.

The dates and the order of Henry's issues have been modified several times since Brooke. The main changes are as follows: BMC 11 preceded 10 and BMC 9 follows 6. The order of BMC 7 and 8 remains uncertain. The issues were not made for equal periods of time, as BMC 15 began in early 1125. The first nine types were probably made between 1100-10, by the time that Matilda's dowry was collected. BMC 10 to 14 were therefore made between 1110-24. The contemporary chronicles mention the round halfpenny (and farthings) and the order to snick whole coins under 1107 or 1108. The halfpennies are now dated to agree with these references when BMC 6 and 9 pennies were current. A few pennies of BMC 6 are snicked as are most of the halfpennies. Snicks continue to be used on coins of BMC 13 and 14, thought the cut is smaller and only a quarter to a half of the coins are snicked. [Brooke 1916; Dolley; Gomm SCMB 1984; Walker SCMB 1984; Archibald and Conté NC 1990; Blackburn RNS 1990 and Rogers BNS June 1992.]

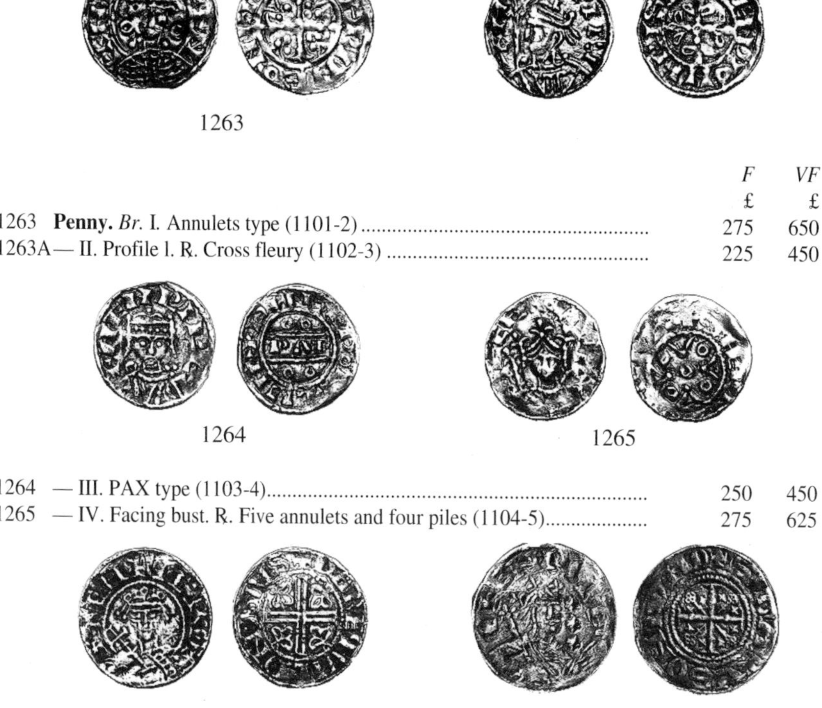

1263

		F	*VF*
		£	£
1263	**Penny.** *Br.* I. Annulets type (1101-2)	275	650
1263A	— II. Profile l. R. Cross fleury (1102-3)	225	450

1264 1265

1264	— III. PAX type (1103-4)	250	450
1265	— IV. Facing bust. R. Five annulets and four piles (1104-5)	275	625

1267

1266	— V. — R. Voided cross with fleur in each angle (1105-6)	450	950
1267	— VI. Pointing bust and stars type (1106-7)	650	1250

1268

		F	*VF*
		£	£
1268	*Br.* VII. Facing bust. ℞. Quatrefoil with piles (1108-9)............................	225	475

1269 1270

1269	— VIII. Large bust 1. ℞. Cross with annulet in each angle (1109-10)......	600	1450
1270	— IX. Facing bust. ℞. Cross in quatrefoil (1107-8)	450	1000

1271 1272

1271	— X. Small facing bust in circle. ℞. Cross fleury (1114-19)	140	300
1272	— XI. Very large bust l. ℞. 'Double inscription' around small cross pattee (1110-14)	350	750

1273 1274

1273	— XII. Small bust 1. ℞. Cross with annulet in each angle (1119-20)	225	550
1274	— XIII. Star in lozenge fleury type (1120-2)	250	500

1275

1276

		F	VF
		£	£
1275	Br. XIV. Pellets in quatrefoil type (1122-4)	125	260
1276	— XV. Quadrilateral on cross fleury type (1125-36)	110	200

*Full flan pieces with good legends may be worth more than the price stated.

1277

1277*	*Halfpenny.* Facing head. ℞. Cross potent with pellets in angles (c.1107)	1500	2750
1277A	— As above ℞. Similar to penny die of type IX (1107-8)		*Unique*

STEPHEN, 1135-1154
and the Civil War and Anarchy, 1138-1153

Stephen of Blois, Count of Boulogne and a nephew of Henry I, hastily crossed the Channel on his uncle's death and secured the throne for himself, despite Henry's wishes that his daughter Matilda should succeed him. She was the widow of the German emperor Henry V, and was then married to Geoffrey, Count of Anjou. Two years later Matilda arrived in England to claim the throne, supported by her half-brother Robert of Gloucester.

During the protracted civil war that ensued Matilda and later her son, Henry of Anjou, set up an alternative court at Bristol and held much of the west of England, striking coins at mints under their control. Many irregular coins were struck during this troubled period, some by barons in their own name. Particularly curious are the coins from the Midlands and E. Anglia which have Stephen's head defaced, now believed to have been issued during the Interdict of 1148. In 1153, following the death of Stephen's son, Eustace, a treaty between the two factions allowed for the succession of Matilda's son Henry and a uniform coinage was once more established throughout the kingdom.

B.M.C. Norman Kings, 2 vols. (1916). *M.*—Mack, R. P., 'Stephen and the Anarchy 1135-54', *BNJ, XXXV* (1966), pp. 38-112.

STEPHEN

Regular regal issues

1278

1280

		F £	VF £
1278	**Penny.** Cross moline (Watford) type. Bust r., with sceptre. ℞. Cross moline with lis in angles. *B.M.C. I; M. 3-42*	90	200
1279	— Similar, but obv. reads PERERIC or PERERICM. *M. 43-50*	350	750
1280	Voided cross type. Facing bust with sceptre. ℞. Voided cross pattee with mullets in angles. *East and South-east mints only. B.M.C. II; M. 53-66*	135	300

1281 1282

		F £	VF £
1281	Cross fleury type. Bust l. with sceptre. ℞. Cross fleury with trefoils in angles. *East and South-east mints only. B.M.C. VI; M. 77-99*	300	700
1282	Cross pommee (Awbridge) type. Bust half-left with sceptre. ℞. Voided cross pommee with lis in angles. *B.M.C. VII; M. 99z-135b*	150	325

For B.M.C. types III, IV & V, see 1300-1302.

Local and irregular issues of the Civil War

A. Coins struck from erased or defaced dies (interdict of 1148)

1283 1288

		F £	VF £
1283	As 1278, with king's bust defaced with long cross. *East Anglian Mints. M. 137-147*	400	950
1284	— Similar, but king's bust defaced with small cross. *Nottingham. M. 149*	350	750
1285	— Similar, but sceptre defaced with bar or cross. *Nottingham, Lincoln and Stamford. M. 148 and 150-154*	300	800
1286	— Similar, but king's name erased. *Nottingham. M. 157*	450	900
1286A	— Other defacements	*Extremely rare*	

B. South-Eastern variant

		F £	VF £
1287	As 1278, but king holds mace instead of sceptre. *Canterbury. M. 158*	*Extremely rare*	

C. Eastern variants

		F £	VF £
1288	As 1278, but roundels in centre or on limbs of cross or in angles. *Suffolk mints. M. 159-168*	700	1500
1288A	As 1278, but star before sceptre and annulets at tips of *fleurs on reverse. Suffolk mints. M. 188*	1000	2500

		F £	*VF* £
1289	As 1278, but thick plain cross with pellet at end of limbs, lis in angles. *Lincoln. M. 169-173*	600	1200
1290	— Similar, but thick plain cross superimposed on cross moline. *M. 174* .	*Extremely rare*	
1290A	As 1278. R. Quadrilateral over voided cross. *M. 176*	*Extremely rare*	
1290B	As 1278. R. Long cross to edge of coin, fleurs outwards in angles. *Lincoln. M. 186-187*	*Extremely rare*	

D. Southern variants

1291	As 1278, but with large rosette of pellets at end of obverse legend. *M. 184-185*	*Extremely rare*	
1292	— Similar, but star at end of obverse legend. *M. 187y*	*Extremely rare*	
1293	Crowned bust r. or l. with rosette of pellets before face in place of sceptre. R. As 1280, but plain instead of voided cross. *M. 181-183*	*Extremely rare*	

1291 1295

1295	As 1278, but usually collar of annulets. R. Voided cross moline with annulet at centre. *Southampton. M. 207-212*	350	750

E. Midland variants

1296

1296	As 1278, but cross moline on reverse has fleured extensions into legend. *Leicester. M. 177-178*	1000	2500
1297	As 1278 but crude work. R. Voided cross with lis outwards in angles. *Tutbury. M. 179*	*Extremely rare*	
1298	Somewhat similar. R. Voided cross with martlets in angles. *Derby. M. 175*	1200	3000

1298

1300

		F £	VF £
1299	As 1278. ℞. Plain cross with T-cross in each angle. *M. 180*	*Extremely rare*	
1300	Facing bust with three annulets on crown. ℞. Cross pattee, fleurs inwards in angles. *Northampton or Huntingdon (?). B.M.C. III; M.67-71*	1200	3000

1301 1302

1301	Facing bust with three fleurs on crown. ℞. Lozenge fleury, annulets in angles. *Lincoln or Nottingham. B.M.C. IV; M. 72-75*	1250	3250
1302	Bust half-right with sceptre. ℞. Lozenge with pellet centre, fleurs inwards in angles. *Leicester. B.M.C. V; M. 76*	1250	3250
1303	**Robert,** Earl of Leicester(?). As 1280, but reading ROBERTVS. *M. 269*	*Extremely rare*	

F. North-east and Scottish border variants

1304	As 1278, but star before sceptre and annulets at tips of fleurs on reverse. *M. 188*	1000	2500
1305	As 1278, but a voided cross extending to outer circle of reverse. *M. 189-192*	*Extremely rare*	
1306	As 1278, but crude style, with Stephen's name. *M. 276-279 and 281-282*	700	1750
1307	— Similar. ℞. Cross crosslet with cross-pattée and crescent in angles. *M. 288*	*Extremely rare*	
1308	David I (K. of Scotland). As 1305, but with name DAVID REX. *M. 280*	1500	3000
1309	**Henry** (Earl of Northumberland, son of K. David). hENRIC ERL. As 1278. *M. 283-285*	1200	3000
1310	— Similar. ℞. Cross fleury. *M. 286-287*	1000	2500
1311	— As 1307, but with name NENCI : COM on obverse. *M. 289*	1200	2750

G. 'Ornamented' series. *So-called 'York Group' but probably minted in Northern France*

1312	As 1278, with obverse inscription NSEPEFETI, STEFINEI or RODBDS. ℞. WISĐ. GNETA, etc., with ornament(s) in legend (sometimes retrograde). *M. 215-216 and 227*	*Extremely rare*	

1313 1315

1313	Flag type. As 1278, but king holds lance with pennant, star to r. ℞. As 1278, mostly with four ornaments in legend. *M. 217*	1250	2500
1313A	— Similar, but with eight ornaments in reverse inscription. *M. 217*	1250	2500

		F £	VF £
1314	As 1278, but STIEN and ornaments, sceptre is topped by pellet in lozenge. ℞. Cross fleury over plain cross, ornaments in place of inscription. *M. 218*	*Extremely rare*	
1314A	King stg. facing, holding sceptre and long standard with triple-tailed pennon. ℞. Cross pattee, crescents and quatrefoils in angles, pellets around, ornaments in legend	*Unique*	
1315	**Stephen and Queen Matilda.** Two standing figures holding sceptre, as illustration. ℞. Ornaments in place of inscription. *M. 220*	2500	5000

1316  1320

1316	**Eustace.** EVSTACIVS, knight stg. r. holding sword. ℞. Cross in quatrefoil, EBORACI EDTS (or EBORACI TDEFL). *M. 221-222*	2250	5000
1317	— Similar, but ThOMHS FILIuS VIF. *M. 223*	2250	5000
1318	— Similar, but mixed letters and ornaments in rev. legend. *M. 224*	1500	4500
1319	[EVSTA] CII . FII . IOANIS, lion passant r, collonnade (or key?) below. ℞. Cross moline with cross-headed sceptres in angles, mixed letters and ornaments in legend. *M. 225*	*Unique*	
1320	Lion rampant r., looped object below, EISTAOhIVS. ℞. Cross fleury with lis in angles, mostly, ornaments in legend. *M. 226*	1400	3250
1321	**Rodbert.** Knight on horse r., RODBЄRTVS IESTV (?). ℞. As 1314. *M. 228*	*Extremely rare*	

1321  1322

1322	**Bishop Henry.** Crowned bust r., crozier and star to r., HЄNRICVS ЄPC. ℞. Somewhat as last, STЄPhANVS RЄX. *M. 229*	*Extremely rare*	

H. Uncertain issues

1323	Crowned bust r. with sceptre, -NEΓ:. ℞. Cross pattée with annulets in angles (as Hen. I type XIII). *M. 272*	*Extremely rare*	
1324	Crowned facing bust with sceptre, star to r. (as Hen. I type XIV). ℞. As last. *M. 274Extr.*	*Extremely rare*	
1325	Other types	*Extremely rare*	

1326

1331

		F £	VF £
1326	**Matilda,** Dowager Empress, Countess of Anjou (in England 1139-1148). As 1278, but cruder style, MATILDI IMP. etc. *M. 230-240*	800	2000
1326A	Obv. similar. ℞. Cross pattee over cross fleury (Cardiff hoard)	800	2000
1326B	Similar, but triple pellets or plumes at end of cross (Cardiff hoard)	*Extremely rare*	
1326C	**Henry of Neubourg,** Bust r., ℞. As 1276A or 1278	*Extremely rare*	
1327	**Duke Henry,** son of Matilda and Geoffrey of Anjou, Duke of Normandy from 1150 (in England 1147-1149-1150 and 1153-1154). As 1278 but hENRICVS, etc. *M. 241-245*	2250	5000
1327A	As 1295 but hENRIC. *M. 246*	*Extremely rare*	
1327B	As 1326B, but hENNENNVS R, etc	*Extremely rare*	
1328	Obverse as 1278. ℞. Cross crosslet in quatrefoil. *M. 254*	*Extremely rare*	
1329	Crowned bust r. with sceptre. ℞. Cross fleury over quadrilateral fleury. *M. 248-253*	2250	4500
1330	Crowned facing bust, star each side. ℞. Cross botonnée over a quadrilateral pommee. *M. 255-258*	2250	5000
1331	Obverse as 1330. ℞. Voided cross botonnee over a quadrilateral pommée. *M. 259-261*	2250	5000
1331A	**Robert, Earl of Gloucester,** 1143-7, Lion. r. ℞. Cross fleury	*Extremely rare*	
1332	**William,** Earl of Gloucester (succeeded his father, Earl Robert, in 1147). Type as Henry of Anjou, no. 1329. *M. 262*	—	5500
1333	Type as Henry of Anjou, no. 1330. *M. 263*	*Unique*	
1334	Type as Henry of Anjou, no. 1331. *M. 264-268*	2500	5500
1334A	— Lion. ℞. Cross fleury	*Extremely rare*	
1335	**Brian Fitzcount,** Lord of Wallingford (?). Type as Henry of Anjou, no. 1330. *M. 270*	*Unique*	
1336	**Patrick,** Earl of Salisbury (?). Helmeted bust r. holding sword, star behind. ℞. As Henry of Anjou, no. 1329. *M. 271*	*Extremely rare*	

PLANTAGENET KINGS

HENRY II, 1154-1189

Cross-and-crosslets ('Tealby') Coinage, 1158-1180

Coins of Stephen's last type continued to be minted until 1158. Then a new coinage bearing Henry's name replaced the currency of the previous reign which contained a high proportion of irregular and sub-standard pennies. The new Cross and Crosslets issue is more commonly referred to as the 'Tealby' coinage, as over 5000 of these pennies were discovered at Tealby, Lincolnshire, in 1807. Thirty mints were employed in this re-coinage, but once the re-minting had been completed not more than a dozen mints were kept open. The issue remained virtually unchanged for twenty-two years apart from minor variations in the king's portrait. The coins tend to be poorly struck on irregular plans.

Cut coins occur with varying degrees of frequency during this issue, according to the type and local area. The price quoted for coins in the above section allows for the usual poor quality strike. However, the illustrations portray coins of unusually high quality for this issue.

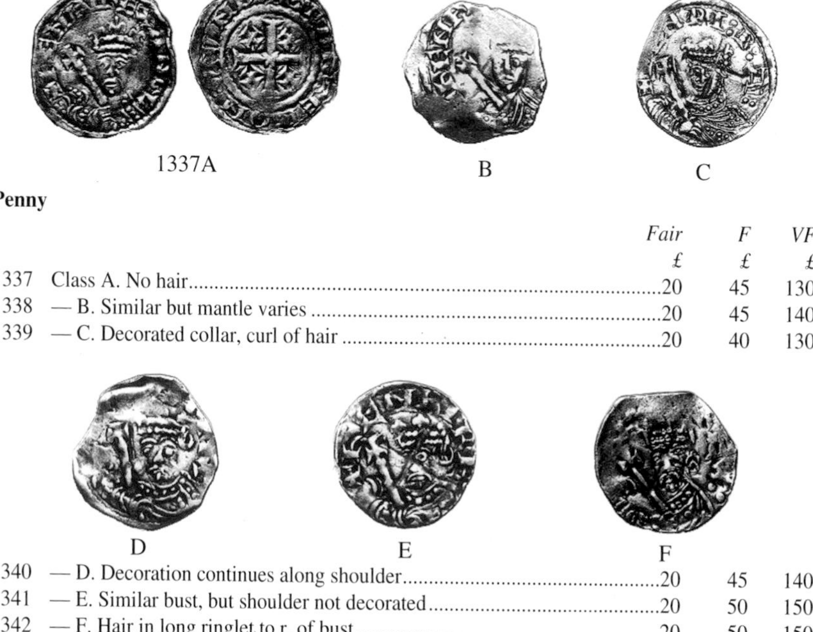

1337A B C

Penny

		Fair	*F*	*VF*
		£	£	£
1337	Class A. No hair	20	45	130
1338	— B. Similar but mantle varies	20	45	140
1339	— C. Decorated collar, curl of hair	20	40	130

D E F

1340	— D. Decoration continues along shoulder	20	45	140
1341	— E. Similar bust, but shoulder not decorated	20	50	150
1342	— F. Hair in long ringlet to r. of bust	20	50	150

Mints and classes of the Cross-and-Crosslets coinage

Approximate dates for the various classes are as follows:

A 1158-1161, B and C 1161-1165, D 1165-1168, E 1168-1170 and F 1170-1180.

Bedford	A - - - - -	Ilchester	A B C D - F	Pembroke	A - - - - -
Bristol	A B C D E F	Ipswich	- B C D E F	Salisbury	A - - - - -
Bury St. Edmunds	A B C D E F	Launceston	A - - - - -	Shrewsbury	A - - - - -
Canterbury	A B C D E F	Leicester	A - - - - -	Stafford	A - C - - -
Carlisle	A - C D E F	Lewes	- - - - ? F	Thetford	A - C D - F
Chester	A - - D - -	Lincoln	A B C D E F	Wallingford	A - - - - -
Colchester	A - C - E -	London	A B C D E F	Wilton	A - - - - -
Durham	A B C - - -	Newcastle	A - C D E F	Winchester	A - C D ? -
Exeter	A B C D - -	Northampton	A - C ? - -	York	A - C D - -
Gloucester	A - - - - -	Norwich	A B C D - F		
Hereford	A - C - - -	Oxford	A - - D E -		

'Short Cross' coinage of Henry II (1180-1189)

In 1180 a coinage of new type, known as the Short Cross coinage, replaced the Tealby issue. The new coinage is remarkable in that it covers not only the latter part of the reign of Henry II, but also the reigns of his sons Richard and John and his grandson Henry III, and the entire issue bears the name 'hЄNRICVS'. There are no English coins with names of Richard or John. The Short Cross coins can be divided chronologically into various classes: eleven mints were operating under Henry II and tables of mints, moneyers and classes are given for each reign.

Cut coins continue and although less common than after 1247, they are still up to ten times commoner than during the Anglo-Saxon period.

1a 1b 1c

		F £	*VF* £
1343	Class 1a. Narrow face, square E, and C, round M	150	375
1343A	1a* Bust of 1a, but round C and Є, square M	80	200
1344	— 1b. Curls usually 2 to l., 5 to r., round Є and C, square M, stop before REX on most coins	35	70
1345	— 1c. First evidence of degradation, more curls to r. than to l., no stop in *obv.* legend on some coins	30	65

Mints, moneyers, and classes for Henry II

London: Aimer (1a, b, c), Alain (1a, b, c), Alain V (1a, b), Alward (1b), Davi (1b, c), Fil. Aimer (1a, b), Gilebert (1c), Godard (1b), Henri (1a, b), Henri Pi (1a, b), Iefrei or Gefrei (1a, b, c), Iohan (1a, b), Osber (1b), Pieres (1a, b, c), Pieres M . (1a, b), Randul (1a, b), Raul (1b, c), Reinald (1b), Willelm (1a, b, c) .... *from* 30

Carlisle: Alain (1b, c) 70

Exeter: Asketil (1a, b), Iordan (1a, b), Osber (1a, b), Raul (1b), Ricard (1b, c), Roger (1b) .... *from* 60

Lincoln: Edmund (1b, c), Girard (1b), Hugo (1b), Lefwine (1b, c), Rodbert (1b), Walter (1b), Will . D.F. (1b), Willelm (1b, c) .... *from* 45

Northampton: Filipe (1a, b), Hugo (1a, b), Raul (1a, b, c), Reinald (1a, b), Simund (1b), Walter (1a, b, c), Willelm (1a, b) .... *from* 40

Norwich: Reinald (1b, c), Willelm (1b) .... *from* 60

(Current research may indicate that these coins are of the Northampton mint).

Oxford: Asketil (1b), Iefrei (1b), Owein (1b), Ricard (1b, c), Rodbert (1b), Rodbt. F. B. (1b), Sagar (1b) .... *from* 70

Wilton: Osber (1a, b), Rodbert (1a, b) .... *from* 65

Winchester: Adam (1b, c), Clement (1a, b), Gocelm (1a, b, c), Henri (1a), Osber (1a, b), Reinier (1b), Ricard (1b), Rodbert (1a, b) .... *from* 35

Worcester: Edrich (1b), Godwine (1b, c), Osber (1b) .... *from* 60

York: Alain (1a, b), Efrard (1a, b, c), Gerard (1b), Hugo (1b, c), Hunfrei (1a, b), Isac (1a, b), Turkil (1a, b, c), Willelm (1a, b) .... *from* 35

RICHARD I, 1189-1199

Pennies of Short Cross type continued to be issued throughout the reign, all bearing the name hЄNRICVS. The coins of class 4, which have very crude portraits, continued to be issued in the early years of the next reign. The only coins bearing Richard's name are from his territories of Aquitaine and Poitou in western France.

2 3a 3b 4a 4b

		F £	VF £
'Short Cross' coinage (reading hЄNRICVS)			
1346	Class 2. Round face; 5 or more pearls in crown; mass of small curls at both sides of head	65	150
1347	— 3a. Large face; 7 or more pearls in crown; 3 or 4 curls at either side of head; beard of small curls, large pellet eyes	50	120
1347A	— 3b. Similar, but smaller face	45	100
1348	— 4a. Similar, but beard of pellets	40	80
1348A	— 4b. Very crude bust, hair represented by only one or two crescents each side	40	75
1348B	— 4a*. As 4a, but colon stops on reverse	55	95

Mints, moneyers, and classes for Richard I

London: Aimer (2-4b), Fulke (4a, b), Goldwine (4a), Henri (4a-4b), Raul (2), Ricard (2-4b), Stivene (2-4b), Willelm (2-4b)	*from*	40
Canterbury: Goldwine (2-4b), Hernaud (4b), Io(h)an (4b), Meinir (2-4b), Reinald (2-4a), Reinaud (4b), Roberd (2-4b), Samuel (4b), Ulard (2-4b)	*from*	40
Carlisle: Alein (3-4b)	*from*	90
Durham: Adam (4a), Alein (4a-b)	*from*	100
Exeter: Ricard (3b)		85
Lichfield: Ioan (2)		*Extremely rare*
Lincoln: Edmund (2), Lefwine (2), Willelm (2)	*from*	50
Northampton: Geferi (4a), Roberd (3), Waltir (3)	*from*	75
Norwich: Randul (4a-b), Willelm (4a-b)	*from*	75
Shrewsbury: Ive (4b), Reinald (4a, 4b), Willelm (4a)	*from*	150
Winchester: Adam (3a), Gocelm (2-3), Osbern (3-4a), Pires (4a), Willelm (2-4)	*from*	50
Worcester: Osbern (2)		*Extremely rare*
York: Davi (4b?), Everard (2-4b), Hue (2-4a), Nicole (4b), Turkil (2-4b)	*from*	45

JOHN, 1199-1216

'Short Cross' coinage *continued.* All with name hЄNRICVS
The Short Cross coins of class 4 will have continued during the early years of John's reign, but in 1205 a re-coinage was initiated and new Short Cross coins of better style replaced the older issues. Coins of classes 5a and 5b were issued in the re-coinage in which sixteen mints were employed. Only ten of these mints were still working by the end of class 5. The only coins to bear John's name are the pennies, halfpence and farthings issues for Ireland.

4c 5a 5b 5c 6a1 6a2

		F	*VF*
		£	£
1349	Class 4c. Somewhat as 4b, but letter S is reversed	40	90
1350	— 5a. New coinage of neat style and execution; realistic face; 5 or more pearls to crown; letter S is reversed; *mm* cross pommée	35	70
1350A	— — with ornamented letters	40	110
1350B	— 5a/5b or 5b/5a mules	45	100
1351	— 5b. Similar, but S normal and *mm* reverts to cross pattee	35	65
1352	— 5c. Similar, but letter X composed of 4 strokes in the form of a St. Andrew's cross	35	65
1353	— 6a1. Coarser style; letter X composed of 2 wedges in the form of a St. Andrew's cross	40	75
1353A	— 6a2. Similar, but letter X has arms at right angles and with rounded ends	40	75

Mints, moneyers and classes for John

London: Abel (5c-6a), Adam (5b-c), Arnaud (5b), Beneit (5b-c), Fulke (4c-5a), Henri (4c-5b), Ilger (5b-6a), Iohan (5b), Rauf (5c-6a), Rener (5b-c), Ricard (4c-5b), Ricard B (5b-c), Ricard T (5b), Walter (5c-6a), Willelm (4c-5c), Willelm B (5b-c), Willelm L (5b-c), Willelm T (5b-c) .... *from* 30

Bury St. Edmunds: Fulke (5b-c) .... *from* 50

Canterbury: Arnaud (5a-c), Coldwine (4c-5c), (H)ernaud (5a-c), Hue (4c-5c), Io(h)an (4c-5c), Iohan B (5b-c), Iohan M (5b-c), Rauf (Vc?), Roberd (4c-5c), Samuel (4c-5c), Simon (5a or c), Simun (4c-5b) .... *from* 30

Carlisle: Tomas (5b) 80

Chichester: Pieres (5b), Rauf (5a-b), Simon (5a- b), Willelm (5b) .... *from* 50

Durham: Pieres (4c-6a) .... *from* 60

Exeter: Gilebert (5a-b), Iohan (5a-b), Ricard (5a-b) .... *from* 50

Ipswich: Alisandre (5b, c), Iohan (5b-c) .... *from* 50

Kings Lynn: Iohan (5b), Nicole (5b), Willelm (5b) .... *from* 120

Lincoln: Alain (5a), Andreu (5a-c), Hue (5b-c), Iohan (5a), Rauf (5a-b), Ricard (5a), Tomas (5a, b) .... *from* 35

Northampton: Adam (5b-c), Randul (4c), Roberd (5b), Roberd T (5b) .... *from* 40

		F £
Norwich: Gifrei (5a-c), Iohan (5a-c), Renald (5a), Renaud (5a-c)	*from*	45
Oxford: Ailwine (5b), Henri (5 b), Miles (5b)	*from*	50
Rhuddlan: An irregular issue probably struck during this reign. Halli, Henricus, Tomas, Simond	*from*	75
Rochester: Alisandre (5b), Hunfrei (5b)	*from*	90
Winchester: Adam (5a-c), Andreu (5b-c), Bartelme (5b-c), Henri (5a), Iohan (5a-c), Lukas (5b, c), Miles (5a-c), Rauf (5b-c), Ricard (5a, b)	*from*	35
York: Davi (4c-5b), Nicole (4c-5c), Renaud (5b), Tomas (5b)	*from*	40

HENRY III, 1216-72

'Short Cross' coinage *continued* (1216-47)
The Short Cross coinage continued for a further thirty years during which time the style of portraiture and workmanship deteriorated. By the 1220s minting had been concentrated at London and Canterbury, one exception being the mint of the Abbot of Bury St. Edmunds.

Halfpenny and farthing dies are recorded early in this issue; a few halfpennies and now two farthings have been discovered. See nos 1357 D-E.

6b  6c  7 early  7 middle  7 late

'Short Cross' coinage, 1216-47

		F £	VF £
1354	Class 6b. Very tall lettering; early coins have a head similar to 6a, but later issues have a long thin face	20	45
1355	— 6c. Pointed face	20	45
1355A	— — Ornamental lettering	40	110
1355B	— 6x. Large face, two curls each side of hd., pellet on chin, letter X only by sceptre	100	200
1355C	— 6d. Tall, straight-sided letters, pellet on crossbar of N on most coins.	20	40
1356	— 7. No stops between words in rev. legend; no neck	20	40

8a  8b1  8b2  8b3

		F £	VF £
1357	— 8a. New style; *mm* cross pattee; letter X curule shaped	*Extremely rare*	
1357A	— 8b1. Similar; *mm* cross pommee	25	75
1357B	— 8b2. Cruder version; wedge-shaped letter X	25	75
1357C	— 8b3. Very crude version; letter X is cross pommée	25	75

1357D

1357E

		F £
1357D	**'Short Cross' coinage.** (*c.* 1221-30). Cl. 7. Halfpenny. hЄNRICVS REX. ℞. TER.RI ON LUND or ELIS ON LUND (London)	*Extremely rare*
1357E	— — Farthing. Similar ℞. TERRI ON LUND or RAVLF ON LUND	*Extremely rare*

Mints, moneyers, and classes for Henry III 'Short Cross' coinage

London: Abel (6b-7), Adam (7), (H)elis (7), Giffrei (7), Ilger (6b-7), Ledulf (7), Nichole (7-8), Rau(l)f (6b-7), Ricard (7), Terri (7), Walter (6b-6c)	*from*	20
Bury St. Edmunds: Io(h)an (7-8), Norman (7), Rauf (6b-7), Simund (7), Willelm (7)	*from*	35
Canterbury: Arnold (6x), Henri (6b-7), Hiun (6b-7), Iun (7), Io(h)an (6b-8), Ioan Chic (7), Ioan F. R. (7), Nicole (7-8), Norman (7), Osmund (7), Roberd (6b), Robert (7), Robert Vi (7), Roger (6b-7), Roger of R (7), Salemun (6x, 7), Samuel (6b-7), Simon (7), Simun (6b-7), Tomas (6d, 7), Walter (6b-7), Willem (7-8), Willem Ta (7)	*from*	20
Durham: Pieres (7)		100
Winchester: Henri (6c)		25
York: Iohan (6c), Peres (6c), Tomas (6c), Wilam (6c)		110

'Long Cross' coinage (1247-72)

By the middle of Henry's reign the coinage in circulation was in a poor state, being worn and clipped. In 1247 a fresh coinage was ordered, the new pennies having the reverse cross extended to the edge of the coin to help safeguard the coins against clipping. The earliest of these coins have no mint or moneyers' names. A number of provincial mints were opened for producing sufficient of the Long Cross coins, but these were closed again in 1250, only the royal mints of London and Canterbury and the ecclesiastical mints of Durham and Bury St. Edmunds remained open.

In 1257, following the introduction of new gold coinages by the Italian cities of Brindisi (1232), Florence (1252) and Genoa (1253), Henry III issued a gold coinage in England. This was a gold 'Penny' valued at 20 silver pence and twice the weight of the silver penny. The coinage was not a success, being undervalued, and coinage ceased to be minted after a few years; few have survived.

Cut halfpennies and farthings are common for this period, with a greater concentration in the early part. They are up to 100 times commoner than in late Anglo-Saxon times.

Without sceptre

Ia

Ib

		F £	VF £
1358	Class Ia. hЄNRICVS: RЄX. ℞. ANGLIЄ TЄRCI	275	575
1359	Ib. hЄNRICVS REX. ANG. ℞. LIE TЄRCI LON *(London),* CAN *(Canterbury)* or AED *(Bury St. Edmunds)* *from*	45	90
1360	—— I/II mule	45	90

II

IIIb

IIIc

		F	VF
		£	£
1361	Class II. hЄNRICVS RЄX TЄ RCI. R. Moneyer and mint	28	50
1362	— IIIa. hЄNRICVS RЄX ·. III, thin face as class II	18	30
1363	— IIIb. Smaller, rounder face	18	30
1364	— IIIc. Face with pointed chin, neck indicated by two lines, usually RЄX: III	18	30

With sceptre

IVa

Va

Vb

Vc

1365	Class IVa. Similar to last, but with sceptre	60	130
1366	— IVb. Similar, but new crown with half-fleurs and large central fleur	70	180
1367	— Va. With class IV bust, round eyes, from now on legend begins at 10 o'clock	20	35
1368	— Vb. Narrower face, wedge-tailed R, round eyes	18	30
1369	— Vc. As last, but almond-shaped eyes	18	30

Vd

Ve

Vf

Vg

Vh

1370	— Vd. Portrait of quite different style; new crown with true-shaped fleur	35	85
1371	— Ve. Similar, with jewelled or beaded crown	125	325
1372	— Vf. New style larger face, double-banded crown	25	55
1373	— Vg. Single band to crown, low central fleur, curule chair shaped X	20	40
1374	— Vh. Crude copy of Vg, with pellets in lieu of fleur	40	80
1375	— Vi. Similar to last, but triple line of pellets for beard	275	525

Vi

1376

		F £	VF £
1376	**Gold penny** of 20d. As illustration ... *A very fine specimen was sold at auction in June 1985 for £65,000.*	*Extremely rare*	

Mints, Moneyers, and classes for Henry III 'Long Cross' coinage

Mint and moneyers		Fine
London: Davi or David (IIIc-Vf), Henri (IIIa-Vd, f, g), Ion, Ioh, Iohs or Iohan (Vc-g), Nicole (Ib/II mule, II-Vc), Renaud (Vg-i), Ricard (IIIc-Vg), Robert (Vg), Thomas (Vg), Walter (Vc-g), Willem (Vc-g and gold penny) ...	*from*	18
Bristol: Elis (IIIa, b, c), Henri (IIIb) , Iacob (IIIa, b, c), Roger (IIIa, b, c), Walter (IIIb, c) ...	*from*	22
Bury St. Edmunds: Ion or Iohs (II-Va, Vg, h, i), Randulf (Va-f), Renaud (Vg), Stephane (Vg) ...	*from*	20
Canterbury: Alein (Vg, h), Ambroci (Vg), Gilbert (II-Vd/c.mule, Vf, g), Ion, Ioh, Iohs, or Iohanes (IIIe-Vd, f, g), Nicole or Nichole (Ib/II mule, II-Vh), Ricard (Vg, h), Robert (Vc-h), Walter (Vc-h), Willem or Willeme (Ib/II mule, II-Vd, f, g)	*from*	18
Carlisle: Adam (IIIa, b), Ion (IIIa, b), Robert (IIIa, b), Willem (IIIa, b) ...	*from*	45
Durham: Philip (IIIb), Ricard (V, b, c), Roger (Vg), Willem (Vg) ...	*from*	55
Exeter: Ion (II-IIIc), Philip (II-IIIc), Robert (II-IIIc), Walter (II-IIIb) ...	*from*	30
Gloucester: Ion (II-IIIc), Lucas (II-IIIc), Ricard (II-IIIc), Roger (II-IIIc) ...	*from*	25
Hereford: Henri (IIIa, b), Ricard (IIIa, b, c), Roger (IIIa, b, c), Walter (IIIa, b, c)	*from*	40
Ilchester: Huge (IIIa, b, c), Ierveis (IIIa, b, c), Randulf (IIIa, b, c), Stephe (IIIa, b, c) ...	*from*	65
Lincoln: Ion (II-IIIc), Ricard (II-IIIc), Walter (II-IIIc), Willem (II-IIIc) ...	*from*	25
Newcastle: Adam (IIIa, b), Henri (IIIa, b, c), Ion (IIIa, b, c), Roger (IIIa, b, c) ..	*from*	22
Northampton: Lucas (II-IIIb), Philip (II-IIIc), Tomas (II-IIIc), Willem (II-IIIc)	*from*	25
Norwich: Huge (II-IIIc), Iacob (II-II Ic), Ion (II-IIIc), Willem (II-IIIc) ...	*from*	35
Oxford: Adam (II-IIIc), Gefrei (II-IIIc), Henri (II-IIIc), Willem (II-IIIc) ...	*from*	35
Shrewsbury: Lorens (IIIa, b, c), Nicole (IIIa, b, c), Peris (IIIa, b, c), Ricard (IIIa, b, c) ...	*from*	45
Wallingford: Alisandre (IIIa, b), Clement (IIIa, b), Ricard (IIIa, b), Robert (IIIa, b) ...	*from*	30
Wilton: Huge (IIIb, c), Ion (IIIa, b, c), Willem (IIIa, b, c) ...	*from*	40
Winchester: Huge (II-IIIc), Iordan (II-IIIc), Nicole (II-IIIc), Willem (II-IIIc)	*from*	22
York: Alain (II-IIIb), Ieremie (II-IIIb), Ion (II-IIIc), Rener (II-IIIc), Tomas (IIIb, c) ...	*from*	25

EDWARD I, 1272-1307

'Long Cross' coinage (1272-79). With name hЄNRICVS
The earliest group of Edward's Long Cross coins are of very crude style and known only of Durham and Bury St. Edmunds. Then, for the last class of the type, pennies of much improved style were issued at London, Durham and Bury, but in 1279 the Long Cross coinage was abandoned and a completely new coinage substituted.

Cut halfpennies and farthings also occur for this issue, and within this context are not especially rare.

VI

VII

		F	*VF*
		£	£
1377	Class VI. Crude face with new realistic curls, Є and N ligate	25	55
1378	— VII. Similar, but of improved style, usually with Lombardic U	50	110

Mints, moneyers, and classes for Edward I 'Long Cross' coinage

London: Phelip (VII), Renaud (VII)	*from*	50
Bury St. Edmunds: Ioce (VII), Ion or Ioh (VI, VII)	*from*	25
Durham: Roberd (VI), Robert (VII)	*from*	175

New Coinage (from 1279).
A major re-coinage was embarked upon in 1279 which introduced new denominations. In addition to the penny, halfpence and farthings were also minted and, for the first time, a fourpenny piece called a 'Groat' (from the French *Gros).*

As mint administration was now very much centralized, the practice of including the moneyer's name in the coinage was abandoned (except for a few years at Bury St. Edmunds). Several provincial mints assisted with the re-coinage during 1279-81, then minting was again restricted to London, Canterbury, Durham and Bury.

The provincial mints were again employed for a subsidiary re-coinage in 1299-1302 in order to remint lightweight coins and the many illegal *esterlings* (foreign copies of the English pennies, mainly from the Low Countries), which were usually a poorer quality than the English coins.

1379

1379	**Groat.** (=4d.; wt. 89 grs.). Type as illustration but several minor varieties *Extant specimens often show traces of having been mounted on the obverse and gilded on the reverse; unmounted coins are worth more.*	900	2250

1a 1b 1c

		F £	VF £
1380	**Penny.** *London.* Class 1a. Crown with plain band, ЄDW RЄX; Lombardic n on obv.	300	650
1381	— 1b. — ЄD RЄX; no drapery on bust, Roman N	375	800
1382	— Ic. — ЄDW RЄX; Roman N, normal or reversed; small lettering	16	40
1383	— Id. — ЄDW R;—; large lettering and face	15	35

1d(1384) 2a 2b

		F £	VF £
1384	— — — Annulet below bust (for the Abbot of Reading)	135	325
1385	— 2a. Crown with band shaped to ornaments; large face and short neck similar to 1d; usually broken left petal to central fleur of crown	16	40
1386	— 2b. — tall bust; long neck; N reversed	14	35

3a 3b 3c

		F £	VF £
1387	— 3a. Crescent-shaped contraction marks; pearls in crown, drapery is foreshortened circle	35	65
1388	— 3b. — — drapery is segment of a circle	25	45
1389	— 3c. — normal crown; drapery in one piece, hollowed in centre	10	25

3e

3f

3g

		F	*VF*
		£	£
1390	— 3d. — — drapery in two pieces, broad face	12	30
1391	— 3e. — long narrow face (mostly Northern mints)	14	32
1392	— 3f. — broad face, large nose, rougher work, late S first used	25	60
1393	— 3g. — small neat bust, narrow face	10	30

4a

4b

4c

4d

4e

1394	— 4a. Comma-shaped contraction mark, late S always used, C and Є open.	12	30
1395	— 4b. Similar, but face and hair shorter	10	25
1396	— 4c. Larger face with more copious hair; unbarred A first used	10	25
1397	— 4d. Pellet at beginning of *obv.* and/or *rev.*inscription	12	30
1398	— 4e. Three pellets on breast; pellet in *rev.* legend	14	32

5a

5b

1399	— 5a. Well spread coins, pellet on breast, A normally unbarred	30	70
1400	— 5b. Coins more spread, tall lettering, long narrow face, pellet on breast....	30	70

6a

6b

7a

7b

		F £	VF £
1401	— 6a. Smaller coins, initial cross almost plain, crown with wide fleurs	80	175
1402	— 6b. Initial cross well pattee; lettering of good style; closed Є (from now on)	50	100
1403	— 7a. Rose on breast; almond-shaped eyes, double barred N	50	130

8a 8b 9a 9b

1404	— 7b. — — longer hair, new crown	55	135
1404A	— Type as 7, but no rose	85	200
1405	— 8a. Smaller crown; top-tilted S; longer neck	25	60
1406	— 8b. Not unlike 9a, but top-tilted S	25	55
1407	— 9a. Narrow face, flatter crown, star on breast	16	35
1408	— 9b. Small coins; Roman N, normal, un-barred, or usually of pot-hook form; often star or pellet on breast	10	30

10ab 10cf 10cf 10cf

1409 } 1410 }	— 10ab. Read ЄDWARR, ЄDWARD, ЄDWR'R'. Ornate Rs. Usually bi-foliate crown from now on. Also very rarely with annulet on breast.	14	28
1411 } 1412 } 1413 } 1414 }	— 10cf. Read ЄDWA. Plain Rs	10	25

For a more detailed classification of Class 10, see 'Sylloge of British Coins, 39, The J. J. North Collection, Edwardian English Silver Coins 1279-1351', The Classification of Class 10, c. 1301-10, by C. Wood.

Prices are for full flan, well struck coins.
The prices for the above types are for London. For coins of the other mints see following pages; types are in brackets, prices are for the commonest type of each mint.

Berwick Type I

Type II

Type III

Type IV

No.	Description		F £	VF £
1415	*Berwick-on-T weed.* (Blunt types I-IV)	*from*	15	40
1416	*Bristol.* (2; 3b; c, d; 3f, g; 9b)	*from*	15	45
1417	*Bury St. Edmunds.* Robert de Hadelie (3c, d, g; 4a, b, c)	*from*	50	120
1418	— Villa Sci Edmundi (4e; 5b; 6b; 7a; 8a-10f)	*from*	18	45
1419	*Canterbury.* (2; 3b-g; 4; 5; 7a; 9;10)	*from*	10	28
1420	*Chester.* (3g; 9b)	*from*	30	60
1421	*Durham.* King's Receiver (9b; 10a, b, e, f)	*from*	15	35
1422	— Bishop de Insula (2; 3b, c, e, g; 4a)	*from*	18	40
1423	— Bishop Bec (4b, c, d; 5b; 6b; 7a; 8b; 9; 10b-f) mostly with *mm.* cross moline	*from*	18	40
1424	— — (4b) cross moline in one angle of *rev.*		130	275
1425	*Exeter.* (9b)		40	110
1426	*Kingston-upon-Hull.* (9b)		40	110
1427	*Lincoln.* (3c, d, f, g)	*from*	15	35
1428	*Newcastle-upon-Tyne.* (3e; 9b; 10)	*from*	20	45
1429	*York.* Royal mint (2; 3b, c, d, f; 9b)	*from*	18	40
1430	— Archbishop's mint (3e, f; 9b). ℞. Quatrefoil in centre	*from*	25	60

1431

1433

1436

No.	Description	F	VF
1431	**Halfpenny,** *London.* Class IIIb. Drapery as segment of circle	30	70
1432	— IIIc. Normal drapery as two wedges	25	60
1433	— IIIg. Similar, larger letters, wider crown	25	65
1433A	— — IV c. Comma abbreviation mark, thick waisted s.	30	75
1433B	— — Pellet before LON	35	85
1434	— IVe. Usually three pellets on breast, one on *rev.*	40	90
1434A	— VI. Double barred N, small lettering	35	85
1435	— VII. Double barred N, large lettering	32	80
1436	— IX. Pot-hook N, usually no star on breast, crown band curved at fleurs	25	60
1437	— X. ЄDWAR R ANGL DNS hYB, thick waisted letters	20	50

The above prices are for London; halfpence of the mints given below were also struck.

No.	Description		F	VF
1438	*Berwick-on-Tweed.* (Blunt types II and III)	*from*	70	175
1439	*Bristol.* (IIIc; IIIg)	*from*	40	100

		F £	VF £
1440	*Lincoln.* (IIIc)	70	165
1441	*Newcastle.* (IIIe). With single pellet in each angle of *rev.*	85	250
1442	*York.* (IIIb)	60	135

1443A 1445 1446

		F	VF
1443	**Farthing,** *London.* Class I. Heavy weight (6.65 grains), ЄDWARDVS REX. ℞. LONDONIЄNSIS, bifoliate crown	40	120
1443A	— — — trifoliate crown	40	100
1444	— II. Similar, but reversed N's (6.62 grs.)	25	70
1445	— IIIc. As class I, but different bust	20	60
1446	— IIIg. Lighter weight (5.5 grs.) Є R ANGLIЄ, no inner circle on obv...	15	40
1446A	— IV Reads CIVITAS LONDON, narrow crown	40	100
1446B	— V — Wider crown	40	100
1447	— VI+VII. Similar, double barred N, pellet eyes	60	140
1448	— VIII. ЄR ANGL DN, closed Є	45	90
1449	— IX. Unbarred Ns	40	90
1450	— X or XI. (Edward II) ЄDWARDVS REX A or AN inner circle both sides	12	35

Types 1449 and 1450 often appear on oval flans.

The above prices are for London; farthings of the mints given below were also struck.

1452

		F	VF
1451	*Berwick-on-Tweed.* (Blunt type III)	140	275
1452	*Bristol.* (II, IIIc (heavy), III (light))	60	125
1453	*Lincoln.* (III)	70	140
1453A	*Newcastle* (IIIe), triple pellet in *rev.* quarters	200	500
1454	*York.* (II; III)	90	200

For further information see J. J. North 'Syllogue of British Coins, 39, The J. J. North Collection, Edwardian Engilsh Silver Coins 1279-1351'.

The coinage of this reign differs only in minor details from that of Edward I. No groats were issued in the years *c.* 1282-1351.

11a 12 13 14

15a 15b 15c

		F £	*VF* £
1455	**Penny,** *London.* Class 11a. Broken spear-head or pearl on l. side of crown; long narrow face, straight-sided N	15	35
1456	— 11b. — Є with angular back (till 15b), N with well-marked serifs	15	35
1457	— 11c. — — A of special form	30	70
1458	— 12. Central fleur of crown formed of three wedges	25	50
1459	— 13. Central fleur of crown as Greek double axe	18	45
1460	— 14. Crown with tall central fleur; large smiling face with leering eyes	16	40
1461	— 15a. Small flat crown with both spear-heads usually bent to l.; face of 14	18	45
1462	— 15b. — very similar, but smaller face	18	45
1463	— 15c. — large face, large Є	20	50

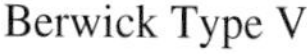

Berwick Type V

Type VI

Type VII

		F £	*VF* £
1464	*Berwick-on-Tweed.* (Blunt types V, VI and VII)	40	80
1465	*Bury St. Edmunds.* (11; 12; 13; 14; 15)	18	40
1466	*Canterbury.* (11; 12; 13; 14; 15)	20	40
1467	*Durham.* King's Receiver (11a), *mm.* plain cross	25	55
1468	— Bishop Bec. (11a), *mm.* cross moline	25	60
1469	— Bishop Kellawe (11; 12; 13), crozier on *rev.*	25	55
1470	— Bishop Beaumont (13; 14; 15), *mm.* lion with lis	30	70
1471	Sede Vacante (15c); *mm.* plain cross	55	135

		F	*VF*
		£	£
1472	**Halfpenny** of *London.* ЄDWARDVS REX A(NG)	60	175
1473	— — *Berwick-on-Tweed.* (Blunt type V)	80	200
1474	**Farthing** of *London.* ЄDWARDVS REX (ANG)	50	125
1475	— *Berwick-on-Tweed.* (Blunt type V)	150	—

The figures in brackets refer to the plate of mintmarks in Appendix III.

EDWARD III, 1327-77

During Edward's early years small quantities of silver coin were minted following the standard of the previous two reigns, but in 1335 halfpence and farthings were produced which were well below the .925 Sterling silver standard. In 1344 an impressive gold coinage was introduced comprising the Florin or Double Leopard valued at six shillings, and its half and quarter, the Leopard and the Helm. The design of the Florin was based on the contemporary gold of Philip de Valois of France.

The first gold coinage was not successful and it was replaced later the same year by a heavier coinage, the Noble, valued at 6s. 8d, i.e., 80 pence, half a mark or one third of a pound, together with its fractions. The Noble was lowered in weight in two stages over the next few years, being stabilized at 120 grains in 1351. With the signing of the Treaty of Bretigni in 1360 Edward's title to the Kingdom of France was omitted from the coinage, but it was resumed again in 1369.

In 1344 the silver coinage had been re-established at the old sterling standard, but the penny was reduced in weight to just over 20 grains and in 1351 to 18 grains. Groats were minted again in 1351 and were issued regularly henceforth until the reign of Elizabeth.

Subsequent to the treaty with France which gave England a cross-channel trading base at Calais, a mint was opened there in 1363 for minting gold and silver coins of English type. In addition to coins of the regular English mints, the Abbot of Reading also minted silver pence and a halfpence with a scallop shell badge while coins from Berwick display one or two boars' or bears' heads.

There is evidence of re -use of dies at later periods, e.g. 3rd coinage halfpennies.

Mintmarks

6 1 2 3 74 4 5 7a

1334-51	Cross pattée (6)	1356	Crown (74)
1351-2	Cross 1 (1)	1356-61	Cross 3 (4)
1351-7	Crozier on cross end (76a, *Durham*)	1361-9	Cross potent (5)
1352-3	Cross 1 broken (2)	1369-77	Cross pattée (6)
1354-5	Cross 2 (3)		Plain cross (7a)

GOLD

Third coinage, 1344-51
First period, 1344

1476

1477

1478

1479

		F £	VF £
1476	**Florin** or **Double Leopard.** (=6s.; wt. 108 grs.). King enthroned beneath canopy; crowned leopard's head each side. ℞. Cross in quatrefoil...........	*Extremely rare*	
1477	**Half-florin** or **Leopard.** Leopard sejant with banner l. ℞. Somewhat as last..........	*Extremely rare*	
1478	**Quarter-florin** or **Helm.** Helmet on fleured field. ℞. Floriate cross........	*Extremely rare*	

Second period, 1344-46

1479	**Noble** (=6s. 8d., wt. 138.46 grs.). King stg. facing in ship with sword and shield. ℞. L in centre of royal cross in tressure..........	*Extremely rare*	
1480	**Quarter-noble.** Shield in tressure. ℞. As last..........	1250	2750

Third period, 1346-51

1481	**Noble** (wt. 128.59 grs.). As 1479, but Є in centre; large letters	700	1500
1482	**Half-noble.** Similar..........	1250	3000
1483	**Quarter-noble.** As 1480, but Є in centre..........	250	550

Fourth coinage, 1351-77
Reference: L. A. Lawrence, *The Coinage of Edward III from 1351.*
Pre-treaty period, 1351-61. With French title.

1488

1498

1484	**Noble** (wt. 120 grs.), series B (1351). Open Є and C, Roman M; *mm.* cross 1 (1)..........	325	600
1485	— — *rev.* of series A (1351). Round lettering, Lombardic M and N; closed inverted Є in centre..........	350	675

	F £	*VF* £
1486 C (1351-1352). Closed Є and C, Lombardic M; *mm.* cross 1 (1)	300	525
1487 D (1352-1353). *O.* of series C. ℞. *Mm.* cross 1 broken (2)	400	700
1488 E (1354-1355). Broken letters, V often has a nick in r. limb; *mm.* cross 2 (3)	300	525
1489 F (1356). *Mm.* crown (74)	375	650
1490 G (1356-1361). *Mm.* cross 3 (4). Many varieties	275	500
1491 **Half-noble,** B. As noble with *rev.* of series A, but closed Є in centre not inverted	225	475
1492 C. *O.* as noble. *Rev.* as last	250	500
1493 E. As noble	450	800
1494 G. As noble. Many varieties	175	375
1495 **Quarter-noble,** B. Pellet below shield. ℞. Closed Є in centre	135	225
1496 C. *O.* of series B. *Rev.* details as noble	140	275
1497 E. *O.* as last. *Rev.* details as noble, pellet in centre	160	300
1498 G. *Mm.* cross 3 (4). Many varieties	110	200

Transitional treaty period, 1361. French title omitted, replaced by that of Aquitaine on the noble and (rarely) on the half-noble, but not on the quarter-noble; irregular sized letters; *mm.* cross potent (5).

1499

1499 **Noble.** ℞. Pellets or annulets at corners of central panel	325	600

1500

1503

1500 **Half-noble.** Similar	175	375
1501 **Quarter-noble.** Similar. Many varieties. Pellet and rarely Є in centre	130	250

Treaty period, 1361-69. Omits FRANC, new letters, usually curule-shaped X; *mm.* cross potent(5).

1502 **Noble.** *London.* Saltire or nothing before ЄDWARD	245	500
1503 — Annulet before ЄDWARD (with, rarely, crescent on forecastle)	235	475
1504 *Calais.* C in centre of *rev.,* flag at stern of ship	275	575
1505 — — without flag	275	575

1506 1508

		F £	VF £
1506	**Half-noble.** *London.* Saltire before ЄDWARD	160	315
1507	— Annulet before ЄDWARD	170	330
1508	*Calais.* C in centre of *rev.*, flag at stern of ship	235	550
1509	— — without flag	250	575
1510	**Quarter-noble.** *London.* As 1498. ℞. Lis in centre	100	200
1511	— — annulet before ЄDWARD	100	200
1512	*Calais.* ℞. Annulet in centre	125	225
1513	— — cross in circle over shield	135	275
1514	— ℞. Quatrefoil in centre; cross over shield	150	325
1515	— — crescent over shield	225	500

Post-treaty period, 1369-1377. French title resumed.

		F £	VF £
1516	**Noble.** *London.* Annulet before ЄD. ℞. Treaty period die	280	530
1517	— — — crescent on forecastle	300	575
1518	— — post-treaty letters. ℞. Є and pellet in centre	275	520
1519	— — — ℞. Є and saltire in centre	325	600
1520	*Calais.* Flag at stern. ℞. Є in centre	260	570

1521

		F £	VF £
1521	— — *Rev.* as 1518, with Є and pellet in centre	260	535
1522	— As 1520, but without flag. ℞. C in centre	280	575
1523	**Half-noble.** *London. O.* Treaty die. *Rev.* as 1518	700	1500
1524	*Calais.* Without AQT, flag at stern. ℞. Є in centre	350	750
1525	— — ℞. Treaty die with C in centre	375	775

SILVER

First coinage, 1327-35 (.925 fineness)

1526

1530

		F	VF
		£	£
1526	**Penny.** *London.* As Edw. II; class XVd with Lombardic n's	325	750
1527	*Bury St. Edmunds.* Similar	*Extremely rare*	
1528	*Canterbury; mm.* cross pattée with pellet centre	250	550
1529	— — three extra pellets in one quarter	250	575
1530	*Durham.* ℞. Small crown in centre	400	850
1531	*York.* As 1526, but quatrefoil in centre of *rev.*	200	475
1532	— — — pellet in each quarter of *mm.*	200	475
1533	— — — three extra pellets in one quarter	200	475
1534	— — — Roman N on *obv.*	200	475
1535	*Berwick* (1333-1342, Blunt type VIII). Bear's head in one quarter of *rev.*	250	650
1536	**Halfpenny.** *London.* If struck then indistinguishable from EDWARD II (cf. 1472)	60	175
1537	*Berwick* (Bl. VIII). Bear's head in one or two quarters	50	125
1538	**Farthing.** *London.* As Edw. II but with curl tailed ℞	70	150
1539	*Berwick* (Bl. VIII). As 1537	40	115

1535

1537

1540

Second coinage, 1335-43 (.833 fineness)

		F	VF
1540	**Halfpenny.** *London.* ЄDWARDVS RЄX A(NG)*, rough work, tall crown	15	35
1541	*Reading.* Escallop in one quarter	300	550
1542	**Farthing.** *London.* Early dies, flat crown. A* or AN *	30	100
1542A	— Later dies, taller crown AIIG*	40	120

Third or florin coinage, 1344-51. Bust with bushy hair. (.925 fine, 20 grs.)

1543

1555

		F £	VF £
1543	**Penny.** *London.* Class 1. ЄDW, Lombardic ꞥ's	20	50
1544	— 2, ЄDWA, ꞥ's, but sometimes N's on *rev.*	18	45
1545	— 3, ЄDW, N's, sometimes reversed or ꞥ's on *rev.*	18	45
1546	— 4, ЄDW, no stops, reversed N's, but on *rev.* sometimes ꞥ's, N's or double-barred N's	18	45
1547	*Canterbury.* ЄDWA, ꞥ's	45	120
1548	— ЄDW, reversed N's	40	110
1549	*Durham,* Sede Vacante (1345). A, ЄDW R. ℞. No marks	35	100
1550	— — B, similar, ЄDWAR R	110	250
1551	— Bp. Hatfield. C, similar, but pellet in centre of *rev.*	65	150
1552	— — — Crozier on *rev.*	65	200
1553	— — — — with pellet in centre of *rev.*	65	200
1554	— — D, ЄDWARDVS RЄX AIꞥ, crozier on *rev.*	125	300
1555	*Reading. obv.* as 1546. ℞. Escallop in one quarter	200	475
1556	*York. obv.* as 1546. ℞. Quatrefoil in centre	25	65
1557	**Halfpenny.** *London.* ЄDWARDVS RЄX(Aꞥ)	15	35
1558	— — pellet either side of crown	25	65
1559	— — saltire either side of crown and in one quarter of *rev.,* or pellet in each quarter	25	65
1560	*Reading. O.* Similar. ℞. Escallop in one quarter	275	500
1561	*Continental imitation.* Mostly reading ЄDWARDIENSIS	20	50
1562	**Farthing.** *London.* ЄDWARDVS REX	30	90
1562A	*Reading.* As last. ℞. As halfpenny	*Unique*	

Fourth coinage, 1351-77

Reference: L. A. Lawrence, *The Coinage of Edward III from 1351.*

Pre-treaty period, 1351-61. With French title.

1565

1567

		F	VF
1563	**Groat** (=4d., 72 grs.). *London,* series B (1351). Roman M, open C and Є; *mm.* cross 1	110	275
1564	— — — crown in each quarter	*Unique*	
1565	— C (1351-2). Lombardic m, closed C and Є, R with wedge-shaped tail; *mm.* cross 1	25	70
1566	— D (1352-3). R with normal tail; *mm.* cross 1 or cross 1 broken (2)	30	90
1567	— E (1354-5). Broken letters, V often with nick in r. limb; *mm.* cross 2 (3)	25	60

		F	VF
		£	£
1568	— — — lis on breast	35	100
1569	— F (1356). *Mm.* crown (74)	35	100

1570 1572

1570	— G (1356-61). Usually with annulet in one quarter and sometimes under bust, *mm.* cross 3 (4). Many varieties	25	70
1571	*York,* series D. As London	65	150
1572	— E. As London	45	115

1573 1574

1573	**Halfgroat.** *London,* series B. As groat	70	170
1574	— C. As groat	15	40
1575	— D. As groat	18	45
1576	— E. As groat	20	50
1577	— F. As groat	25	55
1578	— G. As groat	18	45
1579	— — — annulet below bust	25	70
1580	*York,* series D. As groat	40	100
1581	— E. As groat	35	75
1582	— — — lis on breast	45	125

1584 1587 1591

1583	**Penny.** *London.* Series A (1351). Round letters, Lombardic m and n, annulet in each quarter; *mm.* cross pattee	66	125
1584	— C. Details as groat, but annulet in each quarter	15	35
1585	— D. Details as groat, but annulet in each quarter	15	35
1586	— E. Sometimes annulet in each quarter	15	35
1587	— F. Details as groat	20	40

		F £	VF £
1588	— G. Details as groat	15	35
1589	— — — annulet below bust	20	50
1590	— — — saltire in one quarter	30	60
1591	*Durham,* Bp. Hatfield. Series A. As 1583, but extra pellet in each quarter, VIL LA crozier DVRRЄM	150	350
1592	— C. Details as groat. ℞. Crozier, CIVITAS DVNЄLMIЄ	25	65
1593	— D — — —	35	85
1594	— E — — —	25	65
1595	— F — ℞. Crozier, CIVITAS DVRЄMЄ	35	75
1596	— G — — —	25	65
1597	— — — — — — annulet below bust	35	70
1598	— — — — — — saltire in one quarter	35	80
1599	— — — — — — annulet on each shoulder	35	80
1600	— — — — — — trefoil of pellets on breast	35	70
1601	— — — ℞. Crozier, CIVITAS DVRЄLMIЄ	50	90
1602	*York,* Royal Mint. Series D	30	65
1603	— — E	15	45
1604	— Archb. Thoresby. Series D. ℞. Quatrefoil in centre	25	55
1605	— — G —	15	40
1606	— — — annulet or saltire on breast	25	60
1607	**Halfpenny.** *London.* Series E. ЄDWARDVS RЄX An	100	250
1608	— G, but with *obv.* of F (*mm.* crown). Annulet in one quarter	—	400
1609	**Farthing.** *London.* Series E. ЄDWARDVS RЄX	150	300
1609A	— — Series G. Annulet in one quarter	200	375

Transitional treaty period, 1361. French title omitted, irregular sized letters; *mm.* cross potent (5).

1610	**Groat.** *London.* Annulet each side of crown	135	450
1611	**Halfgroat.** Similar, but only seven arches to tressure	80	200

1611

1612

1612	**Penny,** *London.* Omits RЄX, annulet in two upper qtrs. of *mm*	75	175
1613	*York,* Archb. Thoresby. Similar, but quatrefoil enclosing pellet in centre of *rev.*	50	125
1614	*Durham.* Bp. Hatfield. Similar. ℞. Crozier, CIVITAS DORЄLMЄ	60	150
1615	**Halfpenny.** Two pellets over *mm.,* ЄDWARDVS RЄX An	75	150

Treaty period, 1361-69. French title omitted, new letters, usually 'Treaty' X, rarely curule chair X *mm.* cross potent (5).

1616	**Groat,** *London.* Many varieties	40	110
1617	— Annulet before ЄDWARD	45	120
1618	— Annulet on breast	70	175

1619

		F £	VF £
1619	*Calais.* As last	100	250

1621 1635

		F	VF
1620	**Halfgroat,** *London.* As groat	25	60
1621	— — Annulet before ЄDWARDVS	25	60
1622	— — Annulet on breast	60	125
1623	*Calais.* As last	100	200
1624	**Penny,** *London.* ЄDWARD AnGL R, etc	20	55
1625	— — — pellet before ЄDWARD	25	65
1626	*Calais.* ℞. VILLA CALЄSIE	75	175
1627	*Durham.* ℞. DIVITAS DVNЄLMIS	60	125
1628	— ℞. Crozier, CIVITAS DVRЄMЄ	50	120
1629	*York,* Archb. Thoresby. Quatrefoil in centre of *rev.,* ЄDWARDVS DЄI G RЄX An	45	95
1630	— — — ЄDWARDVS RЄX ANGLI	20	45
1631	— — — — quatrefoil before ЄD and on breast	25	55
1632	— — — — annulet before ЄD	25	55
1633	— — — ЄDWARD AnGL R DnS HYB	35	65
1634	**Halfpenny.** ЄDWARDVS RЄX An, pellet stops	30	60
1635	— Pellet before ЄD, annulet stops	35	70
1636	**Farthing.** ЄDWARDVS RЄX, pellet stops	80	225

Post-treaty period, 1369-77. French title resumed, X like St. Andrew's cross; *mm.* 5, 6, 7a.

1637

		F	VF
1637	**Groat.** Various readings, *mm.* cross pattee	75	200

1639

		F £	VF £
1638	— — row of pellets across breast (chain mail)	150	450
1639	— row of annulets below bust (chain mail); *mm.* cross potent with four pellets	175	550
1640	**Halfgroat.** Various readings	100	275

1640A

1640A	— Thin portrait of Richard II		*Rare*
1641	— row of pellets one side of breast (chain mail)	165	500
1642	**Penny,** *London.* No marks on breast	40	95
1643	— Pellet or annulet on breast	50	120
1644	— Cross or quatrefoil on breast	45	110
1645	Durham, Bp. Hatfield. Mm. 7a, CIVITAS DVnOLM, crozier	45	110
1646	— — — — annulet on breast	50	120
1647	— — — — lis on breast	40	95
1648	*York.* Archb. Thoresby or Neville. ℞. Quatrefoil in centre	25	65
1649	— — — lis on breast	50	105
1650	— — — annulet on breast	30	70
1651	— — — cross on breast	35	80

1652

1652	**Farthing.** EDWARD REX ANGL, large head without neck	150	325

There was no significant change in the coinage during this reign. Noteworthy is the first appearance of symbols on the ship's rudder on some of the gold coins. The earlier silver coins have a portrait like that on the coins of Edward III, but the king's head and the style of lettering were altered on the later issues.

Reference: *Silver coinages of Richard II, Henry IV and V.* (B.N.J. 1959-60 and 1963).

Mintmark: cross pattée (6) 

1655

1657

GOLD

		F £	VF £
1653	**Noble,** *London.* With altered *obv.* and/or *rev.* die of Edw. III	575	1250
1654	— Lettering as Edw. III, lis over sail	475	1100
1655	— Straight-sided letters, annulet over sail	400	900
1656	— Late issue, fish-tail lettering; no marks, or trefoil by shield	450	950
1657	— — — lis on rudder	600	1250
1658	— — small dumpy lettering; escallop or crescent on rudder and/or trefoil over sail or by shield	550	1150

1658

1662

		F £	VF £
1659	*Calais*. Flag at stern, otherwise as 1653	500	1050
1660	— — as 1655, but quatrefoil over sail	475	1025
1661	— — as 1656; no marks	450	975
1662	— — — lion on rudder	600	1350
1663	— — as 1658	475	1025

1664 1672/3 1673 1677

		F £	VF £
1664	**Half-noble,** *London*. As 1653	525	1200
1665	— as 1655	450	1000
1666	— as 1656; lion on rudder	475	1100
1667	— as 1658; crescent on rudder	525	1200
1668	*Calais*. Flag at stern, otherwise as 1653	550	1500
1669	— — as 1655; quatrefoil over sail	550	1500
1670	— — as 1656; lion on rudder	525	1400
1671	— — as 1658, but one var. has saltire behind rudder	700	1600
1672	**Quarter-noble,** *London*. R in centre of *rev*.	225	425
1673	— Lis or pellet in centre of *rev*.	185	350
1674	— — *obv*. die of Edw. III altered	240	475
1675	— — escallop over shield	250	500
1676	— — trefoil of annulets over shield	235	450
1677	— — quatrefoil, cross or slipped trefoil over sheild	215	425

SILVER

1679 1682

		F £	VF £
1678	**Groat.** I. Style of Edw. III, F (*i.e. et*) before FRANC, etc.	225	650
1679	II. New lettering, retrograde Z before FRANC, etc.	175	400
1680	III. Bust with bushy hair, 'fishtail' serifs to letters	200	600
1681	IV. New style bust and crown, crescent on breast	1000	2750
1682	**Halfgroat.** II. New lettering	175	450

		F	VF
		£	£
1683	III. As 1680	225	600
1684	— — with *obv.* die of Edw. III (1640A)	300	700
1685	IV. As 1681, but no crescent	650	1250
1686	**Penny,** *London.* I Lettering as 1678, RICARDVS RЄX AnGLIЄ	175	450
1688	— II. As 1679, Z FRAnC lis on breast	175	450
1689	— III. As 1680, RICARD RЄX AnGLIЄ, fish-tail letters	200	500

1689 1692

		F	VF
1690	*York.* I. Early style, usually with cross or lis on breast, quatrefoil in centre of *rev*	45	145
1691	— II. New bust and letters, no marks on breast	40	140
1692	— Local dies. Pellet above each shoulder, cross on breast, REX AnGLIE or AnGILIE	30	110
1693	— — — RЄX DNS ЄB	50	140
1694	— — — RЄX AnG FRAnC	50	150
1695	— III. As 1680, RЄX AnGL Z FRANC (scallop after TAS)	50	120
1696	— IV. Very bushy hair, new letters, no crescent. ℞. R in centre of quatrefoil	225	475
1697	*Durham.* Cross or lis on breast, DVnOLM	175	450

1698 1699 1701 1704

		F	VF
1698	**Halfpenny.** Early style. LONDON, saltire or annulet on breast	60	150
1699	Intermediate style. LOnDOn, no marks on breast	25	75
1700	Type III. Late style. Similar, but fishtail letters	30	90
1700A	Type IV. Short, stubby lettering	30	85
1701	**Farthing.** Small bust and letters	125	350
1703	Similar but no neck	175	375
1704	Rose in each angle of *rev.* instead of pellets	450	900
1704A	Large head with broad face as Henry IV	375	—

THE HOUSE OF LANCASTER

HENRY IV, 1399-1413

In 1412 the standard weights of the coinage were reduced, the noble by 12 grains and the penny by 3 grains, partly because there was a scarcity of bullion and partly to provide revenue for the king, as Parliament had not renewed the royal subsidies. As in France, the royal arms were altered, three fleur-de-lis taking the place of the four or more lis previously displayed.

Mintmark: cross pattée (6) 

GOLD

Heavy coinage, 1399-1412

1707

1705

No.	Description	F £	VF £
1705	**Noble** (120 grs.), *London.* Old arms with four lis in French quarters; crescent or annulet on rudder	2750	6000
1706	— New arms with three lis; crescent, pellet or no marks on rudder	2750	6000
1707	*Calais.* Flag at stern, old arms; crown on or to l. of rudder	*Extremely rare*	
1708	— — new arms; crown or star on rudder	3250	7500

1708

1710

No.	Description	F £	VF £
1709	**Half-noble,** *London.* Old arms	*Extremely rare*	
1710	— new arms	4000	—
1711	*Calais.* New arms	*Extremely rare*	
1712	**Quarter-noble,** *London.* Crescent over old arms	800	1750
1713	— — — new arms	700	1600
1714	*Calais.* New arms. R. *Mm.* crown	900	1900

1715

		F £	VF £
Light coinage, 1412-13			
1715	**Noble** (108 grs.). Trefoil, or trefoil and annulet, on side of ship. ℞. Trefoil in one quarter	750	1650
1716	**Half-noble.** Similar, but always with annulet	2500	—

1717

1717	**Quarter-noble.** Trefoils, or trefoils and annulets beside shield, lis above. ℞. Lis in centre	375	800

SILVER

Heavy coinage, 1399-1412

1718

1722

1723

1718	**Halfgroat** (36 grs.). Star on breast	1000	2500
1718A	— Muled with Edw. III (1640A) *obv.*		*Rare*
1719	**Penny,** *London.* Similar, early bust with long neck	500	1250
1720	— later bust with shorter neck, no star	500	1250
1721	*York.* Early bust with long neck	250	600
1722	— later bust with broad face, round chin	250	600
1723	**Halfpenny.** Early small bust	140	275
1724	— later large bust, with rounded shoulders, annulets by neck	140	275
1725	**Farthing.** Face without neck	500	950

Light coinage, 1412-13

1728 1731 1737

		F £	*VF* £
1726	**Groat** (60 grs.). I. Pellet to l., annulet to r. of crown; altered die of Richard II	1350	3500
1727	New dies; II. Annulet to l., pellet to r. of crown, 8 or 10 arches to tressure	1250	2750
1728	— III. Similar but 9 arches to tressure	1250	2750
1729	**Halfgroat.** Pellet to l., annulet to r. of crown	650	1500
1730	Annulet to l., pellet to r. of crown	550	1200
1731	**Penny,** *London.* Annulet and pellet by crown; trefoil on breast and before CIVI	400	950
1732	— — annulet or slipped trefoil before LON	400	950
1733	— Pellet and annulet by crown	*Unique*	
1734	*York.* Annulet on breast. ℞. Quatrefoil in centre	175	575
1735	*Durham.* Trefoil on breast, DVnOLM	175	575
1736	**Halfpenny.** Struck from heavy dies	140	275
1737	New dies; annulet either side of crown or none	150	325
1738	**Farthing.** Face, no bust; ?trefoil after RЄX	475	950

There was no change of importance in the coinage of this reign. There was, however, a considerable development in the use of privy marks which distinguished various issues, except for the last issue of the reign when most marks were removed. The Calais mint, which had closed in 1411, did not re-open until early in the next reign.

Mintmarks

Cross pattee (4)

Pierced cross with pellet centre (20)

Pierced cross (18).

GOLD

1744

No.	Description	F £	VF £
1739	**Noble.** A. Quatrefoil over sail and in second quarter of *rev.* Short broad letters, no other marks	*Extremely rare*	
1740	— B. Ordinary letters; similar, or with annulet on rudder	475	800
1741	— C. Mullet by sword arm, annulet on rudder	450	750
1742	— — — broken annulet on side of ship	300	550
1743	—D. Mullet and annulet by sword arm, trefoil by shield, broken annulet on ship	325	625
1744	— E. Mullet, or mullet and annulet by sword arm, trefoil by shield, pellet by sword point and in one quarter, annulet on side of ship	350	650
1745	— — Similar, but trefoil on ship instead of by shield	400	700
1746	— F. Similar, but no pellet at sword point, trefoil in one quarter	400	750
1747	— G. No marks; annulet stops, except for mullet after first word	625	1200
1748	**Half-noble.** B. As noble; Hen. IV *rev.* die	1200	—
1749	— C. Broken annulet on ship, quatrefoil below sail	375	800

1750

No.	Description	F £	VF £
1750	— — Mullet over shield, broken annulet on *rev.*	325	650
1751	— F. Similar, but no annulet on ship, usually trefoil by shield	400	850
1752	— F/E. As last, but pellet in 1st and annulet in 2nd quarter	450	1000

		F £	VF £
1753	— G. As noble, but quatrefoil over sail, mullet sometimes omitted after first word of *rev.*	425	900
1754	**Quarter-noble.** A. Lis over shield and in centre of *rev.* Short broad letters; quatrefoil and annulet beside shield, stars at corners of centre on rev.	300	550
1755	— C. Ordinary letters; quatrefoil to l., quat. and mullet to r. of shield	160	350

1756

1759

1756	— — — annulet to l., mullet to r. of shield	150	275
1757	— F. Ordinary letters; trefoil to l., mullet to r. of shield	175	350
1758	— G. — no marks, except mullet after first word	175	350

SILVER

1759	**Groat.** A. Short broad letters; 'emaciated' bust	400	1050
1760	— — muled with Hen. IV *obv.* or *rev*	375	1000
1761	— — muled with later *rev.* of Hen. V	425	850

1762

1765

1762	B. Ordinary letters; 'scowling' bust	250	525
1762A	— — mullet in centre of breast	250	525
1763	— — muled with Hen. IV or later Hen. V	275	600
1764	C. Normal bust	110	225
1765	— — mullet on r. shoulder	65	140
1766	— — ℞ muled with Hen. IV	350	800
1767	G. Normal bust; no marks	110	225
1768	**Halfgroat.** A. As groat, but usually with annulet and pellet by crown	400	1050
1769	B. Ordinary letters; no marks	125	325
1770	— — muled with Hen. IV or class C (HV) *obv.*	160	350
1771	C. Tall neck, broken annulet to l. of crown	70	160
1772	— — — mullet on r. shoulder	70	180

1773  1774

		F £	VF £
1773	— — — mullet in centre of breast	75	170
1774	F. Annulet and trefoil by crown, mullet on breast	80	190
1775	G. New neat bust: no marks. May sometimes be muled with ℞ of Hen. VI annulet issue	70	175
1776	**Penny.** *London.* A. Letters, bust and marks as 1768	325	700
1777	— B. Altered A *obv.,* with mullet and broken annulet added by crown. ℞. Ordinary letters	200	475

1778  1791

1778	— C. Tall neck, mullet and broken annulet by crown	25	60
1779	— D. Similar, but whole annulet	30	90
1780	— F. Mullet and trefoil by crown	30	100
1781	— G. New neat bust, no marks, DI GRA	30	90
1782	*Durham.* C. As 1778 but quatrefoil at end of legend	45	135
1783	— D. As 1779	40	125
1784	— G. Similar, but new bust. ℞. Annulet in one qtr.	50	160
1785	*York.* C. As 1778, but quatrefoil in centre of *rev.*	20	60
1786	— D. Similar, but whole annulet by crown	20	60
1787	— E. As last, but pellet above mullet	40	110
1788	— F. Mullet and trefoil by crown	30	80
1789	— — Trefoil over mullet to l., annulet to r. of crown	35	90
1790	— G. Mullet and trefoil by crown (London dies)	25	70
1791	— — Mullet and lis by crown, annulet in one qtr. (usually local dies)	25	70
1792	**Halfpenny.** A. Emaciated bust, annulets by crown	40	100
1793	— altered dies of Hen. IV	75	200
1794	C. Ordinary bust, broken annulets by crown	20	50
1795	D. Annulets, sometimes broken, by hair	20	50

1796

1798

1796	F. Annulet and trefoil by crown	20	50
1797	G. New bust; no marks, (usually muled with Henry VI annulet rev.)	65	150
1798	**Farthing.** G. Small face with neck	135	275

The supply of gold began to dwindle early in the reign, which accounts for the rarity of gold after 1426. The Calais mint was reopened in 1424 and for some years a large amount of coin was struck there. It soon stopped minting gold; the mint was finally closed in 1440. A royal mint at York was opened for a short time in 1423/4.

Marks used to denote various issues become more prominent in this reign and can be used to date coins to within a year or so.

Reference: C. A. Whitton *Heavy Coinage of Henry VI.* (B.N.J. 1938-41).

Mintmarks

136 7a 105 18 133 8 9 15

1422-7	Incurved pierced cross (136)	1422-34	Cross pommee (133)
1422-3	Lis (105, York)	1427-34	Cross patonce (8)
1422-60	Plain cross (7a, intermittently		Cross fleury (9)
	Lis (105, on gold)	1434-35	Voided cross (15)
1422-27	Pierced cross (18)	1435-60	Cross fleury (9)
1460	Lis (105, on *rev.* of some groats)		

For Restoration mintmarks see page 138.

GOLD

1799 1805

		F £	VF £
	Annulet issue, 1422-7		
1799	**Noble.** *London.* Annulet by sword arm, and in one spandrel on *rev.*; trefoil stops on *obv.* with lis after hЄNRIC, annulets on *rev.,* with mullet after IhC	275	525
1800	— Similar, but *obv.* from Henry V die	600	1200
1801	— As 1799, but Flemish imitative coinage	225	425
1802	*Calais.* As 1799, but flag at stern and C in centre of *rev*	425	850
1803	— — with h in centre of *rev.*	375	675
1804	*York.* As London, but with lis over stern	400	750
1805	**Half-noble.** *London.* As 1799	200	360
1806	— Similar, but *obv.* from Henry V die	350	700
1807	*Calais.* As noble, with C in centre of *rev.*	550	1100
1808	— — with h in centre of *rev.*	325	675
1809	**York.** As noble	350	725

		F £	VF £
1810	**Quarter-noble.** *London.* Lis over shield; *mm.* large lis	130	225
1811	— — — trefoil below shield	140	275
1812	— — — pellet below shield	*Extremely rare*	
1813	*Calais.* Three lis over shield; *mm.* large lis	180	350

1814 1819

		F £	VF £
1814	— Similar but three lis around shield	200	400
1815	— As 1810, but much smaller *mm.*	160	325
1816	*York.* Two lis over shield	225	400

Rosette-mascle issue, 1427-30

		F £	VF £
1817	**Noble.** *London.* Lis by sword arm and in *rev.* field; stops, rosettes, or rosettes and mascles	525	1100
1818	*Calais.* Similar, with flag at stern	550	1250
1819	**Half-noble.** *London.* Lis in *rev.* field; stops, rosettes and mascles	750	1500
1820	*Calais.* Similar, flag at stern; stops, rosettes	825	1750
1821	**Quarter-noble.** *London.* As 1810; stops, as noble	275	550
1822	— without lis over shield	250	525
1823	*Calais.* Lis over shield, rosettes r. and l., and rosette stops	350	575

Pinecone-mascle issue, 1430-4

		F £	VF £
1824	**Noble.** *London.* Stops, pinecones and mascles	500	1000
1825	**Half-noble.** *London. O.* Rosette-mascle die. ℞. As last	*Extremely rare*	
1826	**Quarter-noble.** As 1810, but pinecone and mascle stops	*Extremely rare*	

Leaf-mascle issue, 1434-5

		F £	VF £
1827	**Noble.** Leaf in waves; stops, saltires with two mascles and one leaf	1500	3000
1828	**Half-noble.** (Fishpool hoard and Reigate hoard)	*Extremely rare*	
1829	**Quarter-noble.** As 1810; stops, saltire and mascle; leaf on inner circle of *rev.*	750	1500

Leaf-trefoil issue, 1435-8

		F £	VF £
1830	**Noble.** Stops, leaves and trefoils	2000	4500
1830A	**Half-noble.** Mule with annulet issue reverse die		*Unique*
1831	**Quarter-noble.** Similar		*Unique*

Trefoil issue, 1438-43

		F £	VF £
1832	**Noble.** Trefoil below shield and in *rev.* legend	1500	3500

Leaf-pellet issue, 1445-54

		F £	VF £
1833	**Noble.** Annulet, lis and leaf below shield	1500	3500

Cross-pellet issue, 1454-60

		F £	VF £
1834	**Noble.** Mascle at end of *obv.* legend		*Unique*

SILVER

Annulet issue, 1422-7

1835 1836 1840

		F £	VF £
1835	**Groat.** *London.* Annulet in two quarters of *rev.*	30	55
1836	*Calais.* Annulets at neck. ℞. Similar	25	50
1837	— — no annulets on *rev.*	45	100
1838	*York.* Lis either side of neck. ℞. As 1835	650	1400
1839	**Halfgroat.** *London.* As groat	25	75
1840	*Calais.* As 1836	20	40
1841	— — no annulets on *rev.*	30	60
1842	— — only one annulet on *rev.* (mule with annulet-trefoil *rev.*)	50	125

1843 1849 1852

		F £	VF £
1843	*York.* As groat	650	1500
1844	**Penny.** *London.* Annulets in two qtrs.	25	60
1845	*Calais.* Annulets at neck. ℞. As above	20	45
1846	— — only one annulet on *rev.*	25	60
1847	*York.* As London, but lis at neck	500	950
1848	**Halfpenny.** *London.* As penny	15	35
1849	*Calais.* Similar, but annulets at neck	15	35
1850	*York.* Similar, but lis at neck	350	700
1851	**Farthing.** *London.* As penny, but *mm.* cross pommée	150	250
1852	*Calais.* Similar, but annulets at neck	225	450

Many mules exist which span two or even three issues, dating from the Annulet issue to the Pinecone-mascle issue inclusive, also later on there is adjacent muling.

Annulet-trefoil sub-issue

		F £	VF £
1854	**Groat.** *Calais*, as 1836 but trefoil to l. of crown.	50	130
1855	**Halfgroat.** *Calais.* Similar, but usually with ann. or rosette mascle *rev.*.	50	125
1856	**Penny.** *Calais.* Similar	60	150
1857	— — only one annulet on *rev*	75	185

Rosette-mascle issue, 1427-30. All with rosettes (early) or rosettes and mascles somewhere in the legends.

		F	*VF*
		£	£
1858	**Groat.** *London.*	45	85
1859	*Calais*	30	60
1860	— mascle in two spandrels (as illus. 1863)	45	120

1859

1861

1861	**Halfgroat.** *London.*	45	100
1862	*Calais*	25	50

1863

1872

1863	— mascle in two spandrels, as illustrated	35	90
1864	**Penny.** *London.*	60	120
1865	*Calais*	30	60
1866	*York.* Archb. Kemp. Crosses by hair, no rosette	25	65
1867	— — Saltires by hair, no rosette	25	65
1868	— — Mullets by crown	25	65
1869	*Durham,* Bp. Langley. Large star to l. of crown, no rosette, DVnOLMI	35	110
1870	**Halfpenny,** *London*	20	50
1871	*Calais*	20	50
1872	**Farthing,** *London*	110	225
1873	*Calais. Mm.* cross pommee	125	325

Pinecone-mascle issue, 1430-4. All with pinecones and mascles in legends.

1875

1879

1874	**Groat,** *London*	35	70
1875	*Calais*	30	60
1876	**Halfgroat,** *London*	40	85
1877	*Calais*	25	50
1878	**Penny,** *London*	50	100
1879	*Calais*	30	75

		F £	VF £
1880	*York,* Archb. Kemp. Mullet by crown, quatrefoil in centre of *rev.*	25	60
1881	— — rosette on breast, no quatrefoil	25	60
1882	— — mullet on breast, no quatrefoil	40	90
1883	*Durham,* Bp. Langley. DVnOLMI	40	110

1884

1888

1884	**Halfpenny,** *London*	20	45
1885	*Calais*	20	50

Full flan coins are difficult to find in the smaller denominations.

1886	**Farthing,** *London*	125	275
1887	*Calais. Mm.* cross pommee	175	425

Leaf-mascle issue, 1434-5. Usually with a mascle in the legend and a leaf somewhere in the design.

1888	**Groat.** *London.* Leaf below bust all appear to read DOnDOn	85	185
1889	— — *rev.* of last or next coinage	50	150
1890	*Calais.* Leaf below bust, and usually below MЄVM	35	110
1891	**Halfgroat.** *London.* Leaf under bust, pellet under TAS and DON	40	100

1892

1897

1892	*Calais.* Leaf below bust, and sometimes on *rev.*	35	85
1893	**Penny.** *London.* Leaf on breast, no stops on *rev.*	40	100
1894	*Calais.* Leaf on breast and below SIЄ	40	100
1895	**Halfpenny.** *London.* Leaf on breast and on *rev.*	25	65
1896	*Calais.* Leaf on breast and below SIЄ	50	110

Leaf-trefoil issue, 1435-8. Mostly with leaves and trefoil of pellets in the legends.

1897	**Groat.** *London.* Leaf on breast	35	80
1898	— without leaf on breast	40	100
1899	*Calais.* Leaf on breast	400	750
1900	**Halfgroat.** *London.* Leaf on breast; *mm.* plain cross	35	85
1901	— *O. mm.* cross fleury; leaf on breast	35	85
1902	— — without leaf on breast	40	100

		F £	*VF* £
1903	**Penny.** *London*. Leaf on breast	50	100
1903A	*Calais*. Similar	200	500
1904	*Durham,* Bp. Neville. Leaf on breast. ℞. Rings in centre, no stops, DVnOLM	80	200
1905	**Halfpenny.** *London*. Leaf on breast	25	50
1906	— without leaf on breast	25	50
1907	**Farthing.** *London*. Leaf on breast; stops, trefoil and saltire on *obv.*	100	325

Trefoil issue, 1438-43. Trefoil of pellets either side of neck and in legend, leaf on breast.

1908 1909 1911A 1911B

1908	**Groat.** *London*. Sometimes a leaf before LON.	40	100
1909	— Fleurs in spandrels, sometimes extra pellet in two qtrs.	50	125
1910	— Trefoils in place of fleurs at shoulders, none by neck, sometimes extra pellets	40	120
1911	*Calais*	100	350
1911A	**Halfgroat,** *London* Similar, but trefoil after DEUM and sometimes after POSUI Mule only with leaf trefoil *obv.*	200	400
1911B	— *Calais* Similar. only known muled with leaf mascle *rev.*	*Extremely rare*	
1912	**Halfpenny,** *London*	30	70

Trefoil pellet issue, 1443-5

1912 1913 1915 1917

1913	**Groat.** Trefoils by neck, pellets by crown, small leaf on breast; sometimes extra pellet in two quarters	40	135

Leaf-pellet issue, 1445-54. Leaf on breast, pellet each side of crown, except where stated.

1914	**Groat.** AnGL; extra pellet in two quarters	30	80
1915	Similar, but AnGLI	35	85
1916	— — trefoil in *obv.* legend	50	110
1917	Leaf on neck, fleur on breast, often extra pellet in two quarters	30	75
1918	As last, but two extra pellets by hair	75	175
1919	**Halfgroat.** As 1914 *mm.*Cross patonce	35	90
1920	Similar, but *mm.* plain cross, some times no leaf on breast, no stops	40	100

		F	VF
1921	**Penny.** *London.* Usually extra pellets in two quarters	35	80
1922	— — pellets by crown omitted	35	80
1923	— — trefoil in legend	40	100
1924	*York,* Archb. Booth. ℞. Quatrefoil and pellet in centre	30	80
1925	— — two extra pellets by hair (local dies)	25	70
1926	*Durham,* Bp. Neville. Trefoil in *obv.* legend. B. Two rings in centre of cross	80	200

1927

1927	— — Similar, but without trefoil	80	200
1928	**Halfpenny.** Usually extra pellet in two quarters	20	50
1929	— *mm.* plain cross	20	50
1930	**Farthing.** As last	150	325

Unmarked issue, 1453-4

1931	**Groat.** No marks on *obv.;* two extra pellets on *rev.*	200	500
1932	— four extra pellets on *rev.*	300	650
1933	**Halfgroat.** As 1931	175	400

Cross-pellet issue, 1454-60

1934	**Groat.** Saltire either side of neck, pellets by crown, leaf and fleur on breast, extra pellets on *rev.*	100	300
1935	Saltire on neck, no leaf, pellets by crown, usually mullets in legend; extra pellets on *rev.*	65	140

1935

1940

1945

1936	— Similar, but mascles in place of mullets on *obv.*	85	215
1937	— — pellets by hair instead of by crown	90	275
1938	**Halfgroat.** Saltire on neck, pellets by crown and on *rev.*, mullets in legend	175	400
1939	**Penny.** *London.* Saltire on neck, pellets by crown and on *rev.*, mascle(s), or mullet and mascle in legend	100	275
1940	*York,* Archb. Wm. Booth. Saltires by neck, usually leaf on breast, pellets by crown. ℞. Cross in quatrefoil in centre. Illustrated below	40	90
1941	*Durham,* Bp. Laurence Booth. Saltire and B at neck, pellets by crown. ℞. Rings in centre	100	240
1942	**Halfpenny.** Saltires by neck, usually two extra pellets on *rev.*	60	125
1943	Similar, but saltire on neck, sometimes mullet after hЄnRIC	35	80
1944	**Farthing.** Saltire on neck, usually pellets by crown and on *rev.*, but known without either.	150	325

Lis-pellet issue, 1456-60

1945	**Groat.** Lis on neck; pellets by crown. ℞. Extra pellets	150	350

Full flan coins are difficult to find in the smaller denominations.

THE HOUSE OF YORK

EDWARD IV, First Reign, 1461-70

In order to increase the supply of bullion to the mint the weight of the penny was reduced to 12 grains in 1464, and the current value of the noble was raised to 8s. 4d. Later, in 1465, a new gold coin was issued, the Ryal or 'Rose Noble', weighing 120 grains and having a value of 10s. However, as 6s. 8d. had become the standard professional fee the old noble was missed, and a new coin was issued to take its place, the Angel of 80 grains.

Royal mints were opened at Canterbury and York to help with the re-coinage, and other mints were set up at Bristol, Coventry and Norwich, though they were not open for long.

Reference: C. E. Blunt and C. A Whitton, *The Coinage of Edward IV and Henry VI (Restored)*, B.N.J. 1945-7.

Mintmarks

105	9	7a	33	99	28	74	11

1461-4	Lis (105)	1467-70	Lis (105, *York*)	
	Cross fleury (9)	1467-8	Crown (74)	(often
	Plain cross (7a)		Sun (28)	combined)
1464-5	Rose (33 and 34)	1468-9	Crown (74)	(sometimes
1464-7	Pall (99, *Canterbury*)		Rose (33)	combined)
1465-6	Sun (28)	1469-70	Long cross	
1466-7	Crown (74)		fitchee (l.c.f) (11)	(often
			Sun (28)	combined)

GOLD

Heavy coinage, 1461-4

		F £	*VF* £
1946	**Noble** (=6s. 8d., wt. 108 grs.). Normal type, but *obv.* legend commences at top left, lis below shield; *mm.*-/lis (Spink's sale May 1993)	3000	6000
1947	— Quatrefoil below sword arm; *mm.* rose/lis	*Extremely rare*	
1948	— ℞. Roses in two spandrels; *mm.* rose	*Extremely rare*	
1949	**Quarter-noble**	*Unique*	

1946 1950

		F £	VF £

Light coinage, 1464-70

		F £	VF £
1950	**Ryal** or rose-noble (=10s., wt. 120 grs.), *London.* As illustration. Large fleurs in spandrels; *mm.* 33-74	300	525
1951	— — Small trefoils in spandrels; *mm.* 74-11	300	525

1952

		F £	VF £
1952	— Flemish imitative coinage (mostly 16th cent. on a large flan)	225	425
1953	*Bristol.* B in waves, large fleurs; *mm.* sun, crown	350	650
1954	— — small fleurs in spandrels; *mm.* sun, crown	375	725
1955	*Coventry.* C in waves; *mm.* sun	650	1400
1956	*Norwich.* n in waves; *mm.* sun, rose?	750	1500
1957	*York.* € in waves, large fleurs in spandrels, *mm.* sun, lis	325	700
1958	— — small fleurs, *mm.* sun. lis	350	750
1959	**Half-ryal.** *London.* As 1950	240	425
1960	*Bristol.* B in waves; *mm.* sun, sun/crown	350	800
1961	*Coventry.* C in waves; *mm.* sun	*Extremely rare*	
1962	*Norwich.* n in waves; *mm.* rose	1200	2500

1963

1965

		F £	VF £
1963	*York.* € in waves; *mm.* 28, 105, 33/105	240	275
1963	Similar but lis instead of € in waves (probably York)	*Extremely rare*	
1964	**Quarter-ryal.** Shield in tressure of eight arcs, rose above. ℞. Somewhat as half ryal; *mm.* sun/rose	*Unique?*	
1965	Shield in quatrefoil, ℞. € above, rose on l., sun on r.; *mm.* 33/28-74/33	175	400
1966	— — sun on l., rose on r.; *mm.* 74-11	190	425

1967 1972

		F £	*VF* £
1967	**Angel** (=6s. 8d., wt. 80 grs.). St. Michael spearing dragon. ℞. Ship, rays of sun at masthead, large rose and sun beside mast; *mm.*-/33	*Extremely rare*	
1968	— — small rose and sun at mast; *mm.*-/74	*Extremely rare*	

SILVER

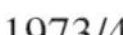
1973/4

1978

Heavy coinage, 1461-4

		F £	*VF* £
1969	**Groat** (60 grs.). Group I, lis on neck, pellets by crown; *mm.* 9, 7a, 105, 9/105 Occasionally ЄDWARD over hЄNRIC *mm.* cross, fleury	70	175
1970	— Lis on breast, no pellets; *mm.* plain cross, 7a/105	75	200
1971	— — with pellets at crown; *mm.* plain cross	75	200
1972	II, quatrefoils by neck, crescent on breast; *mm.* rose	70	165
1973	III, similar but trefoil on breast; *mm.* rose	55	140
1974	— — — eye in *rev.* inner legend, *mm.* rose	55	135
1975	— Similar, but no quatrefoils by bust	75	200
1976	— — Similar, but no trefoil on breast	75	200
1977	IV, annulets by neck, eye after TAS; *mm.* rose	100	250
1978	**Halfgroat.** I, lis on breast, pellets by crown and extra pellets in two qtrs.; *mm.* 9, 7a	200	500
1979	II, quatrefoils at neck, crescent on breast; *mm.* rose	225	475
1980	III, similar, but trefoil on breast, eye on *rev.; mm.* rose	225	475
1981	— Similar, but no mark on breast	210	450
1982	IV, annulets by neck, sometimes eye on *rev.; mm.* rose	200	425
1983	**Penny** (15 grs.), *London.* I, marks as 1978, but mascle after RЄX; *mm.* plain cross	325	750
1984	— II, quatrefoils by neck; *mm.* rose	*Extremely rare*	

1985

		F £	VF £
1985	— III, similar, but eye after TAS; *mm.* rose	160	375
1986	— IV, annulets by neck; *mm.* rose	225	500
1987	*York,* Archb. Booth. Quatrefoils by bust, voided quatrefoil in centre of *rev.; mm.* rose	130	280
1988	*Durham. O.* of Hen. VI. R. DVnOLIn	160	350
	Some of the Durham pennies from local dies may belong to the heavy coinage period, but if so they are indistinguishable from the light coins.		
1989	**Halfpenny.** I, as 1983, but no mascle	100	200
1990	II, quatrefoils by bust; *mm.* rose	45	120
1991	— saltires by bust; *mm.* rose	65	135
1992	III, no marks by bust; *mm.* rose	50	125
1993	IV, annulets by bust; *mm* rose	60	150
1994	**Farthing.** I, as 1989	500	1250

Light coinage, 1464-70. There is a great variety of groats and we give only a selection. Some have pellets in one quarter of the reverse, or trefoils over the crown; early coins have fleurs on the cusps of the tressure, then trefoils or no marks on the cusps, while the late coins have only trefoils.

		F	VF
1995	**Groat** (48 grs.), *London.* Annulets at neck, eye after TAS; *mm.* 33 (struck from heavy dies, IV)	45	120
1996	— — — Similar, but new dies, eye after TAS or DOn	60	140
1997	— Quatrefoils at neck, eye; rose (heavy dies, III)	45	115
1998	— — — Similar, but new dies, eye in *rev.* legend	35	100
1999	— No marks at neck, eye; rose	100	200

2000

2002

		F	VF
2000	— Quatrefoils at neck, no eye; *mm.* 33, 74, 28, 74/28, 74/33, 11/28	30	60
2001	— — — rose or quatrefoil on breast; *mm.* 33, 74/28	30	65
2002	— No marks at neck; *mm.* 28, 74, 11/28, 11	40	85
2003	— Trefoils or crosses at neck; *mm.* 11/33, 11/28, 11	40	80

Light coinage, silver, *continued*	*F* £	*VF* £
2004 *Bristol.* B on breast, quatrefoils at neck; *mm.* 28/33, 28, 28/74, 74, 74/28	35	70
2005 — — trefoils at neck; *mm.* sun	40	100
2006 — — no marks at neck; *mm.* sun	50	135
2007 — Without B, quatrefoils at neck; *mm.* sun	50	135
Bristol is variously rendered as BRESTOLL, BRISTOLL, BRESTOW, BRISTOW.		
2008 *Coventry.* C on breast, quatrefoils at neck, COVETRE; *mm.* 28/33, 28	55	125
2009 — — Local dies, similar; *mm.* rose	65	185
2010 — — — as last, but no C or quatrefoils	70	225
2011 *Norwich.* n on breast, quatrefoils at neck, nORWIC or nORVIC, *mm.* 28/33, 28	55	135
2012 *York.* € on breast, quatrefoils at neck, €BORACI; *mm.* 28, 105/74, 105, 105/28	35	75
2013 — Similar, but without € on breast, *mm.* lis	40	120
2014 — € on breast, trefoils at neck; *mm.* 105/28, 105	35	125
2015 **Halfgroat.** *London.* Annulets by neck (heavy dies); *mm.* 33	*Unique*	
2016 — Quatrefoils by neck; *mm.* 33/-, 28/-, 74, 74/28	45	100
2017 — Saltires by neck; *mm.* 74, 74/28	50	120
2018 — Trefoils by neck; *mm.* 74, 74/28, 11/28	45	110
2019 — No marks by neck; *mm.* 11/28	90	180
2020 — *Bristol.* Saltires or crosses by neck; *mm.* 33/28, 28, 74, 74/-	80	210
2021 — Quatrefoils by neck; *mm.* 28/-, 74, 74/-	70	200
2022 — Trefoils by neck; *mm.* crown	95	225
2023 — No marks by neck; *mm.* 74/28	95	225
2024 *Canterbury,* Archb. Bourchier (1464-7). Knot below bust; quatrefoils by neck; *mm.* 99/-, 99, 99/33, 99/28	25	55
2025 — — — quatrefoils omitted *mm.* 99	25	55
2026 — — — saltires by neck; *mm.* 99/-, 99/28	30	60
2026A — — — trefoils by neck; *mm.* 99	40	90

2027

2030

	F £	*VF* £
2027 — — — wedges by hair and/or neck; *mm.* 99, 99/33, 99/28	30	70
2028 — — As 2024 or 2025, but no knot	35	80
2029 — Royal mint (1467-9). Quatrefoils by neck; *mm.* 74, 74/-	25	75
2030 — — Saltires by neck; *mm.* 74/-, 74	30	75
2031 — — Trefoils by neck; *mm.* 74, 74/-, 74/28, 33	25	55
2032 — No marks by neck; *mm.* sun	50	125
2033 *Coventry.* Crosses by neck; *mm.* sun	*Unique*	
2034 *Norwich.* Saltires by neck; *mm.* sun	*Extremely rare*	

No.	Description	F £	VF £
2035	*York.* Quatrefoils by neck; *mm.* sun, lis , lis/-	60	145
2036	— Saltires by neck; *mm.* lis	50	110
2037	— Trefoils by neck; *mm.* lis, lis/-	50	110
2038	— Є on breast, quatrefoils by neck; *mm.* lis/-	55	115
2039	**Penny** (12 grs.), *London.* Annulets by neck (heavy dies); *mm.* rose	110	250
2040	— Quatrefoils by neck; *mm.* 74, sun. crown	35	70
2041	— Trefoil and quatrefoil by neck; *mm.* crown	40	85
2042	— Saltires by neck; *mm.* crown	40	85
2043	— Trefoils by neck; *mm.* crown, l.c.f	35	70
2044	— No marks by neck; *mm.* l.c.f	*Extremely rare*	
2045	*Bristol.* Crosses, quatrefoils or saltires by neck, BRISTOW; *mm.* crown	100	225
2046	— Quatrefoils by neck; BRI(trefoil)STOLL	100	260
2047	— Trefoil to r. of neck BRISTOLL	125	275
2048	*Canterbury,* Archb. Bourchier. Quatrefoils or saltires by neck, knot on breast; *mm.* pall	80	160
2049	— — Similar, but no marks by neck	90	175
2050	— — As 2048, but no knot	85	170
2051	— — Crosses by neck, no knot	85	170
2052	— Royal mint. Quatrefoils by neck; *mm.* crown	125	325
2053	— *Durham*, King's Receiver (1462-4). Local dies, mostly with rose in centre of *rev.; mm.* 7a, 33	20	70
2054	—·Bp. Lawrence Booth (1465-70). B and D by neck, B on *rev.; mm.* 33	25	75
2055	— — Quatrefoil and B by neck; *mm.* sun	30	80
2056	— — B and quatrefoil by neck; *mm.* crown	*Extremely rare*	
2057	— — D and quatrefoil by neck; *mm.* crown	30	85
2058	— — Quatrefoils by neck; *mm.* crown	30	85
2059	— — Trefoils by neck; *mm.* crown	30	85
2060	— Lis by neck; *mm.* crown	30	85
2061	*York,* Sede Vacante (1464-5). Quatrefoils at neck, no quatrefoil in centre of *rev.*; *mm.* sun, rose	50	125
2062	— Archb. Neville (1465-70). Local dies, G and key by neck, quatrefoil on *rev.; mm.* sun, plain cross	30	75

2063

2068

No.	Description	F £	VF £
2063	— — London-made dies, similar; *mm.* 28, 105, 11	25	75
2064	— — Similar, but no marks by neck; *mm.* large lis	*Extremely rare*	
2065	— — — Quatrefoils by neck; *mm.* large lis	35	85
2066	— — — Trefoils by neck; *mm.* large lis	35	85
2067	**Halfpenny,** *London.* Saltires by neck; *mm.* 34, 28, 74	40	90
2068	— Trefoils by neck; *mm.* 28, 74, 11	30	70
2069	— No marks by neck; *mm.* l.c.f		*Unique?*
2070	*Bristol.* Crosses by neck; *mm.* crown	125	275
2071	— Trefoils by neck; *mm.* crown	100	200

		F	VF
		£	£
2072	*Canterbury.* Archb. Bourchier. No marks; *mm.* pall	100	225
2072A	— — — Trefoils by neck, *mm.* pall	100	225
2073	— Royal mint. Saltires by neck; *mm.* crown	70	140
2074	— — Trefoils by neck; *mm.* crown	60	125
2074A	*Norwich.* Quartrefoils by neck., *mm.* Sun	*Unique*	
2075	*York.* Royal mint. Saltires by neck; *mm.* lis/-, sun/-	70	140
2076	— — Trefoils by neck; *mm.* lis/-	65	125
2077	**Farthing,** *London.* ЄDWARD DI GRA RЄX, no marks at neck, mm. rose	400	—
2077A	— Trefoils by neck, *mm.* crown	600	—

Full flan coins are difficult to find in the smaller denominations.

HENRY VI RESTORED, Oct. 1470-Apr. 1471

The coinage of this short restoration follows closely that of the previous reign. Only angel gold was issued, the ryal being discontinued. Many of the coins have the king's name reading hENRICV—another distinguishing feature is an R that looks like a B.

Mintmarks

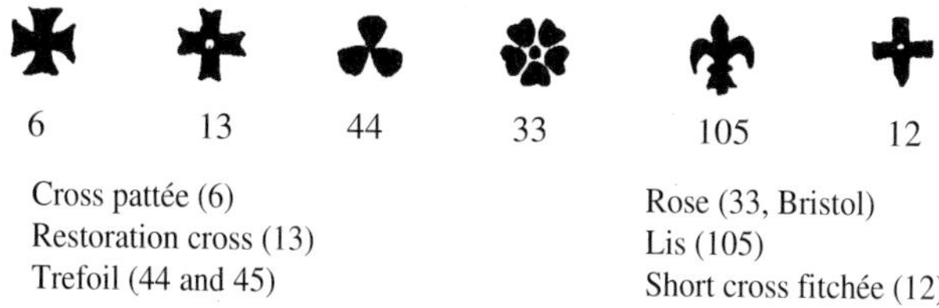

6 13 44 33 105 12

Cross pattée (6)
Restoration cross (13)
Trefoil (44 and 45)
Rose (33, Bristol)
Lis (105)
Short cross fitchée (12)

GOLD

2079

		F £	*VF* £
2078	**Angel,** *London.* As illus. but no B; *mm.* -/6, 13, -/105, none	525	1200
2079	*Bristol.* B in waves; *mm.* -/13, none	850	1800
2080	**Half-angel,** *London.* As 2078; *mm.* -/6, -/13, -/105	1400	3000
2081	*Bristol.* B in waves; *mm.* -/13	*Unique*	

SILVER

2082 2084

2082	**Groat,** *London.* Usual type; *mm.* 6, 6/13, 6/105, 13, 13/6, 13/105, 13 /12	100	200
2083	*Bristol.* B on breast; *mm.* 13, 13/33, 13/44, 44, 44/13, 44/33, 44/12	150	325
2084	*York.* € on breast; *mm.* lis, lis/sun	110	240
2085	**Halfgroat,** *London.* As 2082; *mm.* 13, 13/-	220	450
2086	*York.* € on breast; *mm.* lis	*Extremely rare*	
2087	**Penny,** *London.* Usual type; *mm.* 6, 13, 12	325	750

No.	Description	F £	VF £
2087A	*Bristol.* Similar; *mm.* 12	*Unique?*	
2088	*York.* G and key by neck; *mm.* lis	200	425
2089	**Halfpenny,** *London.* As 2087; *mm.* 12, 13,	150	350
2090	*Bristol.* Similar; *mm.* cross	*Unique?*	

EDWARD IV, Second Reign, 1471-83

The Angel and its half were the only gold denominations issued during this reign. The main types and weight standards remained the same as those of the light coinage of Edward's first reign. The use of the 'initial mark' as a mintmark to denote the date of issue was now firmly established.

Mintmarks

33 105 12 55 44 55 28 56 17

30 37 6 18 19 20 31 11 38

1471-83 Rose (33, *York & Durham*)
Lis (105, *York*)
1471 Short cross fitchee (12)
1471-2 Annulet (large, 55)
Trefoil (44)
Rose (33, *Bristol*)
1471-3 Pansy (30, *Durham*)
1472-3 Annulet (small, 55)
Sun (28, *Bristol*)
1473-7 Pellet in annulet (56)
Cross and four pellets (17)
Cross in circle (37)

1473-7 Cross pattée (6)
Pierced cross 1 (18)
1477-80 Pierced cross and pellet (19)
Pierced cross 2 (18)
Pierced cross, central pellet (20)
Rose (33, *Canterbury*)
1480-3 Heraldic cinquefoil (31)
Long cross fitchee (11, *Canterbury*)
1483 Halved sun and rose (38)
(Listed under Ed. IV/V.)

GOLD

2091 2093

No.	Description	F £	VF £
2091	**Angel.** *London.* Type as illus.; *mm.* 12, 55, 56, 17, 18, 19, 31	200	425
2092	*Bristol.* B in waves; *mm.* small annulet	750	1650
2093	**Half-angel.** As illus.; *mm.* 55, cross in circle, 19, 20/19, 31	175	375
2094	King's name and title on *rev.*; *mm.* 12/-	350	650
2095	King's name and the title both sides; *mm.* 55/-	300	550

SILVER

2096

2101

		F £	VF £
2096	**Groat,** *London.* Trefoils on cusps, no marks by bust; *mm.* 12-37	30	70
2097	— — roses by bust; *mm.* pellet in annulet	45	100
2098	— Fleurs on cusps; no marks by bust; *mm.* 18-20	30	70
2099	— — pellets by bust; *mm.* pierced cross	60	140
2100	— — rose on breast; *mm.* 31	30	70
2101	*Bristol.* B on breast; *mm.* 33, 33/55, 28/55, 55, 55/-, 28 no marks by bust	60	150
2102	*York.* Є on breast; *mm.* lis	70	165
2103	**Halfgroat,** *London.* As 2096; *mm.* 12-31	35	85
2104	*Bristol.* B on breast; *mm.* 33/12	*Extremely rare*	
2105	*Canterbury* (Royal mint). As 2103; *mm.* 33, 11, 11/31, 31	25	70

2106

		F £	VF £
2106	— C on breast; *mm.* rose	25	65
2107	— — ℞. C in centre; *mm.* rose	25	65
2108	— — ℞. Rose in centre; *mm.* rose	25	65
2109	*York.* No. Є on breast; *mm.* lis	90	225
2110	**Penny,** *London.* No marks by bust; *mm.* 12-31	35	85
2111	*Bristol.* Similar; *mm.* rose	300	—
2112	*Canterbury* (Royal). Similar; *mm.* 33, 11	65	140
2113	— C on breast; *mm.* rose	80	175
2114	*Durham,* Bp. Booth (1471-6). No marks by neck; *mm.* 12, 44	23	60

2115

2116

		F £	VF £
2115	— — D in centre of *rev.*; B and trefoil by neck; *mm.* 44, 33, 56	25	65
2116	— — — two lis at neck; *mm.* rose	23	60
2117	— — — crosses over crown, and on breast; *mm.* rose	20	55

		F	VF
		£	£
2118	— — — crosses over crown, V under CIVI; *mm.* rose, pansy	25	70
2119	— — — B to l. of crown, V on breast and under CIVI	20	55
2120	— — — As last but crosses at shoulders	20	55
2121	— Sede Vacante (1476). R. D in centre; *mm.* rose	35	100
2122	— Bp. Dudley (1476-83). V to r. of neck; as last	30	80

2123 2125 2134

2123	— — D and V by neck; as last, but *mm.* 31	20	55
	Nos. 2117-2123 are from locally-made dies.		
2124	*York,* Archb. Neville (1471-2). Quatrefoils by neck. R. Quatrefoil; *mm.* 12 (over lis)	90	225
2125	— — Similar, but G and key by neck; *mm.* 12 (over lis)	18	50
2126	— Neville suspended (1472-5). As last, but no quatrefoil in centre of *rev.*	20	55
2126A	— — no marks by bust, similar; *mm.* annulet	90	225
2127	— — No marks by neck, quatrefoil on *rev.*; *mm.* 55, cross in circle, 33..	20	55
2128	— — Similar but € and rose by neck; *mm.* rose	20	55
2129	— Archb. Neville restored (1475-6). As last, but G and rose	23	60
2130	— — Similar, but G and key by bust	20	50
2131	— Sede Vacante (1476). As 2127, but rose on breast; *mm.* rose	23	55
2132	— Archb. Lawrence Booth (1476-80). B and key by bust, quatrefoil on *rev.; mm.* 33, 31	20	50
2133	— Sede Vacante (1480). Similar, but no quatrefoil on *rev.*; *mm.* rose	20	55
2134	— Archb. Rotherham (1480-3). T and slanting key by neck, quatrefoil on *rev.; mm.* 33	18	55
2135	— — — Similar, but star on breast	90	225
2136	— — — Star on breast and to r. of crown	75	150
2137	**Halfpenny,** *London.* No marks by neck; *mm.* 12-31	20	60
2138	— Pellets at neck; *mm.* pierced cross	30	70
2139	*Canterbury* (Royal). C on breast and in centre of *rev.; mm.* rose	70	150
2140	— C on breast only; *mm.* rose	60	130
2141	— Without C either side; *mm.* 11	70	160
2142	*Durham,* Bp. Booth. No marks by neck. R. DERAM, D in centre; *mm.* rose	120	250
2142A	— — Lis either side of neck. R. D or no mark in centre	*Extremely rare*	
2143	— — — Similar, but V to l. of neck	120	250

Full flan coins are very difficult to find in the small denominations.

EDWARD IV or V

On the death of Edward IV, 9th April, 1483, the 12-year-old Prince Edward was placed under the guardianship of his uncle, Richard, Duke of Gloucester, but within eleven weeks Richard usurped the throne and Edward and his younger brother were confined to the Tower and never seen alive again. The boar's head was a personal badge of Richard, Edward's 'Protector'.
The consensus of opinion now favours the last year of Edward IV for the introduction of the halved-sun and rose mintmark, but it is suggested that all the coins of Edward V's reign were also struck from dies bearing this mint mark. The coins are very rare.

Mintmark: Halved sun and rose. 

GOLD

		F	*VF*
		£	£
2144	**Angel.** As 2091	900	2000
2145	**Half-angel.** As 2093	*Extremely rare*	

2145 2146

SILVER

2146	**Groat.** As 2098 with or without pellet below bust	400	850
2147	**Penny.** As 2110	600	1200
2148	**Halfpenny.** As 2137	225	525

2149

COINS ATTRIBUTABLE TO RICHARD III, 1483

Recent research indicates that coins with the mint marks previously thought to be for Edward V are now attributable to Richard III, even though they bear Edward's name.

Mintmarks: Boar's head on *obv.*, halved sun and rose on *rev.*  

GOLD

2149	**Angel.** As 2091	*Extremely rare*
2150	**Half-angel.** Similar	*Unique*

SILVER

2151

		F	VF
		£	£
2151	**Groat.** As 2098	1850	3500
2152	**Halfgroat.** As 2103		*Unique*
2153	**Penny.** As 2110 (*mm.* uncertain on only known specimen)		*Unknown?*

RICHARD III, 1483-85

Richard's brief reign was brought to an end on the field of Bosworth. His coinage follows the pattern of the previous reigns. The smaller denominations of the London mint are all rare.

Mintmarks

38 62 63 105 33

Halved sun and rose, 3 styles (38, 39 and another with the sun more solid, see *North*).
Boar's head, narrow (62) wide (63).
Lis (105, *Durham*)
Rose only (33).

GOLD

2154	**Angel.** Reading ЄDWARD but with R and rose by mast; *mm.* sun and rose		*Unique*
2155	— Similar, but boar's head *mm.* on *obv*		*Unique*

2156 2158

2156	Reading RICARD or RICAD. ℞. R and rose by mast; *mm.* various combinations	750	1450
2157	— Similar, but R by mast over rose	800	1500
2158	**Half-angel.** ℞. R and rose by mast; *mm.* boar's head		*Extremely rare*

SILVER

2159

2160

		F	VF
		£	£
2159	**Groat,** *London. Mm.* various combinations	240	450
2160	— Pellet below bust	250	475
2161	*York. Mm.* Sun and rose *(obv.)*	350	850
2162	**Halfgroat.** *Mm.* sun and rose on *obv.* only	750	1500
2163	Pellet below bust; *mm.* sun and rose	*Unique*	
2164	— *mm.* boar's head *(obv.)*	850	1750
2165	**Penny.** *London. mm.* boar's head *(obv.)*	*Unique*	

This was the R. Carlyon-Britton specimen. It was stolen from B. A. Seaby Ltd in Feb. 1962.

2168

2169

2166	*York,* Archb. Rotherham. ℞. Quatrefoil in centre; *mm.* sun and rose	300	550
2167	— — T and upright key at neck; *mm.* rose	125	300
2168	— — — *mm.* boar's head	150	350
2169	*Durham,* Bp. Sherwood. S on breast. ℞. D in centre; *mm.* lis	100	250
2170	**Halfpenny,** *London. Mm.* sun and rose	150	375
2171	— *Mm.* boar's head	225	475

Most small denomination coins are short of flan and unevenly struck.

THE HOUSE OF TUDOR

HENRY VII, 1485-1509

For the first four years of his reign Henry's coins differ only in name and mintmark from those of his predecessors, but in 1489 radical changes were made in the coinage. Though the pound sterling had been a denomination of account for centuries, a pound coin had never been minted. Now a magnificent gold pound was issued, and, from the design of the king enthroned in majesty, was called a 'Sovereign'. The reverse had the royal arms set in the centre of a Tudor rose. A few years later the angel was restyled and St. Michael, who is depicted about to thrust Satan into the Pit with a cross-topped lance, is no longer a feathered figure but is clad in armour of Renaissance style. A gold ryal of ten shillings was also minted again for a brief period.

The other major innovation was the introduction of the shilling in the opening years of the 16th century. It is remarkable for the very fine profile portrait of the king which replaces the representational image of a monarch that had served on the coinage for the past couple of centuries. This new portrait was also used on groats and halfgroats but not on the smaller denominations.

Mintmarks

39 41 40 42 33 11 7a 123

105 76b 31 78 30 91 43 57

85 94 118 21 33 53

1485-7	Halved sun and rose (39)
	Lis upon sun and rose (41)
	Lis upon half rose (40)
	Lis-rose dimidiated (42)
	Rose (33, *York*)
1487	Lis (105)
	Cross fitchy (11)
1487-8	Rose (33)
	Plain cross (7a, *Durham*)
1488-9	No marks
1489-93	Cinquefoil (31)
	Crozier (76b, *Durham*)
1492	Cross fitchy (11, gold only)
1493-5	Escallop (78)
	Dragon (118, gold only)
	Lis (105, *Canterbury* and *York*
	Tun (123, *Canterbury*)
1495-8	Pansy (30)
	Tun (123, *Canterbury*)
	Lis (105, *York*)
1498-9	Crowned leopard's head (91)
	Lis issuant from rose (43)
	Tun (123, *Canterbury*)
1499-1502	Anchor (57)
1502-4	Greyhound's head (85)
	Lis (105, profile issue only)
	Martlet (94, *York*)
1504-5	Cross-crosslet (21)
1504-9	Martlet (94, (*York, Canterbury*)
	Rose (33, *York* and *Canterbury*)
1505-9	Pheon (53)

GOLD

No.	Description	F £	VF £
2173	**Sovereign** (20s; wt. 240 gr.). Group I. Large figure of king sitting on backless throne. R. Large shield crowned on large Tudor rose. *mm.* 31...	*Unique*	
2172	— Group II. Somewhat similar but throne has narrow back, lis in background. R. Large Tudor rose bearing small shield. *mm.* -/11	*Extremely rare*	

2174

No.	Description	F £	VF £
2174	— III. King on high-backed very ornamental throne, with greyhound and dragon on side pillars. R. Shield on Tudor rose; *mm.* dragon......	6000	13000
2175	— IV. Similar but throne with high canopy breaking legend and broad seat, *mm.* 105/118, (also with no *obv.* i.c. *mm.* 105/118, very rare)	5500	11000
2176	— Narrow throne with a portcullis below the king's feet (like Henry VIII); *mm.* 105/21, 105/53	5750	11500
2177	**Double-sovereign** and **Treble-sovereign** from same dies as 2176. These piedforts were probably intended as presentation pieces *mm.* 105/21, 105/53 .	*Extremely rare*	

2178

No.	Description	F £	VF £
2178	**Ryal** (10s.). As illustration: *mm.* -/11	6500	15000
2179	**Angel** (6s. 8d). I. Angel of old type with one foot on dragon. R. PЄR CRVCЄM. etc., *mm.* 39, 40, (also muled both ways)..............................	375	850
2179A	— With Irish title, and legend over angel head. *mm.* 33/-	*Extremely rare*	
2180	— — Name altered from RICARD? and h on *rev.* from R. *mm.* 41/39, 41/40, 41/-, 39/?	500	1100

2181

2183

2187

		F	VF
		£	£
2181	II. As 2179, but *mm.* none. 31/-.	275	575
2181A	II/III mule. *mm.* 31/78, ℞. PER CRUC or AVTEM TRANS	300	625
2182	As 2181. ℞. IhC AVTЄM TRAnSIЄnS etc.; *mm.* none, 31/-	300	625
2183	III. New dies, angel with both feet on dragons; (large straight lettering) *mm.* 78-85 except 91 (many mules exist)	200	375
2183A	— Angel with very small wings. *mm.* escallop		*Rare*
2184	— — ℞. IhC AVTEM TRAnSIЄnS, etc.; *mm.* escallop	275	575
2185	IV. Small square lettering; *mm.* 85 (also muled with 2183)	215	475
2186	— Tall thin lettering; *mm.* 21 (also muled with 2185 *obv.*)	215	420
2187	V. Large crook-shaped abbreviation after hЄNRIC; *mm.* 21 and 53 (combinations and mules exist)	185	400
2188	**Half-angel or angelet.** I. *Mm.* 39, 41, (old dies RIII altered)	300	725
2189	III. Angel with both feet on dragon: *mm.* 30, 57/30, -/85 30/85	250	525
2190	IV. Small square lettering; *mm.* rose	300	725
2191	— *Obv.* as last. ℞. Tall thin lettering; *mm.* 33/21	275	675
2192	V. As angel; *mm.* pheon	175	350

SILVER

Facing bust issues. Including 'Sovereign' type pennies.

2193	**Groat.** I. Open crown; *mm.* 40 (rose on bust), 39-42 and none (combinations)	70	150

2194

2195

2194	— — crosses or saltires by neck, 41, 40, 105-33 and none (combinations)	75	165
2195	IIa. Large bust with out-turned hair, crown with two plain arches; *mm.* none, 31, 31/-, 31/78	50	100
2196	— — similar but crosses by neck; *mm.* none, -/105	50	120
2197	— — ℞ . Portcullis over long cross; *mm.* -/lis		*Extremely rare*

2198

2199

2201

		F	*VF*
		£	£
*2198	**Groat.** IIIa. Bust as IIa. Crown with two jewelled arches, *mm.* 31, 78?	60	125
*2198A	IIIb. Similar, but new bust with realistic hair *mm.* 78, 30	40	80
*2199	IIIc. Bust as IIIb, but crown with one plain and one jewelled arch, *mm.* 30-21 and none	35	70
*2199A	IIId. As last, but plainer letters. *mm* 57, 85, 33 and none	40	90
2200	IVa. Wide single arch crown; arch is single or double bar with 4 crockets; *mm.* 85, 85/33, 21	40	85
2201	IVb. — Similar, but arch is double bar with 6 uprights or crockets as jewels; *mm.* 85, 21/85, 21	40	80
	* *mm.*s muled.		
2202	**Halfgroat,** *London.* I. Open crown, tressure unbroken; *mm.* 40/-, 40/39 (R. III mule)	350	750
2203	— IIIa. Double arched crown, rosettes on tressure; *mm.* escallop		*Rare*
2204	— IIIb. Similar, nothing on tressure. ℞. Lozenge panel in centre; *mm.* lis	40	100
2205	— — Similar, but also with lis on breast; *mm.* lis	40	100
2206	— IIIc. Unarched crown with tressure broken. ℞. Lozenge panel in centre; *mm.* lis	30	65
2206A	— — — Similar but smaller dies and much smaller lettering	30	65

2207

2211

2207	*Canterbury,* Archb. Morton. I. Open crown, crosses by neck. ℞. M in centre; *mm.* tun/-	35	75
2208	— — II. Similar, but double-arched crown; no *mm.*	30	65
2209	III King and Archb. jointly. As last but without M; (a) early lettering, trefoil stops; *mm.* lis, tun and lis/lis	30	60
2209A	— Class IIIa/I mule		*Rare*
2210	— — (b) ornate lettering, rosette stops; *mm.* tun, lis in combinations	20	50
2211	— — (c) — saltire or no stops; *mm.* 123, 123 & 30/123	20	50
2212	*York,* Royal mint. (a) Double-arched crown, lis on breast (rarely omitted). ℞. Lozenge panel in centre; *mm.* lis	35	75
2213	— — (b) Similar, but unarched crown, tressure broken, *mm.* lis	30	65

2214 2221 2226

		F £	VF £
2214	— Archb. Savage. (a) Double-arched crown, keys at neck, no tressure; ornate lette ring; *mm.* martlet	25	50
2215	— — (b) Similar, but fleured tressure, small square lettering; *mm.* martlet	25	55
2216	— — (c) As last, but tall thin lettering; *mm.* martlet	25	55
2217	— As last but no keys; *mm.* martlet	35	75
2218	**Penny.** Old type. London; *mm.* 40/-	250	525
2219	— — — crosses by bust, *mm.* small cross (*obv.*)	*Extremely rare*	
2220	— *Canterbury*, Archb. Morton. Open crown, *mm.* tun/- ℞. M in centre	*Extremely rare*	
2221	— — King and Archb. jointly, arched crown; *mm.* tun, tun/-	40	100
2222	— *Durham*, Bp. Sherwood. S on breast. ℞. D in centre; *mm.* 7a/-	75	175
2223	— *York,* Archb. Rotherham. With or without cross on breast, *mm.* 33/-, T and cross or key at neck. ℞. h in centre	35	90
2224	— — — T and trefoil at neck. ℞. Quatrefoil in centre and two extra pellets; *mm.* 41/-	40	100
2225	'Sovereign' type. *London.* Early lettering, no stops, no pillars to throne; no *mm.*	*Extremely rare*	
2226	— — — single pillar on king's right side, trefoil stops; no *mm.* or 31/-	20	60
2227	— — Ornate letters, rosette stops, single pillar; *mm.* lis (can be muled with above)	25	65
2228	— — saltire stops or none, two pillars; *mm.* none, -/30	20	60
2229	— — Similar, but small square lettering; no *mm.*	20	60
2230	— — Similar, but lettering as profile groats two double pillars; *mm.* 21, 53, none (sometimes on one side only)	25	70

2231 2233 2235

		F £	VF £
2231	— *Durham*, Bp. Sherwood. Crozier to r. of king, throne with one pillar. ℞. D and S beside shield	25	65
2232	— — Throne with two pillars, no crozier. ℞. As last	30	75
2233	— — Bp. Fox. Throne with one pillar. ℞. Mitre above shield, RD or DR at sides, no *mm.*	25	65
2234	— — Similar, but two pillars	25	65
2235	*York,* Archb. Rotherham. Keys below shield; early lettering, trefoil stops, no pillars to throne, no *mm.*	25	60

		F £	VF £
2236	— — — single pillar	25	60
2237	— — — ornate lettering, rosette or no stops, single pillar	25	60
2238	— — — — — — — two pillars sometimes with crosses between legs of throne	25	60

2245 2249

		F £	VF £
2239	**Halfpenny,** *London.* I. Open crown; *mm.* 40, 42	60	150
2240	— — — trefoils at neck; no *mm.*, rose	60	150
2241	— — — crosses at neck; *mm.* rose	55	135
2242	— II. Double arched crown; *mm.* cinquefoil, none	25	65
2243	— — — saltires at neck; no *mm.*	25	65
2244	— III. Crown with single arch, ornate lettering; no *mm.*	20	60
2245	— V. Much smaller portrait; *mm.* pheon, lis, none	25	65
2246	*Canterbury,* Archb. Morton. I. Open crown, crosses by neck; ℞. M in centre	140	275
2247	— — II. Similar, but arched crown, saltires by bust; *mm.* profile eye (82)	140	275
2248	— III. King and Archb. Arched crown; *mm.* lis, none	65	150
2249	*York,* Archb. Savage. Arched crown, key below bust	100	250
2250	**Farthing,** *London.* hЄnRIC DI GRA RЄX (A), arched crown	150	300

*No.s 2239-49 have *mm.* on *obv.* only.

Profile issue

2253

2251	**Testoon** (1s.). Type as groat. hЄnRIC (VS); *mm.* lis	4000	8000
2252	— hЄnRIC VII; *mm.* lis	4500	9000
2253	— hЄnRIC SЄPTI M; *mm.* lis	5000	10000

2254 2258

		F	VF
		£	£
2254	**Groat,** *Tentative issue* (contemporary with full-face groats). Double band to crown, hЄnRIC VII; *mm.* none, 105/-, -/105: 105/85, 105, 85, 21	110	225
2255	— — — tressure on *obv.; mm.* cross-crosslet..	2750	5000
2256	— — hЄnRIC (VS); *mm.* 105, -/105, 105/ 85, none..............................	225	550
2257	— — hЄnRIC SЄPTIM; *mm.* -/105	3250	6000
2258	*Regular issue.* Triple band to crown; *mm.* 21, 53 (both *mm.*s may occur on some *obv.* or *rev.*)	50	120
2259	**Halfgroat,** *London.* As last; *mm.* 105, 53/105, 105/53, 53......................	50	125
2260	— — no numeral after King's name, no *mm.*, -/lis................................	*Extremely rare*	

2261 2262

2261	*Canterbury,* King and Archb. As London, but *mm.* 94, 33, 94/33...........	30	75
2262	*York,* Archb. Bainbridge. As London, but two keys below shield; *mm.* 94, 33, 33/94..	30	70
2262A	— Similar but no keys; *mm.* rose..	35	80

2263

2263	— — XB beside shield; *mm.* rose/martlett	750	—

Henry VIII is held in ill-regard by numismatists as being the author of the debasement of England's gold and silver coinage; but there were also other important numismatic innovations during his reign. For the first sixteen years the coinage closely followed the pattern of the previous issues, even to the extent of retaining the portrait of Henry VII on the larger silver coins.

In 1526, in an effort to prevent the drain of gold to continental Europe, the value of English gold was cried up by 10%, the sovereign to 22s. 0d. and the angel to 7s. 4d., and a new coin valued at 4s. 6d.—the Crown of the Rose—was introduced as a competitor to the French *écu au soleil*. The new crown was not a success and within a few months it was replaced by the Crown of the Double Rose valued at 5s but made of gold of only 22 carat fineness, the first time gold had been minted below the standard 23c. At the same time the sovereign was again revalued to 22s. 6d. and the angel to 7s. 6d., with a new coin, the George Noble, valued at 6s. 8d. (one-third pound).

The royal cyphers on some of the gold crowns and half-crowns combine the initial of Henry with those of his queens: Katherine of Aragon, Anne Boleyn and Jane Seymour. The architect of this coinage reform was the chancellor, Cardinal Thomas Wolsey, who besides his other changes had minted at York a groat bearing his initials and cardinal's hat in addition to the other denominations normally authorized for the ecclesiastical mints.

When open debasement of the coinage began in 1544 to help finance Henry's wars, the right to coin of the archbishops of Canterbury and York and of the bishop of Durham was not confirmed. Instead, a second royal mint was opened in the Tower as in subsequent years were six others, at Southwark, York, Canterbury, Bristol, Dublin and Durham House in the Strand. Gold, which fell to 23c. in 1544, 22c. in 1545, and 20c. in 1546 was much less debased than silver which declined to 9oz 2dwt. in 1544, 6oz 2dwt. in 1545 and 4oz 2dwt. in 1546. At this last standard the blanched silver surface of the coins soon wore away to reveal the copper alloy beneath which earned for Henry the nickname 'Old Coppernose'.

Mintmarks

53 69 70 108 33 94 73 11

105 22 23 30 78 15 24 110

52 72a 44 8 65a 114 121 90

36 106 56 S E 116

1509-26	Pheon (53)
	Castle (69)
	Castle with H (70, gold)
	Portcullis crowned (108)
	Rose (33, *Canterbury*)
	Martlet (94, *Canterbury*)
	Pomegranate (73, but broader, *Cant.*)
	Cross fitchée (11, *Cant.*)
	Lis (105, *Canterbury, Durham*)
1509-14	Martlet (94, *York*)
1509-23	Radiant star (22, *Durham & York*)
1513-18	Crowned T *(Tournai)*
1514-26	Star (23, *York & Durham*)
	Pansy (30, *York*)
	Escallop (78, *York*)
	Voided cross (15, *York*)
1523-26	Spur rowel (24, *Durham*)

1526-44	Rose (33)
	Lis (105)
	Sunburst 110)
	Arrow (52)
	Pheon (53)
	Lis (106)
	Star (23, *Durham*)
1526-9	Crescent (72a, *Durham*)
	Trefoil (44 variety, *Durham*)
	Flower of eight petals and circle centre (*Durham*)
1526-30	Cross (7a, sometimes slightly voided, *York*)
	Acorn (65a, *York*)
1526-32	Cross patonce (8, *Cant.*)
	T (114, *Canterbury*)
	Uncertain mark (121, *Canterbury*)
1529-44	Radiant star (22, *Durham*)
1530-44	Key (90, *York*)
1533-44	Catherine wheel (36, *Canterbury*)
1544-7	Lis (105 and 106)
	Pellet in annulet (56)
	S (Southwark)
	Є or E (Southwark)
1546-7	WS monogram (116, *Bristol*)

GOLD

First coinage, 1509-26

		F £	*VF* £
2264	**Sovereign** (20s.). Similar to last sov. of Hen. VII; *mm.* 108	3000	6500
2264A	**Ryal** (10s.) King in ship holding sword and shield. ℞. Similar to 1950, *mm.*-/108		*Unique*
2265	**Angel** (6s. 8d.). As Hen. VIII, but hЄnRIC? VIII DI GRA RЄX, etc.; *mm.* 53, 69, 70, 70/69, 108, ℞. May omit h and rose, or rose only; *mm.* 69, 108	200	400
2266	**Half-angel.** Similar (sometimes without VIII), *mm.* 69, 70, 108/33, 108	160	335

2265

Second coinage, 1526-44

2267

2267	**Sovereign** (22s. 6d.). As 2264, ℞. single or double tressure *mm.* 110, 105, 105/52....................	2500	5000
2268	**Angel** (7s. 6d.). As 2265, hЄnRIC VIII D(I) G(RA) R(EX) etc,; *mm.* 110, 105....................	300	650
2269	**Half-angel.** Similar; *mm.* lis	450	950

Second coinage

2270 2272

		F	VF
		£	£
2270	**George-noble** (6s. 8d.). As illustration; *mm.* rose	2250	5500
2270A	— Similar, but more modern ship with three masts, without initials hR. ℞. St. George brandishing sword behind head.		*Unique*
2271	**Half-George-noble.** Similar to 2270 *mm* rose, lis		*Extremely rare*
2272	**Crown of the rose** (4s. 6d., 23 c. 3 1/2 gr.). As illustration; *mm.* rose, two legend varieties (In May 1994 a specimen fetched £10,000 in auction.)		*Extremely rare*

2279 2285

2273	**Crown of the double-rose** (5s., 22 c). Double-rose crowned, hK (Henry and Katherine of Aragon) both crowned in field. ℞. Shield crowned; *mm.* rose	175	375
2274	— hK both sides; *mm.* rose/lis, lis, arrow	190	400
2275*	— hK/hA or hA/hK; *mm.* arrow	200	600
2276*	— hR/hK or hI/hR; *mm.* arrow	300	650
2277	— hA (Anne Boleyn); *mm.* arrow	225	625
2278	— hA/hR; *mm.* arrow	—	2000
2279	— hI (Jane Seymour); *mm.* arrow	200	450
2280*	— hK/hI; *mm.* arrow	225	650
2281	— hR/hI; *mm.* arrow	225	675
2282	— hR (Rex); *mm.* arrow	200	450
2283	— — but with hIBERIC REX; *mm.* pheon	400	1000
2284	**Halfcrown**. Similar but king's name henric 8 on *rev.*, no initials; *mm.* rose	170	400
2285	— hK uncrowned on *obv.; mm.* rose	150	375
2286	— hK uncrowned both sides; *mm.* rose/lis, lis, arrow	160	385
2287	— hI uncrowned both sides; *mm.* arrow	225	500
2288	— hR uncrowned both sides; hIB REX; *mm.* pheon	325	750

*The hK initials may on later coins refer to Katherine Howard (Henry's fifth wife).

Third coinage, 1544-7

2291

		F £	VF £
2289	**Sovereign,** I (20s., Wt. 200 gr., 23 c.). As illustration but king with larger face and larger design; *mm.* lis	4000	9500
2290	II (20s., wt. 200 or 192 grs., 23, 22 or 20 ct.). *Tower.* As illustration; *mm.* lis, pellet in annulet/lis	1150	3000
2291	— *Southwark.* Similar; *mm.* S, Є/S	1100	2750
2292	— — Similar but Є below shield; *mm.* S/Є	*Extremely rare*	
2293	— *Bristol.* As London but *mm.* WS/-	2750	5000
2294	**Half-sovereign** (wt. 100 or 96 gr.), *Tower.* As illus.; *mm.* lis, pellet in annulet	200	500
2295	— Similar, but with annulet on inner circle (either or both sides)	225	575
2296	*Southwark. Mm.* S	225	550
2297	— Є below shield; *mm.* S, Є, S/Є, Є/S, (known without sceptre; *mm.* S)	200	550
2298	*Bristol.* Lombardic lettering; *mm.* WS, WS/-	350	950

2294

2303 2304

		F £	VF £
2299	**Angel** (8s., 23 c). Annulet by angel's head and on ship, hɛnRIC' 8; *mm.* lis	200	385
2300	— Similar, but annulet one side only or none	215	400
2301	**Half-angel.** Annulet on ship; *mm.* lis	175	425
2302	— No annulet on ship; *mm.* lis	200	475
2303	— Three annulets on ship; *mm.* lis	250	500
2304	**Quarter-angel** Angel wears armour; *mm.* lis	175	400
2304A	— Angel wears tunic; *mm.* lis	200	450

Third coinage

		F £	VF £
2305	**Crown,** *London.* Similar to 2283, but hЄnRIC' 8 ; Lombardic lettering; mm . 56	170	375
2306	— without RVTILAnS; *mm.* 56	180	400
2307	— — — with annulet on inner circle	190	425
2307A	— King's name omitted. DEI GRA both sides, *mm.* 56	*Extremely rare*	
2308	— *Southwark.* As 2306; *mm.* S, Є, E/S, Є/-, E/Є	235	475
2309	*Bristol.* hЄnRIC VIII. ROSA etc. ℞. D G, etc.; *mm.*-/WS	175	400
2310	— Similar but hЄnRIC(VS) 8 ℞. D(EI) G(RA); *mm.* -/WS, WS	175	400
2311	**Halfcrown,** *London.* Similar to 2288; *mm.* 56, 56/-	135	300
2312	— — with annulet on inner circle *mm.* 56	145	325
2313	*Southwark.* As 2311; *mm.* S	170	375
2314	— *O.* hЄnRIC 8 ROSA SINЄ SPIn. ℞. DЄI GRA, etc.; *mm.* Є	235	550
2315	*Bristol. O.* RVTILAn S, etc. ℞. hЄnRIC 8; *mm.* WS/-	260	450

For other gold coins in Henry's name see page 159.

SILVER

First coinage, 1509-26

2316 2327

2316	**Groat.** Portrait of Hen. VII. *London mm.* 53, 69, 108, 108 over 135...50	120	
2317	— *Tournai; mm.* crowned T. ℞. CIVITAS TORnACЄn*	200	500
2318	**Halfgroat.** Portrait of Hen. VII. London; *mm.* 108, 108/-	75	180
2319	— *Canterbury,* Archb. Warham. POSVI *rev.*; *mm.* rose	70	180
2320	— — — WA above shield; *mm.* martlet	40	110
2321	— — — WA beside shield; *mm.* cross fitchee	40	120
2322	— — CIVITAS CAnTOR *rev.,* similar; *mm.* 73, 105, 11/105	35	100
2323	— *York,* POSVI *rev.,* Archb. Bainbridge (1508-14). Keys below shield; *mm.* martlet	45	120
2324	— — — XB beside shield no keys; *mm.* martlet	55	135
2325	— — — Archb. Wolsey (1514-30). Keys and cardinal's hat below shield; *mm.* 94, 22	80	170
2326	— — CIVITAS ЄBORACI *rev.* Similar; *mm.* 22, 23, 30, 78, 15, 15/78	40	80
2327	— — As last with TW beside shield; *mm.* voided cross	60	125
2327A	— *Tournai.* As 2317	*Unique*	

*Other non-portrait groats and half-groats exist of this mint, captured during an invasion of France in 1513. (Restored to France in 1518.)

2332 2335 2336

		F £	VF £
2328	**Penny,** 'Sovereign' type, *London; mm.* 69, 108 /-	30	70
2329	— *Canterbury*. WA above shield; *mm.* martlet	70	150
2330	— — — WA beside shield; *mm.* 73/-	45	90
2331	— *Durham,* Bp. Ruthall (1509-23). TD above shield; *mm.* lis	25	60
2332	— — — TD beside shield; *mm.* lis, radiant star	25	55
2333	— — Bp. Wolsey (1523-9). DW beside shield, cardinal's hat below; spur rowel	100	225
2334	**Halfpenny.** Facing bust, hEnRIC DI GRA REX (AGL). *London; mm.* 69, 108/-	25	60
2335	— *Canterbury*. WA beside bust; *mm.* 73/-, 11	75	160
2335A	— **York**. Key below bust, *mm.* star.	*Extremely rare*	
2336	**Farthing.** *mm.* 108/-, hEnRIC DI GRA REX, portcullis. R. CIVITAS LOnDON, rose in centre of long cross	350	800

Second coinage, 1526-44

2337 2337 D 2337 E

		F £	VF £
2337	**Groat.** His own young portrait. *London;* bust r., with heavy jowls; *mm.* rose, mainly Roman letters, both sides, roses in cross ends	150	325
2337A	— Obv. as last. R. Lombardic letters, saltires in cross ends; *mm.* rose	100	225
2337B	Bust as 2337 but Lombardic letters. R. Lombardic letters but roses in cross ends; *mm.* rose	90	175
2337C	— *Obv.* as last. R. As 2337A; *mm.* rose	55	110
2337D	Second bust, Greek profile, longer hair, less heavy jowls; *mm.* rose ...	40	95
2337E	Third bust, stereotyped as ill. *mm.* 33-53 (muling occurs)	35	85
2338	— — with Irish title HIB; larger flan, saltires in cross ends; *mm.* 53, 105 53/105, 105/53,	225	550
2339	— *York*, Archb. Wolsey. TW beside shield, cardinal's hat below; *mm.* voided cross, acorn, muled (both ways)	65	140
2340	— — — omits TW; *mm.* voided cross	150	375

Second coinage silver

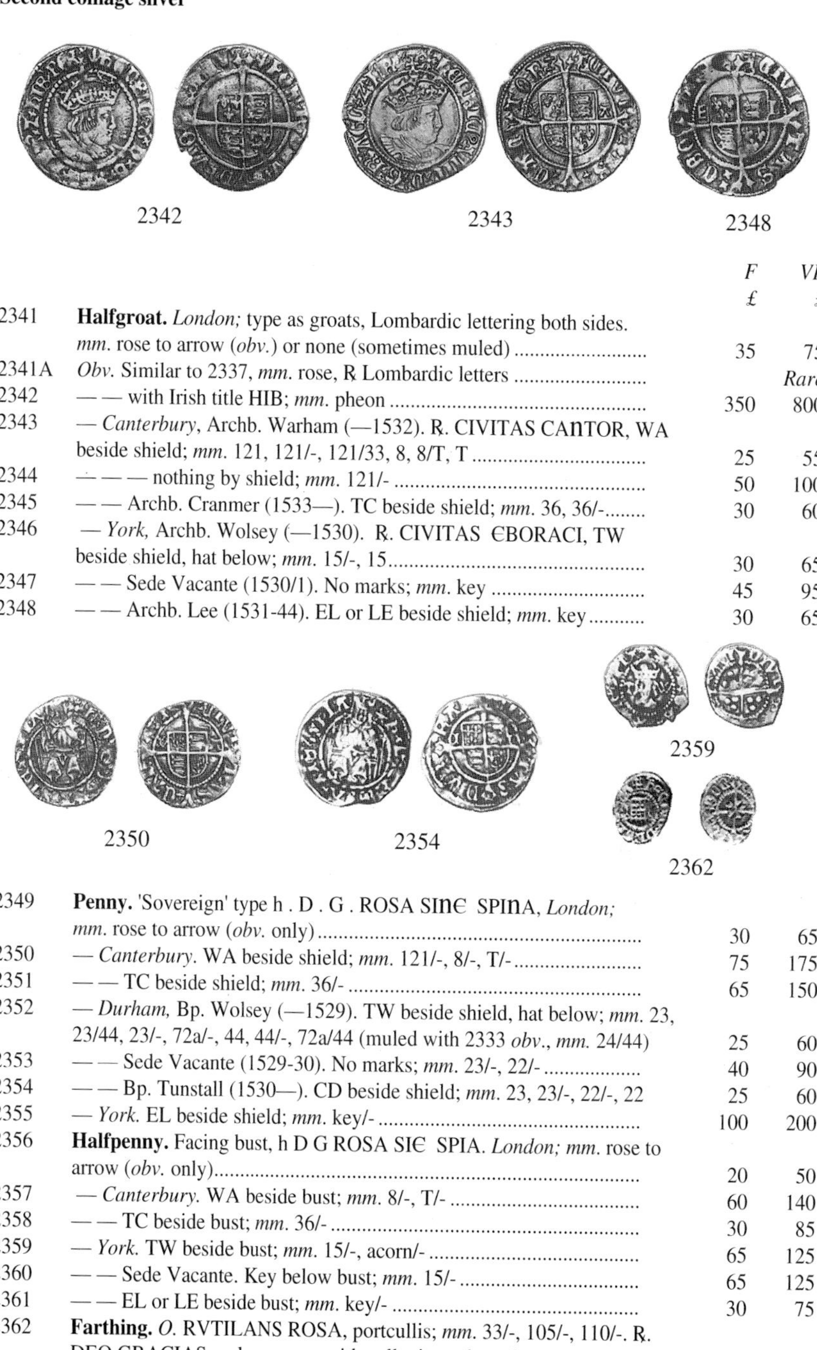

2342 2343 2348

No.		F £	VF £
2341	**Halfgroat.** *London;* type as groats, Lombardic lettering both sides. *mm.* rose to arrow (*obv.*) or none (sometimes muled)	35	75
2341A	*Obv.* Similar to 2337, *mm.* rose, ℞ Lombardic letters		*Rare*
2342	— — with Irish title HIB; *mm.* pheon	350	800
2343	— *Canterbury*, Archb. Warham (—1532). ℞. CIVITAS CANTOR, WA beside shield; *mm.* 121, 121/-, 121/33, 8, 8/T, T	25	55
2344	— — — nothing by shield; *mm.* 121/-	50	100
2345	— — Archb. Cranmer (1533—). TC beside shield; *mm.* 36, 36/-	30	60
2346	— *York,* Archb. Wolsey (—1530). ℞. CIVITAS EBORACI, TW beside shield, hat below; *mm.* 15/-, 15	30	65
2347	— — Sede Vacante (1530/1). No marks; *mm.* key	45	95
2348	— — Archb. Lee (1531-44). EL or LE beside shield; *mm.* key	30	65

2359

2350 2354

2362

No.		F £	VF £
2349	**Penny.** 'Sovereign' type h . D . G . ROSA SINE SPINA, *London; mm.* rose to arrow (*obv.* only)	30	65
2350	— *Canterbury.* WA beside shield; *mm.* 121/-, 8/-, T/-	75	175
2351	— — TC beside shield; *mm.* 36/-	65	150
2352	— *Durham,* Bp. Wolsey (—1529). TW beside shield, hat below; *mm.* 23, 23/44, 23/-, 72a/-, 44, 44/-, 72a/44 (muled with 2333 *obv., mm.* 24/44)	25	60
2353	— — Sede Vacante (1529-30). No marks; *mm.* 23/-, 22/-	40	90
2354	— — Bp. Tunstall (1530—). CD beside shield; *mm.* 23, 23/-, 22/-, 22	25	60
2355	— *York.* EL beside shield; *mm.* key/-	100	200
2356	**Halfpenny.** Facing bust, h D G ROSA SIE SPIA. *London; mm.* rose to arrow (*obv.* only)	20	50
2357	— *Canterbury.* WA beside bust; *mm.* 8/-, T/-	60	140
2358	— — TC beside bust; *mm.* 36/-	30	85
2359	— *York.* TW beside bust; *mm.* 15/-, acorn/-	65	125
2360	— — Sede Vacante. Key below bust; *mm.* 15/-	65	125
2361	— — EL or LE beside bust; *mm.* key/-	30	75
2362	**Farthing.** *O.* RVTILANS ROSA, portcullis; *mm.* 33/-, 105/-, 110/-. ℞. DEO GRACIAS...., long cross with pellet in each angle	350	750
2363	— — *mm.* arrow/- ℞. DEO GRACIAS, rose on long cross	450	925
2363A	— *Canterbury.* O. Similar. ℞. Similar. *mm.* 36/-		*Extremely rare*

Third coinage, 1544-7 (Silver progressively debased. 9oz (2dwt), 6oz (2dwt) 4oz (dwt)).

2364 2365

		Fair	Fine	VF
2364	**Testoon.** *Tower.* hENRIC'. VIII, etc. R. Crowned rose between h and R.POSVI, etc.; *mm.* lis, lis and 56, lis/two lis	130	425	1100
2365	— hENRIC 8, *mm.* 105 and 56, 105/56, 105 and 56/56, 56	130	400	1000
2366	— — annulet on inner circle of rev. or both sides; *mm.* pellet in annulet	140	450	1100
2367	*Southwark.* As 2365. R. CIVITAS LONDON; *mm.* S, E, S/E, E/S	120	400	1000
2368	*Bristol. Mm.*-/WS monogram. (Tower or local dies.)	175	500	1250

2384 Bust 1 Bust 2 Bust 3

2369	**Groat.** *Tower.* As ill. above, busts 1, 2, 3; *mm.* lis/-, lis	45	145
2369A	Bust 1, R. As second coinage; i.e. saltires in forks; *mm.* lis	75	195
2370	Bust 2 or 3 annulet on inner circle, both sides or rev. only	65	185
2371	*Southwark.* As 2367, busts 1, 2, 3, 4; no *mm.* or lis/-; S or S and E or E in forks	55	160
2372	*Bristol. Mm.*-/WS monogram, Bristol bust and Tower bust 2 or 3	60	170
2373	*Canterbury.* Busts 1, 2, (2 var); no *mm*, or lis/–	60	160
2374	*York.* Busts 1 var., 2, 3, no *mm.*	60	150
2375	**Halfgroat.** *Tower.* As 2365, bust 1; *mm.* lis, none	75	150
2376	*Southwark.* As 2367, bust 1; no *mm.*; S or E and S in forks	175	300
2377	*Bristol. Mm.*-/WS monogram	55	160
2378	*Canterbury.* Bust 1; no *mm.*	40	125
2379	*York.* Bust 1; no *mm.*	50	150
2380	**Penny.** *Tower.* Facing bust; no *mm.* or lis/-	45	115
2381	*Southwark.* Facing bust; *mm.* S/-, E/-, -/E	150	250
2382	*Bristol.* Facing bust; no *mm.* (Tower dies or local but truncated at neck)	45	110
2383	*Canterbury.* Facing bust; no *mm.*	45	115
2384	*York.* Facing bust; no *mm.*	45	110
2385	**Halfpenny.** *Tower.* Facing bust; no *mm.* or lis/-, pellet in annulet in *rev.* centre	35	125
2386	*Bristol.* Facing bust; no *mm.*	70	185
2387	*Canterbury.* Facing bust; no *mm.*, (some read H 8)	35	125
2388	*York.* Facing bust; no *mm.*	35	125
2388A	**Farthing** *obv.* Rose. R. Cross and pellets (as 2362)	*Extremely rare*	

These coins were struck during the reign of Edward VI but bear the name and portrait of Henry VIII, except in the case of the half-sovereigns which bear the youthful head of Edward.

Mintmarks

56 105 52 K E 116

66 115 33 122 t 94

1547	Annulet and pellet (56)	1549	TC monogram (115, *Bristol*)
1547-8	Lis (105)		Lis (105, *Canterbury*)
1547-9	Arrow (52)		Rose (33, *Canterbury*)
	K		Grapple (122)
	Roman E (*Southwark*)	1549/50	t (*Canterbury*)
	WS monogram (116, *Bristol*)	1550/1	Martlet (94)
1548-9	Bow (66, *Durham House*)		

GOLD

		F	*VF*
		£	£
2389	**Sovereign** (20 c), *London*. As no. 2290, but Roman lettering; *mm*. lis	1750	4250
2390	— *Bristol*. Similar but *mm*. WS	2000	4750

2391

2391A

2395

		F £	VF £
2391	**Half-sovereign.** As 2294, but with youthful portrait with sceptre. *Tower; mm.* 52, 105, 94 (various combinations)	225	550
2391A	— Similar but no sceptre; *mm.* 52, 52/56	250	600
2392	— — — K below shield; *mm.*-/K, none,. E/-	240	575
2393	— — — grapple below shield; *mm.* 122, none, 122/-, -/122	250	600
2394	— *Southwark. Mm.* E, E/-, -/E, Є /E. Usually Є or E (sometimes retrograde) below shield (sceptre omitted; *mm.* -/E)	225	550
2394A	— — — ℞. As 2296; *mm.*-/S	225	600
2395	**Crown.** Similar to 2305. *London; mm.* 52, 52/-, -/K, 122, 94, K	275	600
2396	— Similar but transposed legends without numeral; *mm.* -/arrow	375	775
2396A	— As 2395, but omitting RVTILANS; *mm.* arrow	*Extremely rare*	
2396B	Similar, but RVTILANS both sides; *mm.* arrow	*Extremely rare*	
2397	— *Southwark.* Similar to 2396; *mm.* E	*Extremely rare*	
2398	— — King's name on *obv.*; *mm.* E/-, E, -/E	400	800
2399	**Halfcrown.** Similar to 2311. *London; mm.* 52, K/[illegible]122/-, 94, -/52	250	600
2399A	As last but E over h on *rev.*, *mm.* 56/52	*Extremely rare*	
2399B	As 2399 but RUTILANS etc. on both sides, *mm.* arrow	*Extremely rare*	
2400	— *Southwark. Mm.* E, E/-, -/E	250	600

SILVER

AR (4oz .333)		*Fair*	F	VF
2401	**Testoon.** *Tower.* As 2365 with lozenge stops one side; -/56, 56	160	575	—
2402	*Southwark.* As 2367; *mm.* S/E	170	600	—

Bust 4

Bust 5

Bust 6

Some of the Bristol testoons, groats and halfgroats with WS monogram were struck after the death of Henry VIII but cannot easily be distinguished from those struck during his reign.

		F	VF
2403	**Groat.** *Tower.* Busts 4, 5, 6 (and, rarely, 2). ℞. POSVI, etc.; *mm.* 105-94 and none (frequently muled)	50	160
2404	*Southwark.* Busts 4, 5, 6. ℞. CIVITAS LONDON; no *mm.* -/E; lis/-, -/lis, K/E; roses or crescents or S and Є in forks, or rarely annulets	55	170
2405	*Durham House.* Bust 6. ℞. REDDE CVIQUE QVOD SVVM EST; *mm.* bow	125	350
2406	*Bristol. Mm.* WS on *rev.* Bristol busts A and B, Tower bust 2 and 3	55	185
2407	— — *Mm.* TC on *rev.* Similar, Bristol bust B	90	275
2408	*Canterbury.* Busts 5, 6; no *mm.* or rose/-	50	150
2409	*York.* Busts 4, 5, 6; no *mm.* or lis/-, -/lis	60	170
2410	**Halfgroat.** Bust 1. *Tower.* POSVI, etc.; *mm.* 52, 52/-, 52/K , -/K, 52/122, 122, -/122	35	110
2411	— *Southwark.* CIVITAS LONDON; *mm.* E, -/E, none, 52/E, K/E	30	100

		F	VF
		£	£
2412	**Halfgroat.** *Durham House.* ℞. REDD, etc.; *mm.* bow, -/bow	250	500
2413	— *Bristol. Mm.* WS on *rev.*	40	120
2414	— — *mm.* TC on *rev.*	60	160
2415	— *Canterbury.* No *mm.* or t/-, -/t, (mms with t are rare)	30	90
2416	— *York.* No *mm.*, bust 1 and three quarter facing	50	150

2418 2422 2427

2417	**Penny.** *Tower.* CIVI TAS LONDON. Facing bust; *mm.* 52/-, -/52, -/K, 122/-, -/122, none	35	100
2418	— — three-quarter bust; no *mm.*	35	100
2419	*Southwark.* As 2417; *mm.* E, -/E	75	225
2420	*Durham House.* As groat but shorter legend; *mm.* -/bow	175	450
2421	*Bristol.* Facing busts, as 2382 but showing more body, no *mm.*	40	140
2422	*Canterbury.* Similar to 2417	30	100
2423	— three-quarters facing bust; no *mm.*	35	120
2424	*York.* Facing bust; no *mm.*	40	110
2425	— three-quarters facing bust; no *mm.*	40	125
2426	***Halfpenny.** *Tower.* 52?, none	30	110
2427	*Canterbury.* No *mm.*, sometimes reads H8	50	125
2428	*York.* No *mm.*	40	115

* *Full weight only, 5gr.*

Coinage in his own name

The 4 oz. 2.5dwt coins of Henry VIII and those issued under Edward in 1547 and 1548 caused much disquiet, yet at the same time government was prevented by continuing financial necessity from abandoning debasement. A stratagem was devised which entailed increasing the fineness of silver coins, thereby making them appear sound, while at the same time reducing their weight in proportion so that in practice they contained no more silver than hitherto. The first issue, ordered on 24 January 1549, at 8 oz.2 dwt. fine produced a shilling which, at 60 gr., was so light that it was rapidly discredited and had to be replaced in April by another at 6 oz. 2 dwt. Weighing 80 gr., these later shillings proved acceptable.

In 1551 there was a brief issue of the worst silver coins of all, 3 oz.2 dwt. fine at 72 s. per lb, before retrenchment came: first, by a 50 per cent devaluation of silver, and, second, by the issue of a fine standard. At 11 oz. 1 dwt. 'out of the fire' this was the equivalent of 11 oz. 3 dwt. at the comixture, which meant that since sterling was only 11 oz. or 2 dwt. this issue which contained four new denominations - the crown, half crown, sixpence and threepence - was in effect the finest ever issued under the Tudors. Some pennies continued to be struck in base silver.

The first dates on English coinage during this reign appear in Roman Numerals i.e. - MDXLVIII = 1548, MDXLIX = 1549, MDL = 1550, MDLI = 1551. In the fine issue the dates on the crown and half crown are in Arabic. However these would not have been struck between April and August 1551, when the 0.25 fine shillings were made. Therefore the base penny and halfpenny of the third period were issued after the two devaluations and were issued as halfpennies and farthings respectively. The base 'penny' and 'halfpenny' of the third period were issued after the two devaluations for use as half pence and farthings respectively.

Mintmarks

66 52 35 115 E 53 122

t T 111 Y 126 94 91A

92 105 y 97 123 78 26

1548-9	Bow (66, *Durham House*)	1550	Martlet (94)
1549	Arrow (52)	1550	Leopard's head (91A)
	Grapple (122)	1550-1	Lion (92)
	Rose (35, *Canterbury*)		Lis (105, *Southwark*)
	TC monogram (115, *Bristol*)		Rose (33)
	Roman E (*Southwark*)	1551	Y or y (117, *Southwark*)
	Pheon (53)		Ostrich's head (97, gold only)
	t or T (*Canterbury*)	1551-3	Tun (123)
1549-50	Swan (111)		Escallop (78)
	Roman Y (*Southwark*)	1552-3	Pierced mullet (26, *York*)
1549-50	6 (126 gold only)		

GOLD

First period, Apr. 1547-Jan. 1549

2429 2431

		F £	VF £
2429	**Half-sovereign** (20 c). As 2391, but reading EDWARD 6. Tower; *mm.* arrow	400	850
2430	— *Southwark* (Sometimes with E or Є below shield); *mm.* E	350	750
2431	**Crown.** RVTILANS, etc., crowned rose between ER both crowned. ℞. EDWARD 6, etc., crowned shield between ER both crowned; *mm.* arrow, E over arrow/-	*Extremely rare*	
2431A	— *Obv.* as last. ℞. As 2305, *mm.* 52/56	*Extremely rare*	
2432	**Halfcrown.** Similar to 2431, but initials not crowned; *mm.* arrow	*Extremely rare*	

Second period, Jan. 1549-Apr. 1550

2433

2433	**Sovereign** (22 ct). As illustration; *mm.* arrow, –/arrow, Y,	1600	3000

2435 2438

		F £	VF £
2434	**Half-sovereign.** Uncrowned bust. *London.* TIMOR etc., MDXLIX on *obv. mm.* arrow	*Extremely rare*	
2435	— — SCVTVM, etc., as illustration; *mm.* arrow, **6,** Y	375	950
2436	— *Durham House.* Uncrowned, 1/2 length bust with MDXLVIII at end of *obv.* legend; *mm.* bow; SCVTVM etc.	*Extremely rare*	
2437	— Normal, uncrowned bust. LVCERNA, etc., on *obv.; mm.* bow	*Extremely rare*	
2438	— Crowned bust. *London.* EDWARD VI, etc. R. SCVTVM, etc.; *mm.* 52, 122, 111/52, 111, Y, 94	350	850
2439	— *Durham House.* Crowned, half-length bust; *mm.* bow	*Unique*	
2440	— — King's name on *obv.* and *rev.; mm.* bow (mule of 2439/37)	4000	7500

2441

2444

**Small denominations often occur creased or straightened.*

		F £	VF £
2441	**Crown.** Uncrowned bust, as 2435; *mm.* 6, Y, 52/-, Y/-	600	1300
2442	— Crowned bust, as 2438; *mm.* 52, 122, 111, Y (usually *obv.* only)	475	1000
2443	**Halfcrown.** Uncrowned bust; R. As 2441, *mm.* arrow, Y, Y/-, 52/-	550	1100
2444	— Crowned bust, as illus. above; *mm.* 52, 52/111, 111, 122, Y, Y/-	450	900
2445	— Similar, but king's name on *rev., mm.* 52, 122	550	1000

Third period, 1550-3

		F £	VF £
2446	**'Fine' sovereign** (30s.). King on throne; *mm.* 97, 123	7500	17,500
2447	**Double sovereign.** From the same dies, *mm.* 97 (a well struck *VF* specimen fetched £80000 in auction, May 1994)	*Extremely rare*	

2448

2451

2448	**Angel** (10s.). As illustration; *mm.* 97, 123	3500	7000
2449	**Half-angel.** Similar, *mm.* 97		*Unique*
2450	**Sovereign**. (=20s.). Half-length figure of king r., crowned and holding sword and orb. ℞. Crowned shield with supporters; *mm.* y, tun	800	1900
2451	**Half-sovereign**. As illustration above; *mm.* y, tun	475	1100
2452	**Crown**. Similar, but *rev.* SCVTVM etc., *mm.* y, tun	650	1500
2453	**Halfcrown**. Similar, *mm.* tun, y	650	1500

SILVER

2459 2460

First period, Apr. 1547-Jan. 1549

		F £	*VF* £
2454	**Groat.** Cr. bust r. *Tower.* ℞. Shield over cross, POSVI, etc.; *mm.* arrow.	300	700
2455	— As last, but EDOARD 6, *mm.* arrow	350	800
2456	— *Southwark. Obv.* as 2454. ℞. CIVITAS LONDON; *mm.*-/E or none, somethimes S in forks	350	800
2457	**Halfgroat**. *Tower. Obv.* as 2454; *mm.* arrow	350	750
2458	*Southwark.* As 2456; *mm.* arrow, E	350	750
2459	*Canterbury.* Similar. No *mm.*, also reads EDOARD (as ill.)	175	475
2460	**Penny**. *Tower.* As halfgroat, but E.D.G. etc. ℞. CIVITAS LONDON; *mm.* arrow	200	575
2461	— *Southwark.* As last, but *mm.* -/E.	250	750
2462	*Bristol.* Similar, but reads ED6DG or E6DG no *mm.*	200	550
2463	**Halfpenny**. *Tower. O.* As 2460, *mm.* E (?). ℞. Cross and pellets	300	750
2464	— *Bristol.* Similar, no *mm.* but reads E6DG or EDG	225	550

Second period, Jan. 1549-Apr. 1550

At all mints except Bristol, the earliest shillings of 1549 were issued at only 60 grains but of 8 oz. 2 dwt standard. This weight and size were soon increased to 80 grains., (S.2466 onwards), but the fineness was reduced to 6 oz. 2 dwt so the silver content remained the same.

2465

2467

		F £	VF £
60 gr; 8oz. 2 dwt.			
2465	**Shilling**. *Tower*. Broad bust with large crown. *Obv*. TIMOR etc. MDXLIX. ℞. Small, oval garnished shield dividing ER. EDWARD VI etc., *mm*. 52, no *mm*; slight bust var. *mm*, –/52	120	300
2465A	*Southwark*. As last, *mm*. Y, EY/Y	125	350
2465B	*Canterbury*. As last, *mm*. -/rose		*Rare*
80 gr; 6oz. 2 dwt.			
2466	*Tower*. Tall, narrow bust with small crown. *Obv*. EDWARD VI etc. MDXLIX or MDL. ℞. As 2465 but TIMOR etc., *mm*. 52-91a (frequently muled)	80	225
2466A	— *Obv*. as last, MDXLIX. ℞. Heavily garnished shield, Durham House style. *mm*. grapple	140	325
2466B	*Southwark*. As 2466, *mm*. Y, Y/swan	80	225
2466C	— — — ℞. as 2466A. *mm*. Y	140	325
2467	*Bristol*. *Obv*. similar to 2466. ℞. Shield with heavy curved garniture or as 2466, *mm*. TC/rose TC, rose TC	600	1250
2468	*Canterbury*. As 2466, *mm*. T, T/t, t/T	100	275
2469	*Durham House*. Bust with elaborate tunic and collar TIMOR etc. MDXLIX. ℞. Oval shield, very heavily garnished in different style. EDWARD VI etc., *mm*. bow	250	500

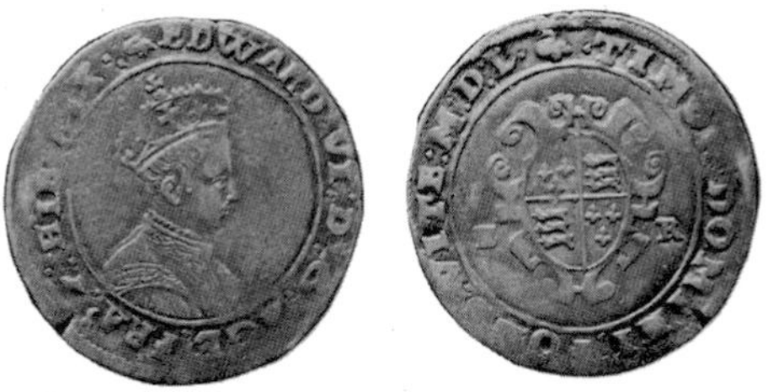

2466 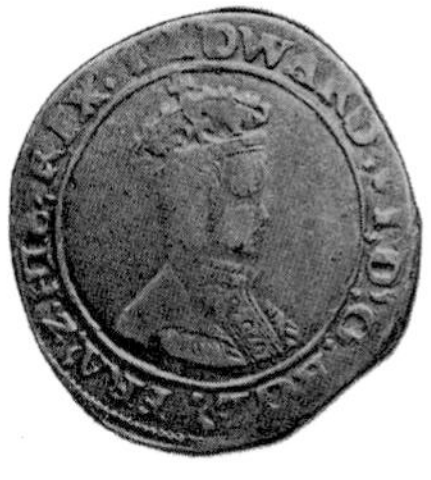 2468

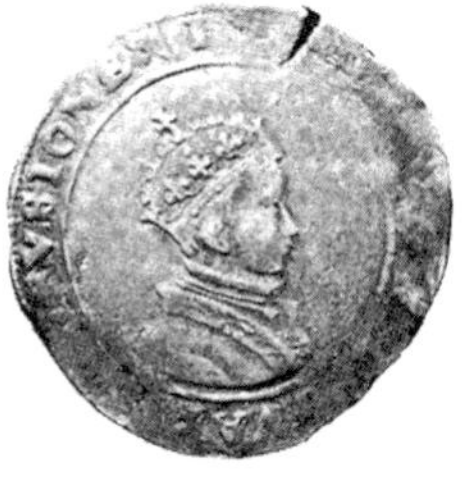

2470 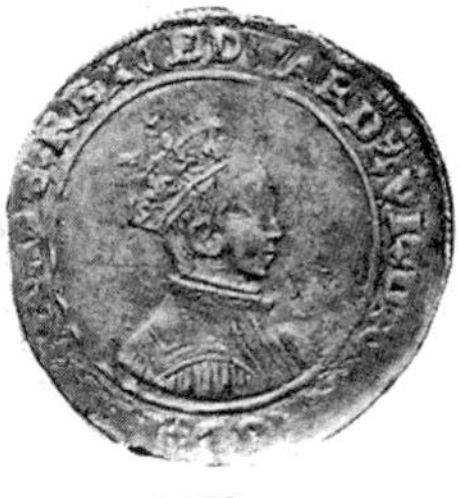 2472 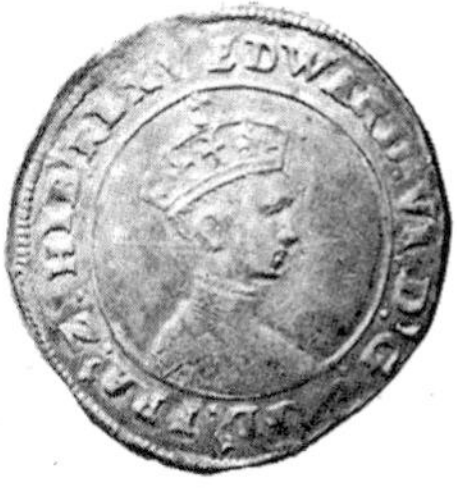 2472C

		F £	VF £
2470	— Bust as last. INIMICOS etc., no date. ℞. EDWARD etc.	175	450
2471	— — As last, but legends transposed	250	600
2472	— Bust similar to 2466. EDWARD VI etc. ℞. INIMICOS etc.	150	400
2472A	As last but legends transposed	225	500
2472B	*Tower*. Elegant bust with extremely thin neck. ℞. As 2466, *mm*. martlett	135	375
2472C	*Southwark*. As last, *mm*. Y	135	375

For coins of Edward VI countermarked, see p. 171

Third period, 1550-3

Very base issue (1551) 3oz. 2 dwt.

2473 2475

		F	VF
		£	£
2473	**Shilling**, *Tower*. As 2472B. MDL or MDLI, *mm.* lion, rose, lion/rose ...	125	350
2473A	*Southwark*. As last, *mm.* lis/Y, Y/lis, lis ...	125	350
2474	**Base Penny**. *London. O.* Rose. ℞. Shield; *mm.* escallop (*obv.*)...	60	135
2475	— — *York. Mm.* mullet (*obv.*) as illustration...	50	110
2476	**Base Halfpenny**. As penny, but single rose ...	175	350

* The base penny and halfpenny were used as halfpenny and farthing respectively.

Fine silver issue, (1551-3) 11oz. 3 dwt.

2478

2478	**Crown**. King on horseback with date below horse. ℞. Shield on cross; *mm.* y. 1551; tun, 1551-3 (1553, wire line inner circle may be missing)	225	475

2479

2479	**Halfcrown**. Walking horse with plume; *mm.* y, 1551 ...	150	375

		F £	VF £
2480	Galloping horse without plume; *mm*. tun, 1551-3	165	500
2481	Large walking horse without plume; *mm*. tun, 1553	450	1000

2482

2483

2482	**Shilling**. Facing bust, rose l., value XII r. *mm*. y, tun (several bust varieties)	50	125
2483	**Sixpence**. *London*. Similar, as illustration; *mm*. y/-, -/y, y, tun (bust varieties)	55	135
2484	*York*. As last, but CIVITAS ЄBORACI; *mm*. mullet	90	225
2485	**Threepence**. *London*. As sixpence, but III; *mm*. tun	125	325

2486

2487A

2486	*York*. As 2484, but III by bust	175	475
2487	**Penny**. 'Sovereign' type; *mm*. tun	—	1400
2487A	**Farthing.** *O*. Portcullis, R Cross and Pellets (previously 2477)	*Extremely Rare*	

Mary brought English coins back to the sterling standard (11 oz. 'Out of the fire' = 11 oz. 2 dwt. at the comixture) and struck all her gold coins at the traditional fineness of 23 c. 3 $^{1}/_{2}$ gr. On the latter the mintmarks appear at the end of the first or second word of the legends.

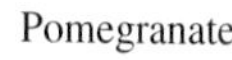  Half-rose (or half-rose and castle) 

GOLD

2488

		F £	VF £
2488	**'Fine' Sovereign** (30s.). Queen enthroned. ℞. Shield on rose, MDLIII, MDLIIII and undated, *mm.* pomegranate, half-rose (or mule)	1600	3400
2489	**Ryal** (15s.). As illus, MDLIII. ℞. As 1950 but A DNO etc. *mm.* pomegranate/-	—	13000
2490	**Angel** (10s.). Usual type; *mm.* pomegranate, half-rose, none? (Known with rose and M transposed)	500	1000
2491	**Half-angel**. Similar; *mm.* pomegranate, pomegranate/-	1650	4000

2489 2492

SILVER

2492	**Groat**. Crowned bust l. ℞. VЄRITAS, etc.; *mm.* pomegranate, pomegranate/-	60	150
2493	**Halfgroat**. Similar	500	1500
2494	**Penny**. Similar, but M. D. G. ROSA, etc.	350	900
2495	— As last. ℞. CIVITAS LONDON; no *mm.*	350	900
2495A	— Base penny. Similar to 2474 but M.D.G. etc.	*All late 19th cent. fabrications*	

PHILIP AND MARY, 1554-58

The groats and smaller silver coins of this period have Mary's portrait only, but the shillings and sixpences show the bust of the queen's husband, Philip of Spain.

Mintmarks

Lis (105) Half-rose and castle

GOLD

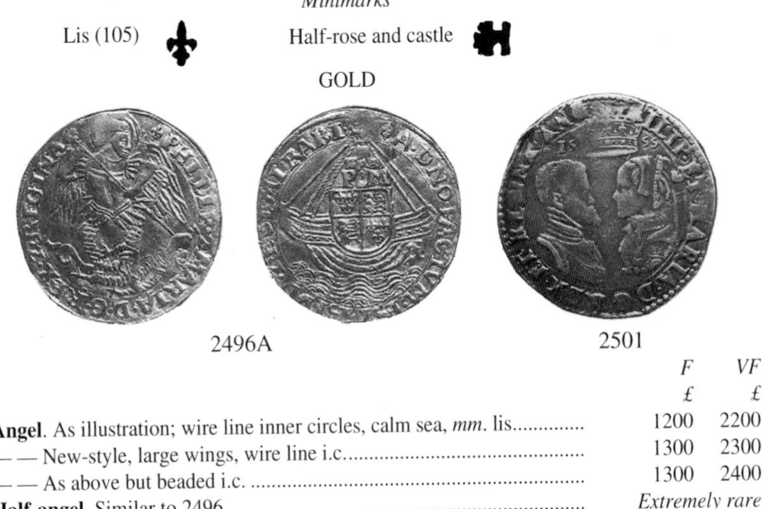

2496A 2501

No.	Description	Fair	F £	VF £
2496	**Angel**. As illustration; wire line inner circles, calm sea, *mm*. lis		1200	2200
2496A	— — New-style, large wings, wire line i.c.		1300	2300
2496B	— — As above but beaded i.c.		1300	2400
2497	**Half-angel**. Similar to 2496		*Extremely rare*	

SILVER

2505  2506  2510

No.	Description	Fair	F £	VF £
2498	**Shilling**. Busts face-to-face, full titles, undated, no *mm*.		135	400
2499	— — — also without mark of value		160	500
2500	— — 1554		135	400
2501	— English titles only 1554, 1555		150	450
2501A	— — undated			*Rare*
2502	— — without mark of value, 1554, 1555 (rare)		165	550
2503	— — date below bust, 1554, 1555	250	—	—
2504	— — As last, but without ANG., 1555	275	—	—
2505	**Sixpence**. Similar. Full titles, 1554 (and undated?)		125	375
2506	— English titles only, 1555 (no *mm*., rare), 1557 (*mm*. lis, 1557 only)		135	400
2506A	— As last but heavy beaded i.c. on obv. 1555. (Irish 4d. obv. mule)		250	600
2507	— — date below bust, 1554, 1557 (very rare)	200	—	—
2508	**Groat**. Crowned bust of Mary 1. ℞. POSUMVS etc.; *mm*. lis		60	160
2509	**Halfgroat**. Similar, but POSVIM, *mm*. lis		300	750
2510	**Penny**. Similar to 2495, but P. Z. M. etc.; *mm*. lis		250	650
2510A	**Base penny**. Similar to 2495A, but P. Z. M . etc.; *mm*. halved rose and castle or castle/–, (used as a halfpenny)		65	175

Similar pence of the York mint were made for currency in Ireland

Elizabeth's coinage is particularly interesting on account of the large number of different denominations issued. 'Crown' gold coins were again issued as well as the 'fine' gold denominations. In 1559 the base shillings of Edward VI's second and third coinages were called in and countermarked for recirculation at reduced values. Smaller debased coins were not only countermarked, but were also devalued. The old debased groat became a three halfpenny and other coins in proportion. The normal silver coinage was initially struck at .916 fineness as in the previous reign but between 1560 and 1577 and after 1582 the old sterling standard of .925 was restored. Between 1578 and 1582 the standard was slightly reduced and the weights were reduced by 1/32nd in 1601. Gold was similarly reduced slightly in quality 1578-82, and there was a slight weight reduction in 1601.

To help alleviate the shortage of small change, and to avoid the expense of minting an impossibly small silver farthing, a threefarthing piece was introduced to provide change if a penny was tendered for a farthing purchase. The sixpence, threepence, threehalfpence and threefarthings were marked with a rose behind the queen's head to distinguish them from the shilling, groat, half-groat and penny.

Coins of exceedingly fine workmanship were produced in a screw press introduced by Eloye Mestrelle, a French moneyer, in 1561. With parts of the machinery powered by a horse-drawn mill, the coins produced came to be known as 'mill money'. Despite the superior quality of the coins produced, the machinery was slow and inefficient compared to striking by hand. Mestrelle's dismissal was engineered in 1572 and six years later he was hanged for counterfeiting.

Mintmarks

106 21 94 23 53 33 107 92

74 71 77 65b 27 7 14

113 60 54 79 72b 86 123 124

90 57 0 1 2

1558-60	Lis (106)	1569-71	Castle (71)	1587-9	Crescent (72b)
1560-1	Cross crosslet (21)	1572-3	Ermine (77)	1590-2	Hand (86)
	Martlet (94)	1573-4	Acorn (65b)	1591-5	Tun (123)
1560-6	Star (23, milled)	1573-7	Eglantine (27)	1594-6	Woolpack (124)
1561-5	Pheon (53)	1578-9	Greek cross (7)	1595-8	Key (90)
1565	Rose (33)	1580-1	Latin cross (14)	1597-1600	Anchor (57)
1566	Portcullis (107)	1582	Sword (113)	1600	**0**
1566-7	Lion (92)	1582-3	Bell (60)	1601-2	**1**
1567-70	Coronet (74)	1582-4	A (54)	1602	**2**
	Lis (105, milled)	1584-6	Escallop (79)		

N.B. *The dates for* mms *sometimes overlap. This is a result of using up old dies, onto which the new mark was punched.*

GOLD

Hammered Coinage

First to Third issues, 1559-78. ('Fine' gold of .994. 'Crown' gold of .916 fineness. Sovereigns of 240 gr.). Mintmarks; lis to eglantine.

2512

		F £	VF £
2511	**'Fine' Sovereign** (30 s.) Queen enthroned, tressure broken by throne, reads Z not ET, no chains to portcullis. ℞. Arms on rose; *mm.* lis.	1700	4000
2512	—— Similar but ET, chains on portcullis; *mm.* crosslet	1600	3600
2513	**Angel**. St. Michael. ℞. Ship. Wire line inner circles; *mm.* lis.	350	800
2513A	— Similar, but beaded i.c. on *obv.*, *mm.* lis	325	725
2514	— — Similar, but beaded inner circles; ship to r.; *mm.* 106, 21, 74, 27,..	275	500
2515	— — — Similar, but ship to l.; *mm.* 77-27	300	550
2516	**Half Angel**. As 2513, wire line inner circles; *mm.* lis	*Extremely rare*	
2516A	— As last, but beaded i.c.s, legend ends. Z.HIB	500	1200
2517	— As 2514, beaded inner circles; *mm.* 106, 21, 74, 77-27	180	450
2518	**Quarter Angel**. Similar; *mm.* 74, 77-27	175	425

2513 2520A

		F £	VF £
2519	**Half Pound** (10 s.) Young crowned bust l. ℞. Arms. Wire line inner circles; *mm.* lis	700	1500
2520	— Similar, but beaded inner circles; *mm.* 21, 33-107	300	675
2520A	— — Smaller bust; *mm.* lion	350	800
2520B	— — Broad bust, ear visible; *mm.* 92, 74, 71	325	750
2521	**Crown**. As 2519; *mm.* lis	*Extremely rare*	
2522	— Similar to 2520; *mm.* 21, 33-107	250	575
2522A	— Similar to 2520B; *mm.* 74, 71, 92	275	650
2523	**Half Crown**. As 2519; *mm.* lis	—	2250
2524	— Similar to 2520; *mm.* 21, 33-107 (2 busts)	275	625
2524A	— Similar to 2520B; *mm.* 107-71	300	675

Fourth Issue, 1578-82 (`Fine' gold only of .992). *Mms* Greek cross, Latin cross and sword.

		F £	*VF* £
2525	**Angel**. As 2514; *mm*. 7, 14, 113	250	550
2526	**Half Angel**. As 2517; *mm*. 7, 14, 113	190	450
2527	— Similar, but without E and rose above ship; *mm*. latin cross	375	800
2528	**Quarter Angel**. As last; *mm*. 7, 14, 113	170	365

Fifth Issue, 1583-1600 (`Fine' gold of .979, `crown' gold of .916; pound of 174.5 grs. wt.). Mintmarks: bell to **O**.

2529

2530

2534

		F £	*VF* £
2529	**Sovereign** (30 s:). As 2512, but tressure not normally broken by back of throne; *mm*. 54-123	1500	2900
2530	**Ryal** (15 s.). Queen in ship. ℞. Similar to 1950; *mm*. 54-86 (*rev*. only) ..	2500	6500
2531	**Angel**. As 2514; *mm*. 60-123, 90-**O**	250	525
2532	**Half Angel**. As 2517; *mm*. 60-86, 90-57	180	450
2533	**Quarter Angel**. As 2518; *mm*. 60-123, 90-57/–	165	375
2534	**Pound** (20 s.). Old bust l., with elaborate dress and profusion of hair; *mm*., lion and tun/tun, 123-**O**	600	1250
2535	**Half Pound**. Similar; *mm*. tun	450	775
2535A	— Similar but smaller bust with less hair; *mm*. 123-**O**	450	775
2536	**Crown**. Similar to 2534; *mm*. 123-90. **O**	300	625
2537	**Half Crown**. Similar; *mm*. -/123, 123-0, **O**	250	575

Sixth Issue, 1601-3 ('Fine' gold of .994, 'crown' gold of .916; Pound of 172 gr.). Mintmarks: **1** and **2**

		F £	VF £
2538	**Angel**. As 2531; *mm.* **1, 2**	325	800
2539	**Pound**. As 2534; *mm.* **1, 2**	650	1400
2540	**Half Pound**. As 2535A; *mm.* **1, 2**	600	1200

2541

2541	**Crown**. As 2536; *mm.* **1, 2**		*Rare*
2542	**Half Crown**. As 2537; *mm.* **1, 2**		*Rare*

Milled Coinage, 1561-70

2543	**Half Pound**. Crowned bust l.; *mm.* star, lis	700	1700
2544	**Crown**. Similar; *mm.* star, lis	750	1800
2545	**Half Crown**. Similar; *mm.* star, lis	1100	2350

For further details on both AV and AR milled coinage, *see* D. G. Borden *'An introduction to the milled coinage of Elizabeth I'.* BNJ 1983

SILVER

Hammered Coinage

Countermarked Edward VI base shillings(1559)

2546

2547

		Fair £	F £
2546	**Fourpence-halfpenny**. Edward VI 2nd period 6oz and 8oz shillings .... cmkd on obv. with a portcullis; *mm.* 66, –/33, 52, t, 111, Y and 122.......	525	1100
2547	**Twopence-farthing**. Edward VI 3rd period 3 oz. shillings countermarked on obverse with a seated greyhound; *mm.* 92. 105, 35 and 87	750	1400

N.B. *Occasionally the wrong countermark was used*

First Issue, 1559-60 (.916 fine, shillings of 96 grs.)

2548 2549

		F £	VF £
2548	**Shilling**. Without rose or date. ELIZABET(H), wire line inner circles, pearls on bodice (three similar busts); *mm.* lis.	250	600
2549	— Similar, ELIZABETH, wire line and beaded inner circles, no pearls on bodice (several busts); *mm.* lis	100	325

2556 2551 2555

2550	**Groat**. Without rose or date, wire line or no inner circles (two busts); *mm.* lis	100	250
2551	— Similar, wire line and beaded inner circles, large bust; circles *mm.* lis	40	110
2551A	— — Small bust and shield (from halfgroat punches); *mm.* lis	100	250
2552	**Halfgroat**. Without rose or date, wire line inner circles; *mm.* lis	150	350
2553	**Penny**. Without rose or date, wire line inner circles; *mm.* lis	165	400
2554	— Similar but dated 1558 on *obv.*; *mm.* lis	—	1500

Second Issue, 1560-1 (.925 fineness, shilling of 96 gr.)

2555	**Shilling**. Without rose or date, beaded inner circles. ET instead of Z (several bust varieties); *mm.* 21, 94	50	160
2555A	— large bust with pearls on bodice as 2548; *mm.* 21, 94	60	200
2556	**Groat**. Without rose or date, bust as 2551; *mm.* 21, 94	25	60
2557	**Halfgroat**. Without rose or date; *mm.* 21, 94	30	65
2558	**Penny**. Without rose or date (three bust varieties); *mm.* 21, 94	15	35

Third Issue, 1561-77 (Same fineness and weight as last)

		F	*VF*
2559	**Sixpence**. With rose and date, large flan (27 *mm.* or more), large bust with hair swept back, 1561; *mm.* pheon	130	300

2560

2561

2560	— Similar, small bust, 1561; *mm.* pheon	40	125
2561	— Smaller flan (26.5 *mm.*). Small regular bust, 1561-6; *mm.* 53-107	25	65
2561A	— Similar, without rose, 1561; *mm.* pheon	*Extremely rare*	
2561B	— Similar, very large bust, with rose, 1563-5; *mm.* pheon	50	150

2562

2563

2562	— Intermediate bust, ear shows, 1566-74; *mm.* 92-65b (also 1567 *mm.* 71/74)	25	65
2562A	— Similar, without date; *mm.* lion, coronet, ermine	*Extremely rare*	
2563	— Larger bust, 1573-7; *mm.* 77-27	25	65
2564	**Threepence**. With rose and date 1561, large flan (20.5 *mm.*); *mm.* pheon	25	75
2565	— smaller flan (19 *mm.*). Regular bust, 1561-7; *mm.* 53-92	20	50
2566	— taller bust, ear shows, 1566-77; *mm.* 92-27, 27/-, 27/65b	20	50
2566A	— Similar, without rose, 1568; *mm.* coronet	*Unique*	

2567

2571

2567	**Halfgroat**. Without rose or date; *mm.* 107-71	35	85
2568	**Threehalfpence**. With rose and date 1561, large flan (17 *mm.*) *mm.* pheon	30	75
2569	— — Smaller flan (16 *mm.*); 1561-2, 1564-70, 1572-7; *mm.* 53-107, 74-27	20	55
2570	**Penny**. Without rose or date; *mm.* 33-71, 65b-27, 33/107, 92/107, 74/107	20	50
2571	**Threefarthings**. With rose and date 1561-2, 1568, 1572-7; *mm.* 53, 74, 77-27	40	120

		F £	VF £

Fourth Issue, 1578-82 (.921 fineness, shilling of 95.6 gr.)

2572

		F	VF
2572	**Sixpence**. As 2563, 1578-82; *mm*. 7-113, 14/113, 14/7	25	65

2573 2575

		F	VF
2573	**Threepence**. As 2566, 1578-82; *mm*. 7-113	20	50
2574	**Threehalfpence**. As 2569, 1578-9, 1581-2; *mm*. 7-113	20	55
2575	**Penny**. As 2570; *mm*. 7-113, 7/14, 14/7	20	45
2576	**Threefarthings**. As 2571, 1578-9, 1581-2; *mm*. 7-113	40	130

Fifth Issue, 1582-1600 (.925 fineness, shilling of 96 gr.)

2577

2578A

2580

2581

		F	VF
2577	**Shilling**. Without rose or date, ELIZAB; ear concealed (two busts) *mm*. 60-72b, ear shows. *mm*. 79-**0** (mules occur)	40	135
2578	**Sixpence**. As 2572, ELIZABETH, 1582, 1583 *mm*. bell	30	75
2578A	— Similar, ELIZAB, 1582-1600; *mm*. 60-**0**, also 1583 *mm*. 79/54	25	65
2579	**Halfgroat**. Without rose or date, two pellets behind bust. R. CIVITAS LONDON; *mm*. 60-**0** (*mm*. bell sometimes without pellets)	12	35
2580	**Penny**. Without rose or date. R. CIVITAS LONDON; *mm*. 60-57, 90/-, 57/-, **0**/-	15	40
2581	**Halfpenny**. Portcullis. R. Cross and pellets; *mm*. none, 54-**0**	20	55

Sixth Issue, 1601-2 (.925 fineness, shilling of 93 gr.)

2582 2583

		F	*VF*
		£	£
2582	**Crown**. Similar to illustration of 2583; *mm*. **1, 2**	375	800
2583	**Halfcrown**. As illustration, *mm*. **1, 2**	225	500

2584

2592

2584	**Shilling**. As 2577; *mm*. **1, 2**	50	150
2585	**Sixpence**. As 2578A, 1601-2; *mm*. **1, 2**	30	85
2586	**Halfgroat**. As 2579, *mm*. **1, 2, 2/-**	15	50
2587	**Penny**. As 2580, *mm*. **1, 2, 2/-**	20	50
2588	**Halfpenny**. As 2581, *mm*. **1, 2**	20	65

Milled coinage

2589	**Shilling**. Without rose or date; *mm*. star. Plain dress, large size (over 31 *mm*.)	325	800
2590	— decorated dress, large size	130	400
2591	— — intermediate size (30-31 *mm*.)	80	250
2592	— — small size (under 30 *mm*.)	70	225

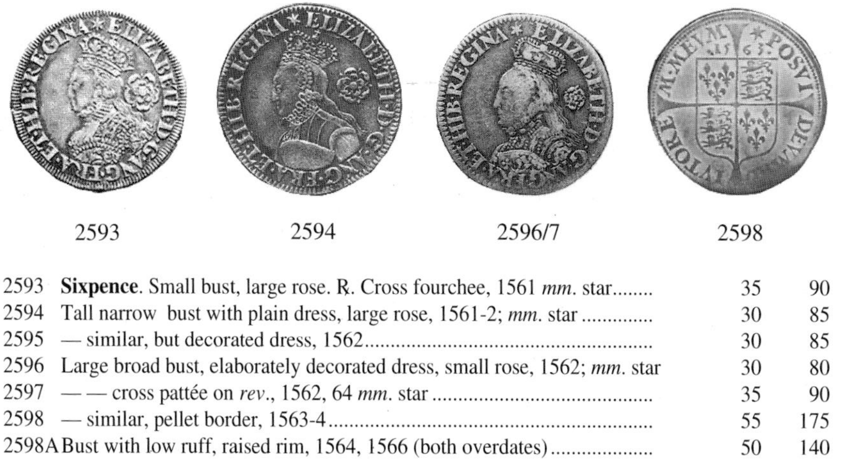

2593 2594 2596/7 2598

2593	**Sixpence**. Small bust, large rose. ℞. Cross fourchee, 1561 *mm.* star........	35	90
2594	Tall narrow bust with plain dress, large rose, 1561-2; *mm.* star	30	85
2595	— similar, but decorated dress, 1562...	30	85
2596	Large broad bust, elaborately decorated dress, small rose, 1562; *mm.* star	30	80
2597	— — cross pattée on *rev.*, 1562, 64 *mm.* star	35	90
2598	— similar, pellet border, 1563-4...	55	175
2598A	Bust with low ruff, raised rim, 1564, 1566 (both overdates)...................	50	140

2599 2600 2601

2599	Small bust, 1567-8, ℞. As 2593; *mm.* lis..	35	100
2600	Large crude bust breaking legend; 1570, *mm.* lis; 1571/0, *mm.* castle (over lis)	90	250
2601	**Groat**. As illustration..	75	275
2602	**Threepence**. With rose, small bust with plain dress, 1561	70	225
2603	Tall narrow decorated bust with medium rose, 1562..............................	50	165
2604	Broad bust with very small rose, 1562...	65	200
2605	Cross pattee on *rev.*, 1564/3..	125	350
2606	**Halfgroat**. As groat	70	235
2607	**Threefarthings**. E . D . G . ROSA, etc., with rose. ℞. CIVITAS LONDON, shield with 1563 above	*Extremely rare*	

Portcullis money

Trade coins of 8, 4, 2, and 1 Testerns were coined at the Tower Mint in 1600/1 for the first voyage of the incorporated 'Company of Merchants of London Trading into the East Indies'. The coins bear the royal arms on the obverse and a portcullis on the reverse and have the *mm.* **O**. They were struck to the weights of the equivalent Spanish silver 8, 4, 2 and 1 reales.

2607A

		£	£
2607A	Eight testerns	650	1400
2607B	Four testerns	375	725
2607C	Two testerns	400	800
2607D	One testern	300	700

THE HOUSE OF STUART AND THE COMMONWEALTH

JAMES I, 1603-25

With the accession of James VI of Scotland to the English throne, the royal titles and coat of arms are altered on the coinage; on the latter the Scottish rampant lion and the Irish harp now appear in the second and third quarters. In 1604 the weight of the gold pound was reduced and the new coin became known as the 'Unite'. Fine gold coins of 23 c. 3 1/2 carat and crown gold of 22 c. were both issued, and a gold four-shilling piece was struck 1604-19. In 1612 all the gold coins had their values raised by 10%; but in 1619 the Unite was replaced by a new, lighter 20s. piece, the 'Laurel', and a lighter rose-ryal, spur-ryal and angel were minted.

In 1613 the king granted Lord Harington a licence to coin farthings of copper as a result of repeated public demands for a low value coinage; this was later taken over by the Duke of Lenox. Towards the end of the reign coins made from silver sent to the mint from the Welsh mines had the Prince of Wales's plumes inserted over the royal arms.

Mintmarks

125 105 33 79 84 74 90

60  25 71 45 32 123 132

72b  7a 16 24 125  105 46

First coinage
1603-4 Thistle (125)
1604-5 Lis (105)

Second coinage
1604-5 Lis (105)
1605-6 Rose (33)
1606-7 Escallop (79)
1607 Grapes (84)
1607-9 Coronet (74)
1609-10 Key (90)
1610-11 Bell (60)
1611-12 Mullet (25)
1612-13 Tower (71)
1613 Trefoil (45)
1613-15 Cinquefoil (32)
1615-16 Tun (123)
1616-17 Book on lectern (132)
1617-18 Crescent (72b, gold)
1618-19 Plain cross (7a)
1619 Saltire cross (16, gold)

Third coinage
1619-20 Spur rowel (24)
1620-1 Rose (33)
1621-3 Thistle (125)
1623-4 Lis (105)
1624 Trefoil (46)

GOLD

2610 2612

First coinage, 1603-4 (Obverse legend reads D' . G' . ANG : SCO : etc.)

		F £	*VF* £
2608	**Sovereign** (20s.). King crowned r., half-length, first bust with plain armour. ℞. EXVRGAT, etc.; *mm.* thistle	600	1250
2609	— second bust with decorated armour; *mm.* thistle, lis	650	1400
2610	**Half-sovereign**. Crowned bust r. ℞. EXVRGAT, etc.; *mm.* thistle	1500	3500
2611	**Crown**. Similar. ℞. TVEATVR, etc.; *mm.* 125, 105/125	700	2000
2612	**Halfcrown**. Similar; *mm.* thistle, lis	200	550

N.B. *The Quarter-Angel of this coinage is considered to be a pattern (possibly a later strike), although coin weights are known.*

2613 2614

Second coinage, 1604-19 (Obverse legend reads D' G' MAG : BRIT : etc.)

		F £	*VF* £
2613	**Rose-ryal** (30s., 33s. from 1612). King enthroned. ℞. Shield on rose; *mm.* 33-90, 25-132	700	1500
2614	**Spur ryal** (15s., 16s. 6d. from 1612). King in ship; *mm.* 33, 79, 74, 25-32, 132	1500	3250
2615	**Angel** (10s., 11s. from 1612). Old type but larger shield; *mm.* 33-74, 60-16	400	800
2616	—— pierced for use as touch-piece	200	400
2617	**Half-angel** (5s., 5s. 6d. from 1612). Similar; *mm.* 71-132, 7a, 16	1300	3000

Second coinage gold

2620

2622 2627

		F £	VF £
2618	**Unite** (20s., 22s. from 1612). Half-length second bust r. ℞. FACIAM etc.; *mm.* lis or rose	235	450
2619	— fourth bust; *mm.* rose to cinquefoil	210	390
2620	— fifth bust; *mm.* cinquefoil to saltire	190	375
2621	**Double-crown**. Third bust r. ℞. HENRICVS, etc.; *mm.* lis or rose	150	335
2622	Fourth bust; *mm.* rose to bell	145	325
2623	Fifth bust; *mm.* key, mullet to saltire	140	300
2624	**Britain crown**. First bust r.; *mm.* lis to coronet	135	250
2625	Third bust; *mm.* key to cinquefoil	115	235
2626	Fifth bust; *mm.* cinquefoil to saltire	125	235
2627	**Thistle crown** (4s.). As illus.; *mm.* lis to plain cross	135	250
2628	— IR on only one side or absent both sides; *mm.* 79, 74, 71-123	150	275
2629	**Halfcrown**. I' D' G' ROSA SINE SPINA. First bust; *mm.* lis to key	110	210
2630	Third bust; *mm.* key to trefoil, trefoil/tower	115	225
2631	Fifth bust; *mm.* cinquefoil to plain cross	105	200

Third coinage, 1619-25

		F £	VF £
2632	**Rose-ryal** (30s.; 196 1/2 grs.). King enthroned. ℞. XXX above shield; lis, lion and rose emblems around; *mm.* 24, 125, 105	900	2000
2633	Similar but plain back to throne; *mm.* trefoil	1100	2500

2634

2635

		F £	VF £
2634	**Spur-ryal** (15s.). As illus. ℞. Somewhat like 2614, but lis are also crowned. *mm.* 24-125, 46	1600	3500
2635	**Angel** (10s.) of new type; *mm.* 24-46	500	1200
2636	— pierced for use as touch-piece	225	450
2637	**Laurel** (20s.; 140 1/2 gr.). First (large) laur, bust l.; *mm.* 24, 24/-	225	485
2638	Second, medium, square headed bust, `SS' tie ends; *mm.* 24, 33	200	375
2638A	Third, small rounded head, ties wider apart; *mm.* 33, 125	200	375
2638B	Fourth head, very small ties; *mm.* 105, 46	200	365

2638C

2640

		F £	VF £
2638C	Fourth head variety, tie ends form a bracket to value; *mm.* lis	210	380
2639	Fifth, small rather crude bust; *mm.* trefoil	650	1600
2640	**Half-laurel**. First bust; *mm.* spur rowel	175	375
2641	— As 2638A; *mm.* rose	160	340

2641A

2642B

		F £	VF £
2641A	— As 2638B; *mm.* 33-46, 105/-	150	325
2642	**Quarter-laurel**. Bust with two loose tie ends; *mm.* 24-105	120	190
2642A	Bust as 2638C; *mm.* 105, 46, 105/46	120	190
2642B	As last but beaded, i.c. on *rev.* or both sides; *mm.* 105, 46	125	210

Rev. mm. on 1/2 and 1/4 laurels normally follows REGNA.

SILVER

2643

		F £	VF £
First coinage, 1603-4			
2643	**Crown**. King on horseback. R. EXVRGAT, etc., shield; *mm*. thistle, lis	375	800
2644	**Halfcrown**. Similar	425	1200
2645	**Shilling**. First bust, square-cut beard. R. EXVRGAT, etc.; *mm*. thistle	40	150

2646

2647 2648

		F £	VF £
2646	— Second bust, beard merges with collar; *mm*. thistle, lis	30	100
2647	**Sixpence**. First bust; 1603; *mm*. thistle	30	110
2648	Second bust; 1603-4; *mm*. thistle, lis	25	100
2649	**Halfgroat**. As illustration 2650 but II; *mm*. thistle, lis	20	55

2650 2651

		F £	VF £
2650	**Penny**. First bust I behind head; *mm.* thistle, lis ?	50	125
2650A	— Second bust; *mm.* thistle, lis	25	90
2651	**Halfpenny**. As illustration; *mm.* thistle, lis	15	45

Second coinage, 1604-19

		F £	VF £
2652	**Crown**. King on horseback. R. QVAE DEVS, etc. *rev.* stops; *mm.* 105-84	300	650
2653	**Halfcrown**. Similar; *mm.* 105-79	575	1400
2654	**Shilling**. Third bust, beard cut square and stands out (*cf.* illus. 2657); *mm.* lis, rose	25	90
2655	— Fourth bust, armour plainer (*cf.* 2658); *mm.* 33-74, 60 over 74	20	80
2656	— Fifth bust, similar, but hair longer; *mm.* 74-7a (several bust varieties)	25	90

2657 2658

		F £	VF £
2657	**Sixpence**. Third bust; 1604-6; *mm.* lis, rose	25	80
2658	— Fourth bust; 1605-15; *mm.* rose to tun, 90/60, 25/60	25	85
2658A	— Fifth bust, 1618; *mm.* plain cross	*Unique*	

2660

2663

		F £	VF £
2659	**Halfgroat**. As illus. but larger crown on *obv.*; *mm.* lis to coronet	15	35
2660	—— Similar, but smaller crown on *obv.*; *mm.* coronet to plain cross	15	40
2660A	As before, but TVEATVR legend both sides; *mm.* plain cross	50	100
2661	**Penny**. As halfgroat but no crowns; *mm.* 105-32,7a and none, -/84, 32/-	12	30
2662	— As before but TVEATVR legend both sides; *mm.* mullet	50	100
2663	**Halfpenny**. As illus.; *mm.* 105- 25 (except 90), 32; all *mms* on *rev.* only	12	30

2665

		F £	VF £
Third coinage, 1619-25			
2664	**Crown**. As 2652, with plain or grass ground line, colon stops on *obv*., no stops on *rev*.; *mm*. 33-46	200	450
2665	— — plume over shield; *mm*. 125-46	225	500
2666	**Halfcrown**. As 2664 but normally plain ground line only; all have bird-headed harp; *mm*. 33-46	90	225

2666

2666A	— — Similar but no ground line; *mm*. rose	*Extremely rare*	
2667	— — Plume over shield; groundline *mm*. 125-46	150	400
2668	**Shilling**. Sixth (large) bust, hair longer and very curly; *mm*. 24-46	30	95

2667

2668/9

2669	— — plume over shield; *mm*. 125-46	50	150

2670 2672

2670	**Sixpence**. Sixth bust; 1621-4; *mm*. 33-46; 1621/0, *mm*. rose	30	100
2671	**Halfgroat**. As 2660 but no stops on *rev*.; *mm*. 24-46 and none, 105 and 46, 46/- *mm*. 24 with *rev*. stops known	12	30
2671A	Similar but no inner circles; *mm*. lis, trefoil	20	60
2672	**Penny**. As illus.; *mm*. 24, 105, two pellets, none, trefoil, many mule *mms*.	12	30
2672A	— Similar but without inner circles on one or both sides; *mm*. lis, two pellets	15	30
2673	**Halfpenny**. As 2663, but no *mm*.	12	25

COPPER

For mintmarks see C. Wilson Peck, *English Copper, Tin and Bronze Coins in the British Museum, 1558-1958.*

2675 2676 2679

		F £	*VF* £
2674	**Farthing**. 'Harington', small size. 1a, letter or other mark below crown (originally tinned surface) *from*	20	45
2675	— — 1b, central jewel on circlet of crown with *mm*. below or crown unmodified	25	45
2676	— 2, normal size of coin; *mm*. on *rev*.	12	25
2677	'Lennox'. 3a; *mm*. *rev*. only	8	20
2678	— 3b; *mm*. both sides	6	18
2679	— — 3c; *mm*. *obv*. only	6	18
2680	— — 3d; larger crown	6	18
2681	— 4; oval type, legend starts at bottom l.	20	45

Numismatically, this reign is one of the most interesting. Some outstanding machine-made coins were produced by Nicholas Briot, a French die-sinker, but they could not be struck at sufficient speed to supplant hand-hammering methods. In 1637 a branch mint was set up at Aberystwyth to coin silver extracted from the Welsh mines. After the king's final breach with Parliament the parliamentary government continued to issue coins at London with Charles's name and portrait until the king's trial and execution. The coinage of copper farthings continued to be manufactured privately under licences held first by the Duchess of Richmond, then by Lord Maltravers and later by various other persons. The licence was finally revoked by Parliament in 1644.

During the Civil War coins were struck at a number of towns to supply coinage for those areas of the country under Royalist control. Many of these coins have an abbreviated form of the 'Declaration' made at Wellington, Shropshire, Sept., 1642, in which Charles promised to uphold the Protestant Religion, the Laws of England and the Liberty of Parliament. Amongst the more spectacular pieces are the gold triple unites and the silver pounds and half-pounds struck at Shrewsbury and Oxford, and the emergency coins, some made from odd-shaped pieces of silver plate and some from proper flans, during the sieges of Newark, Scarborough, Carlisle and Pontefract.

Mintmarks

105 10 96 71 57 88 101 35

87 107 60 75 123 57 119a 23

119b 98 112 81 120 109

Tower Mint under Charles I

1625	Lis (105)
1625-6	Cross Calvary (10)
1626-7	Negro's head (96)
1627-8	Castle (71)
1628-9	Anchor (57)
1629-30	Heart (88)
1630-1	Plume (101)
1631-2	Rose (35)
1632-3	Harp (87)
1633-4	Portcullis (107)
1634-5	Bell (60)
1635-6	Crown (75)
1636-8	Tun (123)
1638-9	Anchor (57)
1639-40	Triangle (119a)
1640-1	Star (23)
1641-3	Triangle in circle (119b)

Tower Mint under Parliament

1643-4	P in brackets (98)
1644-5	R in brackets (112)
1645	Eye (81)
1645-6	Sun (120)
1646-8	Sceptre (109)

Mint mark no. 57 is often horizontal to left or right.

59 B 58 *var* 58

Briot's Mint

1631-2	Flower and B (59)
1632	**B**
1638-9	Anchor (57)
	Anchor and B (58)
	Anchor and mullet

On mint mark no. 58 the 'B' below the anchor is sometimes shown as ᗺ

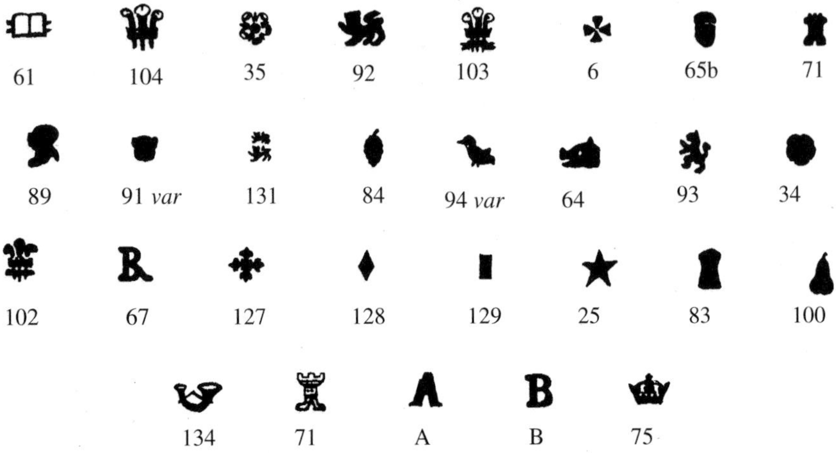

61 104 35 92 103 6 65b 71

89 91 *var* 131 84 94 *var* 64 93 34

102 67 127 128 129 25 83 100

134 71 A B 75

Provincial Mints

1638-42	Book (61, *Aberystwyth*)
1642	Plume (104, *Shrewsbury*)
	Pellets or pellet (*Shrewsbury*)
1642-3	Rose (35, *Truro*)
	Bugle (134, *Truro*)
1642-4	Lion (92, *York*)
1642-6	Plume (103, *Oxford*)
	Pellet or pellets (*Oxford*)
	Lis (105, *Oxford*)
1643	Cross pattee (6, *Bristol*)
	Acorn (65b, *Bristol*)
	Castle (71, *Worcester* or *Shrewsbury*)
	Helmet (89, *Worcester* and *Shrewsbury*)
1643-4	Leopard's head (91 *var. Worcester*)
	Two lions (131, *Worcester*)
	Lis (105, *Worcs.* or *Shrews.*)
	Bunch of grapes (84, *Worcs.* or *Shrews.*)
	Bird (94 var., *Worcs.* or *Shrews.*)
1643-4	Boar's head (64 *Worcs.* or *Shrews.*)
	Lion rampant (93, *Worcs.* or *Shrews.*)
	Rosette (34, *Worcs.* or *Shrews.*)
1643-5	Plume (102, *Bristol*)
	Br. (67, *Bristol*)
	Pellets (*Bristol*)
	Rose (35, *Exeter*)
	Rosette (34, *Oxford*)
1643-6	Floriated cross (127, *Oxford*)
1644	Cross pattee (6, *Oxford*)
	Lozenge (128, *Oxford*)
	Billet (129, *Oxford*)
	Mullet (25, *Oxford*)
1644-5	Gerb (83, *Chester*)
	Pear (100, *Worcester*)
	Lis (105, *Hereford?*)
	Castle (71, *Exeter*)
1645-6	Plume (102, *Ashby, Bridgnorth*)
1645	A (*Ashby*)
1646	B (*Bridgnorth*)
1648-9	Crown (75, *Aberystwyth Furnace*)

GOLD

Tower mint, under the King, 1625-42

Tower Gold

		F £	VF £
2682	**Angel**. As for James I last issue, but *rev*. reads AMOR POPULI etc; without mark of value; *mm*. lis and cross calvary	550	1450
2683	— — pierced for use as touch-piece	250	525
2684	— X in field to r.; *mm*. 96-88, 71 and 96/71, 57 and 71/57	450	1250
2685	— — — pierced for use as touch-piece	250	525
2686	— X in field to l.; *mm*. 96, 88, 35-119b	425	1300

2687

2687	— — — pierced for use as touch-piece	250	525

2688

2697

2688	**Unite** (20s.). First bust with ruff and collar of order, high double-crown. ℞. Square-topped shield; *mm*. lis.	210	390
2688A	— Similar, but extra garnishing to shield; *mm*. lis	235	465
2689	— Similar, but flat single-arched crown; *mm*. lis, cross calvary	210	415
2689A	℞. As 2688A. *mm*. lis	235	480
2690	Second bust with ruff and armour nearly concealed with scarf; ℞. Square-topped shield with slight garnishing *mm*. 10-88	185	390
2690A	Similar but more elongated bust, usually dividing legend. *mm*. 57-101, 88/101	185	400
2691	— As 2690A but *mm*. anchor below bust	350	850
2691A	*Obv*. as 2690A. ℞. As next: *mm*. plume	250	575
2692	Third bust, more armour visible. ℞. Oval shield with CR at sides; *mm*. 101, 35.	190	415
2692A	*Obv*. as next. ℞. As last, *mm*. plume	190	475
2693	Fourth bust, small lace collar with large high crown usually breaking i.c., long hair. Garter ribbon on breast. ℞. Oval shield with crowned CR at sides; *mm*. harp, portcullis	200	440

		F £	VF £
2693A	Similar, but unjewelled crown, within or touching i.c.; *mm.* 107-23	200	390
2694	Sixth (Briot's) bust, large lace collar. ℞. Similar; *mm.* 119a-119b	225	450
2695	Briot's hammered issue, (square-topped shield); *mm.* anchor	—	3000
2696	**Double-crown**. First bust. As 2688. ℞. Square-topped shield; *mm.* lis	155	350
2696A	Similar to last but wider flatter double-arched crown; *mm.* 105, 10	155	350
*2697	Second bust. ℞. Similar to 2690; *mm.* 10-57	150	330
*2697A	Similar to 2690A: *mm.* 57-101	155	350
2697B	*Obv.* as last. ℞. As next: *mm.* plume	160	360

*For these coins inner circles are sometimes omitted on *obv.*, *rev.*, or both. *See also 2704, 2704A and 2707.*

Tower Gold

		F £	VF £
2698	**Double-crown.** Third bust. Flat or domed crown. ℞. Oval shield with CR at sides; *mm.* plume, rose	185	410
2699	Fourth bust, large head, high wide crown. ℞. Oval shield with crowned CR at sides; *mm.* portcullis	175	360
2699A	— Similar to last, but flat crown, jewelled outer arch: *mm.* 87-123	150	330
2699B	— Similar, but smaller head, unjewelled crown: *mm.* 60-57	150	330
2699C	— Sim. to 2699, but bust within i.c.; *mm.* bell	*Extremely rare*	
2700	Fifth bust (Early Aberystwyth style). ℞. Similar; *mm.* anchor	*Extremely rare*	
2700A	— (Late Aberystwyth style). ℞. *mm.* anchor, triangle	200	450
2701	Sixth bust. ℞. Normal; *mm.* 119a-119b	200	450
2702	— ℞. Briot's square-topped shield; *mm.* anchor	*Extremely rare*	

2703 2707

		F £	VF £
2703	**Crown**. First bust with small round crown. ℞. Square-topped shield; *mm.* lis, cross calvary	130	200
2703A	As 2696A. *mm.* cross calvary	130	200
2704	Second bust as 2690. ℞. Similar; *mm.* 10-71	130	200
2704A	As 2690A. *mm.* 57-101, 88/-, 57/-, 101/-	130	200
2704B	As 2691. Wire line i.c.s on *rev.*	200	400
2705	*Obv.* as 2690A. ℞. As next; 101, 35, 101/-	135	260
2706	Third bust. ℞. Oval shield with CR at sides; *mm.* plume	250	500
2707	Fourth bust. ℞. Oval shield with crowned CR at sides; *mm.* -/87, 87-119b, 23/119a, 107/60	130	215
2708	Fifth (Aberystwyth style) bust. ℞. Similar; *mm.* anchor	175	425
2709	Sixth (Briot's) bust. ℞. Similar; *mm.* anchor	*Unique*	

Tower mint, under Parliament, 1642-9. All Charles I types

		F £	VF £
2710	**Unite**. Fourth bust, as 2693A; *mm.* (P), (P)/-	250	525
2711	Sixth bust, as 2694 but crude style; *mm.* (P), (R), 119b	325	700
2712	Seventh bust, crude r style; *mm.* eye, sun, sceptre	335	725
2713	**Double-crown**. Fourth bust, as 2699B; *mm.* eye	*Extremely rare*	

2714

		F	VF
		£	£
2714	Fifth bust, as 2700A; *mm.* sun, sceptre	350	800
2715	Sixth bust, as 2701; *mm.* (P)	375	875
2716	Eighth, dumpy bust with single flat-arched crown; *mm.* sun		*Unique*
2717	**Crown**. Fourth bust, as 2707 jewelled crown; *mm.* -/98 , 98/-, 98-120....	140	300
2717A	Sim. but unjewelled crown. ℞. Small crude shield; *mm.* 81-109	150	325

Nicholas Briot's coinage, 1631-2

2718 **Angel**. Type somewhat as Tower but smaller and neater; *mm.* -/B .... *Extremely rare*

2719

2719	**Unite**. As illustration. ℞. FLORENT etc.; *mm.* flower and B/B	750	1750
2720	**Double-crown**. Similar but X. ℞. CVLTORES, etc. *mm.* flower and B/B	500	1250
2720A	Similar but King's crown unjewelled: *mm.* flower and B/B, B	550	1300
2721	**Crown**. Similar; *mm.* B		*Extremely rare*

**Inner circles sometimes omitted on* obv. *or* rev. *or both.*

BRIOTS HAMMERED GOLD: See No. 2695.

Provincial issues, 1638-49

Chester mint, 1644

2722 **Unite**. As Tower. Somewhat like a crude Tower sixth bust. ℞. Crowned, oval shield, crowned CR, *mm.* plume .... *Extremely rare*

Shrewsbury mint, 1642 (See also 2749)

2723 **Triple unite**, 1642. Half-length figure l holding sword and olive-branch; *mm.*: ℞. EXVRGAT, etc., around RELIG PROT, etc., in two wavy lines. III and three plumes above, date below .... *Extremely rare*

Oxford mint, 1642-6

2724

		F £	*VF* £
2724	**Triple unite**. As last, but *mm.* plume, tall narrow bust, 1642	1800	4000
2725	Similar, but 'Declaration' on continuous scroll, 1642-3	1900	4500
2725A	Large bust of fine style. King holds short olive branch; *mm.* small lis..... *A good EF specimen fetched £48,000 in auction in May, 1989*	*Extremely rare*	
2726	As last, but taller bust, with scarf behind shoulder, 1643, *mm.* plume	2100	4500
2727	Similar, but without scarf, longer olive branch, 1643	1800	3900
2728	Similar, but OXON below 1643, rosette stops	*Extremely rare*	
2729	Smaller size, olive branch varies, bust size varies, 1644 OXON	1900	4400
2730	— Obv. as 2729, 1644 / OX	2100	4600

2731

2731	**Unite**. Tall thin bust. ℞. 'Declaration' in two wavy lines, 1642; *no mm.*	450	1050
2732	— ℞. 'Declaration' in three lines on continuous scroll, 1642-3	450	1050
2733	Tall, well-proportioned bust. ℞. Similar, 1643, no *mm.*	450	1100
2734	Shorter bust, king's elbow not visible. ℞. Similar, 1643; *mm.* plume/-	450	925
2735	Similar but longer olive branch curving to l. 1644 / OX; *mm.* plume	450	1000
2735A	Similar, but dumpy bust breaking lower i.c., small flan	450	1050
2736	Tall bust to edge of coin. ℞. Similar, 1643	625	1450
2737	As 2734. ℞. 'Declaration' in three straight lines, 1644 / OX	*Extremely rare*	
2738	Similar to 2734, but smaller size; small bust, low olive branch. 1645	500	1400
2739	— ℞. Single plume above 'Declaration', 1645-6 / OX; *mm.* plume, rosette, none	550	1250

No.	Description	F £	VF £
2740	**Half-unite**. 'Declaration' in three straight lines, 1642	*Extremely rare*	
2741	'Declaration' on scroll; *mm.* plume; 1642-3	*Extremely rare*	
2742	Bust to bottom of coin, 1643; Oxford plumes	425	950
2743	— 1644 / OX. Three Shrewsbury plumes (neater work)	*Extremely rare*	
	Bristol mint, 1645		
*2744	**Unite**. Somewhat as 2734; Two busts known. *mm.* Br. or Br/ plumelet.; 1645	*Extremely rare*	
2745	**Half-unite**. Similar 1645	*Unique?*	
	**A nearly EF specimen fetched £16,500 in auction Mar. 1988.*		
	Truro mint, 1642–3		
2745A	**Half-Unite**. Crowned bust l. (similar to Tower 4th bust). R. CVLT, etc., crowned shield	*Extremely rare*	
	Exeter mint, 1643–4		
2746	**Unite**. *obv.* sim. to early Oxford bust. R. FLORENT, etc., crowned oval shield between crowned CR, *mm.* rose	*Unique*	
2747	— R. CVLTORES, etc., similar but no CR	*Extremely rare*	
	Worcester mint, 1643-4		
2748	**Unite**. Crude bust R. FLORENT, etc., double annulet stops, crowned oval shield, lion's paws on either side of garniture, no *mm.*	-	12500
	Salopia (Shrewsbury) mint, 1644		
2749	**Unite.** *Obv.* bust in armour. R. Cr. shield, crowned CR. *mm.* lis/-	*Unique?*	
	Colchester besieged, 1648		
2750	**Ten Shillings** Gateway of castle between CR; below OBS CO L 16 S/X 48. Uniface	*Not genuine*	
	Pontefract besieged, 1648-9. After the death of Charles I, in the name of Charles II		
2751	**Unite**. DVM : SPIRO : SPERO around CR crowned. CAROLVS : SECVNDVS : 16 48, castle, OBS on l., PC above.	*Extremely rare*	
	A specimen fetched £29,000 in auction in April, 1989.		
2752	**Unite.** CAROL : II, etc., around HANC : DEVS, etc. R. POST : MORTEM, etc., around castle. *Octagonal*	*Extremely rare*	

SILVER

2759

Tower mint, under the King, 1625-42

No.	Description	F £	VF £
2753	**Crown**. King on horseback with raised sword. 1a. Horse caparisoned with plume on head and crupper. R. Square-topped shield over long cross fourchee; *mm.* lis, cross calvary	200	550
2754	— 1b. Similar, but plume over shield, no cross; *mm.* 105, 10, 71	475	1050
2755	— 2a. Smaller horse, plume on hd. only, cross on housings, king holds sword on shoulder. R. Oval garnished shield over cross fourchee, CR above; *mm.* harp	175	450

No.	Description	F £	VF £
2756	— 2b^1. — — plume divides CR, no cross; *mm.* plume, rose	200	525
2757	— 2b^2. — — — with cross; *mm.* harp	275	675
2758	— 3a. Horse without caparisons. ℞. Oval shield without CR; *mm.* 60-23	175	450
2759	— 3b. — — plume over shield; *mm.* 107, 75, 123	225	575
2760	'Briot' horse with ground-line; *mm.* triangle in circle	*Three known?*	
2761	**Halfcrown**. As 2753. 1a^1. Rose on housings, ground-line; *mm.* lis	100	275
2761A	— Similar, but no rose on housings; *mm.* lis	*Very rare*	

2762

No.	Description	F £	VF £
2762	— 1a^2. Similar, but no rose or ground-line; *mm.* 105, 10 over 105	85	230
2763	— 1a^3. As last but clumsier horse and shield not over cross; *mm.* 10-96, 10 over lis	75	175
2763A	— Similar but only slight garnishing to shield; *mm.* 10, 71	85	190
2763B	— As 2763, but light weight (204 grains as standard) *mm* 10/10 over 105		*Rare*
2764	— 1a^4. — — with ground-line; *mm.* lis	450	900
2765	— 1b. Heavy garnishing, plume over shield; *mm.* 105, 10, 96	400	850
2765A	— Similar but only slight garnishing; *mm.* 96-57	400	850
2766	— 2/1b. As 2755 but rose on housings. ℞. As last; *mm.* heart, plume	*Extremely rare*	
2767	— 2a. As 2755. ℞. Flattened oval garnished shield without cross; *mm.* 101/35 plume, rose, (CR above, divided by rose (rare), lis over rose, lis)	60	125
2768	— 2b. Similar, but large plume between the CR; *mm.* plume, rose	110	300
2769	— 2c. As 2a, but differently garnished oval shield with CR at sides; *mm.* harp, portcullis, 107/87	40	100
2770	— 2d. Similar, but with plume over shield; *mm.* harp	300	650

2771

2775

No.	Description	F £	VF £
2771	— 3a^1. No caparisons on horse, upright sword, scarf flies out from waist. ℞. Round garnished shield, no CR; *mm.* 60-119a, 60/75	35	100
2772	— 3b. — — plume over shield; *mm.* 107-123	75	200
2773	— 3a^2. — cloak flies from king's shoulder; ℞. Shields vary; *mm.* 123-23, 119b, 119b over 119a/119b	35	100

		F £	VF £
2774	— — — — rough ground beneath horse; R. Shields vary; *mm.* 119a, 23,	45	110
2775	— 4. Foreshortened horse, mane before chest, tail between legs; *mm.* 23, 119b	30	95

Most late Tower halfcrowns have irregular flans.

2776 2776A

		F £	VF £
2776	**Shilling**. l. Bust in ruff, high crown, jewelled arches. R. Square-topped shield over cross fourchee; *mm.* lis, (normal weight 92.75 gr.)	45	135
2776A	— Similar but larger crown, plain inner arch; *mm.* 105, 10	40	125
2777	Similar but light weight (81.75 grs.); *mm.* cross calvary	70	185
2778	— 1b[1]. As 2776A, but plume over shield, no cross; *mm.* 105, 10	150	375
2779	— 1a. Bust in ruff and armour concealed by scarf. R. As 2776; 10-71	45	125
2780	— — — — light weight; *mm.* cross Calvary (often extremely small XII)	70	175
2781	— 1b[2]. As 2779, but plume over shield, no cross; *mm.* 10-101 (five bust varieties)	75	200
2781A	— — light weight 1b[2] *mm.* 10	110	275
2782	— 1b[3], — — — cross; *mm.* negro's head	350	750
2783	— 2a. More armour visible. R. Oval shield, CR above; *mm.* 35, 101, 101 over 88/101, (two bust varieties)	30	95
2784	— 2b. — — plume over shield; *mm.* 101, 35, 101 over 88/101, (three bust varieties)	80	275
2785	— 3[1]. Bust with lace collar, (six bust varieties). R. Flattish oval shield, CR at sides; *mm.* harp, portcullis	30	85
2786	— 3[2]. — — plume over shield; *mm.* harp (three bust varieties)	250	600

2787

		F £	VF £
2787	— 3a. — no inner circles, rounder shield without CR; *mm.* 60-123 (five bust varieties)	25	75
2788	— 3b. — — plume over shield; *mm.* 60-123 (Two bust varieties)	50	125
2789	— 4[1]. Large Aberystwyth bust, medium or small XII. R. Square-topped shield over cross fleury; *mm.* tun, 57 over 123 (obv.) small neat cross ends	55	135
2790	— 4[1]. var. Similar, but rounder shoulders, large XII; *mm.* 57, 119a, (cross ends vary)	30	80

2791 2793

		F £	VF £
2790A	— *O* as above. ℞ As Briot hammered issue (lozenge stops) *mm* triangle	—	500
2791	— 4^2. Smaller Aberystwyth bust with small double-arched crown, small XII; *mm*. tun, small neat cross ends, large XII, *mm*. anchor	40 30	115 80
2792	— 4^3. — single-arches, large XII; *mm*. 123, 57, 119a, 119b (cross ends vary)	30	75
2793	— 4^4. Older (Briot's style) bust, very pointed beard; *mm*. 119a-119b	30	75
2793A	— *Obv*. as last. ℞. As 2790A (Briot hammered). *mm*. Δ/Δ over 57	—	450
2794	**Sixpence**. 1. As 2776, but dated 1625-6; *mm*. 105, 10 small bust *mm*. lis, large bust *mm*. lis. 10 (*rare*)	35	125
2794A	— Lightweight, 40.85 grains; large bust *mm* 10, 1625-6		*Rare*
2795	— $1a^1$. As 2779, but dated 1625-9; *mm*. 10-88 (busts vary)	45	150
2796	— $1a^2$. — no cross, 1630; *mm*. harp, plume	75	250

2797

2799

2802

		F £	VF £
2797	— 2a. As 2783, no date; *mm*. plume, rose	35	150
2798	— 2b. — plume dividing CR; *mm*. plume, rose, plume/rose	50	145
2799	— 3. As 2785; *mm*. harp, portcullis (busts and crowns vary)	30	120
2799A	— 3. As above but no CR *mm*. portcullis		*Rare*
2800	— 3a. no inner circles; *mm*. 60-123 (busts and crowns vary)......30	95	
2801	— 4^1. As first Aberystwyth sixpence, double-arch crown, small VI. ℞. Square-topped shield over cross; *mm*. tun	30	100
2801A	— 4^1 Similar but lyre cross ends on *rev*, *mm*. tun	50	125
2802	— 4^1. var. — similar, but large VI; *mm*. tun, anchor	30	100
2803	— 4^2. Second Aberystwyth bust, single-arched crown; *mm*. 123, 57, 119a	25	95
2804	— 4^2. larger bust, *mm*. triangle	50	125
2805	— 4^3. Older (Briot's style) bust; *mm*. 119a-119b (moline cross ends)	25	120

2806 2808

		F £	VF £
2806	**Halfgroat**. 1. Crowned rose type. Beaded and/or wire line inner circles on one or both sides. *mm* 105, 105/–10	15	40
2807	— 1a. —— similar but without inner circles, *mm* 96–101	17	50
2808	— 2a. King's 2nd bust in ruff and mantle. ℞. Oval shield; *mm*. plume, rose	15	35

		F	VF
		£	£
2809	— 2b. Similar, but with plume over shield; *mm.* plume, rose, plume/-....	25	65
2809A	— — 2a Var. 3rd bust, with more armour. breaks i.c. at top. ℞. As last; *mm.* plume, rose	15	35
2809B	— — Sim. but plume over shield; *mm.* plume	25	50
2810	— 3¹. Bust with lace collar. ℞. Oval shield between CR; no inner circles; *mm.* rose harp, crown, portcullis	15	35
2811	— 3²⁻⁴. — — inner circles sometimes only on one side; *mm.* harp, portcullis	15	35
2814	— 3⁵. — — no CR, inner circles; *mm.* portcullis	15	35
2815	— 3⁶. — — — inner circles on *obv.*; *mm.* portcullis	15	35
2816	— 3a¹. — ℞. Rounder shield, different garniture, no i.cs.; *mm.* 60-119a.	15	30
2817	— 3a². — — inner circle on *obv.*; *mm.* triangle, anchor	15	35

2818

2822

		F	VF
2818	— 3a³. — — inner circles both sides; *mm.* 119a-119b	15	35
2819	— 3a⁴. Aberystwyth bust, no inner circles; *mm.* anchor	20	50
2820	— 3a⁵. — inner circle on *rev.*; *mm.* anchor, anchor	20	50
2821	— 3a⁶. Very small bust, no inner circles; *mm.* anchor	20	50
2822	**Penny**. 1. Rose each side; i.cs.; *mm.* 96, :/lis, lis/:, one or two pellets, lis	10	30
2823	— 1a. — no i.cs.; *mm.* lis, one or two pellets, anchor	10	30
2824	— 1b. — i.c. on *rev.*; *mm.* negro's head/two pellets	15	50
2825	— 2. Bust in ruff and mantle. ℞. Oval shield; i.cs.; *mm.* plume, plume/rose, rose	15	50
2826	— 2¹. — — no i.cs.; *mm.* plume, rose	15	35
2827	— 2a¹. More armour visible; no i.cs.; *mm.* plume, rose, plume/rose	12	30

2828

2831

2837

		F	VF
2828	— 2a². — i.c. on *obv.*; *mm.* plume, rose, plume over rose	15	40
2829	— 2a³. — i.cs. both sides; *mm.* plume, rose	12	35
2830	— 2a⁴. — i.c. on *rev.*; *mm.* rose over plume	20	55
2831	— 3¹. Bust in lace collar. ℞. CR at sides of shield; no i.cs.; *mm.* harp, one or two pellets. ··/harp (also *obv.* i.c. *mm.* harp)	12	30
2832	— 3². — similar but no CR; *mm.* 87, 107, 107/··, none	12	35
2833	— 3³. — — i.c. on *obv.*; *mm.* harp,··,	15	40
2834	— 3⁴. — — i.c. on *rev.*; *mm.* harp	15	40
2835	— 3a¹. — similar, but shield almost round and with scroll garniture; no i.cs.; *mm.* bell, triangle, one to four pellets, none, bell/··	10	25
2835A	— 3a¹ variety — i.c. on *obv.*, *rev.* or both sides; *mm.* triangle/two pellets, Δ,··,	15	35
2836	— 3a³. Aberystwyth bust; i.c. on *obv.* or none; *mm.* one or two pellets or none, or mule of these *mms.*	13	25
2837	**Halfpenny**. Rose each side; no legend or *mm.*	15	30

Many small denominations have uneven irregular flans.

		F £	*VF* £
Tower mint, under Parliament, 1642-8. All Charles I type			
2838	**Crown**. 4. Foreshortened horse; *mm*. (P) to sun	210	475
2839	— 5. Tall spirited horse; *mm*. sun	225	600
2840	**Halfcrown**. 3a³. As 2773, but coarse work; *mm*. (P) to sun, 81/120	35	95
2841	— 4. Foreshortened horse; *mm*. (P)	125	275
2842	— 5. Tall horse; *mm*. sun, sceptre	50	150
2843	**Shilling**. 4⁴. Briot style bust, *mm*, (P) (R), coarse work; *mm*. eye, sun ...	30	100

2844 2845 2845A

		F £	*VF* £
2844	— 4⁵. Long narrow coarse bust; *mm*. sun, sceptre	40	120
2845	— 4⁶. Short bust with narrow crown; *mm*. sceptre	40	125
2845A	— — Short broad bust, as illus., broader crown; *mm*. sceptre	40	125
2846	**Sixpence**. 4³. Briot style bust; *mm*. (P) (R)	60	135

2847 2855

		F £	*VF* £
2847	— 4⁴. Late Aberystwyth bust modified; *mm*. (R) to sceptre	45	125
2848	— 4⁵. Squat bust of crude style; *mm*. eye, sun, sun over eye	90	225
2849	**Halfgroat**. 3a³. Sim. to 2818; *mm*. (P) to eye, sceptre, 98/119b	15	55
2850	— 3a⁷. Older, shorter bust, pointed beard; *mm*. eye to sceptre	15	45
2851	**Penny**. 3a². Older bust; *mm*. pellets, i.c. on *obv*. only	20	55

Nicholas Briot's coinage, 1631-9

First milled issue, 1631-2

		F £	*VF* £
2852	**Crown**. King on horseback. ℞. Crowned shield between CR crowned; *mm*. flower and B / B	250	650
2853	**Halfcrown**. Similar	175	425
2854	**Shilling**. Briot's early bust with falling lace collar. ℞. Square-topped shield over long cross fourchee; ℞. Legend starts at top or bottom *mm*. flower and B/B, B	125	275
2855	**Sixpence**. Similar, but VI behind bust; *mm*. flower and B/B, flower and B/-	65	175

2856

2857

		F £	VF £
2856	**Halfgroat**. Briot's bust, B below, II behind. R. IVSTITIA, etc., square-topped shield over long cross fourchee	30	65
2856A	Pattern halfgroat. Uncrowned bust in ruff r. R. crowned, interlocked Cs. (North 2687). (Included because of its relatively regular appearance.)....	30	65
2857	**Penny**. Similar, but I behind bust, B below bust; position of legend may vary	35	65

Second milled issue, 1638-9

2858

2859

		F £	VF £
2858	**Halfcrown**. As 2853, but *mm.* anchor and B	160	375
2859	**Shilling**. Briot's late bust, the falling lace collar is plain with broad lace border, no scarf. R. As 2854 but cross only to inner circle; *mm.* anchor and B, anchor or muled	50	130
2860	**Sixpence**. Similar, but VI; *mm.* anchor, anchor and mullet/anchor	25	70

The two last often exhibit flan reduction marks.

Briot's hammered issue, 1638-9

		F £	VF £
2861	**Halfcrown**. King on Briot's style horse with ground line. R. Square-topped shield; *mm.* anchor, triangle over anchor. Also muled with Tower *rev*....	450	1100
2862	**Shilling**. Sim. to 2859; R. Square-topped shield over short cross fleury; usually *mm.* triangle over anchor. Each *mm.* alone is very rare. Often muled with Tower *obv.* see 2790A, 2793A *or rev*	325	750

Provincial and Civil War issues, 1638-49

York mint, 1643-4. *Mm.* lion

		F £	VF £
2863	**Halfcrown**. 1. Ground-line below horse. R. Square-topped shield between CR	165	500
2864	— 2. — R. Oval shield as Tower 3a, groundline grass or dotted	145	400
2865	— 3. No ground-line. R. Similar	135	375
2866	*— 4. As last, but EBOR below horse with head held low. Base metal, often very base	75	200
2867	— 5. Tall horse, mane in front of chest, EBOR below. R. Crowned square-topped shield between CR, floral spray in legend	125	325

2868

		F	VF
		£	£
2868	— 6. As last, but shield is oval, garnished (*rev.* detail variations)	90	225
2869	— 7. Similar, but horse's tail shows between legs. ℞. Shield as last, but with lion's skin garniture, no CR or floral spray	85	200

2870/2

2870	**Shilling**. 1. Bust in scalloped lace collar 3[1]. ℞. EBOR above square-topped shield over cross fleury	70	150
2871	— 2. Similar, but bust in plain armour, mantle; coarse work	80	185
2872	— 3. *Obv.* as 2870. — ℞. EBOR below oval shield	80	185
2873	— 4. — Similar, but crowned oval shield (*obv.* finer style)	70	150
2874	— 5. — As last, but lion's skin garniture	70	150
2875	**Sixpence**. *Obv.* Sim. to 2870. Crowned oval shield	160	400

2876 2877

2876	— —CR at sides	135	250
2877	**Threepence**. As type 4 shilling, but III behind bust. ℞. As 2870............	35	75

**These pieces are contemporary forgeries (Besly, English Civil War Hoards BM 51, 1987)*

		F £	VF £
	Aberystwyth mint, 1638/9-42. *Mm.* book.		
	Plume 1=with coronet and band. Plume 2=with coronet only		
2878	**Halfcrown**. Horseman similar to 2773, but plume 2 behind. R. Oval garnished shield with large plume above. *Obv.* plume 2, *rev.* plume 1. ...	350	825
2879	— Similar to 2774, plume 1 behind King, ground below horse. *Obv.* squat plume 1, *rev.* plume 1	375	875
2880	As 2773 but more spirited horse, no ground. FRAN ET HIB, plume 2/1	400	925
2881	**Shilling**. Bust with large square lace collar, plume 2 before, small XII. R. As before. No inner circles	160	425

2882 2884

2886

		F £	VF £
2882	— inner circle on *rev.*	140	375
2883	As 2881, but large plume 1 or 2, large XII, inner circles	140	375
2884	As last, but small narrow head, square lace collar, large or square plume	145	400
2885	Small Briot style face, small crown, plume 2	225	575
2885A	**Sixpence**. *Obv.* as Tower bust 3a, plume before. R. as 2889; *mm.* book (*obv.* only)	—	600
2886	Somewhat as 2881, but double-arched crown, small VI; no inner circles, or with rev. inner circle as 2889	140	325
2887	Similar to 2886, but single arched crown, plume 2, inner circle *obv.* Large VI	165	375
2888	Similar, but with inner circles both sides	150	350
2889	— — *Rev.* with small squat-shaped plume above, sometimes no *rev. mm.*	145	325
2890	Bust as the first Oxford sixpence; with crown cutting inner circle	210	450

2891

2894

2895-9

		F £	VF £
2891	**Groat**. Large bust, lace collar, no armour on shoulder. Crown breaks or touches inner circle. ℞. Shield, plume 1 or 2	25	50
2892	— Similar, armour on shoulder, shorter collar. ℞. Similar	30	60
2893	— Smaller, neater bust well within circle. ℞. Similar	25	50
2894	**Threepence**. Small bust, plume 2 before. ℞. Shield, plume 1 or 2 above, *obv.* legend variations	25	50
2895-9	— Similar, but crown cuts i.c. squat pl. on *obv.*, ℞. Pl. 2, *Obv.* legend variations	25	55
2900	**Halfgroat**. Bust as Tower type 3. ℞. Large plume. No inner circles, *mm.* pellet/book,book	50	90

2900A

2905

2907

		F £	VF £
2900A	Bust as 2886. ℞. As last, no inner circle	40	115
2901	Bust with round lace collar; single arch crown, inner circles, colon stops	35	75
2902	After Briot's bust, square lace collar: inner circles	40	90
2903	**Penny**. As 2901; CARO; no inner circles	70	150
2904	As 2901; CARO; inner circles	65	140
2905	As last but reads CAROLVS; inner circles	75	160
2906	*Obv.* similar to 2890, tall narrow bust, crown touches inner circle	80	185
2907	**Halfpenny**. No legend. *O.* Rose. ℞. Plume	125	275

Aberystwyth-Furnace mint, 1648/9. *Mm.* crown

		F £	VF £
2908	**Halfcrown**. King on horseback. ℞. Sim. to 2878	1000	2000
2909	**Shilling**. Aberystwyth type, but *mm.* crown	*Extremely rare*	
2910	**Sixpence**. Similar	*Extremely rare*	

2911 2913

		Fair	F	VF
		£	£	£
2911	**Groat**. Similar		140	300
2912	**Threepence**. Similar		150	325
2913	**Halfgroat**. Similar. ℞. Large plume		200	425
2914	**Penny**. Similar		550	1200

Uncertain mint (? Hereford) 1644-5

2915 2930/1

		Fair	F	VF
2915	**Halfcrown**. As illustration, dated 1645 or undated	500	1250	—
2915A	— Scarf with long sash ends. CH below horse. ℞. Oval shield 1644			*Rare*
2915B	— ℞. Crowned oval shield, lion paws			*Rare*

Shrewsbury mint, 1642. Plume without band used as *mm.* or in field.

		F	VF
2917	**Pound**. King on horseback, plume behind, similar to Tower grp. 3 crowns. ℞. Declaration between two straight lines, XX and three Shrewsbury plumes above, 1642 below; *mm.* pellets, pellets/-	750	2000
2918	Similar, but Shrewsbury horse walking over pile of arms; no *mm.*, pellets	700	1750
2919	As last, but cannon amongst arms and only single plume and XX above Declaration, no *mm.*	1000	2350
2920	**Half-pound**. As 2917, but X; *mm.* pellets	350	850
2921	Similar, but only two plumes on *rev.*; *mm.*, pellets	500	1100
2922	Shrewsbury horseman with ground-line, three plumes on *rev.*; *mm.*, none, pellets/-	325	850
2923	— with cannon and arms or arms below horse; *mm.* pellets/-	300	800
2924	— no cannon in arms, no plume in *obv.* field; *mm.* plume/pellets, plume/-	275	650
2925	**Crown**. Aberystwyth horseman, no ground line	*Extremely rare*	

2926

		F £	VF £
2926	Shrewsbury horseman with ground-line; *mm.* -/pellets, pellets/-, none....	250	650
2927	**Halfcrown**. *O.* From Aberystwyth die; (S2880); *mm.* book. ℞. Single plume above Declaration, 1642	*Extremely rare*	
2928	Sim. to Aberystwyth die, fat plume behind. ℞. Three plumes above Declaration; *mm.* pellets, pellets/-	225	500
2929	Shrewsbury horseman, no ground line. ℞. As 2927, single plume, no *mm.*	220	550
2929A	— — ℞. As 2933	*Extremely rare*	
2930	— ℞. 2: plume; 6, above Declaration	500	1100
2931	— with ground-line. ℞. Similar	450	1000
2932	— — ℞. As 2927, single plume	220	550
2933	— — ℞. Three plumes above Declaration; *mm.* none or pellets	185	400
2933A	*Obv.* as last. ℞. Aberystwyth die, plume over shield; *mm.* -/book		*Rare*
2934	— — — no plume behind king; *mm.* plume/pellets	185	400
2935	**Shilling**. *O.* From Aberystwyth die; S2885 *mm.* book. ℞. Declaration type	450	1000
2936	*O.* From Shrewsbury die. ℞. Similar	500	1100

Oxford mint, 1642/3-6. *Mm.* usually plume with band, except on the smaller denominations when it is lis or pellets. There were so many dies used at this mint that we can give only a selection of the more easily identifiable varieties.

2937

		F £	VF £
2937	**Pound**. Large horseman over arms, no exergual line, fine workmanship. ℞. Three Shrewsbury plumes and XX above Declaration, 1642 below; *mm.* plume/pellets	1100	3000

		F £	VF £
2938	— Similar, but three Oxford plumes, 1643; *mm.* as last	1200	3250
2939	Shrewsbury horseman trampling on arms, exergual line. ℞. As last, 1642	700	2350
2940	— — cannon amongst arms, 1642-3; *mm.* similar	650	1750
2941	— as last but exergue is chequered, 1642; *mm.* similar	750	2350
2942	Briot's horseman, 1643; *mm.* similar	1500	4500
2943	*O.* As 2937. ℞. Declaration in cartouche, single large plume above, 1644 OX below	1500	4500
2944	**Half-pound**. As next. ℞. Shrewsbury die, 1642; *mm.* plume/-	275	600
2945	Oxford dies both sides, 1642-3; *mm.* plume/pellets	250	525
2946	**Crown**. *O.* Shrewsbury die with ground-line. ℞. As last but V, 1642-3	275	625
2947	Oxford horseman with grass below, 1643	350	875
2948	By Rawlins. King riding over a view of the city. ℞. Floral scrolls above and below Declaration, 1644 / OXON below (Beware forgeries!)	*Extremely rare*	
	An extremely fine specimen sold at auction in May, 1989 for £24,750.		
2949	**Halfcrown**. *O.* From Shrewsbury die S2931 or 2934. ℞. 3 Ox plumes over 'Dec' 1642	175	425
2950	Ox plume, Shrewsbury horse. ℞. From Shrewsbury die, 1642	150	325

2951

2954

		F £	VF £
2951	Both Oxford dies, but Shrewsbury type horse, ground-line, 1642	70	220
2952	— — without ground-line, 1642	90	275
2953	Oxford type horse, ground-line, 1643	75	225
2954	— without ground-line, 1643	75	220
2954A	— — ℞. 3 Shrewsbury plumes, 1642	100	300
2955	Briot's horse, grass below, 1643, 1643 / OX below date	80	225
2956	— — large central plume, 1643, 1643 / OX, 1644 / OX	90	275
2957	— lumpy ground, 1643, 1643 / OX	80	225
2958	— — large central plume, 1643-4 / OX	80	225

2959-61

		F £	VF £
2959	— plain ground, 1644- 5 / OX	80	225

		F £	VF £
2960	— — large central plume, 1644 / OX	80	225
2960A	Similar. but 2 very small Shrewsbury plumes at sides	100	300
2961	— — — Similar, but large date in script	105	325
2962	Rocky ground, two small plumes at date, 1644 / OX	225	500
2963	Large horse (as Briot's, but clumsier), plain ground, 1644-5 / OX	90	275
2964	— lumpy ground, 1644-5 / OX	90	275
2965	— — large central plume, 1644 / OX	90	275
2966	— pebbly ground, 1645-6 / OX	85	260
2967	— — pellets or annulets by plumes and at date, 1645-6 / OX	85	275
2968	— grass below, 1645-6 / OX	90	300
2969	— — rosettes by plumes and at date, 1645 / OX	110	400
2970	**Shilling**. *O*. From Shrewsbury die. ℞. Declaration type, 1642	150	350
2971	Both Oxford dies. Small bust, 1642-3	80	200
2972	Similar, but coarser work, 1643	80	200
2973	Large bust of fine work, 1643	80	200
2974	— 1644-6 / OX	95	225

2974A

		F £	VF £
2974A	— — 1644 OX. Large date in script	100	215
2975	Bust with bent crown, 1643	120	280
2976	— 1644 / OX	120	280
2977	Rawlins' dies. Fine bust with R on truncation, 1644	165	475
2978	— — 1644 / OX	175	475
2979	Small size, 1646, annulets or pellets at date	125	275

2980

		F £	VF £
2980	**Sixpence**. *O*. Aberystwyth die S2890. ℞. With three Oxford plumes, 1642-3; *mm*. book/-	110	250

2985 2991

		F	VF
		£	£
2981	— R. With three Shrewsbury plumes, 1643; *mm.* book/-	110	235
2982	— R. With Shrewsbury plume and two lis, 1644 / OX; *mm.* book/ -	*Extremely rare*	
2983	**Groat**. *O.* Aberystwyth die S2892. R. As 2985	50	135
2984	As last but three plumes above Declaration	75	200
2985	As illustration, with lion's head on shoulder	45	120
2885A	*Obv.* as last R. 3 Shrewsbury plumes, 1644 / OX	75	185
2986	Large bust reaching to top of coin. R. As 2985	60	150
2987	Large bust to bottom of coin, lion's head on shoulder, legend starts at bottom l. R. As last	70	170
2988	Rawlins' die; similar, but no i.c., and with R on shoulder. R. As last	70	180
2989	*O.* As 2985. R. Large single plume and scroll above Declaration, 1645	80	175
2990	*O.* As 2987. R. As last	65	150
2991	*O.* As 2988. R. Large single plume above Declaration, which is in cartouche, 1645-6 (over 5)	85	200
2992	**Threepence**. *O.* Aberystwyth die; *mm.* book R. Declaration type, 1644 / OX	50	125
2993	Rawlins' die, R below shoulder; *mm.* lis. R. Aberystwyth die with oval shield; *mm.* book	45	125
2994	— R. Declaration type, three lis above, 1644 below; *mm.* lis/-	35	85

2995 2999

		F	VF
2995	— Similar, without the R, 1646 (over 1644); no *mm.*	40	90
2996	**Halfgroat**. R. Aberystwyth type with large plume, *mm* cross/-, cross/lis	75	150
2997	— R. Declaration type, 1644 / OX; *mm.* cross	90	175
2998	**Penny**. *O.* Aberystwyth die S2904; *mm.* book. R. Type, small plume	100	250
2999	As 2906 R. Type, large plume	100	250
3000	— Rawlins' BUST as 2995 R. Type, small plume	100	250
3001	— Wider bust similar to the halfgroat. R. Similar	90	225
3002	— — R. Declaration type, 1644	350	800

		F £	VF £
	Bristol mint, 1643-5. *Mm.* usually plume or Br., except on small denominations		
3003	**Halfcrown**. *O.* Oxford die with or without ground-line. R. Declaration, three Bristol plumes above, 1643 below	100	300
3004	— Obv. as above. R as above, but *mm.* Br. 1643	100	300
3005	King wears unusual flat crown, *obv. mm.* acorn? between four pellets. R. As 3003, 1643	100	275
3006	— Obv. as above. R as 3004 but 1643-4	100	260
3007	Shrewsbury plume behind king. R. As last	80	210
3008	— Obv. as above. R as 3004 but Br below date instead of as *mm* . 1644	100	250

3009

		F £	VF £
3009	— Obv. as 3007 but Br below horse. R as above but 1644-5	90	215
3010	— Obv. as above. R as 3004 but Br. as *mm.* as well as 1644-5	90	250
3011	**Shilling**. *O.* Oxford die. R. Declaration, 1643, 3 crude plumes above, no *mm.*	100	325

3012 3014 3015 3017

		F £	VF £
3012	— — R Similar, but *mm.* Br., 1643-4, less crude plumes	100	265
3013	—Obv. Coarse bust. R. As 3011, no *mm.*	115	300
3014	— — Coarse bust, R. as 3012, *mm.* Br, but 1644	115	300
3015	Obv. Bust of good style, plumelet before face. R. As 3012 *mm.* Br. but 1644-5	100	250
3016	— — R.as 3012, 1644, but Br below date instead of *mm.*	100	265
3016A	— — R as 3012, 1644 but plume and plumelet either side	125	250
3017	—Obv. Taller bust with high crown, no plumelets before, *mm.* Br. on its side. R As 3016 but 3 even plumes, Br.below 1644-5	125	325
3018	—Obv. As 3017 but no *mm.* R as above but *mm..* no Br. below 1644-5..	135	350
3018A	— — R as above but plume and plumelets, 1645	135	350
3019	**Sixpence**. Small bust, nothing before. R. Declaration, 1643; *mm.* ./Br....	200	500
3020	Fine style bust. Plumelet before face, 1644; *mm.* ./Br. (on its side)	125	260
3021	**Groat**. Bust l. R. Declaration, 1644	120	250
3022	— Plumelet before face, 1644	100	230
3023	— Br. below date, 1644	100	225

3024

3027

		F	*VF*
		£	£
3024	**Threepence**. *O*. As 2992. Aberystwyth die; *mm*. book. ℞. Declaration, 1644	120	300
3025	Bristol die, plume before face, no *mm*., 1644	130	375
3026	**Halfgroat**. Br. in place of date below Declaration	185	400
3027	**Penny**. Similar bust, I behind. ℞. Large plume with bands	275	650

Late `Declaration' issues, 1645-6

(Previously given as Lundy Island and/or Appledore and Barnstaple/Bideford, it seems likely that coins marked A, 1645 may be Ashby de la Zouch and the coins marked B or with plumes may be Bridgnorth on Severn.)

3028	**Halfcrown**. A below horse and date and as *rev. mm*. 1645	700	2000
3029	Similar but *rev*. from altered Bristol die (i.e. the A's are over Br.)	600	1500
3030	As 3028 but without A below date 1645	575	1450
3031	A below horse and as *rev. mm*. Scroll above Declaration, B below 1646	*Extremely rare*	
3032	Plumelet below horse struck over A. ℞. *Mm*. Shrewsbury plumes; scroll above Declaration, 1646	350	900

3033

3033	— Similar, but plumelet below date	400	1000
3034	**Shilling**. Crowned bust l., *mm*. plume. ℞. Declaration type; *mm*. A and A below 1645	475	950
3035	— Similar, but plumelet before face	475	950
3036	— — Scroll above 'Declaration', 1646; *mm* plume/plumelet	175	350
3036A	— Bristol obv. die, no plumelet, similar to 3018 *mm*. Br. ℞. As last but *mm*. pellet. 1646.	—	450
3037	Obv as above, but Shrewsbury plume before face. plume over Br. *mm*. ℞. As above	185	375
3038	**Sixpence**. *O*. Plumelet before face; *mm*. A; ℞. 1645, 3 plumelets over 'Dec'	250	525

3039

		F £	VF £
3039	*O*. Large Shrewsbury plume before face; *mm*. B. ℞. Scroll above Declaration, 1646, Shrewsbury plume and two plume plumelets	75	140
3040	**Groat**. As 3038	*Extremely rare*	
3041	Somewhat similar, but *obv. mm.* plumelet; ℞ *mm.* pellet or plume,1646 .	70	150
3042	**Threepence**. Somewhat as last but only single plumelet above Declaration, no line below, 1645; no *mm.*	150	325
3043	— Scroll in place of line above, 1646 below	75	150
3044	**Halfgroat**. Bust l., II behind. ℞. Large plume with bands dividing 1646; no *mm.*	300	700

The penny listed under Bristol may belong to this series. It has the same reverse plume punch as 3044.

Truro mint, 1642-3. *Mm.* rose except where stated

Entries from here to 3092 have been revised to follow E. Besly (BNJ 1992). The original catalogue numbers are therefore no longer sequential.

		F £	VF £
3048	**Crown.** King on horseback, head in profile, sash flies out in two ends. ℞. CHRISTO, etc., round garnished shield	150	350
3048A	**Halfcrown**. King on walking horse, groundline below, ℞. Oblong shield, CR above, *mm.* bugle/–	*Extremely rare*	
3050	Galloping horse, king holds baton. ℞. Oblong shield, CR at sides	850	2500
3054	Walking horse, king holds sword. ℞. Similar	350	825
3055	— ℞. Similar, but CR above	400	950
3051	Galloping horse, king holds sword. ℞. Similar, but CR at sides	650	2300
3052	— ℞. Similar, but CR above	600	2000

3053

3054

		F £	VF £
3053	Trotting horse. R. Similar, but CR at sides	375	850
3056	**Shilling**. Small bust of good style. R. Oblong shield	*Extremely rare*	

Exeter mint, 1643-6. Undated or dated 1644-6 *Mm.* rose except where stated

		F	VF
3045	**Half-pound**. King on horseback, face towards viewer, sash in large bow. R. CHRISTO, etc., round garnished shield. Struck from crown dies on a thick flan	*Extremely rare*	
3046	**Crown**. King on horseback, sash in large bow. R. Round garnished shield	135	320
3047	— Shield garnished with twelve even scrolls	160	375
3070	As 3046, R Date divided by *mm.* 16 rose 44	135	290
3071	— R Date to l. of *mm.* 1644	120	275
3072	— *mm*: rose/EX, 1645	150	320
3073	King's sash flies out in two ends; *mm.* castle/rose, 1645	300	550
3074	— *mm.* castle/EX, 1645	160	335
3075	— *mm.* castle, 1645	125	260

3064

3067-9, 3079

		F	VF
3062	**Halfcrown**. King on horseback, sash tied in bow. R. Oblong shield CR at sides	175	475
3063	— R. Round shield with eight even scrolls	100	225
3064	— R. Round shield with five short and two long scrolls	90	200
3066	— R. Oblong shield with angular garnish of triple lines	*Extremely rare*	
3067	Briot's horseman with lumpy ground. R. As 3063	125	350
3069	— R. As 3064	125	350
3068	— R. As 3066	*Extremely rare*	
3079	— R. As 3064, date to l. of *mm.* 1644	135	425

3049

3080

		F £	*VF* £
3049	King on spirited horse galloping over arms. ℞. Oval garnished shield, 1642 in cartouche below	900	3000
3076	— ℞. As 3079, date to l. of *mm*. 1644-5	*Extremely rare*	
3077	— ℞. *mm*. castle, 1645	*Extremely rare*	
3078	Short portly king, leaning backwards on ill-proportioned horse, 1644, 16 rose 44	250	550
3065	Horse with twisted tail, sash flies out in two ends ℞. As 3063	150	425
3080	— ℞. As 3079, date divided by *mm*. 16 rose 44, or date to l. of *mm*. 1644-5	135	350
3081	— ℞. *mm*. castle, 1645	200	500
3082	— ℞. *mm*. EX, 1645	200	500
3083	— ℞. Declaration type; *mm*. EX. 1644-5	1000	2100
3084	— ℞. Similar, EX also below declaration, 1644	900	1750
3057	**Shilling.** Large Oxford style bust. ℞. Round shield with eight even scrolls	450	1000
3058	— ℞. Oval shield with CR at sides	400	900
3060	Normal bust with lank hair. ℞. As 3057	400	850
3059	— ℞. As 3058	375	750
3061	— ℞. Round shield with six scrolls	300	550

3059-61, 3085/6

3085	— ℞. Similar, date to r. of *mm*. 1644, divided 16 rose 44, or to left of *mm*. 1644-5	150	330
3086	— ℞. Declaration type, 1645	450	1250
3087	**Sixpence**. Similar to 3085, 1644, 16 rose 44, small or large VI	135	340
3088	**Groat**. Somewhat similar but 1644 at beginning of *obv*. legend	55	125

3089

3091

		F	VF
		£	£
3089	**Threepence**. Similar. ℞. Square shield, 1644 above	60	140
3090	**Halfgroat**. Similar, but II. ℞. Oval shield, 1644	70	200
3091	— ℞. Large rose, 1644	90	225
3092	**Penny**. As last but I behind head	190	425

Worcester mint 1643-4

3093	**Halfcrown**. King on horseback l., W below; *mm.* two lions. ℞. Declaration type 1644; *mm.* pellets	400	950
3094	— ℞. Square-topped shield; *mm.* helmet, castle	275	900
3095	— ℞. Oval shield; *mm.* helmet	325	875

3096

3096	Similar but grass indicated; *mm.* castle. ℞. Square-topped shield; *mm.* helmet or pellets. (Illustrated above)	275	750
3097	— ℞. Oval draped shield, lis or lions in legend	300	825
3098	— ℞. Oval shield CR at sides, roses in legend	325	875
3099	— ℞. FLORENT etc., oval garnished shield with lion's paws each side .	400	1000
3100	Tall king, no W or *mm.* ℞. Oval shield, lis, roses, lions or stars in legend	300	750
3101	— ℞. Square-topped shield; *mm.* helmet	325	950
3102	— ℞. FLORENT, etc., oval shield; no *mm.*	400	1000
3103	Briot type horse, sword slopes forward, ground-line. ℞. Oval shield, roses in legend; *mm.* 91v, 105, none (combinations)	300	900
3104	— Similar, but CR at sides, 91v/-	325	900
3105	Dumpy, portly king, crude horse. ℞. As 3100; *mm.* 91v, 105, none	275	750
3106	Thin king and horse. ℞. Oval shield, stars in legend; *mm.* 91v, none	275	750

3106

Worcester or Salopia (Shrewsbury)

		F £	VF £
3107	**Shilling**. Bust of king l., adequately rendered. R. Square-topped shield; *mm.* castle	450	1250
3108	— R. CR above shield; *mm.* helmet and lion	450	1250
3109	— R. Oval shield; *mm.* lion, pear	425	1250
3110	— Bust a somewhat crude copy of last (two varieties); *mm.* bird, lis. R. Square-topped shield with lion's paws above and at sides; *mm.* boar's head, helmet	550	1400

3111

3111	— — CR above	550	1400
3112	— R. Oval shield, lis in legend; *mm.* lis	525	1300
3113	— R. Round shield; *mm.* lis, 3 lis	575	1350
3114	Bust r.; *mm.* pear/-, pear/lis. R. Dr., oval shield with or without CR. (Halfcrown reverse dies)	*Extremely rare*	
3115	**Sixpence**. As 3110; *mm.* castle, castle/boar's hd	500	1250

3116

3117

3116	**Groat**. As 3112; *mm.* lis/helmet, rose/helmet	375	750
3117	**Threepence**. Similar; *mm.* lis *obv.*	200	425
3118	**Halfgroat**. Similar; *mm.* lis (*O.*) various (R.)	325	700

Salopia (Shrewsbury) mint, 1644

3119	**Halfcrown**. King on horseback l. SA below; *mm.* lis. R. (*mm.*s lis, helmet, lion rampant, none). Cr. oval shield; CHRISTO etc. *mm.* helmet	*Extremely rare*	
3120	— R. FLORENT, etc., crowned oval shield, no *mm.*	*Extremely rare*	
3121	— SA erased or replaced by large pellet or cannon ball; *mm.* lis in legend, helmet. R. As 3119	1200	2750
3122	Tall horse and king, no thing below; *mm.* lis. R. Large round shield with crude garniture; *mm.* helmet	475	1100
3123	— R. Uncrowned square-topped shield with lion's paw above and at sides; *mm.* helmet	575	1400
3124	— R. Small crowned oval shield; *mm.* various	475	1100
3125	— R. As 3120	550	1300
3126	Finer work with little or no mane before horse. R. Cr. round or oval shield	500	1150
3127	Grass beneath horse. R. Similar; *mm.* lis or rose	650	1400
3128	Ground below horse. R. As 3120	575	1400

Hartlebury Castle (Worcs.) mint, 1646

3129

		F £	VF £
3129	**Halfcrown**. *O. Mm.* pear. R. HC (Hartlebury Castle) in garniture below shield; *mm.* three pears	1000	2350

Chester mint, 1644

3130

		F	VF
3130	**Halfcrown**. As illus. R. Oval shield; *mm.* three gerbs and sword	400	900
3131	— Similar, but without plume or CHST; R. Cr. oval shield with lion skin; *mm.* prostrate gerb; -/cinquefoil, -/.·.	450	950
3132	— R. Crowned square-topped shield with CR at sides both crowned *rev.*; *mm.* cinquefoil	500	1300
3133	As 3130, but without plume or CHST. R. Declaration type, 1644 *rev.*; *mm.* plume	450	1250
3133A	**Shilling**. Bust l. R. Oval garnished shield; *mm.* .·. (obv. only)	*Extremely rare*	
3133B	— R. Square-topped shield; *mm.* as last	*Extremely rare*	
3133C	— R . Shield over long cross	*Extremely rare*	
3134	**Threepence**. R. Square-topped shield; *mm.*-/ prostrate gerb	300	650

3135

		F £	VF £
Welsh Marches mint? 1644			
3135	**Halfcrown**. Crude horseman, l. ℞. Declaration of Bristol style divided by a dotted line, 3 plumes above, 1644 below	500	950
Carlisle besieged, 1644-5			
3136	**Three shillings**. Large crown above C. R /.III. S. ℞. OBS . CARL /. 1645	1500	3200
3137	Similar but : OBS :/-: CARL :./.1645	1500	3700

3138

		F £	VF £
3138	**Shilling**. As illustration	1000	2750
3139	℞. Legend and date in two lines	1200	3000

Note. *(3136-39) Round or Octagonal pieces exist.*

Newark besieged, several times 1645-6, surrendered May 1646

3140 3144

		F £	VF £
3140	**Halfcrown**. Large crown between CR ; below, XXX. ℞. OBS / NEWARK / 1645 or 1646	300	525
3141	**Shilling**. Similar but curious flat shaped crown, NEWARKE, 1645	225	425
3142	Similar but high arched crown, 1645	210	385
3143	— NEWARK, 1645 or 1646	200	375
3144	**Ninepence**. As halfcrown but IX, 1645 or 1646	200	400
3145	— NEWARKE, 1645	190	375
3146	**Sixpence**. As halfcrown but VI, 1646	175	400

Pontefract besieged, June 1648-March 1648-9

		F £	*VF* £
3147	**Two shillings** (lozenge shaped). DVM : SPIRO : SPERO around CR crowned. ℞. Castle surrounded by OBS, PC, sword and 1648	*Extremely rare*	
3148	**Shilling** (lozenge shaped, octagonal or round). Similar	475	1000
3149	— Similar but XII on r. dividing PC	475	975

After the death of Charles I (30 Jan. 1648/9), in the name of Charles II

3148

3149 3150

3150	**Shilling** (octagonal). *O*. As last. ℞. CAROLVS : SECVNDVS : 1648, castle gateway with flag dividing PC, OBS on l., cannon protrudes on r.	475	1000
3151	CAROL : II : etc., around HANC : DE / VS : DEDIT 1648. ℞. POST : MORTEM : PATRIS : PRO : FILIO around gateway etc. as last	475	1025

Scarborough besieged, July 1644-July 1645

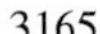

3165

3168

		£
Type I. Castle with gateway to left, value punched below or to side		
3152	**Five shillings and eightpence**	*Extremely rare*
3153	**Crown**. Similar but SC also punched	*Extremely rare*
3154	**Three shillings and fourpence**. As 3152	*Extremely rare*
3155	**Three shillings**. Similar	*Extremely rare*
3156	**Two shillings and tenpence**. Similar	5500
3157	**Halfcrown**. Similar	4750
3158	**Two shillings and fourpence**. Similar	*Extremely rare*
3159	**Two shillings and twopence**. Similar	*Extremely rare*
3160	**Two shillings.** Similar	*Extremely rare*
3161	**One shilling and ninepence**. Similar	*Extremely rare*
3162	**One shilling and sixpence**. Similar	*Extremely rare*
3163	**One shilling and fourpence**. Similar	*Extremely rare*
3164	**One shilling and threepence**. Similar	4000
3165	**Shilling**. As illustration	*Extremely rare*
3166	**Sixpence**. Similar	*Extremely rare*
3167	**Groat**. Similar	*Extremely rare*
Type II. Castle with two turrets, value punched below		
3168	**Two shillings**. Two castles	*Extremely rare*
3170	**One shilling and sixpence**. Single castle	*Extremely rare*
3171	**One shilling and fourpence**. Similar	4000
3172	**One shilling and threepence**. Similar	*Extremely rare*
3173	**One shilling and twopence**. Similar	*Extremely rare*
3174	**One shilling and one penny**. Similar	*Extremely rare*
3175	**Shilling**. Similar	4500
3176	**Elevenpence**. Similar	*Extremely rare*
3177	**Tenpence**. Similar	*Extremely rare*
3178	**Ninepence**. Similar	*Extremely rare*
3179	**Sevenpence**. Similar	*Extremely rare*
3180	**Sixpence**. Similar	*Extremely rare*

COPPER

For mintmarks see C. Wilson Peck, *English Copper, Tin and Bronze Coins in the British Museum, 1558-1958.*

3185

3191

3194

		F £	*VF* £
3181	**Royal farthing**. 'Richmond' round, colon stops, 1a. CARO over IACO; *mm.* on *obv.*	8	22
3182	— — 1b. CARA; *mm.* on *obv.*	75	150
3183	— — 1c. CARO; *mm.* on *obv.*	5	15

		F £	VF £
Royal farthing.			
3184	'Richmond' round apostrophe stops. 1d. Eagle-headed harp	8	22
3185	— 1e. Beaded harp	6	17
3186	— 1f. Scroll-fronted harp, 5 jewels on circlet	12	35
3187	— 1g. — — 7 jewels on circlet	6	17
3188	Transitional issue, double-arched crowns	18	50
3189	'Maltravers' round, 3a; *mm.* on *obv. only*	9	24
3190	— 3b. *Mm.* both sides	5	15
3191	— 3c. Different *mm.* either side	6	18
3192	'Richmond' oval. 4a. CARO over IACO; *mm.* both sides	18	45
3193	— — — *mm.* on *obv.*	18	45
3194	— 4b. CARO, colon stops; *mm.* on *obv.*	15	40
3195	— — — — *mm.* on *rev.*	15	40
3196	— — — — *mm.* both sides	15	40
3197	— 4c. apostrophe stops; *mm.* rose on *obv.*	18	45
3198	— — — *mm.* rose both sides	18	45
3199	— — — *mm.* rose (*obv.*); scroll (*rev.*)	18	45
3200	'Maltravers' oval. 5. CAROLVS; *mm.* lis both sides	22	50

3201

3207

3201	**Rose farthing**. 1a. Double-arched crowns; double rose; sceptres within inner circle, BRIT; *mm.* on *obv.* or *rev.* or both sides, or different each side	9	24
3202	— 1b. — — sceptres just break circle, BRIT; *mm.* on *obv.* or both sides or no *mm.*	7	20
3203	— 1c. — — sceptres almost to outer circle, BRIT; *mm.*s as 3201	6	18
3204	— 1d. — — — BRI; *mm.* on *obv.* or both sides, or different each side	6	18
3205	Transitional mules of types 1d/2, with double and single arched crowns; *mm.* as 3204	9	24
3206	— 2. Single-arched crowns; single rose; *mm.* as 3204	4	12
3207	— 3. Sceptres below crown; *mm.* mullet	18	45

COMMONWEALTH, 1649-60

The coins struck during the Commonwealth have inscriptions in English instead of Latin which was considered to savour too much of papacy. St. George's cross and the Irish harp take the place of the royal arms. The silver halfpenny was issued for the last time. Coins with *mm.* anchor were struck during the protectorship of Richard Cromwell.

Mintmarks

1649-57 Sun 1658-60 Anchor

3208  3213

GOLD

		Fair £	*F* £	*VF* £
3208	**Unite.** As illustration; *mm.* sun, 1649-57		400	750
3209	Similar, *mm.* anchor, 1658, 1660		1000	2650
3210	**Double-crown.** As illus., but X; *mm.* sun, 1649-57		325	600
3211	Similar, *mm.* anchor, 1660		900	2250
3212	**Crown.** Similar, but V; *mm.* sun, 1649-57		250	450
3213	As illus., *mm.* anchor, 1658, 60		900	2250

SILVER

		Fair £	*F* £	*VF* £
3214	**Crown.** Same type; *mm.* sun, 1649, 51-4, 56		300	600
3215	**Halfcrown.** Similar; *mm.* sun, 1649, 1651-6		110	225
3216	— *mm.* anchor, 1658-1660	150	400	825
3217	**Shilling.** Similar; *mm.* sun, 1649, 1651-7		70	140
3218	— *mm.* anchor, 1658-60	125	300	625
3219	**Sixpence.** Similar; *mm.* sun, 1649, 1651-7		70	150
3220	— *mm.* anchor, 1658-60	110	250	525

3221

3223

		F £	*VF* £
3221	**Halfgroat**. As illustration	25	60
3222	**Penny**. Similar, but I above shields	20	50
3223	**Halfpenny.** As illustration	20	45

OLIVER CROMWELL

Patterns. Although often referred to as patterns, there is in fact nothing to suggest that the portrait coins of Oliver Cromwell were not intended for circulation. Authorised in 1656, the first full production came in 1657 and was followed by a second more plentiful one before Cromwell's death. All coins were struck from dies by Thomas Simon in the presses of the Frenchman, Pierre Blondeau.

GOLD

		F £	*VF* £	*EF* £
3224	**Fifty shillings**. Head l. ℞. Shield, 1656. Inscribed edge			15000

3225

		F £	*VF* £	*EF* £
3225	**Broad.** (=20s.). Similar, but grained edge		1600	3750

SILVER

3227A

		F £	*VF* £	*EF* £
3226	**Crown.** Bust l. ℞. Shield, 1658. Inscribed edge	475	900	1650
3227	**Halfcrown.** Similar, 1656	600	—	—
3227A	— 1658	225	450	850
3228	**Shilling.** Similar, but grained edge, 1658	200	400	700
3229	**Sixpence.** Similar	*Extremely rare*		

COPPER

3230

		F £	*VF* £	*EF* £
3230	**Farthing.** Dr. bust l. ℞. CHARITIE AND CHANGE, shield	1200	2250	—

There are also other reverse types for this coin.

SEVENTEENTH-CENTURY TOKENS

As there was no authorized copper coinage under the Commonwealth, towns and traders took it into their own hands to issue small change. Between 1648 and 1672 there was an enormous and very varied issue of these tokens. They were mostly farthings and halfpennies, but there were also some pennies. No collection is truly representative unless it contains at least a few. Many collectors specialize in those of their own town or county.

	F
	£
Price of commoner pennies	30
— — — heart shaped pennies	175
— — — round halfpennies	8
— — — octagonal halfpennies	20
— — — heart-shaped halfpennies	110
— — — square or lozenge-shaped halfpennies	125
— — — round farthings	5
— — — square farthings	75
— — — octagonal farthings	30

For further details of seventeenth-century tokens, see *Trade Tokens issued in the Seventeenth Century* by G. C. Williamson, also Seaby's *British Tokens and their Values,* and *Seventeenth Century Tokens of the British Isles and their Values* by Michael Dickinson, 1986.

CHARLES II, 1660-85

For the first two years after the Restoration the same denominations, apart from the silver crown, were struck as were issued during the Commonwealth. Then, early in 1663, the ancient hand hammering process was finally superceded by the machinery of Blondeau. The Roettiers engraved the dies as a safeguard against clipping, the larger coins were made with the edge inscribed DECVS ET TVTAMEN and the regnal year. The medium-sized coins were given a grained edge.

The new gold coins were current for 100s., 20s. and 10s., and they came to be called 'guineas' as the gold from which some of them were made was imported from Guinea by the Africa Company (whose badge was the Elephant and Castle). It was not until some years later that the guinea increased in value to 21s. and more. The Africa Co. badge is also found on some silver and so is the plume symbol indicating silver from the Welsh mines. The four smallest silver denominations, though known today as 'Maundy Money', were actually issued for general circulation: at this period the silver penny was probably the only coin distributed at the royal Maundy ceremonies. Though never part of the original agreement smaller coins were eventually also struck by machinery.

A good regal copper coinage was issued for the first time in 1672, but later in the reign, farthings were struck in tin (with a copper plug) in order to help the Cornish tin industry.

For the emergency issues struck in the name of Charles II in 1648/9, see the siege pieces of Pontefract listed under Charles I, nos. 3150-1.

Mintmark: Crown. 

GOLD

Hammered coinage, 1660-2

First issue. Without mark of value

3302

3305

		F	*VF*
		£	£
3301	**Unite** (20s.). Type as illustration	500	1150
3302	**Double-crown**. As illustration	500	1100
3303	**Crown**. Similar	450	900
	Second issue. With mark of value		
3304	**Unite.** Type as illustration	450	950
3305	**Double-crown**. As illustration	425	800
3306	**Crown**. Similar	500	850

SILVER

		F	VF
	First issue. Without inner circles or mark of value	£	£
3307	**Halfcrown.** Crowned bust, as 3308	450	1000

3308

3309

3308	**Shilling**. Similar	140	350
3309	**Sixpence**. Similar	125	300
3310	**Twopence**. Similar	25	70
3311	**Penny**. Similar	25	70
3312	As last, but without mintmark	25	70
	Second issue. Without inner circles, but with mark of value		

3313

3322

3313	**Halfcrown**. Crowned bust	475	1500
3314	**Shilling**. Similar	250	650
3315	**Sixpence**. Similar	500	1350
3316	**Twopence**. Similar, but mm. on obv. only	135	300

3310  3317  3326

3317	Similar, but mm. both sides (machine made)	15	30
3318	Bust to edge of coin, legend starts at bottom l. (machine made, single arch crown)	15	30
3319	**Penny**. As 3317	15	30
3320	As 3318 (single arch crown)	15	30

No.	Description	F £	VF £	EF £
	Third issue. With inner circles and mark of value			
3321	**Halfcrown**. Crowned bust to i.c. (and rarely to edge of coin)		100	275
3322	**Shilling**. Similar		65	175
3323	**Sixpence**. Similar		55	160
3324	**Fourpence**. Similar		20	50
3325	**Threepence**. Similar		25	55
3326	**Twopence**. Similar		10	30
3327	**Penny**. Similar		30	60

GOLD

Milled coinage

3328

3328 Five guineas. First bust, pointed truncation

Date	F £	VF £	EF £	Date	F £	VF £	EF £
1668	700	1300	3750	1674	800	1400	3900
1669	750	1300	3750	1675	750	1250	3600
1670	700	1200	3500	1676	800	1400	3900
1671	800	1450	3900	1677	750	1300	3750
1672	700	1300	3750	1678/7	700	1300	3750
1673	700	1300	3750				

3329 — with elephant below bust

Date	F £	VF £	EF £	Date	F £	VF £	EF £
1668	700	1200	3750	1675	950	1800	4750
1669	950	1800	4750	1677/5		*Extremely rare*	

3330 — with elephant and castle below

Date	F £	VF £	EF £	Date	F £	VF £	EF £
1675		*Extremely rare*		1677	800	1400	3900
1676	750	1300	3750	1678/7	850	1500	4250

3331 Second bust, rounded truncation

Date	F £	VF £	EF £	Date	F £	VF £	EF £
1678/7	850	1500	4500	1682	700	1200	3600
1679	700	1200	3600	1683	700	1300	3750
1680	750	1300	3750	1684	700	1200	3600
1681	700	1200	3600				

3332 with elephant and castle below

Date	F £	VF £	EF £	Date	F £	VF £	EF £
1680		*Extremely rare*		1683	850	1500	4500
1681	850	1500	4500	1684	700	1200	3600
1682	750	1300	3750				

3333 Two guineas. First bust, pointed truncation

Date	F £	VF £	EF £	Date	F £	VF £	EF £
1664	350	800	3250	1669		*Extremely rare*	
1665		*Extremely rare*		1671	400	900	3500

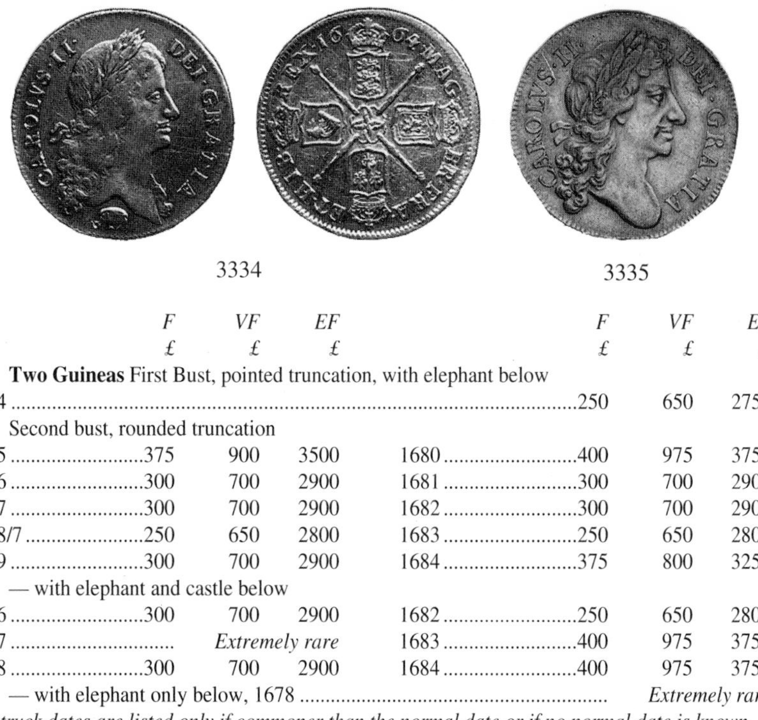

3334 3335

	F £	VF £	EF £		F £	VF £	EF £
3334 Two Guineas First Bust, pointed truncation, with elephant below							
1664					250	650	2750
3335 Second bust, rounded truncation							
1675	375	900	3500	1680	400	975	3750
1676	300	700	2900	1681	300	700	2900
1677	300	700	2900	1682	300	700	2900
1678/7	250	650	2800	1683	250	650	2800
1679	300	700	2900	1684	375	800	3250
3336 — with elephant and castle below							
1676	300	700	2900	1682	250	650	2800
1677		*Extremely rare*		1683	400	975	3750
1678	300	700	2900	1684	400	975	3750
3337 — with elephant only below, 1678						*Extremely rare*	

Overstruck dates are listed only if commoner than the normal date or if no normal date is known.

	F £	VF £	EF £		F £	VF £	EF £
3338 Guinea. First bust, 1663					500	1450	3250
3339 — with elephant below, 1663					400	1150	3000
3340 Second bust, 1664					350	950	2500
3341 — with elephant below, 1664						*Extremely rare*	
3342 Third bust, normal portrait							
1664	200	650	1900	1669	250	750	2000
1665	200	600	1750	1670	200	600	1750
1666	200	600	1750	1671	200	600	1750
1667	200	600	1750	1672	275	800	2250
1668	200	600	1750	1673	350	950	2500

3343

3345

3343 — with elephant below

	F £	VF £	EF £
1664	275	800	2250
1665	250	750	2000
1668	*Extremely rare*		

3344 Fourth bust, rounded truncation

	F £	VF £	EF £
1672	175	500	1550
1673	175	500	1550
1674	250	750	2000
1675	200	600	1750
1676	150	450	1450
1677	150	450	1450
1678	150	450	1450
1679	150	450	1450
1680	150	450	1450
1681	200	600	1750
1682	175	500	1550
1683	150	450	1450
1684	175	500	1550

3345 Guinea. Fourth bust, with elephant and castle below

	F £	VF £	EF £
1674	*Extremely rare*		
1675	350	950	2400
1676	175	500	1600
1677	175	550	1800
1678	250	750	2250
1679	250	750	2250
1680	400	1000	3000
1681	250	750	2200
1682	275	800	2000
1683	400	1000	3000
1684	275	800	2000

3346 — — with elephant below

	F £	VF £	EF £
1677	*Extremely rare*		
1678	*Extremely rare*		

3347 Half-guinea. First bust, pointed truncation

	F £	VF £	EF £
1669	175	500	1800
1670	150	350	1500
1671	225	650	2000
1672	200	650	2000

3348

3348 Second bust, rounded truncation

	F £	VF £	EF £
1672	175	400	1600
1673	300	750	2250
1674	300	750	2500
1675	*Extremely rare*		
1676	175	375	1500
1677	175	400	1600
1678	175	450	1800
1679	135	350	1500
1680	300	750	2250
1681	300	750	2250
1682	200	750	2250
1683	175	400	1600
1684	135	325	1500

3349 Half guinea. Second bust, rounded truncation, with elephant and castle below

	F £	VF £	EF £		F £	VF £	EF £
1676	350	850	—	1682	300	800	2400
1677	300	800	2400	1683		*Extremely rare*	
1678/7	225	650	2000	1684	175	450	1800
1680		*Extremely rare*					

3350

SILVER

		F	VF	EF
3350	**Crown**. First bust, rose below, edge undated, 1662	40	200	950
3351	— — edge dated, 1662	50	250	1100
3352	— no rose, edge dated, 1662	55	300	1250
3353	— — edge not dated, 1662	50	250	1100
3354	— — new reverse, shields altered, 1663, regnal year on edge in Roman figures ANNO REGNI XV	45	225	1100

3355

3355 Second bust, regnal year on edge in Roman figures

	F	VF	EF		F	VF	EF
1664	50	250	1100	1666	65	300	1200
1665	165	600	—				

3356 — — elephant below bust, 1666 ... 130 | 500 | —

3357 — regnal year on edge in words (e.g. 1667= DECIMO NONO)

	F	VF	EF		F	VF	EF
1667	50	250	1100	1670	50	250	1100
1668	45	225	1000	1671	45	225	1000
1669	125	450	—				

3358 Third bust

	F	VF	EF		F	VF	EF
1671	45	225	1000	1676	45	225	1000
1672	45	225	1000	1677	50	250	1100
1673	45	225	1000	1678/7	100	400	—
1674		*Extremely rare*		1679	45	225	1000
1675/3	165	600	—	1680/79	55	250	1100

		F £	VF £	EF £		F £	VF £	EF £
3359	Fourth bust							
	1679	45	225	1000	1682/1	50	250	1100
	1680	45	250	1100	1683	130	500	—
	1681	45	250	1100	1684	90	350	—
3360	— elephant and castle below bust, 1681					950	2250	—
3361	**Halfcrown.** First bust, regnal year on edge in Roman figures 1663					40	175	800
3362	Second bust, 1664					60	275	1000
3363	Third bust, 1666					500	1750	—
3364	— elephant below bust, 1666					300	650	—
3365	— regnal date on edge in words							
	1667/4		*Extremely rare*		1669/4	110	350	—
	1668/4	110	350	—	1670	35	150	750
3366	Third bust variety							
	1671	30	100	650	1672	35	150	750

3367

3369

3370

		F £	VF £	EF £		F £	VF £	EF £
3367	Fourth bust							
	1672	40	150	700	1679	30	100	650
	1673	30	100	650	1680	100	300	—
	1674	75	250	1000	1681	40	175	800
	1675	40	175	800	1682	50	225	900
	1676	30	90	550	1683	35	150	750
	1677	40	150	700	1684/3	90	350	—
	1678	125	350	—				
3368	— plume below bust							
	1673	1000	—	—	1683		*Extremely rare*	
3369	— plume below bust and in centre of *rev*., 1673						*Extremely rare*	
3370	— elephant and castle below bust, 1681					fair 350 —	—	—

3371

		F £	VF £	EF £		F £	VF £	EF £
3371	**Shilling**. First bust, 1663					20	75	275
3372	First bust variety							
	1663	20	75	275	1668	150	400	—
	1666		*Extremely rare*		1669/6		*Extremely rare*	

	F £	VF £	EF £		F £	VF £	EF £
3373 Shilling. First bust variety elephant below bust, 1666					150	500	1750
3374 Guinea head, elephant below bust, 1666					400	1100	—
3375 Shilling Second bust							
1666		*Extremely rare*		1676	30	90	450
1668	20	60	275	1677	30	90	450
1669		*Extremely rare*		1678	60	175	650
1670	60	175	650	1679	30	100	450
1671	90	275	750	1680		*Extremely rare*	
1672	30	120	500	1681	90	275	750
1673	60	175	750	1682/1	225	500	—
1674	60	175	750	1683		*Extremely rare*	
1675	90	300	—				

3376

3380

	F £	VF £	EF £		F £	VF £	EF £
3376 — plume below bust and in centre of *rev.*							
1671	120	350	—	1676	120	400	—
1673	120	400	—	1679	150	500	—
1674	120	350	—	1680	175	600	—
1675	120	400	—				
3377 — plume *rev.* only, 1674					150	500	—
3378 — plume *obv.* *only*							
1677	150	500	—	1679	120	450	—
3379 — elephant and castle below bust, 1681/0					750	—	—
3380 Third (large) bust							
1674	150	475	—	1675	100	275	1000
3381 Fourth (large) bust, older features							
1683	90	200	850	1684	75	175	750
3382 Sixpence							
1674	15	45	150	1680	25	90	300
1675	15	45	150	1681	15	45	150
1676	25	90	300	1682/1	18	65	200
1677	15	45	150	1683	15	45	150
1678/7	18	65	200	1684	15	50	180
1679	18	65	200				
3383 Fourpence. Undated. Crowned bust l. to edge of coin, value behind. R. Shield					7	15	30
3384 Dated. *O.* As illustration 3384. Four Cs							
1670	5	10	35	1678	5	9	30
1671	5	10	35	1679	5	9	30
1672/1	5	10	35	1680	5	9	30
1673	5	10	35	1681	5	9	30
1674	5	10	35	1682	5	9	30
1675	5	10	35	1683	5	9	30
1676	5	10	35	1684/3	5	9	30
1677	5	9	30				
3385 Threepence. Undated. As 3383					9	18	40

3384 3386 3388 3390

3386 Threepence. Dated. As illustration

	F £	VF £	EF £		F £	VF £	EF £
1670	5	9	27	1678	5	8	25
1671	5	8	25	1679	5	7	25
1672/1	5	8	25	1680	5	9	27
1673	5	8	25	1681	5	9	27
1674	5	8	25	1682	5	9	27
1675	5	9	27	1683	5	9	27
1676	5	8	25	1684	5	9	27
1677	5	8	25				

3387 Twopence. Undated. As 3383 (double arch crown) 6 12 25

3388 Dated. As illustration

	F £	VF £	EF £		F £	VF £	EF £
1668	5	8	25	1677	5	8	25
1670	5	8	25	1678	5	8	25
1671	5	8	25	1679	5	8	25
1672/1	5	8	25	1680	5	8	25
1673	5	8	25	1681	5	8	25
1674	5	8	25	1682	5	8	25
1675	5	8	25	1683	5	8	25
1676	5	8	25	1684	5	8	25

3389 Penny. Undated. As 3383 (double arch crown) 8 17 40

3390 Dated. As illustration

	F £	VF £	EF £		F £	VF £	EF £
1670	7	16	35	1678	7	16	35
1671	7	16	35	1679	13	25	45
1672/1	7	16	35	1680	7	16	35
1673	7	16	35	1681	8	18	40
1674	7	16	35	1682	8	17	38
1675	7	16	35	1683	7	16	35
1676	8	17	38	1684	8	17	38
1677	7	16	35				

3391 Maundy Set. Undated. The four coins 45 100 150

3392 Dated. The four coins. Uniform dates

	F £	VF £	EF £		F £	VF £	EF £
1670	32	65	175	1678	35	70	180
1671	30	60	165	1679	32	65	175
1672	32	65	175	1680	30	60	165
1673	30	60	165	1681	35	70	180
1674	30	60	165	1682	32	65	175
1675	30	60	165	1683	30	60	165
1676	30	60	165	1684	32	65	175
1677	30	60	165				

COPPER AND TIN

3393 3394

	F £	VF £	EF £		F £	VF £	EF £
3393 Copper **halfpenny**							
1672	25	60	225	1675	25	60	225
1673	25	60	225				
3394 Copper **farthing.** As illustration							
1672	20	40	175	1675	20	40	175
1673	20	40	175	1679	25	60	225
1674	20	40	175				

3395

	Fair £	F £	VF £	EF £
3395 Tin **farthing.** Somewhat similar, but with copper plug, edge inscribed NUMMORVM FAMVLVS, and date on edge only				
1684	25	65	175	550
1685			*Extremely rare*	

Tin halfpence and farthings provided the only base metal coinage during this short reign. All genuine tin coins of this period have a copper plug.

GOLD

		F £	VF £	EF £		F £	VF £	EF £
3396	**Five guineas.** First bust l., sceptres misplaced, 1686					950	1600	4000
3397	— sceptres normal.							
	1687	900	1500	3600	1688	850	1450	3600
3397A	Second bust							
	1687	900	1500	3600	1688	850	1450	3600
3398	First bust. Elephant and castle below bust							
	1687	1000	1650	4500	1688	1000	1650	4500
3399	**Two guineas.** Similar							
	1687	450	1300	3250	1688/7	500	1400	3500
3400	**Guinea.** First bust							
	1685	180	450	1250	1686	225	600	1900
3401	— elephant and castle below							
	1685	225	650	2150	1686		*Extremely rare*	
3402	Second bust							
	1686	180	450	1250	1688	180	450	1250
	1687	180	450	1250				

3403

3404

		F £	VF £	EF £		F £	VF £	EF £
3403	— elephant and castle below							
	1686	300	950	—	1688	200	500	1700
	1687	200	500	1700				
3404	**Half-guinea**							
	1686	150	325	1350	1688	175	375	1500
	1687	225	475	1800				
3405	Elephant and castle below, 1686					450	1500	—

3406

SILVER

	F £	VF £	EF £		F £	VF £	EF £
3406 Crown. First bust, 1686					70	275	650
3407 Second bust							
1687	55	175	450	1688	65	225	550

3408

1st bust

2nd bust

	F £	VF £	EF £		F £	VF £	EF £
3408 Halfcrown. First bust							
1685	50	165	500	1687	50	165	500
1686	50	165	500				
3409 Second bust							
1687	60	200	600	1688	50	155	550

3410

3412

	F £	VF £	EF £		F £	VF £	EF £
3410 Shilling							
1685	40	150	375	1687/6	50	165	450
1686	40	150	375	1688	50	165	450
3411 Plume in centre of *rev.*, 1685						*Extremely rare*	
3412 Sixpence. Early type shields							
1686	40	120	250	1687	45	130	275

3414  3415  3416  3417

	F £	*VF* £	*EF* £
3413 Late type shields			
1687	40	120	250
1688	45	130	275
3414 **Fourpence.** *O.* As illus. R. IIII crowned			
1686	6	14	30
1687/6	6	13	28
1688	6	14	30
3415 **Threepence.** As illustration			
1685	6	13	27
1686	6	13	27
1687/6	6	13	27
1688	8	18	30
3416 **Twopence.** As illustration			
1686	6	13	25
1687	6	13	25
1688	6	13	25
3417 **Penny.** As illustration			
1685	8	18	30
1686	8	18	30
1687	8	18	30
1688	8	18	30
3418 **Maundy Set.** As last four. Uniform dates			
1686	35	70	150
1687	35	70	150
1688	35	70	150

TIN

3419

	Fair £	*F* £	*VF* £	*EF* £
3419 **Halfpenny.** Draped bust				
1685	25	50	175	550
1686	27	55	200	600
1687	25	50	175	550

3420

3420 **Farthing.** Cuirassed bust

1684			*Extremely rare*	
1685	25	50	175	550
1686	27	55	200	600
1687			*Extremely rare*	
3421 Draped bust, 1687	30	60	225	650

WILLIAM AND MARY, 1688-94

Due to the poor state of the silver coinage, much of it worn hammered coin, the guinea, which wasvalued at 21s. 6d. at the beginning of the reign, circulated for as much as 30s. by 1694. The tin halfpennies and farthings were replaced by copper coins in 1694. The rampant lion of Orange is now placed as an inescutcheon on the centre of the royal arms.

GOLD

	F £	*VF* £	*EF* £		*F* £	*VF* £	*EF* £
3422 Five guineas. Conjoined heads r.							
1691	750	1500	3500	1693	750	1500	3500
1692	750	1500	3500	1694/2	800	1600	3750

3422

	F £	*VF* £	*EF* £		*F* £	*VF* £	*EF* £
3423 — elephant and castle below							
1691	850	1800	4000	1693	1100	2100	4500
1692	900	1800	4000	1694/2	1000	2000	4250
3424 Two guineas. Conjoined heads r.							
1693	400	900	3000	1694/3	400	900	3000
3425 — elephant and castle below							
1691	*Extremely rare*			1694/3	650	1400	4000
1693	650	1400	4000				
3426 Guinea. Conjoined heads r.							
1689	180	450	1500	1692	225	650	1900
1690	200	550	1750	1693	225	600	1750
1691	225	600	1750	1694	180	500	1600

3427

	F £	*VF* £	*EF* £		*F* £	*VF* £	*EF* £
3427 — elephant and castle below							
1689	200	500	1600	1692	250	600	1800
1690	270	750	2400	1693	*Extremely rare*		
1691	225	550	1750	1694	250	600	1800
3428 — elephant only below							
1692	325	900	2250	1693	*Extremely rare*		

Overstruck dates are listed only if commoner than the normal date or if no normal date is known.

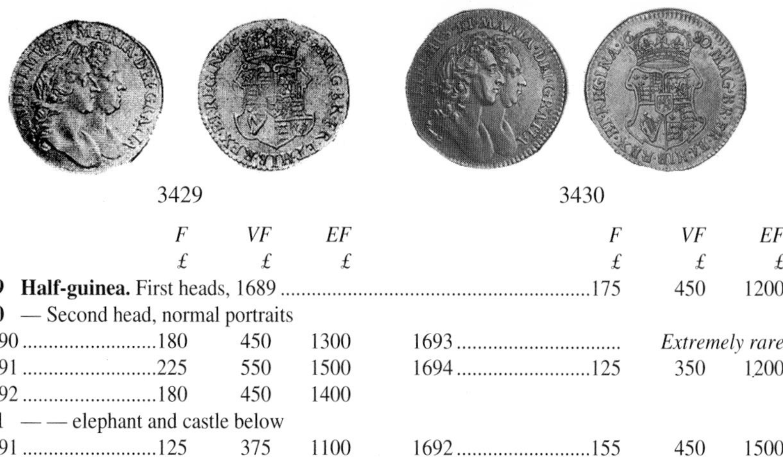

3429 3430

		F £	VF £	EF £		F £	VF £	EF £
3429	**Half-guinea.** First heads, 1689					175	450	1200
3430	— Second head, normal portraits							
	1690	180	450	1300	1693	*Extremely rare*		
	1691	225	550	1500	1694	125	350	1200
	1692	180	450	1400				
3431	— — elephant and castle below							
	1691	125	375	1100	1692	155	450	1500
3432	— — elephant only below, 1692					*Extremely rare*		

SILVER

3433

		F £	VF £	EF £		F £	VF £	EF £
3433	**Crown.** Conjoined busts							
	1691	145	350	1000	1692	145	350	1000

3434 3435

		F £	VF £	EF £		F £	VF £	EF £
3434	**Halfcrown.** First busts, first shields, 1689					25	85	300
3435	— second shield							
	1689	30	95	375	1690	35	135	450

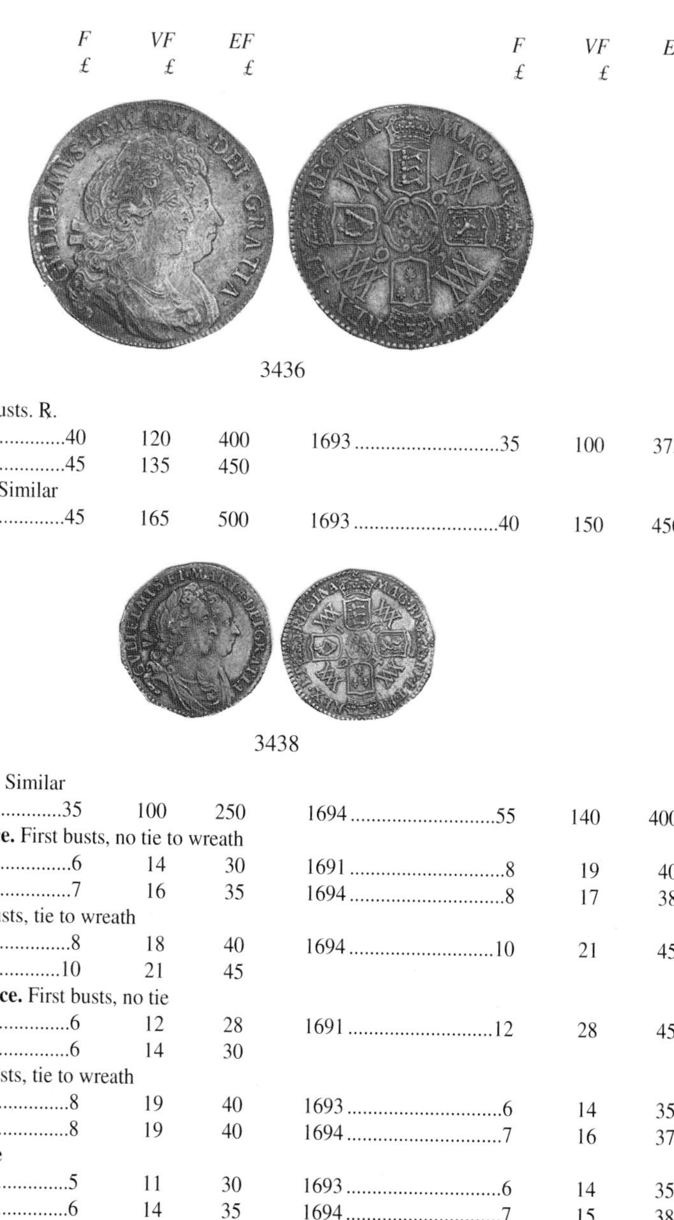

3436

3438

	F £	VF £	EF £		F £	VF £	EF £
3436 Second busts. R.							
1691	40	120	400	1693	35	100	375
1692	45	135	450				
3437 **Shilling.** Similar							
1692	45	165	500	1693	40	150	450
3438 **Sixpence.** Similar							
1693	35	100	250	1694	55	140	400
3439 **Fourpence.** First busts, no tie to wreath							
1689	6	14	30	1691	8	19	40
1690	7	16	35	1694	8	17	38
3440 Second busts, tie to wreath							
1692	8	18	40	1694	10	21	45
1693	10	21	45				
3441 **Threepence.** First busts, no tie							
1689	6	12	28	1691	12	28	45
1690	6	14	30				
3442 Second busts, tie to wreath							
1691	8	19	40	1693	6	14	35
1692	8	19	40	1694	7	16	37
3443 **Twopence**							
1689	5	11	30	1693	6	14	35
1691	6	14	35	1694	7	15	38
1692	6	14	35				
3444 **Penny.** Legend continuous over heads, 1689					90	200	375
3445 Legend broken by heads							
1690	12	25	50	1693	12	25	50
1691	12	25	50	1694	12	25	50
1692	12	25	50				

3446

	F £	VF £	EF £		F £	VF £	EF £
3446 Maundy Set. As last pieces. Uniform dates							
1689	130	275	500	1693	60	120	210
1691	50	110	200	1694	50	110	200
1692	50	110	200				

TIN AND COPPER

3448

3451

	Fair £	F £	VF £	EF £
3447 Tin **Halfpenny.** Small draped busts, 1689	175	350	900	—
3448 Large cuirassed busts; date only on edge				
1690	25	50	175	500
3449 — date in exergue and on edge				
1691	25	50	175	500
1692	25	50	175	500
3450 Tin **Farthing.** Small draped busts				
1689	90	175	500	—
1689, edge 1690			*Extremely rare*	
3451 Large cuirassed busts				
1690, edge 1689			*Extremely rare*	
1690	25	55	175	525
1691	25	55	175	525
1692	27	60	190	575

3452

3453

	F	VF	EF
3452 Copper **Halfpenny,** 1694	20	50	300
3453 Copper **Farthing,** 1694	25	60	350

In 1696 a great re-coinage was undertaken to replace the hammered silver that made up most of the coinage in circulation, much of it being clipped and badly worn. Branch mints were set up at Bristol, Chester, Exeter, Norwich and York to help with the re-coinage. For a short time before they were finally demonetized, unclipped hammered coins were allowed to circulate freely provided they were officially pierced in the centre. Silver coins with roses between the coats of arms were made from silver obtained from the West of England mines.

GOLD

3456

3457

No.		*F* £	*VF* £	*EF* £		*F* £	*VF* £	*EF* £
3454	**Five guineas.** First bust							
	1699	850	1450	3000	1700	850	1450	3250
3455	— elephant and castle below, 1699					1000	2000	4250
3456	Second bust ('fine work'), 1701. Plain or ornamental sceptres					850	1700	3750
3457	**Two guineas** ('fine work'), 1701					900	1550	3600

3458

3460

No.		F	VF	EF		F	VF	EF
3458	**Guinea**. First bust							
	1695	150	375	900	1697	180	450	1100
	1696	180	450	1100				
3459	— elephant and castle below							
	1695	200	500	1300	1696	*Extremely rare*		
3460	Second bust, human-headed harp							
	1697	180	450	1000	1699	200	500	1300
	1698	150	325	750	1700	150	325	750
3461	— elephant and castle below							
	1697	350	1000	—	1699	*Extremely rare*		
	1698	225	600	1450	1700	400	1100	—
3462	**Guinea.** Second bust. R. Human headed harp. Large lettering and large date, 1698					150	350	900
3463	— R. Narrow crowns, usually with strolled harp, 1701					150	350	900
3464	— — elephant and castle, 1701					*Extremely rare*		
3465	Third bust ('fine work'), 1701					300	700	2500

3466

	F £	VF £	EF £		F £	VF £	EF £
3466 **Half-guinea**. ℞. With early harp, 1695					100	250	650
3467 — Elephant and castle. ℞. With early harp							
1695	225	550	1500	1696	150	350	900
3468 ℞. With late harp							
1697	160	400	1300	1700	110	250	600
1698	110	250	600	1701	110	250	600
1699	*Extremely rare*						
3469 — elephant and castle, 1698					180	450	1300

SILVER

3470

	F £	VF £	EF £		F £	VF £	EF £
3470 **Crown**. First bust, first harp							
1695	35	120	300	1696	35	110	275
3471 Second bust (hair across breast), 1696							*Unique*
3472 Third bust, first harp, 1696					35	120	300
3473 — second harp, 1697					250	800	—

3474

	F £	VF £	EF £
3474 Third bust variety, third harp, 1700	35	125	325
3475 **Halfcrown.** Small shields, 1696	20	50	175
3476 — B (*Bristol*) below bust, 1696	25	70	225

No.	Description	F £	VF £	EF £		F £	VF £	EF £
3477	— C (*Chester*) below bust, 1696					75	200	450
3478	— E (*Exeter*) below bust, 1696					90	250	600
3479	— N (*Norwich*) below bust, 1696					40	125	275
3480	— y (*York*) below bust, 1696					75	200	450
3481	Large shield, early harp, 1696					20	50	175
3482	— — B (*Bristol*) below bust, 1696					25	70	225
3483	— — C (*Chester*) below bust, 1696					30	110	275
3484	— — E (*Exeter*) below bust, 1696					35	135	375
3485	— — N (*Norwich*) below bust, 1696					55	175	500
3486	— — y (*York*) below bust, 1696					40	125	300
3487	Large shields, ordinary harp							
	1696	55	175	500	1697	20	50	175

3488

3490

No.	Description	F £	VF £	EF £		F £	VF £	EF £
3488	— — B (*Bristol*) below bust, 1697					25	80	250
3489	— — C (*Chester*) below bust							
	1696	55	175	500	1697	25	70	225
3490	— — E (*Exeter*) below bust							
	1696	55	175	500	1697	20	55	195
3491	—— N (*Norwich*) below bust							
	1696	90	250	600	1697	25	70	225
3492	— — y (*York*) below bust, 1697					20	55	195
3493	Second bust (hair across breast), 1696						*Unique*	
3494	Modified large shields							
	1698	20	55	200	1700	20	65	250
	1699	40	125	375	1701	25	75	275
3495	Elephant and castle below bust, 1701 ... *Fair* 375							
3496	Plumes in angles on *rev.*, 1701					40	125	350

1st bust 2nd bust 3rd bust 3507

3rd bust var. 4th bust 5th bust

		F £	VF £	EF £		F £	VF £	EF £
3497	**Shilling.** First bust							
	1695	18	50	150	1697	10	25	80
	1696	10	25	80				
3498	— B (*Bristol)* below bust							
	1699	18	45	135	1697	20	50	150
3499	— C (*Chester)* below bust							
	1696	20	50	150	1697	20	50	150
3500	— E (*Exeter)* below bust							
	1696	20	50	150	1697	20	50	150
3501	**Shilling.** First bust N (*Norwich)* below bust							
	1696	20	50	150	1697	20	50	150
3502	— y (*York)* below bust							
	1696	20	50	150	1697	20	50	150
3503	— Y (*York)* below bust							
	1696	22	60	175	1697	22	60	175
3504	Second bust (hair across breast), 1696							*Unique*
3505	Third bust, 1697					10	25	80
3506	— B (*Bristol)* below bust, 1697					22	60	175
3507	— C (*Chester)* below bust							
	1696	45	150	450	1697	20	50	150
3508	— E (*Exeter)* below bust, 1697					22	60	175
3509	— N (*Norwich)* below bust, 1697					20	60	175
3510	— y (*York)* below bust							
	1696		*Extremely rare*		1697	22	60	175
3511	Third bust variety							
	1697	10	25	85	1698	18	50	150
3512	— B (*Bristol)* below bust, 1697					22	60	175
3513	Third bust variety C (*Chester)* below bust, 1697					50	150	450
3514	— R. Plumes in angles, 1698					55	175	525
3515	Fourth bust ('flaming hair')							
	1698	30	70	250	1699	30	70	250
3516	Fifth bust (hair high)							
	1699	22	60	200	1701	22	60	200
	1700	15	35	100				
3517	— R. Plumes in angles							
	1699	40	115	350	1701	40	115	350
3518	— R. Roses in angles, 1699					55	150	450
3519	— plume below bust, 1700					750	—	—

3520

No.	Description	F £	VF £	EF £		F £	VF £	EF £
3520	**Sixpence.** First bust, early harp 1695	20	60	175	1696	6	18	50
3521	— — B below bust, 1696					8	22	65
3522	— — C below bust, 1696					15	45	135
3523	— — E below bust, 1696					20	60	175
3524	— — N below bust, 1696					12	40	120
3525	— — y below bust, 1696					10	30	90
3526	— — Y below bust, 1696					20	60	175
3527	— later harp, large crowns, 1696					25	75	225
3528	— — — B below bust 1696	25	75	225	1697	20	60	175
3529	— — — C below bust, 1697					25	75	225
3530	— — — E below bust, 1697					22	70	225
3531	— — small crowns 1696	20	65	190	1697	8	22	65
3532	— — — B below bust 1696	18	55	160	1697	12	40	120
3533	— — — C below bust 1696	35	10	300	1697	12	40	120
3534	— — — E below bust, 1697					15	45	135
3535	— — — N below bust 1696	30	90	275	1697	10	30	90
3536	— — — y below bust, 1697					25	75	225
3537	Second bust 1696	150	300	—	1697	35	120	350
3538	Third bust, large crowns 1697	6	18	50	1700	8	22	65
	1698	8	22	65	1701	11	35	90
	1699	27	80	240				
3539	— — B below bust, 1697					15	45	135
3540	— — C below bust, 1697					25	70	200
3541	— — E below bust, 1697					30	90	275
3542	Third bust, small crowns, 1697					10	30	90
3543	— — C below bust, 1697					22	65	180
3544	— — E below bust, 1697					16	50	150
3545	— — Y below bust, 1697					25	80	240
3546	— ℞. Plumes in angles 1698	15	35	110	1699	14	40	120
3547	— ℞. Roses in angles, 1699					25	75	225
3548*	— plume below bust, 1700						*Extremely rare*	

**An extremely fine specimen sold at auction in October 1985 for £3500.*

3549 Fourpence. ℞. 4 crowned

	F £	VF £	EF £
1697			*Unique*
1698	10	22	50
1699	9	22	50
1700	9	20	45
1701	10	24	55
1702	9	20	45

3550 Threepence. ℞. 3 crowned

	F £	VF £	EF £
1698	9	20	45
1699	10	22	48
1700	9	20	45
1701	9	20	45

3551 Twopence. ℞. Crown to edge of coin, large figure 2

	F £	VF £	EF £
1698	9	19	38
1699	9	18	36
1700	9	19	38
1701	9	18	38

3551A ℞ Crown within inner circle of legend, smaller figure 2

	F £	VF £	EF £
1699	9	18	36
1700	9	19	38
1701	9	18	38

3552 Penny. ℞. 1 crowned

	F £	VF £	EF £
1698	9	19	38
1699	10	20	40
1700	10	20	40
1701	9	19	38

3553

3553 Maundy Set. As last four. Uniform dates

	F £	VF £	EF £
1698	50	105	180
1699	55	115	190
1700	55	115	190
1701	50	105	180

COPPER

3554

3554 Halfpenny. First issue. Britannia with r. hand raised

	F £	VF £	EF £
1695	12	35	175
1696	12	35	175
1697	12	35	175
1698	15	40	200

3555 Second issue. ℞. Date in legend

	F £	VF £	EF £
1698	12	35	175
1699	12	35	175

3556 Third issue. ℞. Britannia with r. hand on knee

	F £	VF £	EF £
1699	12	35	175
1700	12	35	175
1701	12	35	175

3557

3558

	F £	VF £	EF £		F £	VF £	EF £
3557 Farthing. First issue							
1695	15	40	250	1698	60	175	—
1696	12	35	225	1699	12	35	225
1697	12	35	225	1700	12	35	225
3558 Second issue. R. Date at end of legend							
1698	30	75	400	1699	14	45	275

The Act of Union of 1707, which effected the unification of the ancient kingdoms of England and Scotland into a single realm, resulted in a change in the royal arms—on the after-Union coinage the English lions and Scottish lion are emblazoned per pale on the top and bottom shields. After the Union the rose in the centre of the reverse of the gold coins is replaced by the Garter star.

Following a successful Anglo-Dutch expedition against Spain, bullion seized in Vigo Bay was sent to be minted into coin, and the coins made from this metal had the word VIGO placed below the queen's bust.

GOLD

Before Union with Scotland

	F £	*VF* £	*EF* £		*F* £	*VF* £	*EF* £
3560 Five guineas							
1705	1000	2250	5000	1706	950	2000	4500
3561 VIGO below bust, 1703					6000	15,000	40,000

3562 3564

	F £	*VF* £	*EF* £		*F* £	*VF* £	*EF* £
3562 Guinea							
1702	175	550	1750	1706	275	700	2250
1705	275	675	2150	1707	325	800	2500
3563 VIGO below bust, 1703					3000	7000	—
3564 Half-guinea							
1702	225	550	1750	1705	225	550	1750
3565 VIGO below bust, 1703					2250	5000	—

After Union with Scotland. The shields on the reverse are changed

3566

	F £	*VF* £	*EF* £		*F* £	*VF* £	*EF* £
3566 Five guineas. Ordinary bust, 1706					950	2000	5000
3567 Narrower shields, tall narrow crowns, larger rev. letters, 1709					950	1900	4500
3568 Broader shields							
1711	850	1900	4500	1714/3	850	1900	4500
1713	950	1900	4500				

3569

	F £	VF £	EF £		F £	VF £	EF £
3569 Two guineas							
1709	350	800	1750	1713	350	800	1750
1711	350	800	1750	1714/3	400	900	2500
3570 Guinea. First bust							
1707	200	400	1100	1708		*Extremely rare*	
3571 — elephant and castle below							
1707	400	950	2500	1708		*Extremely rare*	
3572 Second bust							
1707		*Extremely rare*		1709	200	425	1250
1708	180	375	1000				
3573 — elephant and castle below							
1708	350	900	2500	1709	325	800	2250

3574

	F £	VF £	EF £		F £	VF £	EF £
3574 Third bust							
1710	150	300	700	1713	150	275	650
1711	150	300	700	1714	150	275	650
1712	200	400	1100				
3575 Half-guinea							
1707	160	325	900	1711	135	260	700
1708	200	450	1200	1712	160	325	900
1709	135	275	750	1713	135	275	750
1710	120	260	700	1714	135	275	750

SILVER

Before Union with Scotland

3576

No.		F £	VF £	EF £		F £	VF £	EF £
3576	**Crown.** VIGO below bust, 1703					90	275	750
3577	℞. Plumes in angles, 1705					150	450	1350
3578	℞. Roses and plumes in angles							
	1706	70	225	600	1707	65	200	600
3579	**Halfcrown**. No marks below bust or on *rev.* (i.e. plain), 1703					275	750	—
3580	VIGO below bust, 1703					35	95	275
3581	℞. Plumes in angles							
	1704	50	200	500	1705	40	120	375
3582	℞. Roses and plumes in angles							
	1706	30	90	275	1707	20	70	200

3583 3589

No.		F £	VF £	EF £		F £	VF £	EF £
3583	**Shilling.** First bust, 1702					35	90	225
3584	— ℞. Plumes in angles, 1702					35	100	275
3585	— VIGO below bust, 1702					35	100	275
3586	Second bust, VIGO below, 1703					25	60	150
3587	— plain							
	1704	225	500	—	1705	40	100	275
3588	— ℞. Plumes in angles							
	1704	40	120	300	1705	30	90	250
3589	— ℞. Roses and plumes in angles							
	1705	25	75	200	1707	30	85	225

3593 3594 Early Shield Late Shield

No.	Description	F £	VF £	EF £
3590	**Sixpence.** VIGO below bust, 1703	12	35	95
3591	Plain, 1705	20	70	200
3592	℞. Early shields, plumes in angles, 1705	16	50	150
3593	℞. Late shields, plumes in angles, 1705	20	60	175

3594 ℞. Roses and plumes in angles

	F £	VF £	EF £		F £	VF £	EF £
1705	18	60	200	1707	16	45	125

3595 **Fourpence.** First bust, small face, curls at back of head point downwards. ℞ Small crown above the figure 4

	F £	VF £	EF £		F £	VF £	EF £
1703	7	15	30	1704	6	14	28

3595A Second bust, larger face, curls at back of head point upwards

	F £	VF £	EF £		F £	VF £	EF £
1705	7	15	30	1709	6	14	28
1706	6	14	28	1710	6	14	28
1708	6	14	28				

3595B ℞ Large crown with pearls on arch, larger serifs on the figure 4

	F £	VF £	EF £		F £	VF £	EF £
1710	6	14	28	1713	6	14	28

3595C Second bust, but with re-engraved hair.

	F £	VF £	EF £		F £	VF £	EF £
1710	6	14	28	1713	6	14	28

3596 **Threepence.** First head, broad bust, tie riband pointing outwards. ℞. Crowned 3

	F £	VF £	EF £
1703	7	15	35

3596A Second head, taller and narrow bust, tie riband pointing inwards

	F £	VF £	EF £		F £	VF £	EF £
1704	6	12	26	1706	6	14	28
1705	6	12	26				

3596B Third Head, similar to first bust but larger and hair more finely engraved

	F £	VF £	EF £		F £	VF £	EF £
1707	6	14	28	1710	6	14	28
1708	6	14	28	1713	6	14	28
1709	6	14	28				

3597 **Twopence.** First bust, as fourpence ℞. Crown to edge of coin, small figure 2

	F £	VF £	EF £		F £	VF £	EF £
1703	6	13	27	1706	6	13	27
1704	6	12	26	1707	6	13	27
1705	6	12	26	1708	6	12	26

3597A Second bust, as fourpence ℞ Crown within inner circle of legend, large figure 2.

	F £	VF £	EF £		F £	VF £	EF £
1708	6	12	26	1709	6	13	27

3598 **Penny.** ℞. Crowned 1

	F £	VF £	EF £		F £	VF £	EF £
1703	9	18	35	1709	8	16	32
1705	8	16	32	1710	9	18	35
1706	8	16	32	1713	9	18	35
1708	10	20	40				

3599

3599 Maundy Set. As last four. Uniform dates

1703 40	75	175	1709 40	75	175
1705 40	75	175	1710 45	80	180
1706 35	70	165	1713 40	75	125
1708 40	75	175			

After Union with Scotland

The shields on reverse are changed. The Edinburgh coins have been included here as they are now coins of Great Britain.

3600

	F £	*VF* £	*EF* £		*F* £	*VF* £	*EF* £
3600 Crown. Second bust, E (Edinburgh) below							
1707	50	150	450	1708	50	165	500
3601 — plain							
1707	50	150	450	1708	75	200	550
3602 ℞. Plumes in angles, 1708					55	225	675
3603 Third bust. ℞. Roses and plumes, 1713					50	150	450

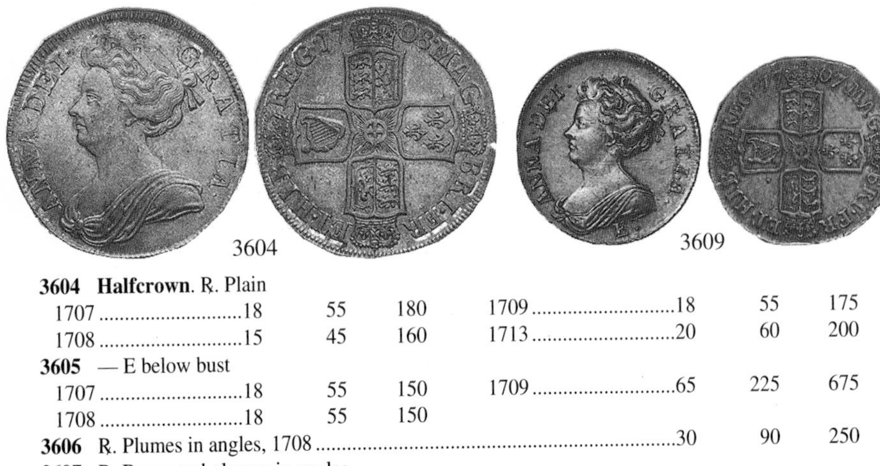

3604 3609

3604 Halfcrown. ℞. Plain						
1707 18	55	180	1709 18	55	175
1708 15	45	160	1713 20	60	200
3605 — E below bust						
1707 18	55	150	1709 65	225	675
1708 18	55	150			
3606 ℞. Plumes in angles, 1708			30	90	250
3607 ℞. Roses and plumes in angles					
1710 25	90	250	1713 22	90	250
1712 22	80	225	1714 22	80	225

	F £	VF £	EF £		F £	VF £	EF £
3608 **Shilling.** Second bust, E below							
1707	18	50	150	1708	30	95	300
3609 — E* below							
1707	35	110	350	1708	20	60	175
3610 Third bust. ℞. Plain.							
1707	12	35	90	1709	12	35	90
1708	10	25	75	1711	40	150	450
3611 — ℞. Plumes in angles							
1707	22	60	175	1708	15	45	135
3612 — E below							
1707	15	40	120	1708	25	80	250
3613 Second bust. ℞. Roses and plumes, 1708					50	150	450
3614 Third bust. ℞. Roses and plumes							
1708	25	70	200	1710	12	35	90
3615 — 'Edinburgh' bust, E* below							
1707	*Extremely rare*			1709	30	95	275
1708	25	80	250				
3616 — E below, 1709						*Extremely rare*	
3617 Fourth bust. ℞. Roses and plumes							
1710	25	90	250	1713/2	15	50	150
1712	12	35	90	1714	12	35	90
3618 — plain, 1711					10	20	60
3619 **Sixpence.** Normal bust. ℞. Plain							
1707	10	22	65	1711	8	16	50
1708	12	30	90				

3620

3623

	F £	VF £	EF £		F £	VF £	EF £
3620 — E below bust							
1707	12	30	90	1708	15	40	120
3621 — E* below bust, 1708					15	50	150
3622 'Edinburgh' bust, E* below, 1708					15	55	165
3623 Normal bust. ℞. Plumes in angles							
1707	12	35	95	1708	15	40	120
3624 — ℞. Roses and plumes in angles, 1710					15	50	150

COPPER

3625

3625 **Farthing,** 1714 .... 90 165 350

THE HOUSE OF HANOVER
GEORGE I, 1714-27

The coins of the first of the Hanoverian kings have the arms of the Duchy of Brunswick and Luneberg on one of the four shields, the object in the centre of the shield being the crown of Charlemagne. The king's German titles also appear, in abbreviated form, and name him 'Duke of Brunswick and Luneberg. Arch-treasurer of the Holy Roman Empire, and Elector', and on the guinea of 1714, 'Prince Elector'. A quarter-guinea was struck for the first time in 1718, but it was an inconvenient size and the issue was discontinued.

Silver coined from bullion supplied to the mint by the South Sea Company in 1723 shows the company's initials S.S.C.; similarly Welsh Copper Company bullion has the letters W.C.C. below the king's bust and plumes and an interlinked CC on the reverse. Roses and plumes together on the reverse indicate silver supplied by the Company for Smelting Pit Coale and Sea Coale.

GOLD

3626

	F £	*VF* £	*EF* £		*F* £	*VF* £	*EF* £
3626 Five guineas							
1716	1000	2100	4750	1720	1250	2250	5000
1717	1250	2250	5000	1726	1000	2250	4750

3627 3628

	F £	*VF* £	*EF* £		*F* £	*VF* £	*EF* £
3627 Two guineas							
1717	450	800	2750	1726	425	750	2600
1720	450	800	2750				

	F £	*VF* £	*EF* £
3628 Guinea. First head. ℞. Legend ends ET PR . EL (Prince Elector), 1714	300	750	2000
3629 Second head, tie with two ends, 1715	175	375	900
3630 Third head, no hair below truncation			

	F £	*VF* £	*EF* £		*F* £	*VF* £	*EF* £
1715	150	300	850	1716	200	450	1000

	F £	VF £	EF £		F £	VF £	EF £
3631 Guinea. Fourth head, tie with loop at one end							
1716	150	300	850	1720	150	300	850
1717	175	350	1000	1721	175	450	1100
1718		*Extremely rare*		1722	150	300	850
1719	150	300	850	1723	175	400	1000
3632 — elephant and castle below							
1721		*Extremely rare*		1722		*Extremely rare*	

3633 3638

	F £	VF £	EF £		F £	VF £	EF £
3633 Fifth (older) head, tie with two ends							
1723	200	400	1000	1726	150	350	800
1724	200	400	1000	1727	225	500	1350
1725	200	400	1000				
3634 — elephant and castle below, 1726					500	1100	—
3635 Half-guinea. First head							
1715	150	300	800	1721		*Extremely rare*	
1717	125	250	650	1722	125	250	650
1718	100	200	600	1723		*Extremely rare*	
1719	100	200	600	1724	150	300	700
1720	175	375	900				
3636 — elephant and castle below, 1721						*Extremely rare*	
3637 Second (older) bust							
1725	90	225	500	1727	100	250	650
1726	100	250	650				
3638 Quarter-guinea, 1718					35	85	165

SILVER

3639

	F £	VF £	EF £		F £	VF £	EF £
3639 Crown. R. Roses and plumes in angles							
1716	115	250	850	1720/18	175	350	1100
1718/6	175	350	1100	1726	125	300	950
3640 R. SSC (South Sea Company) in angles, 1723					125	300	950

3641 Halfcrown. Plain (proof only), 1715 *FDC* £4000

3642 ℞. Roses and plumes in angles

	F £	*VF* £	*EF* £		*F* £	*VF* £	*EF* £
1715	50	150	500	1720/17	50	150	500
1717	50	150	500				

3643 3647

	F £	*VF* £	*EF* £
3643 ℞. SSC in angles, 1723	45	150	450
3644 ℞. Small roses and plumes, 1726	1000	—	—

3645 Shilling. First bust. ℞. Roses and plumes

	F £	*VF* £	*EF* £		*F* £	*VF* £	*EF* £
1715	18	45	150	1720	18	45	150
1716	40	120	350	1721/0	20	55	175
1717	18	45	150	1722	18	45	150
1718	18	40	135	1723	30	75	250
1719	40	120	325				

3646 — plain (i.e. no marks either side)

	F £	*VF* £	*EF* £		*F* £	*VF* £	*EF* £
1720	18	45	140	1721	55	200	500

	F £	*VF* £	*EF* £
3647 ℞. SSC in angles, 1723	10	25	75
3648 Second bust, bow to tie. ℞. Similar, 1723	18	45	135

3649 — ℞. Roses and plumes

	F £	*VF* £	*EF* £		*F* £	*VF* £	*EF* £
1723	20	55	175	1726	125	450	1250
1724	20	55	175	1727	110	400	1100
1725	20	55	175				

3650 3652

3650 — W.C.C. (Welsh Copper Company) below

	F £	*VF* £	*EF* £		*F* £	*VF* £	*EF* £
1723	120	325	850	1725	120	350	900
1724	120	350	900	1726	120	350	900

3651 Sixpence. ℞. Roses and plumes in angles

	F £	*VF* £	*EF* £		*F* £	*VF* £	*EF* £
1717	30	90	225	1720/17	30	90	225

	F £	*VF* £	*EF* £
3652 ℞. SSC in angles, 1723	7	22	65
3653 ℞. Small roses and plumes, 1726	20	50	150

	F £	VF £	EF £		F £	VF £	EF £
3654 Fourpence							
1717	8	18	36	1723	8	18	36
1721	8	18	36	1727	8	19	38
3655 Threepence							
1717	8	19	33	1723	9	20	35
1721	9	20	35	1727	9	20	35
3656 Twopence							
1717	5	10	22	1726	5	9	20
1721	5	9	20	1727	5	10	22
1723	5	10	22				
3657 Penny							
1716	4	8	18	1725	4	8	18
1718	4	8	18	1726	5	10	22
1720	4	8	18	1727	5	10	22
1723	4	8	18				

3658

3658 Maundy Set. As last four. Uniform dates

	F	VF	EF		F	VF	EF
1723	35	80	175	1727	35	80	175

COPPER

	F	VF	EF		F	VF	EF
3659 Halfpenny. 'Dump' issue							
1717	12	40	175	1718	12	40	175
3660 Second issue							
1719	10	35	175	1722	10	35	175
1720	10	35	175	1723	10	35	175
1721	10	35	175	1724	10	35	175

3661 3662

	F	VF	EF		F	VF	EF
3661 Farthing. 'Dump' issue, 1717	75	175	400				
3662 Second issue							
1719	10	30	175	1722	10	35	190
1720	10	30	175	1723	10	35	190
1721	10	30	175	1724	10	35	190

Silver was coined only spasmodically by the Mint during this reign and no copper was struck after 1754. Gold coins made from bullion supplied by the East India Company bear the company's initials. Some of the treasure seized by Admiral Anson during his circumnavigation of the globe, 1740-4, and by other privateers, was made into coin which had the word LIMA below the king's bust to celebrate the expedition's successful harassment of the Spanish colonies in the New World. Hammered gold was finally demonetized in 1733.

GOLD

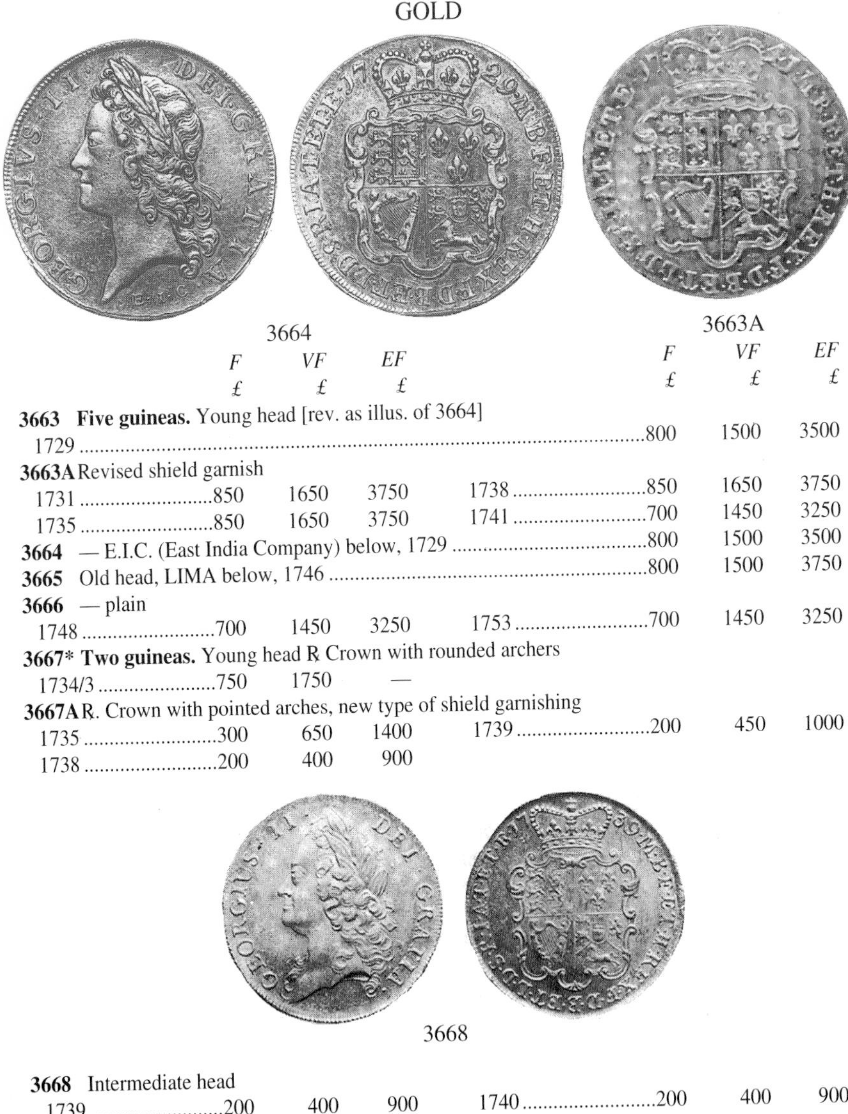

3664 3663A

	F £	VF £	EF £		F £	VF £	EF £
3663 Five guineas. Young head [rev. as illus. of 3664]							
1729					800	1500	3500
3663A Revised shield garnish							
1731	850	1650	3750	1738	850	1650	3750
1735	850	1650	3750	1741	700	1450	3250
3664 — E.I.C. (East India Company) below, 1729					800	1500	3500
3665 Old head, LIMA below, 1746					800	1500	3750
3666 — plain							
1748	700	1450	3250	1753	700	1450	3250
3667* Two guineas. Young head R Crown with rounded archers							
1734/3	750	1750	—				
3667A R. Crown with pointed arches, new type of shield garnishing							
1735	300	650	1400	1739	200	450	1000
1738	200	400	900				

3668

	F £	VF £	EF £		F £	VF £	EF £
3668 Intermediate head							
1739	200	400	900	1740	200	400	900
3669* Old head							
1748	300	700	1500	1753	400	950	2000

**Beware recent forgeries.*
Overstruck dates are listed only if commoner than normal date or if no normal date is known.

3671

3674

		F £	VF £	EF £		F £	VF £	EF £
3670	**Guinea.** First young head, small lettering, 1727					350	1000	2200
3671	— larger lettering, smaller shield							
	1727	250	650	1500	1728	300	700	1650
3672	Second (narrower) young head							
	1729 *proof only FDC £3600*				1731	160	400	1250
	1730	200	400	1500	1732	200	500	1500
3673	— E.I.C. below							
	1729	350	900	2500	1732	250	600	1650
	1731	250	600	1650				
3674	— larger lettering on *obv.*							
	1732	225	500	1450	1736	180	450	1250
	1733	150	375	950	1737	200	500	1450
	1734	150	375	950	1738	180	450	1250
	1735	160	350	1100				
3675	— — E.I.C. below, 1732					300	700	1750
3676	Intermediate head							
	1739	150	375	900	1741/39		*Extremely rare*	
	1740	160	450	1250	1743*		*Extremely rare*	
3677	— E.I.C. below, 1739					300	700	1750
3678	— larger lettering on *obv.,* GEORGIUS							
	1745					225	500	1450
3678A	As last but reads GEORGIVS							
	1746					200	450	1000

3679

		F £	VF £	EF £		F £	VF £	EF £
3679	— LIMA below, 1745					300	600	1800
3680	Old head							
	1747	150	300	700	1753	125	250	600
	1748	125	250	600	1755	175	325	750
	1749	125	250	600	1756	125	225	550
	1750	150	250	600	1758	115	200	500
	1751	125	225	550	1759	115	200	500
	1752	125	225	550	1760	120	225	550

**A good very fine specimen sold at auction in May 1994 for £2700 plus 10% buyer's premium.*

3681

	F £	VF £	EF £		F £	VF £	EF £
3681 Half-guinea. Young head							
1728	150	375	900	1734	120	350	800
1729	175	450	1200	1735			*?exists*
1730	400	—	—	1736	150	400	1000
1731	200	600	1500	1737		*Extremely rare*	
1732	150	425	1100	1738	110	325	800
1733			*?exists*	1739	110	325	800
3682 — E.I.C. below							
1729	250	500	1500	1732		*Extremely rare*	
1730	300	1000	—	1739		*Extremely rare*	
1731		*Extremely rare*					
3683 Intermediate head							
1740	200	600	1500	1745	200	600	1500
1743			*?Unique*	1746	120	350	750
3684 — LIMA below, 1745					350	900	2250

3685

	F £	VF £	EF £		F £	VF £	EF £
3685 Old head							
1747	160	500	1200	1753	100	250	500
1748	130	300	625	1755	100	250	450
1749		*Extremely rare*		1756	90	225	450
1750	110	325	750	1758	90	225	450
1751	120	325	700	1759	80	175	400
1752	120	325	700	1760	80	175	400

3686

SILVER

	F £	VF £	EF £		F £	VF £	EF £
3686 Crown. Young bust. ℞. Roses and plumes in angles							
1732	90	250	600	1735	90	250	600
1734	110	275	750	1736	90	250	650
3687 — ℞. Roses in angles							
1739	80	225	500	1741	80	225	500

3688

	F £	VF £	EF £
3688 Old head. ℞. Roses in angles, 1743	80	225	500
3689 — LIMA below, 1746	80	225	500

3690 — Plain (i.e. no marks either side)
1746 Proof only *FDC* £1750

	F £	VF £	EF £		F £	VF £	EF £
1750	100	275	650	1751	135	325	750

3691 Halfcrown. Young bust ℞. plain (proof only), 1731 *FDC* £1800

3692

	F £	VF £	EF £		F £	VF £	EF £
3692 — ℞. Roses and plumes							
1731	25	80	350	1735	30	90	400
1732	25	80	350	1736	35	125	500
1734	30	90	400				
3693 — ℞. Roses							
1739	22	70	225	1741	22	75	300
3694 Old bust. ℞. Roses							
1743	20	65	200	1745	20	65	200
3695 — LIMA below							
1745	18	45	135	1746	18	45	135
3696 — ℞. Plain							
1746 *proof only FDC* £700							
1750	35	130	350	1751	50	175	500
3697 Shilling. Young bust. R. Plumes							
1727	35	100	300	1731	50	175	450

	F £	VF £	EF £
3698 **Shilling**. Young bust R. Roses and plumes			
1727	20	50	135
1728	30	75	175
1729	30	75	175
1731	20	50	135
1732	30	75	175
3699 — larger lettering. R. Roses and plumes			
1734	12	35	110
1735	12	35	110
1736	12	35	110
1737	12	35	110
3700 — R. plain, 1728	40	150	400

3701

3702

	F £	VF £	EF £
3701 — R. Roses			
1739	10	35	95
1741	12	35	110
3702 Old bust. R. Roses			
1743	10	30	75
1745	20	55	150
1747	12	35	100
3703 — LIMA below			
1745	10	30	75
1746	30	90	250
3704 — R. plain			
1746 Proof only *FDC* £450			
1750	20	55	125
1751	30	90	200
1758	4	12	35
3705 **Sixpence.** Young bust. R. Plain, 1728	30	100	250
3706 — R. Plumes, 1728	25	70	175
3707 — R. Roses and plumes			
1728	12	32	90
1731	12	32	90
1732	12	32	90
1734	25	50	135
1735	25	50	135
1736	20	45	125

3708

3710

	F £	VF £	EF £
3708 — R. Roses			
1739	12	32	90
1741	12	32	90
3709 Old bust. R. Roses			
1743	15	35	95
1745	15	35	100
3710 — LIMA below			
1745	10	30	75
1746	7	20	50

3711 — plain

1746 *proof only FDC* £325

Date	F £	VF £	EF £	Date	F £	VF £	EF £
1750	20	50	145	1757	3	8	22
1751	25	75	200	1758	3	8	22

3712 **Fourpence.** Young head. R. Small dome-shaped crown without pearls on arch, figure 4

Date	F £	VF £	EF £	Date	F £	VF £	EF £
1729	5	10	22	1731	5	10	22

3712A R.Double domed crown with pearls, large figure 4

Date	F £	VF £	EF £	Date	F £	VF £	EF £
1732	5	10	22	1740	5	10	22
1735	5	10	22	1743	5	10	22
1737	5	10	22	1746	5	10	22
1739	5	10	22	1760	5	10	22

3713 **Threepence.** Young head. R. Crowned 3, pearls on arch

Date	F £	VF £	EF £
1729	5	10	22

3713A R Ornate arch

Date	F £	VF £	EF £	Date	F £	VF £	EF £
1731	5	10	22	1732	5	10	22

3713B R. Double domed crown with pearls

Date	F £	VF £	EF £	Date	F £	VF £	EF £
1735	5	10	22	1743	5	10	22
1737	5	10	22	1746	5	10	22
1739	5	10	22	1760	5	10	22
1740	5	10	22				

3714 **Twopence.** Young head. R. Small crown and figure 2

Date	F £	VF £	EF £	Date	F £	VF £	EF £
1729	4	8	18	1731	4	8	18

3714A R. Large crown

Date	F £	VF £	EF £	Date	F £	VF £	EF £
1732	4	8	18	1743	4	8	18
1735	4	8	18	1746	4	8	18
1737	4	8	18	1756	4	8	18
1739	4	8	18	1759	4	8	18
1740	5	9	20	1760	4	8	18

3715 **Penny.** Young head. R. Date over small crown and figure 1

Date	F £	VF £	EF £	Date	F £	VF £	EF £
1729	3	6	12	1731	3	6	12

3715A R. Large crown dividing date

Date	F £	VF £	EF £	Date	F £	VF £	EF £
1732	4	7	14	1753	4	7	14
1735	4	7	14	1754	4	7	14
1737	4	7	14	1755	4	7	14
1739	4	7	14	1756	4	7	14
1740	4	7	14	1757	4	7	14
1743	4	7	14	1758	4	7	14
1746	4	7	14	1759	4	7	14
1750	4	7	14	1760	4	7	14
1752	4	7	14				

3716

3716 **Maundy Set.** As last four. Uniform dates

Date	F £	VF £	EF £	Date	F £	VF £	EF £
1729	27	50	110	1739	25	50	90
1731	27	50	110	1740	25	50	100
1732	27	55	110	1743	25	50	100
1735	25	55	100	1746	25	50	100
1737	25	55	100	1760	27	55	110

COPPER

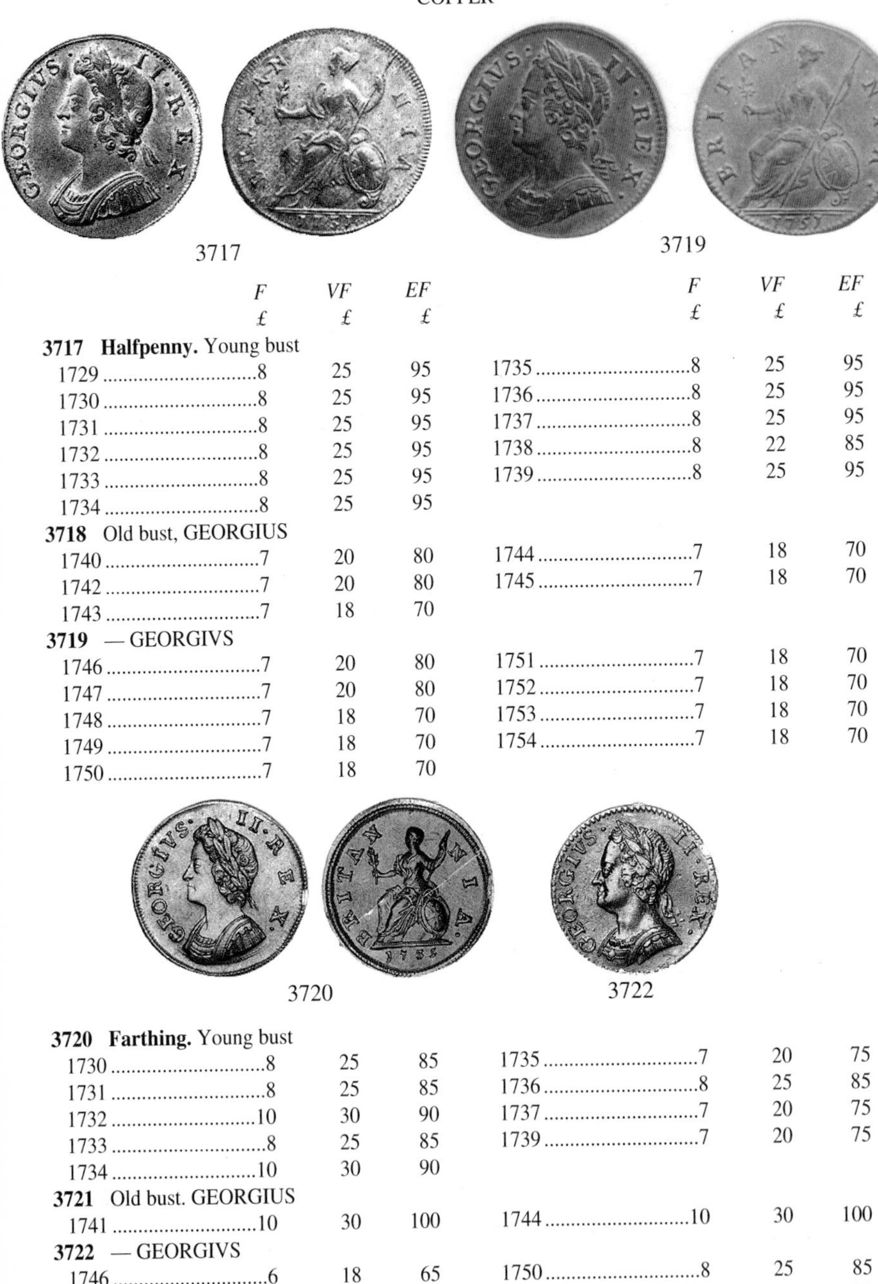

3717 3719

3720 3722

	F £	VF £	EF £
3717 Halfpenny. Young bust			
1729	8	25	95
1730	8	25	95
1731	8	25	95
1732	8	25	95
1733	8	25	95
1734	8	25	95
1735	8	25	95
1736	8	25	95
1737	8	25	95
1738	8	22	85
1739	8	25	95
3718 Old bust, GEORGIUS			
1740	7	20	80
1742	7	20	80
1743	7	18	70
1744	7	18	70
1745	7	18	70
3719 — GEORGIVS			
1746	7	20	80
1747	7	20	80
1748	7	18	70
1749	7	18	70
1750	7	18	70
1751	7	18	70
1752	7	18	70
1753	7	18	70
1754	7	18	70

	F £	VF £	EF £
3720 Farthing. Young bust			
1730	8	25	85
1731	8	25	85
1732	10	30	90
1733	8	25	85
1734	10	30	90
1735	7	20	75
1736	8	25	85
1737	7	20	75
1739	7	20	75
3721 Old bust. GEORGIUS			
1741	10	30	100
1744	10	30	100
3722 — GEORGIVS			
1746	6	18	65
1749	7	22	70
1750	8	25	85
1754	4	10	35

During the second half of the 18th century very little silver or copper was minted. In 1797 Matthew Boulton's 'cartwheels', the first copper pennies and twopences, demonstrated the improvement from the application of steam power to the coining press.

During the Napoleonic Wars bank notes came into general use when the issue of guineas was stopped between 1797 and 1813, but gold 7s. pieces were minted to relieve the shortage of smaller money. As an emergency measure Spanish 'dollars' were put into circulation for a short period after being countermarked, and in 1804 Spanish dollars were overstruck and issued as Bank of England dollars.

The transition to a 'token' silver coinage began in 1811 when the Bank of England had 3s and 1s. 6d. tokens made for general circulation. Private issues of token money in the years 1788-95 and 1811-15 helped to alleviate the shortage of regal coinage. A change over to a gold standard and a regular 'token' silver coinage came in 1816 when the Mint, which was moved from its old quarters in the Tower of London to a new site on Tower Hill, began a complete re-coinage. The guinea was replaced by a 20s. sovereign, and silver coins were made which had an intrinsic value lower than their face value. The St. George design used on the sovereign and crown was the work of Benedetto Pistrucci.

Early coinages

GOLD

3724

3723 Five guineas. Pattern only
1770 *FDC* £62,000
1773 *FDC* £62,000
1777 *FDC* £62,000

3724 Two guineas. Pattern only
1768 *FDC* £22,000
1773 *FDC* £22,000
1777 *FDC* £22,000

There are six different bust varieties for 3723 and 3724, for further details see Douglas-Morris, November 1974, lots 127-132.

	F £	*VF* £	*EF* £
3725 Guinea. First head, 1761 (also with three leaves at top of wreath)	375	850	2500

3725 3726 3727

3726 Second head

	F £	*VF* £	*EF* £
1763	250	500	1250
1764	200	400	1000

3727 Guinea Third head

	F £	VF £	EF £
1765	110	200	450
1766	85	150	325
1767	125	225	525
1768	100	175	400
1769	100	175	400
1770	120	225	475
1771	100	175	425
1772	85	150	325
1773	85	150	325

3728

3729

3728 Fourth head

	F £	VF £	EF £
1774	75	135	300
1775	75	135	300
1776	75	135	300
1777	75	135	300
1778	95	175	375
1779	85	160	350
1781	85	160	350
1782	85	160	350
1783	85	160	350
1784	85	160	350
1785	75	135	300
1786	75	135	300

3729 Fifth head. ℞. 'Spade'-shaped shield

	F £	VF £	EF £
1787	75	130	250
1788	75	130	250
1789	75	135	275
1790	75	130	250
1791	75	130	250
1792	75	135	250
1793	75	130	250
1794	75	130	250
1795	100	175	400
1796	100	175	400
1797	80	140	275
1798*	75	130	250
1799	90	150	350

* *Beware counterfeits*

3730

3730 Sixth head. ℞. Shield in Garter, known as the Military guinea, 1813........ 350 700

3731 Half-guinea. First head

	F £	VF £	EF £
1762	150	400	1200
1763	200	600	1350

3732 Second head

	F £	VF £	EF £
1764	90	225	475
1765	250	600	—
1766	90	250	500
1768	90	250	550
1769	90	275	700
1772		*Extremely rare*	
1773	90	250	550
1774	150	300	1000
1775	200	450	1200

3733

3734

3737

	F £	VF £	EF £		F £	VF £	EF £
3733 Half-guinea Third head (less fine style)							
1774	*Extremely rare*			1775	175	450	1250
3734 Fourth head							
1775	70	135	275	1781	80	150	350
1776	70	135	275	1783	300	800	—
1777	65	120	250	1784	70	135	275
1778	80	140	300	1785	65	120	250
1779	95	200	500	1786	65	120	250
3735 Fifth head. R. 'Spade' type							
1787	60	115	225	1794	60	125	250
1788	60	115	225	1795	90	185	350
1789	80	175	300	1796	65	125	250
1790	60	115	225	1797	60	115	225
1791	65	125	250	1798	60	115	225
1792	350	850	—	1800	125	350	—
1793	60	115	225				
3736 Sixth head. R. Shield in Garter							
1801	45	60	125	1803	45	65	135
1802	45	65	135				
3737 Seventh head. with short hair. R. As last							
1804	45	60	125	1809	45	65	135
1805	*Extremely rare*			1810	45	65	135
1806	45	65	135	1811	75	150	350
1808	45	65	135	1813	65	135	275

3738

	F	VF	EF		F	VF	EF
3738 Third-guinea. I. First head							
1797	30	50	115	1799	35	70	175
1798	30	50	115	1800	30	50	115
3739 II. Similar but date not in legend							
1801	30	50	120	1803	30	50	120
1802	30	50	120				

3740 3741

	F £	VF £	EF £
3740 Third Guinea III. Second head with short hair			
1804	30	50	120
1806	30	50	120
1808	30	50	120
1809	30	50	120
1810	30	50	120
1811	125	300	650
1813	75	150	300
3741 Quarter-guinea, 1762	35	75	150

For gold of the 'new coinage', 1817-20, see page 268.

SILVER

3742

	F £	VF £	EF £
3742 Shilling. Young bust, known as the 'Northumberland' shilling, 1763	100	175	375
3743 Older bust, no semée of hearts in the Hanoverian shield, 1787	5	10	30
3744 — — no stop over head, 1787	7	12	40
3745 — — no stops at date, 1787	7	12	45
3745A — — no stops on *obv.*, 1787	50	150	400

3746

no hearts

with hearts

	F £	VF £	EF £
3746 — with semée of hearts, 1787	5	10	30
3747 — no stop over head, 1798: known as the 'Dorrien and Magens' shilling *UNC* £3500			
3748 Sixpence. Without hearts, 1787	4	8	22
3749 — with hearts, 1787	4	8	25

3750

3751

3755

	F £	VF £	EF £		F £	VF £	EF £
3750 Fourpence. Young bust							
1763	5	8	16	1776	5	8	16
1765	100	250	650	1780	5	8	16
1766	5	9	18	1784	5	9	18
1770	5	9	18	1786	5	9	18
1772	5	9	18				
3751 Older bust. R. Thin 4 ('Wire Money'), 1792					7	15	30
3752 — R. Normal 4							
1795	5	8	16	1800	5	8	16
3753 Threepence. Young bust							
1762	3	5	10	1772	4	7	15
1763	3	5	10	1780	4	7	15
1765	100	250	500	1784	4	7	16
1766	4	7	15	1786	4	7	15
1770	4	7	15				
3754 Older bust. R. Thin 3 ('Wire Money'), 1792					7	15	30
3755 — R. Normal 3							
1795	4	7	15	1800	4	7	15
3756 Twopence. Young bust							
1763	3	6	12	1776	3	6	12
1765	75	175	450	1780	3	6	12
1766	3	6	12	1784	3	6	12
1772	3	6	12	1786	3	6	12
3757 Older bust. R. Thin 2 ('Wire Money'), 1792					6	12	25
3758 — R. Normal 2							
1795	3	5	9	1800	3	5	9
3759 Penny. Young bust							
1763	3	6	12	1779	3	6	11
1766	3	6	11	1780	3	6	12
1770	3	6	11	1781	3	6	11
1772	3	6	11	1784	3	6	11
1776	3	6	12	1786	3	6	11
3760 Older bust. R. Thin 1 ('Wire Money'), 1792					3	5	10
3761 — R. Normal 1							
1795	2	4	8	1800	2	4	8
3762 Maundy Set. Young bust. Uniform dates							
1763	26	45	115	1780	26	45	115
1766	26	45	115	1784	26	45	115
1772	26	45	115	1786	26	45	115
3763 — Older bust. R. Thin numerals ('Wire Money'), 1792					50	80	175
3764 — R. Normal numerals. Uniform dates							
1795	20	35	80	1800	20	35	75

3765 3767 3766

Emergency issue

		F £	*VF* £	*EF* £
3765	**Dollar** (current for 4s. 9d.). Spanish American 8 *reales* counter -marked with head of George III in oval	50	125	250
3766	— octagonal countermark	80	175	350
3767	**Half-dollar** with similar oval countermark	65	150	300

Bank of England issue

3768

3768	**Dollar** (current for 5s.). Laureate bust of king. ℞. Britannia seated l., 1804	35	75	175

These dollars were re-struck from Spanish-American 8 reales until at least 1811. Dollars that show dates of original coin are worth rather more.

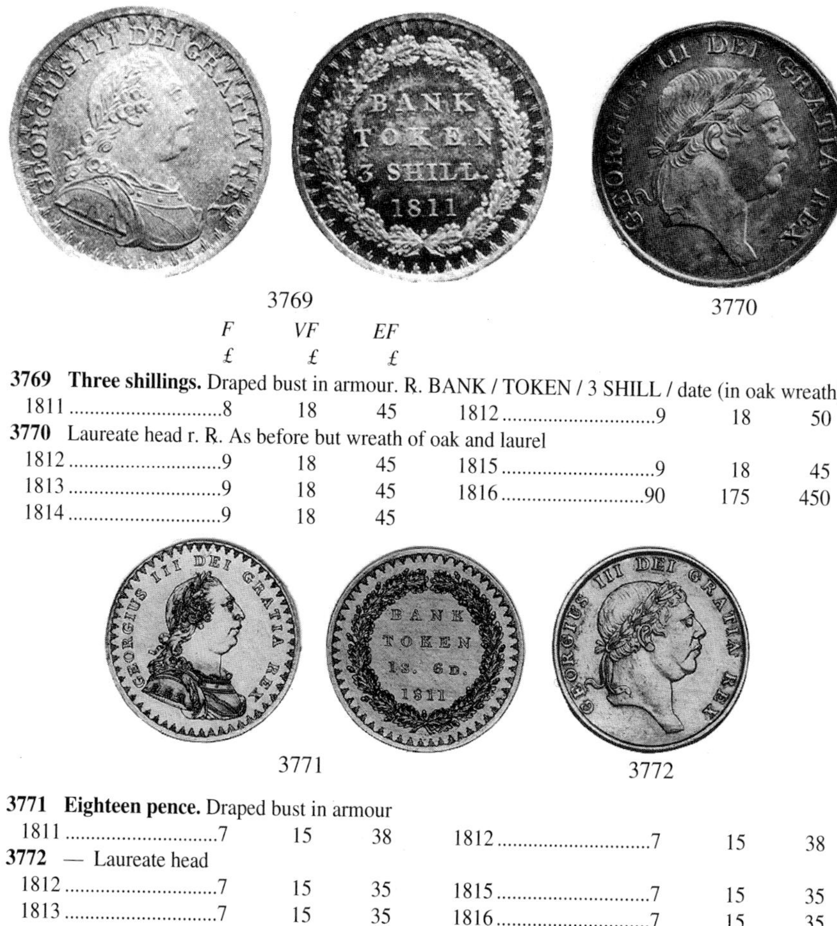

3769 3770

	F £	*VF* £	*EF* £

3769 **Three shillings.** Draped bust in armour. ℞. BANK / TOKEN / 3 SHILL / date (in oak wreath)

1811	8	18	45	1812	9	18	50

3770 Laureate head r. ℞. As before but wreath of oak and laurel

1812	9	18	45	1815	9	18	45
1813	9	18	45	1816	90	175	450
1814	9	18	45				

3771 3772

3771 **Eighteen pence.** Draped bust in armour

1811	7	15	38	1812	7	15	38

3772 — Laureate head

1812	7	15	35	1815	7	15	35
1813	7	15	35	1816	7	15	35
1814	7	15	35				

3773 **Ninepence.** Similar, 1812 (pattern only) *FDC* £900

COPPER

First issue — London

3774

	F £	VF £	EF £		F £	VF £	EF £
3774 Halfpenny. Cuirassed bust r. R. Britannia							
1770	7	15	60	1773	7	15	55
1771	7	15	55	1774	7	15	60
1772	7	15	55	1775	7	18	65

3775

	F £	VF £	EF £		F £	VF £	EF £
3775 Farthing							
1771	15	35	110	1774	7	18	65
1773	7	15	50	1775	7	18	70

Second issue—Soho mint. 'Cartwheel' coinage

3776

	F £	VF £	EF £
3776 Twopence. Legends incuse on raised rim, 1797	10	30	95
3777 Penny, 1797. Similar	9	25	70

Halfpence and farthings of this issue are patterns.

Third issue—Soho mint

3778

	F £	VF £	EF £
3778 Halfpenny. Draped bust r., 1799	2	6	30
3779 Farthing, 1799	2	6	30

Fourth issue—Soho mint

3780

3782

	F £	VF £	EF £		F £	VF £	EF £
3780 Penny. Different bust							
1806	3	9	50	1807	3	9	55
3781 Halfpenny							
1806	1	5	30	1807	2	6	40
3782 Farthing							
1806	1	5	30	1807	2	6	40

In 1787 the regal copper coinage was very scanty, and so pennies and halfpennies were struck by the Anglesey Copper Mining Company and a fresh token epoch began. They present an immense variety of types, persons, buildings, coats of arms, local legends, political events, etc., all drawn upon for subjects of design. They were struck by many firms in most cities and towns in the country and are to be found in good condition. Circulated specimens are so common that they have little value.

For further details of 18th-century tokens see *The Provincial Token-Coinage of the Eighteenth Century,* by Dalton and Hamer, and Seaby's *British Tokens and Their Values.*

	VF	*EF*
	£	£
Price of the commoner **pennies**	5	14
— **halfpennies**	4	11
— **farthings**	3	9

Bury St. Edmunds penny

Anglesey penny

Coventry halfpenny

Isaac Newton Farthing

With the issue of the copper coinage of 1797 tokens were made illegal, but the dearth of silver currency was still felt. During the Napoleonic wars, a small wave of prosperity in the industrial districts brought the inevitable need for small change, so in 1811 tokens again made their appearance. On this occasion silver ones were made as well as copper. These, with two exceptions were suppressed before the last coinage of George III.

For further details of 19th-century silver tokens see *The Nineteenth Century Token Coinage* by W. J. Davis and *Silver Token-Coinage 1811-1812,* by R. Dalton, also Seaby's *British Tokens and Their Values.*

	VF £	*EF* £
Price of the commoner **five shillings**	350	700
— **four shillings**	125	250
— **three shillings**	135	275
— **halfcrowns**	60	120
— **two shillings**	55	110
— **eighteen pence**	20	40
— **shillings**	11	22
— **sixpences**	10	20

Sheffield Shilling

Charing Cross Sixpence

Price of the commoner **threepences**	25	125
— **twopences**	12	50
— **pennies**	3	13
— **halfpennies**	2	8
— **farthings**	2	9

Withymoor Scythe Works Penny, 1813

Last or new coinage, 1816-20

The year 1816 is a landmark in the history of our coinage. For some years at the beginning of the 19th century Mint production was virtually confined to small gold denominations, regular full production being resumed only after the Mint had been moved from the Tower of London to a new site on Tower Hill. Steam powered minting machinery made by Boulton and Watt replaced the old hand-operated presses and these produced coins which were technically much superior to the older milled coins.

In 1816 for the first time British silver coins were produced with an intrinsic value substantially below their face value, the first official token coinage.

Our present 'silver' coins are made to the same weight standard and are still legal tender from 1816 with the exception of the halfcrown shilling and sixpence. The old guinea was replaced by a sovereign of twenty shillings in 1817, the standard of 22 carat (.916) fineness still being retained.

Engraver's and/or designer's initials:

B.P. (Benedetto Pistrucci)

GOLD

3783

3783* Five pounds, 1820 (Pattern only) *FDC*. . . . . *Extremely rare*

A good extremely fine specimen sold at auction in May 1994 for £41,000 plus 10% buyer's premium.

**Beware counterfeits*

	F £	*VF* £	*EF* £	*UNC* £		*F* £	*VF* £	*EF* £	*UNC* £
3784 Two pounds, 1820 (Pattern only) *FDC*. £12,000									
3785 Sovereign. Coarse hair, legend type A (Descending colon after BRITANNIAR, no space between REX and F:D:). R. St. George									
1817	90	150	375	500	1819*				*Extremely rare*
1818	95	175	450	600					

**An almost VF specimen sold at auction in March 1992 for £15,500 plus 10% buyer's premium.*

3785A— legend type B (Ascending colon after BRITANNIAR, space between REX and F:D:)

1818 .... 95 175 450 600

3785B Wiry curls, legend type A.

1818 .... *Extremely rare*

3785C— legend type B.

1818 .... *Extremely rare* 1820 .... 90 150 375 500

3785

3785A

3786

	F £	VF £	EF £	UNC £		F £	VF £	EF £	UNC £
3786 Half-sovereign. ℞. Crowned shield									
1817	55	85	175	300	1820	60	90	200	350
1818	60	90	200	350					

SILVER

3787

3787 Crown. Laureate head r. ℞. Pistrucci's St. George and dragon within Garter

		F	VF	EF	UNC
1818, edge	LVIII	12	30	125	250
— —	LIX	14	35	130	250
1819 —	LIX	12	30	125	250
— —	LX	14	35	130	250
1820 —	LX	12	30	125	250

3788

3788 Halfcrown. Large or 'bull' head

	F	VF	EF	UNC		F	VF	EF	UNC
1816	8	20	80	175	1817	8	20	80	175

3789

	F £	VF £	EF £	UNC £
3789 Halfcrown. Small head				
1817	7	18	80	175
1818	8	20	90	175
1819	8	20	90	175
1820	10	28	130	225

3790

3791

	F £	VF £	EF £	UNC £
3790 Shilling. R. Shield in Garter				
1816	4	8	25	45
1817	5	9	30	50
1818	7	20	85	150
1819	5	9	30	50
1820	5	9	30	50
3791 Sixpence. R. Shield in Garter				
1816	3	7	22	35
1817	4	8	25	35
1818	5	9	30	40
1819	5	9	30	40
1820	5	9	30	40

3792

	VF £	EF £	FDC £
3792 Maundy Set (4d., 3d., 2d. and 1d.)			
1817	50	80	150
1818	50	80	150
1820	50	80	150
3793 — fourpence, 1817, 1818, 1820 ... *from*		14	30
3794 — threepence, 1817, 1818, 1820 ... *from*		14	30
3795 — twopence, 1817, 1818, 1820 ... *from*		8	13
3796 — penny, 1817, 1818, 1820 ... *from*		7	11

The Mint resumed the coinage of copper farthings in 1821, and pennies and halfpennies in 1825. A gold two pound piece was first issued for general circulation in 1823.

Engraver's and/or designer's initials:
B. P. (Benedetto Pistrucci)
J. B. M. (Jean Baptiste Merlen)

GOLD

3797

3797 **Five pounds,** 1826 (proof only). R. Shield, *FDC* £8000

3798

	VF £	*EF* £	*UNC* £
3798 **Two pounds,** 1823. Large bare head. R. St. George	275	550	900

3799 1826. Type as 3797 (proof only), *FDC* £2750

3800

3800 **Sovereign.** Laureate head. R. St. George

	F £	*VF* £	*EF* £	*UNC* £
1821	90	150	375	500
1822*	90	150	400	550
1823	125	325	1200	—
1824	90	150	400	550
1825	110	300	1000	—

**Beware counterfeits.*

3801

3801 Sovereign. Bare head. R. Crowned shield

Date	F £	VF £	EF £	UNC £
1825	90	150	300	500
1826	90	150	300	500
— Proof *FDC* £2000				
1827*	95	150	325	550
1828*	600	1500	3500	—
1829	90	150	325	550
1830	90	150	325	550

**Beware counterfeits*

3802

3803

3804

Date	F £	VF £	EF £	UNC £
3802 Half-sovereign. Laureate head. R. Ornately garnished shield.				
1821	175	375	1000	1500
3803 — R. Plain shield				
1823	70	125	350	475
1824	65	120	325	450
1825	65	110	300	425
3804 — Bare head. R. Garnished shield				
1826	65	110	300	425
— Proof *FDC* £1000				
1827	65	110	300	425
1828	60	100	250	400
3804A — with extra tuft of hair to l. ear, much heavier border				
1826	65	110	300	425
— Proof *FDC* £1000				
1827	65	110	300	425
1828	60	100	250	400

SILVER

3805

Date	F £	VF £	EF £	UNC £
3805 Crown. Laureate head. R. St. George				
1821, edge SECUNDO	14	40	250	450
1822 — SECUNDO	15	50	325	550
— — TERTIO	14	45	275	475

3806

3806 Crown. Bare head. R. Shield with crest (proof only), 1826 *FDC* £2250

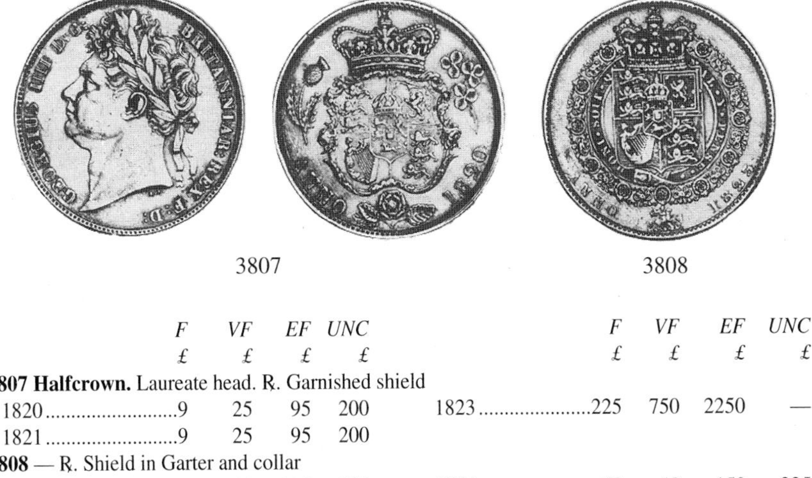
3807 3808

	F £	VF £	EF £	UNC £		F £	VF £	EF £	UNC £
3807 Halfcrown. Laureate head. R. Garnished shield									
1820	9	25	95	200	1823	225	750	2250	—
1821	9	25	95	200					
3808 — R. Shield in Garter and collar									
1823	9	30	110	250	1824	12	40	150	325

3809

	F £	VF £	EF £	UNC £		F £	VF £	EF £	UNC £
3809 Bare head. R. Shield with crest									
1824	*Extremely rare*				1826 Proof *FDC* £400				
1825	9	25	85	175	1828	12	40	175	400
1826	8	22	80	175	1829	10	35	150	325

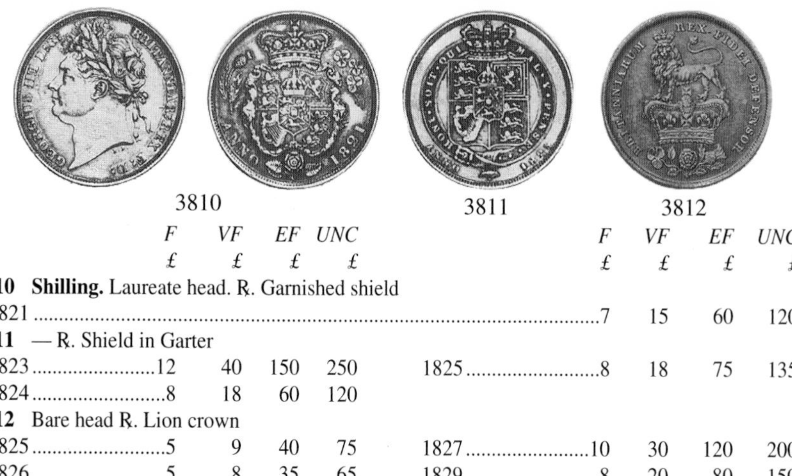

3810 3811 3812

	F £	VF £	EF £	UNC £		F £	VF £	EF £	UNC £
3810 Shilling. Laureate head. ℞. Garnished shield									
1821						7	15	60	120
3811 — ℞. Shield in Garter									
1823	12	40	150	250	1825	8	18	75	135
1824	8	18	60	120					
3812 Bare head ℞. Lion crown									
1825	5	9	40	75	1827	10	30	120	200
1826	5	8	35	65	1829	8	20	80	150
— Proof *FDC* £175									

3813

3814

3815

	F £	VF £	EF £	UNC £		F £	VF £	EF £	UNC £
3813 Sixpence. Laureate head. ℞. Garnished shield									
1821						5	10	45	75
3814 — ℞. Shield in Garter									
1824	5	10	45	75	1826	15	45	150	300
1825	5	10	45	75					
3815 Bare head. ℞. Lion on crown									
1826	3	8	30	60	1828	6	15	60	120
— Proof *FDC* £110					1829	5	10	45	75
1827	10	40	125	200					

3816

	EF £	FDC £		EF £	FDC £
3816 Maundy Set (4d., 3d., 2d. and 1d.)					
1822	65	130	1827	55	110
1823	55	110	1828	55	110
1824	60	120	1829	55	110
1825	55	110	1830	55	110
1826	55	110			

		EF	FDC
		£	£
3817	**Maundy fourpence,** 1822-30 ... *from*	11	18
3818	— **threepence**, small head, 1822 ...	20	35
3819	— — normal head, 1823-30 ... *from*	10	17
3820	— **twopence,** 1822-30 ... *from*	8	10
3821	— **penny,** 1822-30 ... *from*	5	8

COPPER

First issue, 1821-6

3822

	F	VF	EF	UNC
	£	£	£	£
3822 Farthing. Laureate bust, draped				
1821	2	5	20	40
1822	2	5	18	35
1823	2	5	22	45
1825	2	5	18	35
1826	4	8	30	55

Second issue, 1825-30

3823

	F	VF	EF	UNC
3823 Penny. Laureate head. R. Britannia				
1825	6	15	50	90
1826	6	12	40	75
1826 Proof *FDC £200*				
1827	45	100	900	—
3824 Halfpenny. Similar				
1825	10	25	90	175
1826	3	6	25	45
1826 Proof *FDC £100*				
1827	5	10	40	70
3825 Farthing. Similar				
1826	2	5	15	35
— Proof *FDC £100*				
1827	3	6	25	50
1828	2	5	20	45
1829	3	7	35	70
1830	2	5	20	45
3826 Half-farthing (for use in Ceylon). Similar				
1828	7	15	45	95
1830	7	15	45	95

3827

	VF	EF	UNC
3827 Third-farthing (for use in Malta). Similar			
1827	5	18	30

Copper coins graded in this catalogue as UNC have full mint lustre.

In order to prevent confusion between the sixpence and half-sovereign the size of the latter was reduced in 1834, but the smaller gold piece was not acceptable to the public and in the following year it was made to the normal size. In 1836 the silver groat was again issued for general circulation: it is the only British silver coin which has a seated Britannia as the type. Crowns were not struck during this reign for general circulation; but proofs or patterns of this denomination were made and are greatly sought after. Silver threepences and three-halfpence were minted for use in the Colonies.

Engraver's and/or designer's initials:
W. W. (William Wyon)

GOLD

3828

3828 **Two pounds,** 1831 (proof only) ....*FDC* £5000

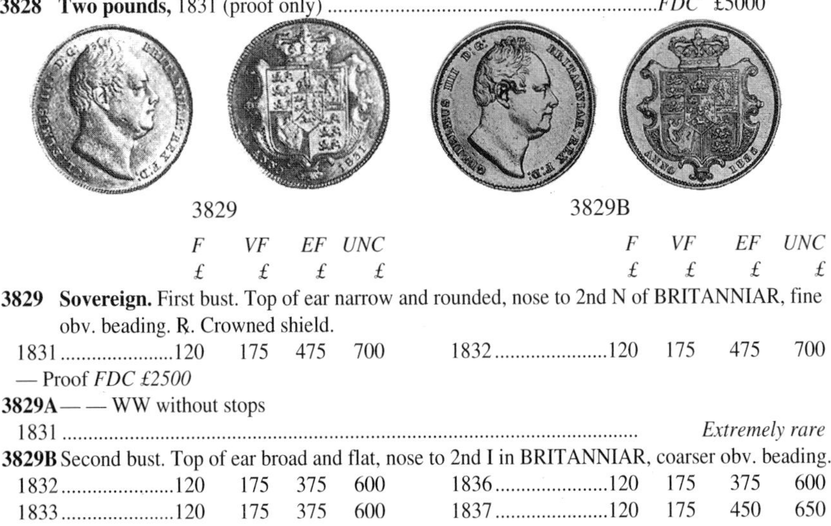

3829 3829B

	F £	*VF* £	*EF* £	*UNC* £		*F* £	*VF* £	*EF* £	*UNC* £

3829 **Sovereign.** First bust. Top of ear narrow and rounded, nose to 2nd N of BRITANNIAR, fine obv. beading. R. Crowned shield.

1831	120	175	475	700	1832	120	175	475	700

— Proof *FDC £2500*

3829A — — WW without stops

1831 .... *Extremely rare*

3829B Second bust. Top of ear broad and flat, nose to 2nd I in BRITANNIAR, coarser obv. beading.

1832	120	175	375	600	1836	120	175	375	600
1833	120	175	375	600	1837	120	175	450	650
1835	120	175	400	625					

3830 3831

3830 **Half-sovereign**. Small size

1831 Proof *FDC* £1250				1834	90	150	400	600

	F £	VF £	EF £	UNC £
3831 Large size				
1835	75	150	400	600
1836	100	225	500	700
1837	90	165	450	650
3832 *Obv.* struck from 6d. die, 1836	500	950	2250	—

SILVER

3833

3833 Crown. ℞. Shield on mantle, 1831 (proof only) ....*FDC* £4000

3834

3834 Halfcrown. ℞. Shield on mantle

	F £	VF £	EF £	UNC £
1831 Proof *FDC* £400				
1834	10	25	95	200
1835	15	50	175	350
1836	12	30	110	200
1837	15	50	200	375

3835

3836

3835 Shilling. ℞. Value in wreath

	F £	VF £	EF £	UNC £
1831 Proof *FDC £225*				
1834	8	20	70	120
1835	10	25	80	135
1836	8	20	80	135
1837	12	35	125	200

3836 Sixpence. ℞. Value in wreath

	F £	VF £	EF £	UNC £
1831	5	12	40	70
— Proof *FDC* £150				
1834	5	12	40	70
1835	5	12	40	70
1836	8	20	90	160
1837	6	18	80	150

3837

	F £	VF £	EF £	UNC £		F £	VF £	EF £	UNC £
3837 Groat. ℞. Britannia seated									
1836	2	6	18	30	1837	2	6	18	30
3838 Threepence (for use in the West Indies). As Maundy threepence but with a dull surface									
1834	2	6	30	65	1836	2	5	28	60
1835	2	5	28	60	1837	3	7	36	80

3839

3839 Three-halfpence (for Colonial use). ℞. Value									
1834	2	5	16	28	1836	2	5	20	35
1835/4	2	5	18	30	1837	5	20	75	150

3840

	EF £	FDC £		EF £	FDC £
3840 Maundy Set (4d., 3d., 2d. and 1d.).					
1831	80	150	1834	75	140
— Proof *FDC £250*			1835	75	140
1832	75	140	1836	75	140
1833	75	140	1837	75	140
3841 — fourpence, 1831-7 *from*				11	20
3842 — threepence, 1831-7 *from*				20	30
3843 — twopence, 1831-7 *from*				7	13
3844 — penny, 1831-7 *from*				7	12

COPPER

3845

	F £	VF £	EF £	UNC £
3845 Penny. No initials on truncation				
1831	8	25	90	200
— Proof *FDC £225*				
1834	9	30	100	225
1837	12	40	150	350
3846 WW on truncation, 1831	9	35	125	300
3847 Halfpenny. As penny				
1831	4	9	30	55
— Proof *FDC £125*				
1834	4	9	35	60
1837	3	8	25	45

3847

3848

	F £	VF £	EF £	UNC £
3848 Farthing. Similar				
1831	2	5	16	35
— Proof *FDC £120*				
1834	2	5	16	35
1835	2	5	16	35
1836	3	6	20	45
1837	2	5	16	35
3849 Half-farthing (for use in Ceylon). Similar				
1837	15	45	175	300
3850 Third-farthing (for use in Malta). Similar				
1835	2	5	16	30

3849

3850

In 1849, as a first step towards decimalization, a silver florin (1/10 th pound) was introduced, but the coins of 1849 omitted the usual *Dei Gratia* and these so-called 'Godless' florins were replaced in 1851 by the 'Gothic' issue. The halfcrown was temporarily discontinued but was minted again from 1874 onwards. Between 1863 and 1880 reverse dies of the gold and silver coins were numbered in the course of Mint experiments into the wear of dies. The exception was the florin where the die number is on the obverse below the bust.

The gold and silver coins were redesigned for the Queen's Golden Jubilee in 1887. The double-florin which was then issued was abandoned after only four years; the Jubilee sixpence of 1887, known as the 'withdrawn' type, was changed to avoid confusion with the half-sovereign. Gold and silver were again redesigned in 1893 with an older portrait of the Queen, but the 'old head' was not used on the bronze coinage until 1895. The heavy copper penny had been replaced by the lighter bronze 'bun' penny in 1860. In 1874-6 and 1881-2 some of the bronze was made by Heaton in Birmingham, and these have a letter H below the date. From 1897 farthings were issued with a dark surface.

Early sovereigns had a shield-type reverse, but Pistrucci's St. George design was used again from 1871. In order to increase the output of gold coinage, branches of the Royal Mint were set up in Australia at Sydney and Melbourne and, later, at Perth for coining gold of imperial type.

Engraver's and/or designer's initials:

W. W. (William Wyon)
L. C. W. (Leonard Charles Wyon)
J. E. B. (Joseph Boehm)
T. B. (Thomas Brock)

GOLD

Young head coinage, 1838-87

3851

3851 Five pounds. 1839. ℞. 'Una and the lion' (proof only) varieties occur *FDC* £16,500

3852D

3852F

3852A

3852F

3852 Sovereign. Type I, first (small) young head. ℞. First shield. London mint

Date	F £	VF £	EF £	UNC £
1838	90	135	300	500
1839	100	200	800	1250
— Proof *FDC* £2000				
1841	400	800	2500	—
1842	80	95	150	225
1843	80	95	150	225
1844	80	95	150	225
1845	80	95	150	225
1846	80	95	150	225
1847	80	95	150	225
1848	*Extremely rare*			

3825A— ℞ similar but leaves of the wreath arranged differently with tops of leaves closer to crown.

1838 .... *Extremely rare*

**A good EF specmen sold at auction in June 1993 for £1300 plus buyers premium.*

3852B*— narrower shield. Considerably modified floral emblems

1843 .... *Extremely rare*

**A practically EF specimen was sold at auction in March 1992 for £2500 plus 10% buyers premium.*

3852C Type I, second (large) head. W W still in relief. ℞. Shield with repositioned legend

Date	F £	VF £	EF £	UNC £
1848	80	95	150	225
1849	80	95	150	225
1850	85	100	160	250
1851	80	95	140	225
1852	80	95	130	200
1853	80	95	130	200
1854	80	95	140	225
1855	80	95	130	200
1872	80	95	130	200

3852D— — WW incuse

Date	F £	VF £	EF £	UNC £
1853	80	95	130	200
— Proof *FDC £4500*				
1854	80	95	140	225
1855	80	95	130	200
1856	80	95	140	225
1857	80	95	130	200
1858	85	110	190	275
1859	80	95	140	225
1860	80	95	130	200
1861	80	95	130	200
1862	80	95	130	200
1863	80	95	130	200

3852E— — As 3852D 'Ansell' ribbon. Additional raised line on the lower part of the ribbon

Date	F £	VF £	EF £	UNC £
1859	175	350	1100	—

3852F *— — As 3852D with 827 on truncation

1863 .... *Extremely rare*

** A VF specimen sold at auction in June 1993 for £1600 plus buyer's premium.*

3852C

3853

3853 — — As 3852D die number below wreath

Date	F £	VF £	EF £	UNC £
1863	80	95	130	200
1864	80	90	120	175
1865	80	95	140	225
1866	80	90	120	175
1868	80	95	130	200
1869	80	90	120	175
1870	85	100	160	250

3853A— — As 3853 with 827 on truncation (Always die no 22)

1863 .... *Extremely rare*

3853B — — WW in relief die number below wreath

Date	F £	VF £	EF £	UNC £
1870	80	95	130	200
1871	80	90	120	175
1872	80	90	120	175
1873	80	95	130	200
1874	—	1100	—	—

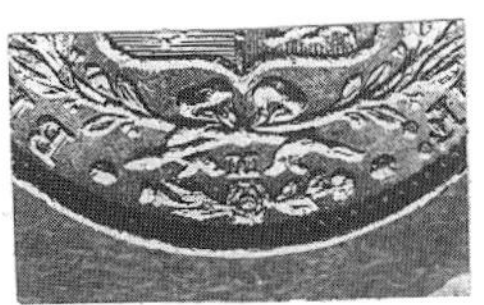

3854 3855

3854 Sovereign., second (large) head. As 3853B but with M below wreath for Melbourne

	F £	VF £	EF £	UNC £		F £	VF £	EF £	UNC £
1872 M	80	95	175	325	1882 M	80	95	175	325
1873 M		*Extremely rare*			1883 M	125	200	600	900
1874 M	80	95	175	325	1884 M	80	95	175	325
1879 M		*Extremely rare*			1885 M	80	75	175	325
1880 M	350	900	2750	—	1886 M	500	1400	3250	—
1881 M	85	110	250	450	1887 M	350	700	2000	—

3854A— — As 3853 W W incuse but with S below wreath for Sydney

	F £	VF £	EF £	UNC £
1871 S	85	100	200	350

3855 — — As 3854 but with S below wreath for Sydney

	F £	VF £	EF £	UNC £		F £	VF £	EF £	UNC £
1871 S	75	90	130	200	1881 S	70	80	110	175
1872 S	75	90	130	200	1882 S	70	80	110	175
1873 S	75	90	130	200	1883 S	70	80	110	175
1875 S	75	80	110	175	1884 S	70	80	110	175
1877 S	75	80	110	175	1885 S	75	90	130	200
1878 S	75	80	110	175	1886 S	75	90	130	200
1879 S	75	80	110	175	1887 S	75	90	130	200
1880 S	75	80	110	175					

3856A

3856 — Type II, first young head. WW buried in narrow truncation. ℞. St. George. London mint. Horse with short tail. Large BP

	F £	VF £	EF £	UNC £
1871	70	80	110	175

3856A — — As 3856 ℞. Horse with long tail. Small BP

	F £	VF £	EF £	UNC £		F £	VF £	EF £	UNC £
1871			90	150	1876			90	150
1872			90	150	1878			100	160
1873			100	160	1879	110	175	600	—
1874	70	80	110	175	1880			90	150

3856B — — As 3856 but with small BP

	F £	VF £	EF £	UNC £		F £	VF £	EF £	UNC £
1880			90	150	1885	70	80	110	175
1884			100	160					

3856C — — As 3856 but no BP

	F £	VF £	EF £	UNC £
1880			90	150

	F	VF	EF	UNC		F	VF	EF	UNC
	£	£	£	£		£	£	£	£

3856D — — Second head. WW on broad truncation. ℞. Horse with long tail, small BP

	F	VF	EF	UNC
1880	70	80	110	175

3856E — — As 3856D but horse with short tail. No BP

	F	VF	EF	UNC
1880			90	150

3856F — — As 3856E but small BP

	F	VF	EF	UNC		F	VF	EF	UNC
1884			100	160	1885	70	80	110	175

3857

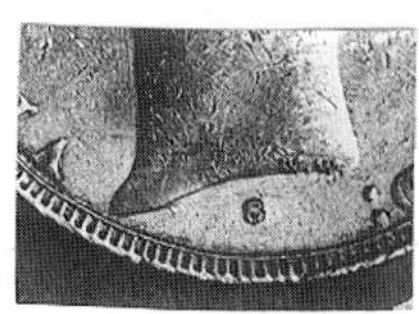

3858

3857 — — First head. WW buried in truncation, M below head for Melbourne mint. ℞. Horse with long tail, small BP

	F	VF	EF	UNC		F	VF	EF	UNC
1872 M	90	120	270	375	1877 M			95	155
1873 M	75	90	160	225	1878 M			95	155
1874 M	75	90	160	225	1879 M	70	80	115	175
1875 M	70	80	115	175	1880 M			95	155
1876 M	70	80	115	175	1881 M			95	155

3857A — — As 3857 but horse with short tail, no BP

	F	VF	EF	UNC		F	VF	EF	UNC
1881 M			95	155	1882 M			95	155

3857B— — As 3857A but with small BP

	F	VF	EF	UNC		F	VF	EF	UNC
1882 M			95	155	1884 M			95	155
1883 M			95	155	1885 M			95	155

3857C— — Second head. WW on broad truncation. ℞. Horse with short tail, small BP

	F	VF	EF	UNC		F	VF	EF	UNC
1882 M			95	155	1885 M			95	155
1883 M			95	155	1886 M			95	155
1884 M			95	155	1887 M			95	155

3858 — — First head. WW buried in narrow truncation, S below head for Sydney mint. ℞. Horse with short tail, large BP

	F	VF	EF	UNC
1871 S	85	100	200	350

3858A— — As 3858 but horse with long tail, small BP

	F	VF	EF	UNC		F	VF	EF	UNC
1871 S	80	95	180	275	1876 S			90	150
1872 S	75	90	160	250	1877 S			*Extremely rare*	
1873 S	70	85	140	225	1879 S	75	90	160	250
1874 S			90	150	1880 S			95	155
1875 S			90	150					

3858B — — As 3858 but with no BP

	F	VF	EF	UNC		F	VF	EF	UNC
1880 S			95	155	1881 S			95	155

3858C Sovereign. Second head. WW on broad truncation. R. Horse with long tail, small BP

	EF £	UNC £		F £	VF £	EF £	UNC £
1880 S				70	80	110	175

3858D — — As 3858C but horse with short tail, no BP

	EF £	UNC £		F £	VF £	EF £	UNC £
1881 S	95	155	1882 S			95	155

3858E — — As 3858D but small BP

	EF £	UNC £		F £	VF £	EF £	UNC £
1882 S	95	155	1885 S			95	155
1883 S	95	155	1886 S			95	155
1884 S	95	155	1887 S			95	155

3859 3860

3859 Half-sovereign. Type A1, first (smallest) young head. R. First shield

	F £	VF £	EF £	UNC £		F £	VF £	EF £	UNC £
1838	50	75	200	350	1850	95	200	600	—
1839 Proof only *FDC* £900					1851		65	150	275
1841	55	90	250	400	1852	55	80	175	300
1842		60	135	250	1853		60	135	250
1843	55	90	250	400	— Proof *FDC* £2750				
1844	50	70	200	350	1854		*Extremely rare*		
1845	100	250	800	—	1855		65	140	250
1846	50	75	200	350	1856		65	140	250
1847	50	75	200	350	1857	55	80	175	300
1848	50	75	200	350	1858	55	80	175	300
1849		65	150	275					

3859A Type A2, second (larger) young head. R. As last

	F £	VF £	EF £	UNC £		F £	VF £	EF £	UNC £
1858		60	140	250	1861		60	140	250
1859		60	140	250	1862		750	—	—
1860		60	140	250	1863		60	140	250

3860 As last but with die number below shield

	F £	VF £	EF £	UNC £		F £	VF £	EF £	UNC £
1863	55	80	200	350	1867		60	135	250
1864		60	135	250	1869		60	135	250
1865		60	135	250	1870	50	70	140	250
1866		60	135	250	1871		60	135	250

3860A — R. Re-engraved shield legend and rosettes closer to border, coarse teeth both sides, with die number

	F £	VF £	EF £	UNC £		F £	VF £	EF £	UNC £
1870	75	175	500	—	1871	75	175	500	—

3860B — R. As last but with normal border and no die number

	F £	VF £	EF £	UNC £
1871		*Extremely rare*		

3860C — obv. with repositioned legend, nose points to T in VICTORIA.
R similar to last but with die number

	F £	VF £	EF £	UNC £		F £	VF £	EF £	UNC £
1871	95	200	600	—	1872	80	175	500	—

3860D Type A3, third (larger still) young head. R. As 3860A

	F £	VF £	EF £	UNC £		F £	VF £	EF £	UNC £
1872		60	135	250	1875		55	125	225
1873		60	135	250	1876		55	125	225
1874		65	135	250	1877		55	125	225

3860E Type A4, fourth young head, hair ribbon now narrow. R. As last with die number

	F £	VF £	EF £	UNC £		F £	VF £	EF £	UNC £
1876		55	130	225	1878		55	130	225
1877		55	130	225	1879	50	75	250	400

3860F Type A5, fifth young head, in very low relief. R. As last with die number

	F £	VF £	EF £	UNC £
1880		65	250	400

3861 Obv. as last. R. Cross on crown buried in border. Legend and rosettes very close to heavy border, no die number

	F £	VF £	EF £	UNC £		F £	VF £	EF £	UNC £
1880		65	150	275	1884		55	115	175
1883		55	115	175	1885		55	115	175

3862

3863

3862 Type A2, second (larger) young head. R. First shield with S below for Sydney mint

	F £	VF £	EF £	UNC £
1871 S	60	95	475	—

3862A — obv. with repositioned legend, nose points to T in VICTORIA. R Re-engraved shield

	F £	VF £	EF £	UNC £
1872 S	70	110	500	—

3862B Type A3, third (larger still) young head. R. As last

	F £	VF £	EF £	UNC £
1875 S	65	100	475	—

3862C Type A4, fourth young head, hair ribbon now narrow. R. As last

	F £	VF £	EF £	UNC £
1879 S	70	110	500	—

3862D Type A5, fifth young head,in low relief. R as last.

	F £	VF £	EF £	UNC £		F £	VF £	EF £	UNC £
1882 S		250	950	—	1883 S	70	110	450	—

3862E — R. Cross on crown buried in border, legend and rosettes very close to heavy border

	F £	VF £	EF £	UNC £		F £	VF £	EF £	UNC £
1880 S	70	110	500	—	1883 S	70	110	450	—
1881 S	90	150	650	—	1886 S	60	95	350	—
1882 S	110	250	950	—	1887 S	60	95	350	—

3863 Type A3, third (larger still) young head. R. Re-engraved shield with M below for Melbourne mint

	F £	VF £	EF £	UNC £		F £	VF £	EF £	UNC £
1873 M	80	125	500	—	1877 M	65	100	450	—

3863A Type A4, third (larger still) young head. hair ribbon now narrow. R. As last

	F £	VF £	EF £	UNC £		F £	VF £	EF £	UNC £
1877 M	65	100	450	—	1882 M	80	125	500	—

3863B Type A5, fifth young head, in low relief. R. As last

	F £	VF £	EF £	UNC £		F £	VF £	EF £	UNC £
1881 M	100	200	700	—	1885 M	135	300	1250	—
1882 M	80	125	500	—	1886 M	80	125	500	—
1884 M	100	200	700	—	1887 M	110	250	1000	—

Jubilee coinage, 1887-93

3864

	EF £	UNC £		F £	VF £	EF £	UNC £
3864 Five pounds. ℞. St. George 1887				325	400	550	750
— Proof *FDC* £2000							
3864A ℞. St George, S on ground for Sydney mint 1887S						*Extremely rare*	
3865 Two pounds. Similar 1887				135	175	300	450
— Proof *FDC* £750							
3865A ℞. St George, S on ground for Sydney mint 1887S						*Extremely rare*	

3866 3867c 3869

	EF £	UNC £		F £	VF £	EF £	UNC £
3866 Sovereign. Normal JEB initials. ℞. St. George. London mint							
1887	95	135	1888			95	135
3866A with tiny initials							
1887						*Extremely rare*	
3866B Reposioned legend. G: of D:G: now close to crown. Normal initials							
1887 Proof *FDC* £450.			1889			95	135
1888	95	135	1890			95	135
3866C Obv. as last. ℞. Horse with long tail							
1891	95	135	1892			95	135
3867 With small spread initials. ℞. M on ground for Melbourne mint							
1887M					75	150	250
3867A With normal initials 1887M						95	135
3867B Repositioned legend. G: of D: G: now close to crown. Normal initials							
1887M	95	135	1889M			95	135
1888M	90	135	1890M			95	135
3867C Obv. as last. ℞. Horse with long tail							
1891M	95	135	1893M			95	135
1892M	95	135					
3868 With small spread initials. ℞. S on ground for Sydney mint							
1887S					150	350	600
3868A With normal initials 1888S						110	150
3868B Repositioned legend. G: of D:G: now close to crown. Normal initials							
1888S	110	150	1890S			95	135
1889S	95	135					
3868C Obv. as last. ℞. Horse with long tail							
1891S	95	135	1893S			100	140
1892S	100	140					
3869 Half-sovereign. Obv. normal JEB. ℞. High Shield							
1887	70	95	1890			*Extremely rare*	
— Proof *FDC* £225							
3869A Tiny close JEB. ℞. As last 1887						*Extremely rare*	
3869B Normal JEB. ℞. Low shield, date spread							
1890	*Extremely rare*		1892			*Extremely rare*	

	F £	VF £	EF £	UNC £		F £	VF £	EF £	UNC £
3869C No JEB. R. High Shield									
1887	75	125	350	—	1891		*Extremely rare*		
1890			70	95	1892		*Extremely rare*		
3869D As last. R. Low Shield, date spread									
1890			70	95	1892			70	95
1891			95	125	1893			100	135

	F £	VF £	EF £	UNC £
3870 Small very extended JEB. R. High shield M below for Melbourne mint				
1887M	65	95	275	500
3870A Small close JEB. R. As last				
1887M	65	95	275	500
3870B Normal JEB. R. Low shield, date spread				
1893M	75	110	350	—
3871 Small very extended JEB. R. high shield S below for Sydney				
1887S	60	90	250	450
3871A Small close JEB. R as last.				
1887S	60	90	250	450
3871B Normal JEB. R. Low shield, date spread				
1889S	75	110	350	—
3871C As last. R. High shield				
1891S	60	90	250	450
3871D No JEB. R. As last				
1891S	60	90	250	450

Old head coinage, 1893-1901

	F £	VF £	EF £	UNC £
3872 Five pounds. R. St. George				
1893	350	500	850	1100
— Proof *FDC* £2000				

3873

	F £	VF £	EF £	UNC £
3873 Two pounds. Similar				
1893	150	250	400	550
— Proof *FDC* £850				

3874 Sovereign. R. St. George, London mint

1893	BV	1898	BV
— Proof *FDC* £450		1899	BV
1894	BV	1900	BV
1895	BV	1901	BV
1896	BV		

3875 — R. St. George. M on ground for Melbourne mint

1893 M	BV	1898 M	BV
1894 M	BV	1899 M	BV
1895 M	BV	1900 M	BV
1896 M	BV	1901 M	BV
1897 M	BV		

3876 3877

3876 Sovereign. R. St. George, P on ground for Perth mint

	F £	VF £	EF £	UNC £
1899 P			95	135
1900 P				BV
1901 P				BV

3877 — — S on ground for Sydney mint

	F £	VF £	EF £	UNC £
1893 S				BV
1894 S				BV
1895 S				BV
1896 S				BV
1897 S				BV
1898 S				BV
1899 S				BV
1900 S				BV
1901 S				BV

3878

3878 Half-sovereign. R. St. George. London mint

	F £	VF £	EF £	UNC £
1893			60	85
— Proof *FDC* £300				
1894			60	85
1895			60	85
1896			60	85
1897			60	85
1898			60	85
1899			60	85
1900			60	85
1901			60	85

3879 — — M on ground for Melbourne mint

	F £	VF £	EF £	UNC £
1893 M	*Extremely rare*			
1896 M	55	95	300	—
1899 M	55	95	300	—
1900 M	55	95	300	—

3880 — — P on ground for Perth mint

	F £	VF £	EF £	UNC £
1899 P	Proof *unique*			
1900 P	65	110	400	—

3881 — — S on ground for Sydney mint

	F £	VF £	EF £	UNC £
1893 S	55	95	300	—
1897 S	55	95	300	—
1900 S		60	150	300

SILVER

Young head coinage

3882

	F	VF	EF	UNC
	£	£	£	£
3882 Crown. Young head. ℞. Crowned shield				
1839 Proof only *FDC £2500*				
1844	20	75	450	900
1845	20	75	400	900
1847	22	90	550	1100
3883*'Gothic' type, as illustration; inscribed edge, mdcccxlvii=1847	160	275	450	850
— Proof, Plain edge *FDC £950*				

**Beware of recent forgeries.*

3884 — — mdcccliii=1853. Proof *FDC £3000*

3883

3888

3885

	F	VF	EF	UNC
3885 Halfcrown. Type A[1]. Young head with one ornate and one plain fillet binding hair. WW in relief on truncation, 1839	250	600	2000	—

3886 Halfcrown Type A[1] — Proof *FDC* £600

3887 Type A[3]. Two plain fillets. WW incuse

Date	*F* £	*VF* £	*EF* £	*UNC* £
1839	250	600	2250	—
1840	20	50	200	350

3888 — Type A[4]. Similar but no initials on truncation

Date	*F* £	*VF* £	*EF* £	*UNC* £
1841	50	135	550	900
1842	18	45	150	275
1843	22	75	275	500
1844	16	40	130	250
1845	16	40	130	250
1846	16	40	130	250
1848/6	45	120	450	900
1849	20	60	225	450
1850	18	55	200	400
1853 Proof *FDC* £1000				

3889 — Type A[5]. As last but inferior workmanship

Date	*F* £	*VF* £	*EF* £	*UNC* £
1874	8	20	75	150
1875	8	24	70	135
1876	8	24	85	160
1877	8	24	80	150
1878	8	24	80	150
1879	9	35	110	200
1880	8	24	80	150
1881	8	20	75	150
1882	8	24	90	175
1883	8	20	70	135
1884	8	20	75	150
1885	8	20	75	150
1886	8	20	75	150
1887	8	20	90	175

3890

3892

	F £	*VF* £	*EF* £	*UNC* £
3890 Florin, 'Godless' type (i.e. without D.G.), 1849	9	20	65	125

3891 'Gothic' type B[1]. Reads brit:, WW below bust, date at end of obverse legend in gothic numerals (1851 to 1863)

Date	*F* £	*VF* £	*EF* £	*UNC* £
mdcccli	*Extremely rare*			
mdccclii	9	22	95	165
mdcccliii	9	20	85	150
— Proof *FDC £1100*				
mdcccliv	225	500	1750	—
mdccclv	10	25	100	175
mdccclvi	10	27	120	200
mdccclvii	10	25	100	175
mdcclviii	10	25	100	175
mdcclix	10	25	100	175
mdcclx	10	30	135	225
mdcclxii	27	100	300	600
mdcclxiii	50	175	650	1000

3892 — type B[2]. As last but die number below bust (1864 to 1867)

Date	*F* £	*VF* £	*EF* £	*UNC* £
mdccclxiv	10	25	100	175
mdccclxv	10	27	110	185
mdccclxvi	10	30	130	225
mdccclxvii	18	60	175	275

3893 — type B³. Reads britt:, die number (1868 to 1879)

	F £	VF £	EF £	UNC £
mdccclxviii	10	27	120	200
mdccclxix	10	25	100	175
mdccclxx	10	25	100	175
mdccclxxi	10	25	100	175
mdccclxxii	9	20	80	150
mdccclxxiii	9	20	80	150
mdccclxxiv	10	25	100	175
mdccclxxv	10	25	100	175
mdccclxxvii	10	25	110	185
mdccclxxvii	10	25	110	185
mdccclxxix	*Extremely rare*			

3894 — type B⁴. As last but with border of 48 arcs and no WW

	F £	VF £	EF £	UNC £
1877 mdccclxxvii	*Extremely rare*			

3895 — type B⁵. Similar but 42 arcs (1867, 1877 and 1878)

	F £	VF £	EF £	UNC £
mdccclxvii	*Extremely rare*			
mdccclxxvii	10	25	110	185
mdccclxxviii	10	25	100	175

3896 — type B⁵/6. As last but no die number (1877, 1879)

	F £	VF £	EF £	UNC £
mdccclxxvii	*Extremely rare*			
mdccclxxix	*Extremely rare*			

3897 — type B⁶. Reads britt:, WW; 48 arcs (1879)

	F £	VF £	EF £	UNC £
mdccclxxix	10	25	100	175

3898 — type B⁷. As last but no WW, 38 arcs (1879)

	F £	VF £	EF £	UNC £
mdccclxxix	10	25	100	175

3899 — type B³/8. As next but younger portrait (1880)

	F £	VF £	EF £	UNC £
mdccclxxx	*Extremely rare*			

3900 — type B⁸. Similar but 34 arcs (1880 to 1887)

	F £	VF £	EF £	UNC £
mdccclxxx	10	25	100	175
mdccclxxxi	9	20	90	165
mdccclxxxiii	9	20	90	165
mdccclxxxiv	9	20	90	165
mdccclxxxv	9	20	90	165
mdccclxxxvi	9	22	95	165
mdccclxxxvii				*? exists*

3901 — type B⁹. Similar but 46 arcs

	F £	VF £	EF £	UNC £
1887 mdccclxxxvii	10	30	140	225

3902 Shilling. Type A¹. First head, WW on truncation

	F £	VF £	EF £	UNC £
1838	7	16	60	110
1839	7	16	65	110

3903 Type A². Second head, WW (proof only), 1839 *FDC £225*

3904 Type A³. Second head, no initials on truncation

	F £	VF £	EF £	UNC £
1839	8	16	50	85
1840	12	30	110	180
1841	12	30	110	180
1842	8	16	55	90
1843	10	25	85	140
1844	8	16	55	90
1845	8	16	65	110
1846	8	16	55	90
1848 over 6	25	70	350	500
1849	9	20	70	120
1850	90	300	800	—
1851	25	75	250	400
1852	8	16	55	90
1853	8	16	50	85
— Proof *FDC £400*				
1854	40	125	450	800
1855	8	16	50	85
1856	8	16	50	85
1857	8	16	50	85
1858	8	16	50	85
1859	8	16	50	85
1860	10	22	80	135
1861	10	22	80	135
1862	15	35	110	175
1863	20	55	225	400

3905 Type A⁴. As before but die number above date

	F £	VF £	EF £	UNC £
1864	8	16	50	85
1865	8	16	50	85
1866	8	16	50	85
1867	8	16	55	90

3906

3906 Shilling. Type A⁶. Third head, die number above date

	F £	VF £	EF £	UNC £
1867	30	90	375	—
1868	8	16	50	85
1869	9	20	70	135
1870	9	20	70	135
1871	6	12	35	55
1872	6	12	35	55
1873	6	12	35	55
1874	6	12	35	55
1875	6	12	35	55
1876	8	16	55	90
1877	6	12	35	55
1878	6	12	35	55
1879	20	50	175	300

3907 — Type A⁷. Fourth head, no die number

	F £	VF £	EF £	UNC £
1879	8	20	50	85
1880	5	10	27	50
1881	5	10	27	50
1882	12	32	80	135
1883	5	10	27	50
1884	5	10	27	50
1885	5	10	25	45
1886	5	10	25	45
1887	8	22	60	110

3908 Sixpence. Type A. First head

	F £	VF £	EF £	UNC £
1838	5	12	35	60
1839	5	12	35	60
— Proof *FDC* £150				
1840	6	13	40	70

3909

3912

	F £	VF £	EF £	UNC £
1841	7	15	50	85
1842	6	13	40	70
1843	6	13	40	70
1844	5	12	35	60
1845	6	13	40	70
1846	5	12	35	60
1848	25	65	275	400
1850	6	13	40	70
1851	6	13	40	70
1852	3	10	40	70
1853	5	12	35	60
— Proof *FDC* £275				
1854	40	110	400	700
1855	5	12	35	60
1856	6	13	40	70
1857	6	13	40	70
1858	6	13	40	70
1859	5	12	35	60
1860	6	13	40	70
1862	25	65	275	400
1863	15	35	175	300
1866			*Extremely rare*	

3909 Type A². First head; die number above date

	F £	VF £	EF £	UNC £
1864	6	13	40	70
1865	7	15	50	85
1866	6	13	40	70

3910 Type A³. Second head; die number above date

	F £	VF £	EF £	UNC £
1867	8	16	55	95
1868	8	16	55	95
1869	4	20	80	150
1870	4	20	80	150
1871	6	13	40	70
1872	6	13	40	70
1873	4	10	35	60
1874	4	10	35	60
1875	4	10	35	60
1876	8	16	60	110
1877	4	10	35	60
1878	4	10	35	60
1879	8	16	60	110

3911 Type A4. Second head; no die number

	F £	VF £	EF £	UNC £
1871	7	15	50	85
1877	6	13	40	70
1879	6	13	40	70
1880	7	15	50	85

3912 Type A5. Third head

	F £	VF £	EF £	UNC £
1880	4	8	22	40
1881	4	8	20	35
1882	9	20	60	110
1883	4	8	20	35
1884	4	8	20	35
1885	4	8	20	35
1886	4	8	20	35
1887	3	7	18	30

3913 Groat (4d.). R. Britannia

	F £	VF £	EF £	UNC £
1838	2	6	20	35
1839	3	8	25	40
— Proof *FDC £110*				
1840	3	8	22	40
1841	4	9	32	50
1842	4	9	30	50
1843	4	9	30	50
1844	4	9	30	50
1845	4	9	30	50
1846	4	9	30	50
1847/6 (or 8)	12	40	135	—
1848	3	8	22	40
1849	3	8	22	40
1851	15	50	150	275
1852	22	75	225	350
1853	30	90	275	400
— Proof *FDC £275*				
1854	3	8	22	40
1855	3	8	22	40

3914

3914A

3914C

3914D

Threepence. R. Crowned 3; as Maundy threepence but with a less prooflike surface

3914 — Type A1. First bust, young head, high relief, ear fully visible.
R Tie ribbon closer to tooth border, cross on crown further from tooth border, figure 3

	F £	VF £	EF £	UNC £
1838*	2	6	30	60
1839*	3	9	40	75
— Proof (see Maundy)				
1840*	3	9	45	80
1841*	4	10	50	90
1842*	4	10	50	90
1843*	2	6	30	60
1844*	3	9	45	80
1845	1	4	22	40
1846	5	12	60	110
1847*		—	300	—
1848*		—	275	—
1849	3	9	45	80
1850	1	4	25	45
1851	2	6	35	65
1852*		—	250	—
1853	4	12	60	110
1854	2	6	35	65
1855	4	10	50	90
1856	3	9	45	80
1857	3	9	45	80
1858	2	6	35	65
1859	1	4	20	40
1860	3	9	45	80
1861	1	4	25	45

3914A — Type A2. First bust variety, slightly older portrait with aquiline nose

	F £	VF £	EF £	UNC £
1859	1	4	20	37
1860	2	6	30	60
1861	2	5	25	45
1862	2	6	35	65
1863	3	9	45	80
1864	2	6	30	60
1865	3	9	45	80
1866	2	6	30	60
1867	2	6	35	65
1868	2	5	25	45

3914B — Type A3. Second Bust, slightly larger, lower relief, mouth fuller, nose more pronounced, rounded truncation

	F £	VF £	EF £	UNC £
1867	3	9	45	80

3914C Threepence Type A^3. Obv. as last. R. Tie ribbon further from tooth border, cross on crown nearer to tooth border

	F £	VF £	EF £	UNC £		F £	VF £	EF £	UNC £
1867	2	6	35	65	1874	2	5	18	35
1869	4	10	55	95	1875	2	5	18	35
1870	2	5	22	40	1876	2	5	18	35
1871	2	6	30	60	1877	2	5	18	35
1872	2	5	25	45	1878	2	5	18	35
1873	2	5	18	35	1879	2	5	18	35

3914D— Type A^4. Third bust, older features, mouth closed, hair strands leading from 'bun' vary

	F £	VF £	EF £	UNC £		F £	VF £	EF £	UNC £
1880	1	4	20	40	1884	1	4	15	30
1881	1	4	20	40	1885	1	4	15	30
1882	2	6	35	65	1886	1	4	15	30
1883	1	4	15	30	1887	1	4	15	30

**Issued for Colonial use only.*

3915 Three-halfpence (for Colonial use). R. Value, etc.

	F £	VF £	EF £	UNC £		F £	VF £	EF £	UNC £
1838	2	6	18	35	1842	3	8	25	45
1839	2	6	16	35	1843	2	5	14	30
1840	3	10	35	60	1860	3	10	40	70
1841	2	6	16	35	1862	3	10	35	60

3916

3916 Maundy Set (4d., 3d., 2d. and 1.)

	EF £	FDC £		EF £	FDC £
1838	40	65	1862	40	60
1839	40	65	1863	40	60
— Proof *FDC £200*			1864	40	60
1840	40	65	1865	40	60
1841	40	65	1866	40	60
1842	40	65	1867	40	60
1843	40	65	1868	40	60
1844	40	65	1869	40	60
1845	40	65	1870	35	55
1846	40	65	1871	35	55
1847	40	65	1872	35	55
1848	40	65	1873	35	55
1849	45	75	1874	35	55
1850	40	65	1875	35	55
1851	40	65	1876	35	55
1852	40	65	1877	35	55
1853	40	65	1878	35	55
— Proof *FDC £300*			1879	35	55
1854	40	65	1880	35	55
1855	45	75	1881	35	55
1856	40	65	1882	35	55
1857	40	65	1883	35	55
1858	40	65	1884	35	55
1859	40	65	1885	35	55
1860	40	65	1886	35	55
1861	40	65	1887	35	55

		EF £	FDC £
3917 — **fourpence,** 1838-87	*from*	6	10
3918 — **threepence**, 1838-87	*from*	12	22
3919 — **twopence**, 1838-87	*from*	4	8
3920 — **penny**, 1838-87	*from*	3	7

Maundy Sets in the original dated cases are worth approximately £5 more than the prices quoted.

Jubilee Coinage

3921

	F £	*VF* £	*EF* £	*UNC* £
3921 Crown. ℞. St. George				
1887	11	18	30	60
— Proof *FDC £375*				
1888	11	22	50	85
1889	11	18	30	60
1890	11	22	55	90
1891	12	24	65	120
1892	14	25	70	130

3922

	F £	*VF* £	*EF* £	*UNC* £
3922 Double-florin (4s.). ℞. Cruciform shields. Roman I in date				
1887	9	15	25	45
3923 Similar but Arabic 1 in date				
1887	9	15	25	45
— Proof *FDC £175*				
1888	10	17	35	60
1889	10	16	30	55
1890	10	17	35	60

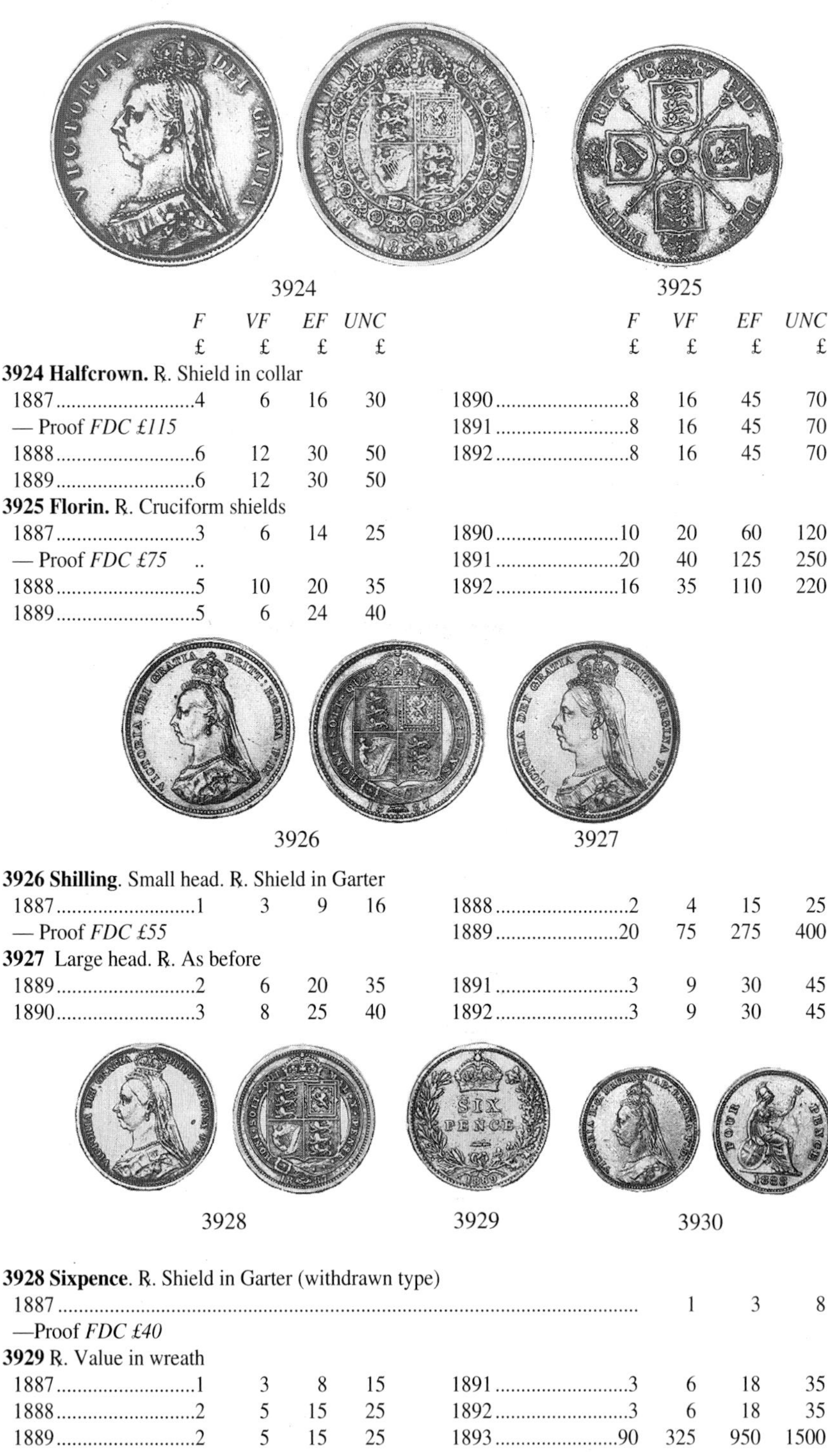

3924 3925

3926 3927

3928 3929 3930

	F £	VF £	EF £	UNC £
3924 Halfcrown. ℞. Shield in collar				
1887	4	6	16	30
— Proof *FDC £115*				
1888	6	12	30	50
1889	6	12	30	50
1890	8	16	45	70
1891	8	16	45	70
1892	8	16	45	70
3925 Florin. ℞. Cruciform shields				
1887	3	6	14	25
— Proof *FDC £75* ..				
1888	5	10	20	35
1889	5	6	24	40
1890	10	20	60	120
1891	20	40	125	250
1892	16	35	110	220
3926 Shilling. Small head. ℞. Shield in Garter				
1887	1	3	9	16
— Proof *FDC £55*				
1888	2	4	15	25
1889	20	75	275	400
3927 Large head. ℞. As before				
1889	2	6	20	35
1890	3	8	25	40
1891	3	9	30	45
1892	3	9	30	45
3928 Sixpence. ℞. Shield in Garter (withdrawn type)				
1887		1	3	8
—Proof *FDC £40*				
3929 ℞. Value in wreath				
1887	1	3	8	15
1888	2	5	15	25
1889	2	5	15	25
1890	2	5	16	30
1891	3	6	18	35
1892	3	6	18	35
1893	90	325	950	1500

	F £	VF £	EF £	UNC £		F £	VF £	EF £	UNC £
3930 Groat (for use in British Guiana). ℞. Britannia									
1888	4	12	25	40					
3931 Threepence. As Maundy but less prooflike surface									
1887		1	4	7	1890	1	2	7	12
— Proof *FDC £27*					1891	1	2	7	12
1888	1	3	9	16	1892	1	3	10	18
1889	1	2	7	12	1893	8	25	75	120

3932

	EF £	FDC £		EF £	FDC £
3932 Maundy Set (4d., 3d., 2d. and 1d.)					
1888	35	60	1891	35	60
1889	35	60	1892	35	60
1890	35	60			

Maundy Sets in the original dated cases are worth approximately £5 more than the prices quoted.

		EF £	FDC £
3933 — fourpence, 1888-92	*from*	9	13
3934 — threepence, 1888-92	*from*	11	21
3935 — twopence, 1888-92	*from*	5	10
3936 — penny, 1888-92	*from*	5	10

Old head coinage

3937

		F £	VF £	EF £	UNC £
3937 Crown. ℞. St. George. Regnal date on edge					
1893 —	LVI	12	24	90	150
— —	Proof *FDC £400*				
— —	LVII	15	35	150	250
1894 —	LVII	12	26	120	175
— —	LVIII	12	26	120	175
1895 —	LVIII	12	25	110	165
— —	LIX	12	25	110	165
1896 —	LIX	14	30	135	200
— —	LX	12	25	110	165
1897 —	LX	12	25	110	165
— —	LXI	12	24	100	150
1898 —	LXI	15	35	150	250
— —	LXII	12	25	115	175
1899 —	LXII	12	25	115	175
— —	LXIII	12	25	115	175
1900 —	LXIII	12	24	100	150
— —	LXIV	12	24	100	150

3938

3938 Halfcrown. ℞. Shield in collar

	F £	VF £	EF £	UNC £		F £	VF £	EF £	UNC £
1893	6	12	25	50	1897	6	12	25	50
— Proof *FDC £150*					1898	6	12	30	60
1894	8	16	45	85	1899	6	12	30	60
1895	6	12	30	60	1900	6	12	25	50
1896	6	12	30	60	1901	6	12	25	50

3939

3939 Florin. ℞. Three shields within Garter

	F £	VF £	EF £	UNC £		F £	VF £	EF £	UNC £
1893	5	10	25	45	1897	5	10	25	45
— Proof *FDC £95*					1898	5	10	30	55
1894	5	8	45	80	1899	5	10	25	45
1895	6	12	35	60	1900	5	10	25	45
1896	5	10	30	55	1901	5	10	25	45

3940

3941

3940 Shilling. ℞. Three shields within Garter

	F £	VF £	EF £	UNC £		F £	VF £	EF £	UNC £
1893	3	6	12	25	1897	3	6	12	25
— Proof *FDC £60*					1898	3	6	12	25
1894	4	8	18	35	1899	3	6	14	28
1895	3	6	14	28	1900	3	6	12	25
1896	3	6	12	25	1901	3	6	12	25

3941 Sixpence. ℞. Value in wreath

	F £	VF £	EF £	UNC £		F £	VF £	EF £	UNC £
1893	2	5	10	20	1897	3	6	12	25
— Proof *FDC £40*					1898	3	6	12	25
1894	4	8	16	30	1899	3	6	14	25
1895	3	6	12	25	1900	3	6	12	20
1896	3	6	12	25	1901	3	6	12	20

3942 Threepence. ℞. Crowned 3. As Maundy but less prooflike surface

	F £	VF £	EF £	UNC £		F £	VF £	EF £	UNC £
1893	1	2	4	8	1897	1	2	5	10
— Proof *FDC £30*					1898	1	2	5	10
1894	1	3	7	15	1899	1	2	4	8
1895	1	3	7	15	1900	1	2	4	8
1896	1	2	5	10	1901	1	2	4	8

3943

	EF £	*FDC* £		*EF* £	*FDC* £
3943 Maundy Set (4d., 3d., 2d. and 1d.)					
1893	30	50	1898	30	50
1894	30	50	1899	30	50
1895	30	50	1900	30	50
1896	30	50	1901	30	50
1897	30	50			
3944 — fourpence, 1893-1901			*from*	5	9
3945 — threepence, 1893-1901			*from*	10	17
3946 — twopence, 1893-1901			*from*	5	8
3947 — penny, 1893-1901			*from*	5	8

Maundy Sets in the original dated cases are worth approximately £5 more than the prices quoted.

Young head copper coinage, 1838-60

3948

	F £	*VF* £	*EF* £	*UNC* £		*F* £	*VF* £	*EF* £	*UNC* £
3948 Penny. ℞. Britannia									
1839 Bronzed proof *FDC £225*					1853	3	7	16	45
1841	4	8	25	60	— Proof *FDC £225*				
1843	20	75	300	—	1854	3	7	16	45
1844	5	9	35	80	1855	3	7	16	45
1845	7	15	60	150	1856	10	25	90	200
1846	6	10	45	120	1857	3	7	20	55
1847	5	9	35	80	1858	3	7	18	50
1848/7	5	9	30	70	1859	4	8	22	55
1849	30	100	350	—	1860/59*		275	475	—
1851	6	10	45	120					

3949

3949 Halfpenny. ℞. Britannia

	F £	VF £	EF £	UNC £		F £	VF £	EF £	UNC £
1838	3	6	16	40	1852	4	8	24	55
1839 Bronzed proof *FDC £90*					1853	2	4	9	25
1841	3	6	14	35	— Proof *FDC £125*				
1843	6	12	40	100	1854	2	4	9	25
1844	3	7	20	50	1855	2	4	9	25
1845	20	50	150	—	1856	4	8	22	55
1846	4	9	25	60	1857	3	6	14	35
1847	4	9	25	60	1858	3	6	16	40
1848	5	10	30	70	1859	3	7	18	45
1851	4	8	22	55	1860*		—	2750	—

Overstruck dates are listed only if commoner than normal date, or if no normal date is known.

3950

3950 Farthing. ℞. Britannia

	F £	VF £	EF £	UNC £		F £	VF £	EF £	UNC £
1838	3	6	20	40	1850	4	7	22	45
1839	3	6	18	35	1851	5	11	45	90
— Bronzed proof *FDC £110*					1852	5	11	45	90
1840	3	6	18	35	1853	4	7	22	45
1841	3	6	18	35	— Proof *FDC £250*				
1842	5	11	45	90	1854	4	7	22	45
1843	3	6	18	35	1855	4	8	25	50
1844	20	45	150	—	1856	5	10	40	80
1845	4	7	22	45	1857	4	7	22	45
1846	5	10	35	70	1858	4	7	22	45
1847	4	7	22	45	1859	7	15	45	90
1848	4	7	22	45	1860*	—	—	3000	—
1849	12	35	110	—					

**These 1860 large copper pieces not to be confused with the smaller and commoner bronze issue with date on reverse (nos. 3954, 3956 and 3958).*

3951 3952 3953

3951 Half-farthing. R. Value

	F £	VF £	EF £	UNC £
1839	12	5	16	30
1842	2	5	16	30
1843		2	6	15
1844		2	6	15
1847	1	4	12	25
1851	2	6	18	35
1852	1	6	18	35
1853	3	10	32	50
— Proof *FDC £200*				
1854	4	15	45	75
1856	4	15	45	75

3952 Third-farthing (for use in Malta). R. Britannia

	F £	VF £	EF £	UNC £
1844	8	20	60	90

3953 Quarter-farthing (for use in Ceylon). R. Value

	F £	VF £	EF £	UNC £
1839	6	12	27	45
1851	7	14	30	50
1852	6	12	27	45
1853	7	14	30	50
— Proof *FDC £250*				

Copper coins graded in this catalogue as UNC have full mint lustre

Bronze coinage, 'bun head' issue, 1860-95

3954

3954 Penny. R. Britannia

	F £	VF £	EF £	UNC £
1860	2	6	24	55
1861	2	6	24	55
1862	1	5	22	50
1863	1	5	22	50
1864	7	25	150	300
1865	2	8	40	80
1866	2	7	27	60
1867	3	9	45	90
1868	5	15	75	150
1869	25	75	300	—
1870	4	12	60	120
1871	15	45	150	300
1872	2	7	27	60
1873	2	7	27	60
1874	2	8	40	80
1875	1	5	20	45
1877	1	5	20	45
1878	2	8	35	70
1879	1	5	18	35
1880	2	8	35	70
1881	2	8	40	80
1882*		*Extremely rare*		
1883	2	7	27	60
1884	1	5	15	30
1885	1	5	15	30
1886	1	5	18	35
1887	1	5	15	30
1888	1	5	18	35
1889	1	4	14	30
1890	1	4	14	30
1891	1	4	12	25
1892	1	4	14	30
1892	1	4	14	30
1894	2	6	25	55

3955

3956

3955 — H (Ralph Heaton & Sons, Birmingham) below date

	F £	*VF* £	*EF* £	*UNC* £
1874 H	2	8	35	70
1875 H	16	50	175	—
1876 H	2	6	20	45
1881 H	2	7	26	60
1882 H	1	5	18	35

**1882 without `H' was sold in auction, condition extremely fine for £1700, March 1988.*

3956 Halfpenny. ℞. Britannia

	F £	*VF* £	*EF* £	*UNC* £
1860	1	4	15	35
1861	1	4	15	35
1862	1	4	13	30
1863	2	5	25	55
1864	2	6	30	65
1865	3	7	40	85
1866	2	5	30	65
1867	3	7	40	85
1868	2	6	32	65
1869	5	25	90	165
1870	2	5	26	55
1871	7	30	100	175
1872	2	5	24	55
1873	2	6	30	65
1874	4	10	60	120
1875	1	4	20	45
1877	1	4	20	45
1878	3	7	40	85
1879	1	4	15	35
1880	2	5	25	55
1881	2	5	25	55
1883	1	4	22	45
1884	1	3	12	25
1885	1	3	12	25
1886	1	3	12	25
1887	1	3	10	22
1888	1	3	12	25
1889	1	3	12	25
1890	1	3	10	22
1891	1	3	10	22
1892	1	3	20	45
1893	1	3	12	25
1894	1	4	22	45

3957 — H below date

	F £	*VF* £	*EF* £	*UNC* £
1874 H	1	4	22	45
1875 H	2	5	28	60
1876 H	1	4	20	45
1881 H	1	3	20	45
1882 H	1	3	20	45

3958

3960

	F	VF	EF	UNC		F	VF	EF	UNC
	£	£	£	£		£	£	£	£
3958 Farthing. ℞. Britannia									
1860		3	10	25	1880		3	14	35
1861		3	12	30	1881		2	8	20
1862		3	12	30	1883		5	20	45
1863	12	30	90	200	1884			5	12
1864		5	18	40	1885			5	12
1865		3	12	30	1886			5	12
1866		3	10	25	1887		2	8	20
1867		4	16	40	1888			7	16
1868		4	16	40	1890			7	16
1869		6	22	50	1891			5	12
1872		3	12	30	1892	2	6	20	45
1873		2	9	20	1893			5	12
1875	5	10	35	65	1894			7	16
1878			7	16	1895	5	10	30	55
1879			7	16					

Bronze coins graded in this catalogue as UNC have full mint

	F	VF	EF	UNC		F	VF	EF	UNC
3959 ℞. Britannia. H below date									
1874 H	2	5	14	35	1881 H	2	4	12	30
1875 H		2	6	15	1882 H	2	14	12	30
1876 H	5	10	30	55					
3960 Third-farthing (for use in Malta). ℞. Value									
1866	1	3	8	20	1881	2	4	10	22
1868	1	3	9	20	1884	1	3	9	20
1876	2	4	10	22	1885	1	3	9	20
1878	1	3	9	20					

Old head issue, 1885-1901

3961

	VF £	EF £	UNC £
3961 Penny. R. Britannia			
1895	2	6	15
1896	1	5	12
1897	1	5	12
1898	3	10	25
1899	1	5	12
1900		3	8
1901		2	5

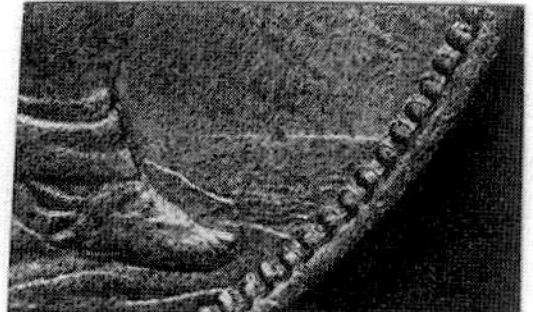

3961 'High Tide'

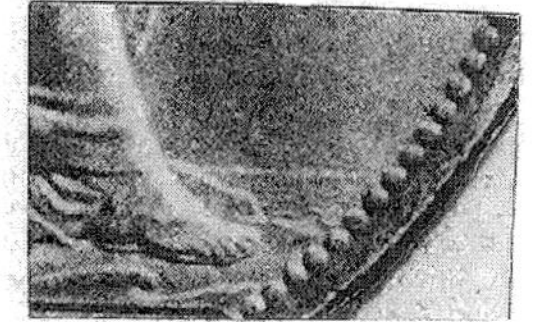

3961A 'Low Tide'

	VF £	EF £	UNC £
3961A As last but 'Low tide', 1895	18	75	150
3962 Halfpenny. Type as Penny. R. Britannia			
1895	2	6	12
1896	1	5	10
1897	1	5	10
1898	1	5	10
1899		4	8
1900		3	6
1901		2	4
3963 Farthing. R. Britannia. Bright finish			
1895	2	4	9
1896	2	4	9
1897	2	5	12

3964

	VF £	EF £	UNC £
3964 — Dark finish			
1897	2	4	9
1898	2	4	9
1899	2	4	9
1900	1	3	8
1901		2	5

THE HOUSE OF SAXE-COBURG GOTHA

EDWARD VII, 1901-10

Five pound pieces, two pound pieces and crowns were only issued in 1902. A branch of the Royal Mint was opened at Ottawa and coined sovereigns of imperial type from 1908.

Unlike the coins in most other proof sets, the proofs issued for the Coronation in 1902 have a matt surface in place of the more usual brilliant finish.

Designer's initials: De S. (G. W. de Saulles)

GOLD

3965

	VF £	EF £	UNC £
3965 **Five pounds.** 1902. R. St. George	375	500	650
3966 — Proof. 1902. *Matt surface FDC £600*			
3966A — Proof 1902S. S on ground for Sydney mint			*Extremely rare*

3967 3969

	EF £	UNC £	
3967 **Two pounds.** 1902. Similar	175	250	350
3968 — Proof. 1902. *Matt surface FDC £325*			
3968A — Proof 1902S. S on ground for Sydney mint			*Extremely rare*

3969 Sovereign. R . St. George. London mint

1902 Matt proof *FDC £110*		1906	BV
1902	BV	1907	BV
1903	BV	1908	BV
1904	BV	1909	BV
1905	BV	1910	BV

3970 — C on ground for Ottawa mint

1908 C (Satin proof only) *FDC £2750*			1910 C	200	300
1909 C	200	300			

3971 — M on ground for Melbourne mint

1902 M	BV	1907 M	BV
1903 M	BV	1908 M	BV
1904 M	BV	1909 M	BV
1905 M	BV	1910 M	BV
1906 M	BV		

3972 — P on ground for Perth mint

1902 P	BV	1907 P	BV
1903 P	BV	1908 P	BV
1904 P	BV	1909 P	BV
1905 P	BV	1910 P	BV
1906 P	BV		

3973 — S on ground for Sydney mint

1902 S	BV	1906 S	BV
— Proof	*Extremely rare*	1907 S	BV
1903 S	BV	1908 S	BV
1904 S	BV	1909 S	BV
1905 S	BV	1910 S	BV

3974

	VF £	*EF* £	*UNC* £		*VF* £	*EF* £	*UNC* £
3974 Half-sovereign. ℞. St. George. London mint							
1902 Matt proof *FDC £80*				1906		45	50
1902		45	50	1907		45	50
1903		45	50	1908		45	50
1904		45	50	1909		45	50
1905		45	50	1910		45	50
3975 — M on ground for Melbourne mint							
1906 M	55	80	175	1908 M	55	80	200
1907 M	55	80	175	1909 M	55	80	175
3976 — P on ground for Perth mint							
1904 P	175	550	—	1909 P	140	400	—
1908 P	175	600	—				
3977 — S on ground for Sydney mint							
1902 S	60	125	250	1906 S	55	110	175
— Proof		*Extremely rare*		1908 S	55	110	175
1903 S	55	110	175	1910 S	55	110	175

SILVER

3978

	F £	VF £	EF £	UNC £
3978 Crown. ℞. St. George				
1902	25	35	70	130

3979 — *matt proof FDC £100*

3980

	F £	VF £	EF £	UNC £
3980 Halfcrown. ℞. Shield in Garter				
1902	5	10	30	55
— Matt proof *FDC £55*				
1903	35	90	350	550
1904	25	65	250	400
1905*	110	250	750	975
1906	8	20	70	120
1907	8	20	75	120
1908	10	25	100	150
1909	8	20	80	130
1910	6	15	55	90
3981 Florin. ℞. Britannia standing				
1902	3	8	30	50
— Matt proof *FDC £40*				
1903	5	12	50	75
1904	6	15	60	100
1905*	20	50	175	300
1906	5	12	50	75
1907	6	16	60	100
1908	8	20	80	130
1909	8	20	75	120
1910	4	10	40	65

**Beware of forgeries.*

3981  3982  3983

	F £	VF £	EF £	UNC £		F £	VF £	EF £	UNC £
3982 Shilling. R. Lion on crown									
1902	1	4	15	25	1906	2	6	20	35
— Matt proof *FDC £25*					1907	3	8	25	40
1903	5	15	50	90	1908	6	16	60	90
1904	5	12	40	65	1909	6	15	50	85
1905*	35	90	300	500	1910	1	4	15	25

**Beware of recent forgeries.*

	F £	VF £	EF £	UNC £		F £	VF £	EF £	UNC £
3983 Sixpence. R. Value in wreath									
1902	1	3	15	25	1906	2	6	20	35
— Matt proof *FDC £20*					1907	2	6	25	40
1903	2	6	20	35	1908	3	8	30	50
1904	3	9	35	55	1909	2	6	25	40
1905	3	7	25	40	1910	1	4	15	25
3984 Threepence. As Maundy but dull finish									
1902		1	3	5	1907	1	2	8	15
1903	1	2	8	14	1908	1	2	8	15
1904	3	7	30	45	1909	1	2	8	15
1905	2	6	20	35	1910		1	6	10
1906	2	5	20	35					

3985

	EF £	FDC £		EF £	FDC £
3985 Maundy Set (4d., 3d., 2d. and 1d.)					
1902	30	45	1906	30	45
— Matt proof *FDC £45*			1907	30	45
1903	30	45	1908	30	45
1904	30	45	1909	30	50
1905	30	45	1910	35	55

	EF £	FDC £
3986 — **fourpence,** 1902-10 .... *from*	5	9
3987 — **threepence**, 1902-10 .... *from*	5	11
3988 — **twopence,** 1902-10 .... *from*	5	8
3989 — **penny,** 1902-10 .... *from*	5	8

Maundy sets in the original dated cases are worth approximately £5 more than the prices quoted.

BRONZE

3990

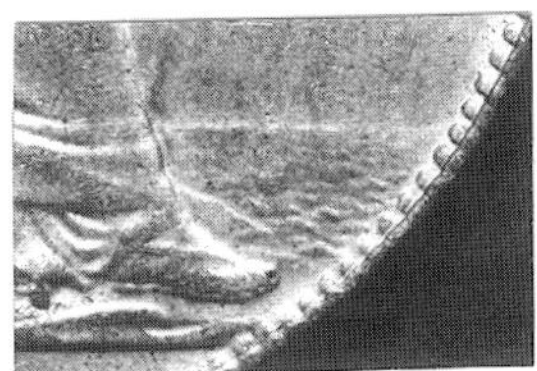

3990 'High Tide'

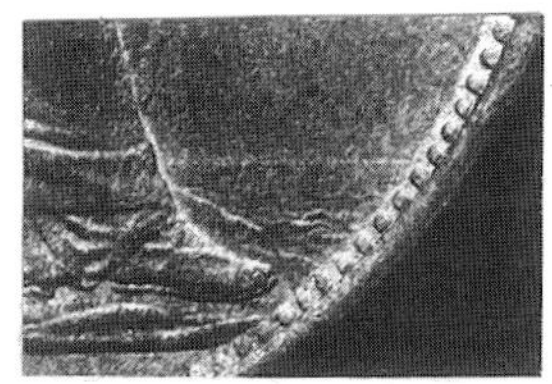

3990A 'Low Tide'

	VF £	EF £	UNC £
3990 Penny. ℞. Britannia			
1902	1	4	9
1903	2	8	20
1904	3	12	25
1905	2	10	22
1906	2	8	20
1907	2	8	20
1908	2	8	20
1909	2	8	20
1910	1	7	15

	F £	VF £	EF £	UNC £
3990A As last but 'Low tide', 1902	2	4	20	40

3991

	F £	VF £	EF £	UNC £
3991 Halfpenny. R. Britannia				
1902		1	4	9
1903		2	6	14
1904		2	8	20
1905		2	8	20
1906		2	7	15
1907		1	5	12
1908		1	5	12
1909		2	8	20
1910		2	7	15
3991A As last but 'Low tide', 1902	7	15	30	55

3992

3993

	VF £	EF £	UNC £
3992 Farthing. Britannia. Dark finish			
1902		3	6
1903	1	5	10
1904	2	7	15
1905	1	5	10
1906	1	5	10
1907	1	5	10
1908	1	5	10
1909	1	5	10
1910	2	7	15
3993 Third-farthing (for use in Malta)			
1902 R. Value		3	7

No proofs of the bronze coins were issued in 1902

THE HOUSE OF WINDSOR

GEORGE V, 1910-36

Paper money issued by the Treasury during the First World War replaced gold for internal use after 1915 but the branch mints in Australia and South Africa (the main Commonwealth gold producing countries) continued striking sovereigns until 1930-2. Owing to the steep rise in the price of silver in 1919/20 the issue of standard (.925) silver was discontinued and coins of .500 silver were minted.

In 1912, 1918 and 1919 some pennies were made under contract by private mints in Birmingham. In 1918, as half-sovereigns were no longer being minted, farthings were again issued with the ordinary bright bronze finish. Crown pieces had not been issued for general circulation but they were struck in small numbers about Christmas time for people to give as presents in the years 1927-36, and in 1935 a special commemorative crown was issued in celebration of the Silver Jubilee.

As George V died in January, it is likely that all coins dated 1936 were struck during the reign of Edward VIII.

Designer's initials:
B. M. (Bertram Mackennal) P. M. (Percy Metcalfe) K. G. (Kruger Gray)

GOLD

3994

	FDC £
3994 Five pounds.* ℞. St. George, 1911 (Proof only)	1200
3995 Two pounds.* ℞. St. George, 1911 (Proof only)	525

3996

VF £ *EF* £ *UNC* £

3996 Sovereign. ℞. St. George. London mint

	VF	*EF*	*UNC*
1911			BV
— Proof *FDC £250*			
1912			BV
1913			BV
1914			BV
1915			BV
1916			90
1917*	1250	2500	—
1925			BV

**Forgeries exist of these and of most other dates and mints.*

3997 — C on ground for the Ottawa mint

	VF £	EF £	UNC £
1911 C		95	110
1913 C	175	350	—
1914 C	90	200	—
1916 C		7500	—
1917 C		95	110
1918 C		95	110
1919 C		95	110

3997

3998

4004

	VF £	EF £	UNC £
3998 — I on ground for India (Bombay) mint, 1918			100

3999 — M on ground for Melbourne mint

	VF £	EF £	UNC £
1911 M			BV
1912 M			BV
1913 M			BV
1914 M			BV
1915 M			BV
1916 M			BV
1917 M			BV
1918 M			BV
1919 M			100
1920 M	800	1700	—
1921 M		3750	—
1922 M	1200	3500	—
1923 M			BV
1924 M			BV
1925 M			BV
1926 M			BV
1928 M	550	1500	—

4000 — small head

	VF £	EF £	UNC £
1929 M	250	950	—
1930 M		90	150
1931 M	75	125	250

4001

4002

4001 — P on ground for Perth mint

	VF £	EF £	UNC £
1911 P			BV
1912 P			BV
1913 P			BV
1914 P			BV
1915 P			BV
1916 P			BV
1917 P			BV
1918 P			BV
1919 P			BV
1920 P			BV
1921 P			BV
1922 P			BV
1923 P			BV
1924 P			BV
1925 P			BV
1926 P			BV
1927 P			BV
1928 P			BV

4002 Sovereign. — — small head

	VF £	EF £	UNC £
1929 P			BV
1930 P			BV
1931 P			BV

4003 — S on ground for Sydney mint

	VF £	EF £	UNC £
1911 S			BV
1912 S			BV
1913 S			BV
1914 S			BV
1915 S			BV
1916 S			BV
1917 S			BV
1918 S			BV
1919 S			BV
1920 S*	*Extremely rare*		
1921 S	500	1200	—
1922 S**	*Extremely rare*		
1923 S***	*Extremely rare*		
1924 S	300	600	1000
1925 S			BV
1926 S****	*Extremely rare*		

4004 — SA on ground for Pretoria mint

	VF £	EF £	UNC £
1923 SA		1200	2500
1923 SA Proof *FDC £600*			
1924 SA		1500	—
1925 SA			BV
1926 SA			BV
1927 SA			BV
1928 SA			BV

4005 — — small head

	VF £	EF £	UNC £
1929 SA			BV
1930 SA			BV
1931 SA			BV
1932 SA			100

* *A good EF specimen sold at auction in March 1992 for £104,000 plus buyer's premium.*

** *An EF specimen sold at auction in March 1992 for £11,000 plus buyer's premium.*

*** *An EF Speciem sold at auction in March 1992 for £5,800 plus buyer's premium.*

**** *An EF Specimen sold at auction in March 1992 for £16,000 plus buyer's premium.*

4006

4006 Half-sovereign. R. St. George. London mint

	VF £	EF £	UNC £
1911		45	50
— Proof *FDC £175*			
1912		45	50
1913		45	50
1914		45	50
1915		45	50

4007 — M on ground for Melbourne mint

	VF £	EF £	UNC £
1915 M	55	80	125

4008 — P on ground for Perth mint

	VF £	EF £	UNC £
1911 P	55	70	80
1915 P	55	70	80
1918 P	200	350	500

4009 — S on ground for Sydney mint

	VF £	EF £	UNC £
1911 S	50	70	90
1912 S	50	70	90
1914 S	50	60	75
1915 S	45	50	60
1916 S	45	50	60

4010 — SA on ground for Pretoria mint

	VF £	EF £	UNC £
1923 SA Proof *FDC £475*			
1925 SA		45	50
1926 SA		45	50

SILVER

First coinage. Sterling silver (.925 fine)

4011

4011 Halfcrown. ℞. Crowned shield in Garter

	VF £	EF £	UNC £		VF £	EF £	UNC £
1911	6	25	50	1915	4	12	25
— Proof *FDC £70*				1916	4	12	25
1912	7	30	55	1917	5	18	35
1913	8	35	70	1918	4	12	25
1914	4	12	30	1919	5	18	35

4012

4012 Florin. ℞. Cruciform shields

	VF £	EF £	UNC £		VF £	EF £	UNC £
1911	6	20	40	1915	3	12	25
— Proof *FDC £50*				1916	3	12	25
1912	6	25	45	1917	4	18	35
1913	8	35	65	1918	3	12	25
1914	3	12	25	1919	4	18	35

4013 Shilling. ℞. Lion on crown, inner circles

	VF £	EF £	UNC £		VF £	EF £	UNC £
1911	2	8	18	1915	2	8	18
— Proof *FDC £35*				1916	2	8	18
1912	4	18	35	1917	2	10	20
1913	6	25	50	1918	2	8	18
1914	2	8	18	1919	3	12	25

4013

4014

	VF £	EF £	UNC £		VF £	EF £	UNC £
4014 Sixpence. R. Similar							
1911		8	15	1916		8	18
— Proof *FDC £30*				1917	3	14	40
1912	3	12	25	1918		8	18
1913	4	16	30	1919	2	10	20
1914		8	18	1920	3	12	25
1915		8	18				
4015 Threepences. As Maundy but dull finish							
1911		3	5	1916		3	5
1912		3	5	1917		3	5
1913		3	5	1918		3	5
1914		3	5	1919		3	5
1915		3	5	1920		4	6

4016

	EF £	FDC £		EF £	FDC £
4016 Maundy Set (4d., 3d., 2d. and 1d.)					
1911	30	45	1916	30	45
— Proof *FDC £60*			1917	30	45
1912	30	45	1918	30	45
1913	30	45	1919	30	45
1914	30	45	1920	30	45
1915	30	45			

	EF £	FDC £
4017 — fourpence, 1911-20 *from*	5	8
4018 — threepence, 1911-20 *from*	8	12
4019 — twopence, 1911-20 *from*	5	8
4020 — penny, 1911-20 *from*	7	10

Second coinage. Debased silver (.500 fine). Types as before.

	EF £	UNC £		VF £	EF £	UNC £
4021 Halfcrown						
1920	20	40	1924		30	50
1921	25	50	1925	15	100	175
1922	20	40	1926		30	55
1923	12	20				
4022 Florin						
1920	20	35	1924		30	50
1921	20	35	1925	8	75	135
1922	16	30	1926		30	50
1923	14	25				
4023 Shilling						
1920	16	30	1924		20	35
1921	20	50	1925		35	55
1922	16	30	1926		12	27
1923	14	25				
4024 Sixpence						
1920	10	18	1923		16	30
1921	10	18	1924		10	18
1922	11	20	1925		12	20

4025

4026

	EF £	UNC £		EF £	UNC £
4025— new beading and broader rim					
1925	10	18	1926	12	20
4026 Threepence					
1920	3	5	1925	10	20
1921	3	5	1926	10	20
1922	4	6			

	EF £	FDC £		EF £	FDC £
4027 Maundy Set (4d., 3d., 2d. and 1d.)					
1921	30	45	1925	30	45
1922	30	45	1926	30	45
1923	30	45	1927	30	45
1924	30	45			
4028 — fourpence, 1921-7			*from*	6	9
4029 — threepence, 1921-7			*from*	8	12
4030 — twopence, 1921-7			*from*	6	10
4031 — penny, 1921-7			*from*	7	11

2nd coinage

3rd coinage

Third coinage. As before but modified effigy, with details of head more clearly defined. The BM on truncation is nearer to the back of the neck and without stops; beading is more pronounced.

	VF £	*EF* £	*UNC* £		*VF* £	*EF* £	*UNC* £
4032 Halfcrown							
1926	4	30	50	1927		18	30
4033 Shilling							
1926		12	20	1927		18	30
4034 Sixpence							
1926		6	14	1927		10	18
4035 Threepence							
1926						3	5

Fourth coinage. New types, 1927-36

4036

4036 Crown. ℞. Crown in wreath

	VF	*EF*	*UNC*		*VF*	*EF*	*UNC*
1927 Proof only *FDC £110*				1932	65	140	200
1928	35	80	135	1933	40	95	150
1929	40	95	150	1934	400	600	950
1930	40	95	150	1936	65	140	200
1931	45	110	175				

4037

4038

4037 Halfcrown. ℞. Shield

	VF £	EF £	UNC £
1927 Proof only *FDC £30*			
1928		8	14
1929		8	14
1930	10	75	130
1931		9	16
1932		10	30
1933		9	16
1934		25	40
1935		6	12
1936		5	10

4038 Florin. ℞. Cruciform sceptres, shield in each angle

	VF £	EF £	UNC £
1927 Proof only *FDC £35*			
1928		7	12
1929		7	12
1930		11	18
1931		8	18
1932	9	70	125
1933		9	16
1935		7	12
1936		6	10

4039

4040

4039 Shilling. ℞. Lion on crown, no inner circles

	VF £	EF £	UNC £
1927		12	20
— Proof *FDC £20*			
1928		7	12
1929		7	12
1930		18	30
1931		8	14
1932		8	14
1933		7	12
1934		14	25
1935		7	12
1936		6	10

4040 Sixpence. ℞. Three oak sprigs with six acorns

	VF £	EF £	UNC £
1927 Proof only *FDC £18*			
1928		3	6
1929		3	6
1930		4	6

4041 — closer milling

	VF £	EF £	UNC £
1931		7	14
1932		12	20
1933		6	12
1934		8	16
1935		5	10
1936		3	6

4042

4042 Threepence. ℞. Three oak sprigs with three acorns

	EF £	UNC £		EF £	UNC £
1927 Proof only *FDC £35*			1933	1	2
1928	10	20	1934	1	2
1930	8	15	1935	1	2
1931	1	2	1936	1	2
1932	1	2			

4043 Maundy Set. As earlier sets

	EF £	FDC £		EF £	FDC £
1928	30	50	1933	30	50
1929	30	50	1934	30	50
1930	30	50	1935	30	50
1931	30	50	1936	35	55
1932	30	50			

	EF £	FDC £
4044 — fourpence, 1928-36 ... *from*	6	10
4045 — threepence, 1928-36 ... *from*	7	12
4046 — twopence, 1928-36 ... *from*	6	9
4047 — penny, 1928-36 ... *from*	8	13

Silver Jubilee Commemorative issue

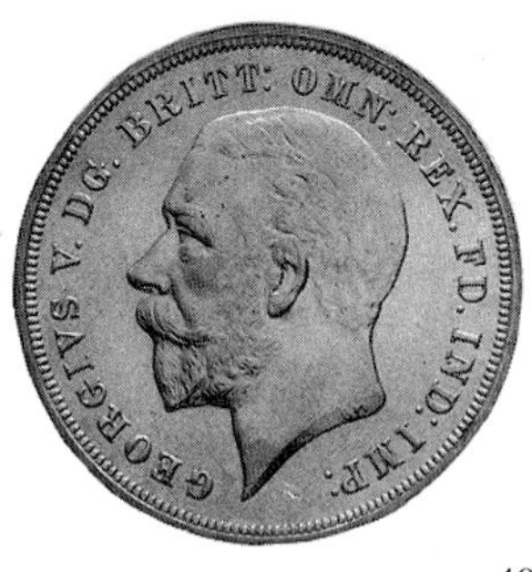

4048

	VF £	EF £	UNC £
4048 Crown, 1935. ℞. St. George, incuse lettering on edge	8	12	20
4049 — Specimen striking issued in box			35
4050 — raised lettering on edge .Proof (.925 Æ) *FDC £225*			

BRONZE

4052

4051 Penny. R. Britannia

	F £	VF £	EF £	UNC £
1911			4	10
1912			4	10
1913			4	10
1914			5	14
1915			5	14
1916			4	10
1917			3	8
1918			4	10
1919			3	8
1920			3	8
1921			3	8
1922			12	25
1926			15	35

4052 — H (The Mint, Birmingham, Ltd.) to l. of date

	F £	VF £	EF £	UNC £
1912 H		1	20	50
1918 H		8	75	150
1919 H		7	65	135

4053 — KN (King's Norton Metal Co.) to l. of date

	F £	VF £	EF £	UNC £
1918 KN	2	10	90	200
1919 KN	2	12	110	225

4054 — modified effigy

	F £	VF £	EF £	UNC £
1926	3	25	250	550
1927			3	5

4055 — small head

	F £	VF £	EF £	UNC £
1928			3	5
1929			3	5
1930			4	6
1931			5	9
1932			12	20
1933*			*Extremely rare*	
1934			10	18
1935			2	4
1936			1	2

4056 Halfpenny. R. Britannia

	F £	VF £	EF £	UNC £
1911			4	9
1912			4	9
1913			4	9
1914			4	9
1915			4	9
1916			4	9
1917			4	9
1918			4	9
1919			4	9
1920			4	9
1921			4	9
1922			7	15
1923			5	11
1924			4	9
1925			5	11

4057 — modified effigy

	F £	VF £	EF £	UNC £
1925			7	15
1926			6	14
1927			4	9

**An extremely fine specimen sold at auction in November 1994 for £23,000 plus 10% buyer's premium.*

4056

4058

	EF £	UNC £		EF £	UNC £
4058 Halfpenny small head					
1928	2	5	1933	2	5
1929	2	5	1934	4	9
1930	2	5	1935	2	5
1931	2	5	1936	1	2
1932	2	5			

4059

4062

	EF £	UNC £		EF £	UNC £
4059 Farthing. R. Britannia. Dark finish					
1911	3	6	1915	4	8
1912	2	4	1916	2	4
1913	2	4	1917	1	2
1914	2	4	1918	9	18
4060 — Bright finish, 1918-25				1	2
4061 — Modified effigy					
1926	1	2	1932	0.50	1
1927	1	2	1933	1	2
1928	1	2	1934	2	4
1929	1	2	1935	2	4
1930	1	2	1936	0.75	2
1931	1	2			
4062 Third-farthing (for use in Malta). R. Value					
1913				3	5

EDWARD VIII, Jan.-Dec. 1936

Abdicated 10 December. Created Duke of Windsor (1936-72)

No coins of Edward VIII were issued for currency within the United Kingdom bearing his name and portrait. The mint had commenced work on a new coinage prior to the Abdication, and various patterns were made. No proof sets were issued for sale and only a small number of sets were struck.

Coins bearing Edward's name, but not his portrait, were issued for the colonial territories of British East Africa, British West Africa, Fiji and New Guinea. The projected U.K. coins were to include a shilling of essentially `Scottish' type and a nickel brass threepence with twelve sides which might supplement and possibly supersede the inconveniently small silver threepence.

Designer's initials:
H. P. (T. Humphrey Paget)
K. G. (Kruger Gray)
W. P. (Wilson Parker)

4063

4063* Proof Set

Gold, £5, £2 and £1, 1937 .... *not issued*

Silver Crown, Halfcrown, Florin, Scottish shilling, sixpence and threepence, 1937 *not issued*

The following coins were sold at auction in December 1984 and October 1985.

	£
Sovereign, *brilliant, with some hair lines in field*	40,000
Halfcrown, *brilliant mint state*	16,000
Shilling, *pattern*	20,000
Sixpence, *brilliant mint state*	9,500

Nickel brass. Threepence, 1937	*not issued*
Bronze. Penny. Halfpenny and Farthing, 1937	*not issued*

Pattern

4064 Nickel brass dodecagonal threepence, 1937. ℞. Thrift plant of more naturalistic style than the modified proof coin. A small number of these coins were produced for experimental purposes and a few did get into circulation 24,750

Colonial issues

4068 4071

	UNC £
4065 British East Africa. Bronze 10 cents, 1936	4
4066 — — 5 cents, 1936	3
4067 British West Africa. Cupro-nickel penny, 1936	2
4068 — — Halfpenny, 1936	2
4069 — — One-tenth penny, 1936	1
4070 Fiji. Cupro-nickel penny, 1936	4
4071 New Guinea. Bronze penny, 1936	3

The coins of East Africa and West Africa occur without mm. (London) and with H (Heaton) Birmingham and KN (King's Norton) Birmingham. The prices quoted are for the commonest of each type, regardless of mm.

GEORGE VI, 1936-52

Though they were at first issued concurrently, the twelve-sided nickel-brass threepence superseded the small silver threepence in 1942. Those dated 1943-4 were not issued for circulation in the U.K. In addition to the usual English 'lion' shilling, a shilling, of Scottish type was issued concurrently. This depicts the Scottish lion and crown flanked by the shield of St. Andrew and a thistle. In 1947, as silver was needed to repay the bullion lent by the U.S.A. during the war, silver coins were replaced by coins of the same type and weight made of cupro-nickel. In 1949, after India had attained independence, the title *Indiae Imperator* was dropped from the coinage. Commemorative crown pieces were issued for the Coronation and the 1951 Festival of Britain.

Designer's initials:
K. G. (Kruger Gray)
H. P. (T. Humphrey Paget)
W. P. (Wilson Parker)

GOLD

4074

	FDC £
4074 Five pounds. ℞. St. George, 1937. Proof	600
4075 Two pounds. Similar, 1937. Proof	375
4076 Sovereign. Similar, 1937. Proof	350
4077 Half-sovereign. Similar, 1937. Proof	125

SILVER

First coinage. Silver, .500 fine, with title IND:IMP

4078

	VF £	EF £	UNC £
4078 Crown. Coronation commemorative, 1937. R. Arms and supporters	8	13	22
4079 — — Proof *FDC* £35			

4080

4081

4080 Halfcrown. R. Shield

	EF £	UNC £		UNC £
1937		6	1942	5
— Proof *FDC* £10			1943	6
1938	3	16	1944	4
1939		6	1945	4
1940		6	1946	4
1941		6		

4081 Florin. R. Crowned rose, etc.

	EF £	UNC £		UNC £
1937		6	1942	4
— Proof *FDC* £8			1943	4
1938	3	15	1944	4
1939		5	1945	4
1940		5	1946	4
1941		4		

4082

4083

4082 Shilling. 'English'. R. Lion on large crown

	EF £	UNC £		UNC £
1937		5	1942	4
— Proof *FDC £6*			1943	4
1938	2	15	1944	4
1939		5	1945	3
1940		5	1946	3
1941		5		

4083 Shilling. 'Scottish'. ℞. Lion seated facing on crown, etc.

	EF £	UNC £		VF £	EF £	UNC £
1937		5	1942			5
— Proof *FDC £7*			1943			5
1938	2	15	1944			5
1939		5	1945			3
1940		6	1946			3
1941		6				

4084 4085

4084 Sixpence. ℞. GRI crowned

	EF £	UNC £		VF £	EF £	UNC £
1937		3	1942			2
— Proof *FDC £4*			1943			2
1938	1	6	1944			2
1939		4	1945			2
1940		4	1946			2
1941		4				

4085 Threepence. ℞. Shield on rose

	EF £	UNC £		VF £	EF £	UNC £
1937		2	1941		1	3
— Proof *FDC £4*			1942*	1	5	12
1938		2	1943*	2	8	15
1939	3	8	1944*	3	12	25
1940		3	1945		*Extremely rare*	

**For colonial use only.*

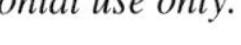

4086

4086 Maundy Set. Silver, .500 fine. Uniform dates

	FDC £		FDC £
1937	45	1942	45
— Proof *FDC £50*		1943	45
1938	45	1944	45
1939	45	1945	45
1940	45	1946	45
1941	45		

	FDC £
4087 — fourpence, 1937-46 ... *from*	9
4088 — threepence, 1937-46 ... *from*	9
4089 — twopence, 1937-46 ... *from*	9
4090 — penny, 1937-46 ... *from*	12

Second coinage. Silver, .925 fine, with title IND.IMP (Maundy only)
4091 Maundy Set (4d., 3d., 2d. and 1d.). Uniform dates

	FDC £		FDC £
1947	45	1948	45

	FDC £
4092 — fourpence, 1947-8	9
4093 — threepence, 1947-8	10
4094 — twopence, 1947-8	9
4095 — penny, 1947-8	12

Third coinage. Silver, .925 fine, but omitting IND.IMP. (Maundy only)
4096 Maundy Set (4d., 3d., 2d. and 1d.). Uniform dates

	FDC £		FDC £
1949	45	1951	45
1950	45	1952	45

The 1952 Maundy was distributed by Queen Elizabeth II.

	FDC £
4097 — fourpence, 1949-52 ... *from*	9
4098 — threepence, 1949-52 ... *from*	9
4099 — twopence, 1949-52 ... *from*	9
4100 — penny, 1949-52 ... *from*	12

CUPRO-NICKEL

Second coinage. Types as first (silver) coinage, IND.IMP.

	UNC £		UNC £
4101 Halfcrown. ℞. Shield			
1947	4	1948	4
4102 Florin. ℞. Crowned rose			
1947	4	1948	3
4103 Shilling. 'English' type			
1947	5	1948	3
4104 'Scottish' type			
1947	4	1948	3
4105 Sixpence. GRI crowned			
1947	3	1948	2

Third coinage. Types as before but title IND.IMP. omitted

4106

	UNC £		VF £	EF £	UNC £
4106 Halfcrown					
1949	5	1951			7
1950	6	— Proof *FDC* £9			
— Proof *FDC* £9		1952			*Extremely rare*
4107 Florin					
1949	7	1951			7
1950	7	— Proof *FDC* £8			
— Proof *FDC* £8					
4108 Shilling. 'English' type					
1949	6	1951			6
1950	6	— Proof *FDC* £6			
— Proof *FDC* £6					
4109 'Scottish' type					
1949	8	1951			7
1950	7	— Proof *FDC* £6			
— Proof *FDC* £6					

4110

	UNC £		VF £	EF £	UNC £
4110 Sixpence. As illustration					
1949	4	1951			4
1950	4	— Proof *FDC* £4			
— Proof *FDC* £4		1952	1	10	30

Festival of Britain issue

4111

	EF £	UNC £
4111 Crown. ℞. St. George, 1951. *Proof-like*	4	8

NICKEL BRASS

First issue, with title IND.IMP.

4112 4113

4112 Threepence (dodecagonal). ℞. Thrift

	VF £	EF £	UNC £
1937			2
—Proof *FDC* £4			
1938		2	6
1939		3	16
1940			5
1941			3
1942			2
1943			2
1944			3
1945			5
1946	3	35	125
1948		3	15

Second issue, omitting IND.IMP.

4113

	VF £	EF £	UNC £
1949	4	40	140
1950		8	30
— Proof *FDC* £25			
1951		8	35
— Proof *FDC* £25			
1952			3

BRONZE

First issue, with title IND.IMP.

4114

	UNC £		UNC £
4114 Penny. ℞. Britannia			
1937	2	1944	7
— Proof *FDC* £6		1945	5
1938	2	1946	2
1939	5	1947	2
1940	6	1948	2

4115

4116

4115 Halfpenny. ℞. Ship			
1937	2	1943	2
— Proof *FDC* £4		1944	2
1938	3	1945	3
1939	4	1946	6
1940	6	1947	3
1941	5	1948	2
1942	2		
4116 Farthing. ℞. Wren			
1937	1	1943	0.65
— Proof *FDC* £4		1944	0.65
1938	2	1945	0.65
1939	0.65	1946	0.65
1940	1	1947	0.65
1941	0.75	1948	0.75
1942	0.75		

Second issue, without IND.IMP. Types as before

4117 Penny

	VF £	EF £	UNC £
1949			2
1950	4	10	20
— Proof *FDC* £16			
1951	6	12	18
— Proof *FDC* £16			

4118

4119

4118 Halfpenny

	UNC £
1949	5
1950	4
— Proof *FDC* £4	
1951	5
— Proof *FDC* £4	
1952	3

4119 Farthing

	UNC £
1949	1
1950	0.70
— Proof *FDC* £4	
1951	0.70
— Proof *FDC* £3	
1952	0.80

The coins dated 1952 were issued during the reign of Elizabeth II.

ELIZABETH II, acc. 1952

The earliest coins of this reign have the title BRITT.OMN, but in 1954 this was omitted from the Queen's titles owing to the changing status of so many Commonwealth territories. The minting of 'English' and 'Scottish' shillings was continued. A Coronation commemorative crown was issued in 1953, another crown was struck on the occasion of the 1960 British Exhibition in New York and a third was issued in honour of Sir Winston Churchill in 1965. A very small number of proof gold coins were struck in 1953 for the national museum collections, but between 1957 and 1968 gold sovereigns were minted again in quantity for sale in the international bullion market and to counteract the activities of counterfeiters.

Owing to inflation the farthing had now become practically valueless; production of these coins ceased after 1956 and the coins were demonetized at the end of 1960. In 1965 it was decided to change to a decimal system of coinage in the year 1971. As part of the transition to decimal coinage the halfpenny was demonetized in August 1969 and the halfcrown in January 1970. (See also introduction to Decimal Coinage.

Designer's initials:
- G. L. (Gilbert Ledward)
- W. P. (Wilson Parker)
- M. G. (Mary Gillick)
- W. G. (William Gardner)
- E. F. (Edgar Fuller)
- C. T. (Cecil Thomas)
- P. N. (Philip Nathan)
- R. D. M. (Raphael David Maklouf)
- N. S. (Norman Sillman)

Other designers whose initials do not appear on the coins:
- Christopher Ironside
- Arnold Machin
- David Wynne
- Professor Richard Guyatt
- Eric Sewel
- Leslie Durbin
- Derek Gorringe

PRE-DECIMAL ISSUES

GOLD

First coinage, with title BRITT.OMN, 1953. *Proof only*

4120 Five pounds. ℞. St. George .... *None issued for collectors*
4121 Two pounds. Similar .... *None issued for collectors*
4122* Sovereign. Similar .... *None issued for collectors*

**A brilliant mint state specimen sold at auction for £24,000 in June 1985.*

4123 Half-sovereign. Similar .... *None issued for collectors*

Second issue, BRITT.OMN omitted

4125

4124 Sovereign. ℞. St. George
1957 .... BV

4125 Similar, but coarser graining on edge

1958	BV	1965	BV
1959	BV	1966	BV
1962	BV	1967	BV
1963	BV	1968	BV
1964	BV		

SILVER

The Queen's Maundy are now the only coins struck regularly in silver.
The location of the Maundy ceremony is given for each year.

First issue, with title BRITT.OMN.

	FDC £
4126 Maundy Set (4d., 3d., 2d. and 1d.), 1953. St Paul's	225
4127 — fourpence, 1953	45
4128 — threepence, 1953	45
4129 — twopence, 1953	45
4130 — penny, 1953	55

Second issue, with BRITT.OMN omitted

4131

4131 Maundy Set (4d., 3d., 2d. and 1d.). Uniform dates

	FDC £		
1954 *Westminster*	50	1963 *Chelmsford*	50
1955 *Southwark*	50	1964 *Westminster*	50
1956 *Westminster*	50	1965 *Canterbury*	50
1957 *St. Albans*	50	1966 *Westminster*	50
1958 *Westminster*	50	1967 *Durham*	50
1959 *Windsor*	50	1968 *Westminster*	50
1960 *Westminster*	50	1969 *Selby*	50
1961 *Rochester*	50	1970 *Westminster*	50
1962 *Westminster*	50		

4132 — fourpence, 1954-70	*from*	10
4133 — threepence, 1954-70	*from*	10
4134 — twopence, 1954-70	*from*	10
4135 — penny, 1954-70	*from*	11

CUPRO-NICKEL

First issue, 1953, with title BRITT.OMN.

4136

	EF	UNC	PROOF FDC
	£	£	£
4136 Crown. Queen on horseback. ℞. Crown in centre of cross, shield in each angle, 1953	6	7	25

4137 4138

	EF	UNC	PROOF FDC
4137 Halfcrown, with title BRITT.OMN. ℞. Arms, 1953		3	8
4138 Florin. ℞. Double rose, 1953		3	6

4139 4140 4141

	EF	UNC	PROOF FDC
4139 Shilling. 'English'. ℞. Three lions, 1953		1	4
4140 'Scottish'. ℞. Lion rampant in shield, 1953		1	4
4141 Sixpence. ℞. Interlaced rose, thistle, shamrock and leek, 1953		0.70	3
4142 Set of 9 uncirculated cu-ni, ni-br and Æ coins (2/6 to 1/4d.) in Royal Mint plastic envelope		8	

Second issue, similar types but omitting BRITT.OMN.

4143 4144

	EF	UNC
	£	£
4143 Crown, 1960. Bust r. ℞. As 4136	6	7
— — Similar, from polished dies (New York Exhibition issue)	6	18
4144 Churchill commemorative, 1965. As illustration. ℞. Bust of Winston Churchill r.		1
— — Similar, satin- finish. *Specimen*		250

4145 Halfcrown. ℞. As 4137

	EF £	UNC £		EF £	UNC £		EF £	UNC £
1954	2	15	1960		3	1965		1
1955		4	1961		1	1966		0.60
1956		5	1961 Polished die		3	1967		0.60
1957		2	1962		1	1970 Proof *FDC £3*		
1958	2	12	1963		1			
1959	2	15	1964		3			

4146

4146 Florin. ℞. As 4138

	EF	UNC		EF	UNC
1954	3	30	1962		1
1955		3	1963		1
1956		3	1964		1
1957	2	20	1965		1
1958	1	10	1966		1
1959	2	25	1967		1
1960		2	1970 Proof *FDC £3*		
1961		2			

4147 Shilling. 'English' type. R. As 4139

Date	*EF* £	*UNC* £
1954		2
1955		2
1956		7
1957		1
1958	2	15
1959		1
1960		1
1961		0.75
1962		0.50
1963		0.25
1964		0.30
1965		0.30
1966		0.30

1970 Proof *FDC £3*

4148 'Scottish' type. R. As 4140

Date	*EF* £	*UNC* £
1954		2
1955		3
1956		7
1957	2	15
1958		1
1959	2	15
1960		1
1961		5
1962		1
1963		0.25
1964		0.50
1965		0.50
1966		0.30

1970 Proof *FDC £3*

4149 Sixpence. R. As 4141

Date	*EF* £	*UNC* £
1954		3
1955		1
1956		1
1957		0.65
1958		4
1959		0.35
1960		4
1961		3
1962		0.30
1963		0.25
1964		0.20
1965		0.15
1966		0.15
1967		0.15

1970 Proof *FDC £2*

NICKEL BRASS

First issue, with title BRITT.OMN.

4152 4153

4152 Threepence (dodecagonal). R. Crowned portcullis, 1953 1

— Proof *FDC* £4

Second issue (omitting BRIT.OMN)

4153 Similar type

Date	*UNC* £
1954	4
1955	5
1956	5
1957	3
1958	6
1959	3
1960	3
1961	0.35
1962	0.30
1963	0.20
1964	0.20
1965	0.20
1966	0.15
1967	0.15

1970 Proof *FDC £2*

BRONZE

First issue, with title BRITT.OMN.

4154 4155

	VF £	*EF* £	*UNC* £	*Proof FDC* £
4154 Penny. ℞. Britannia (only issued with Royal Mint set in plastic envelope), 1953	0.60	2	5	6
4155 Halfpenny. ℞. Ship, 1953			2	4
4156 Farthing. ℞. Wren, 1953			0.75	3

Second issue, omitting BRITT.OMN.

4157 Penny. ℞. Britannia (1954-60 *not issued)*

	UNC £		*UNC* £
1954	*Extremely rare*	1965	0.10
1961	0.50	1966	0.10
1962	0.15	1967	0.10
1963	0.15	1970 Proof *FDC £3*	
1964	0.10		

4158 Halfpenny. ℞. Ship (1961 *not issued)*

1954	4	1962	0.10
1955	4	1963	0.10
1956	4	1964	0.10
1957	0.60	1965	0.10
1958	0.35	1966	0.10
1959	0.20	1967	0.10
1960	0.10	1970 Proof *FDC £2*	

4156 4159

4159 Farthing. ℞. Wren

	UNC £		*EF* £	*UNC* £
1954	0.80	1956	0.55	2
1955	0.75			

DECIMAL COINAGE

A decision to adopt decimal currency was announced in February 1968 following the recommendation of the Halsbury Committee appointed in 1961. A major re-coinage was required and as part of the Government's policy to move goverment departments out of London, a decision was made to build a new mint at Llantrisant in South Wales. The first phase was completed by December 1968 when Her Majesty the Queen struck the first decimal coins at the official opening. The second phase was completed during late 1975; at the same time all coin production at Tower Hill ceased.

Though the official change-over to a decimal currency did not take place until 15 February 1971, three decimal denominations were circulated prior to this date. The 10 and 5 new pence, equivalent to the former florin (2/-) and shilling, were introduced in 1968 and the seven-sided 50 new pence (equal to ten shillings) was issued during October 1969. Two coins which were not required in the decimal system were withdrawn and demonetized: the halfpenny on 1 August 1969 and the halfcrown on 1 January 1970.

To familiarise the public with the decimal coins a small blue wallet was issued during 1968 containing the 10 and 5 new pence coins dated 1968, and the bronze 2, 1 and half new pence dated 1971, although the bronze coins were not legalized for current use until 'Decimal Day' 1971.

In 1982 the word 'new' was omitted from the reverse design which from that date bore the denomination in words and figures. The first ever 20 pence coin was also issued in 1982, and the following year saw the first circulating non-precious metal £1 coin. The reverse design of the £1 coin was changed each year from 1984 to 1988 and from 1989 the designs repeat again from the 1984 variation onwards. 1993 saw the repeat of the 1983 design but with the new portrait. It was decided to issue a further set of four regional variants from 1994-1997. The half (new) pence was demonetized in December 1984, and coins dated that year were only issued in sets.

The first of a number of changes to the coinage took place in 1990 with the introduction of a smaller 5p thus bringing to an end the specification for the 5p and its former 1/- equivalent first introduced in 1816. A life span of 174 years may well make it the longest period of life for any coin from any country. A smaller size 10p was issued in 1992 as were 1p and 2p coins made of copper plated steel instead of bronze. All pre-decimal 1/- coins plus the same size 5p coins ceased to be legal tender on 31 December 1990, and the pre-decimal 2/- coins plus the same size 10p coins ceased to be legal tender from 30 June 1993.

Some base metal coins from 50p downwards only appear in Royal Mint uncirculated sets and these are indicated in the texts by asterisks following the dates. The base metal proofs from £5 downwards are only issued within proof sets (except for the 50p coin of 1973) and those from 1971-80 are presented in sonic sealed cases. However, over the years sets have been broken up, so the individual proof coins are priced in order to provide a complete decimal listing.

An interesting error was discovered during 1991 - a 2p coin of 1983 with 'new pence' on the reverse instead of 'two pence'. Three pieces have so far been recorded and as no 2p coins were issued for circulation that year all the error coins must have come from specimen sets. Reports are received fairly frequently of coins struck on wrong size or wrong metal blanks but, given the generally very high mintages of all decimal coins destined for circulation, this is to be expected from modern mass production processes. Such examples, although interesting to the specialist collector, are outside the scope of this catalogue.

Several commemorative coins have been issued, the first being in 1973 when the United Kingdom's admission to the European Community was commemorated by a 50p piece. The same denomination was used for a double commemoration in 1992-93 - the

UK's Presidency of the EC from July-December 1992 and the completion of the Single Market from 1 January 1993. A third 50p commemorative coin was issued in 1994 to mark the 50th anniversary of the D-Day landings in Normandy.

Crown size 25 pence pieces (equivalent to 5/-) were issued in 1972 to celebrate the Silver Wedding of Her Majesty the Queen and Prince Philip, the Queen's Silver Jubilee in 1977, the 80th birthday of Queen Elizabeth, the Queen Mother, in 1980, and for the wedding of Prince Charles and Lady Diana Spencer in 1981. Further crown sized coins were issued in 1990 for the 90th birthday of Queen Elizabeth, the Queen Mother, and in 1993 for the 40th anniversary of the Coronation. Another crown is expected in 1996 for the Queen's 70th birthday. The crowns from 1990 onwards have a face value of £5 although they retain the same specifications as the earlier 25p issues, thus continuing the traditional crown size piece into another era. The face value of a cupro-nickel crown had been five shillings or 25 pence since 1951, although the equivalent of 5/- in 1951 was £3.27 in 1990. It is hoped that the new £5 face value will stand for many years.

In 1986 the Royal Mint introduced a nickel-brass £2 piece in honour of the XIII Commonwealth Games held in Scotland. Two further £2 pieces were issued in 1989 for the 300th anniversary of the Bill of Rights (in England and Wales) and the Claim of Right (in Scotland). A fourth piece was issued in 1994 for the Bank of England's 300th anniversary and two more were issued in 1995 for the 50th anniversaries of the end of the Second World War and the establishment of the United Nations. These coins, although legal tender, were not intended to circulate.

The Maundy coins continue to be presented each year in the traditional ceremony on Maundy Thursday, with the old denominations being retained as 'new pence'. In the early years of the present reign the ceremony tended to alternate between Westminster Abbey and a cathedral, usually close to London, but in more recent years the Queen has travelled to cathedrals right across the country thus bringing this ancient ceremony to the people and increasing public awareness of these coins, steeped as they are in our great British heritage.

The first decimal coins bore a portrait of the Queen by Arnold Machin, but in 1985 a new portrait by Raphael Maklouf was introduced. The Maundy coins continue to portray the Mary Gillick portrait and we understand there are no plans to alter this.

All silver (Æ) coins are minted in .925 sterling silver unless otherwise stated. The Silver Jubilee proof crown and all proof coins minted from 1980 onwards have frosted relief and mirror-like field which provide a sharp contrast.

There have been developments with the gold coinage. In 1979 the first proof sovereign since 1937 was issued, and 1980 saw a proof five pound, two pound and half-sovereign. Further four coin gold proof sets were issued in 1982 and 1985 and a commemorative set in 1989 to mark the 500th anniversary of the sovereign. Annual issues have appeared since.

The trend developed by gold-producing nations to issue bullion gold coins in sizes based on one ounce was taken up in 1987 by the issue of Britannias. Proof sets as well as uncirculated standard pieces issued at bullion price-related levels have appeared each year, although numbers sold in more recent years are probably quite low, perhaps making these coins more valuable in the future.

What of the future? No firm decisions for the further development of the coinage have been announced but there was a Royal Mint Coinage Review document issued during 1994 covering both the future of the 50p coin and a possible £2 circulation coin. The review does state in bold print that 'Change is not a foregone conclusion'. The options for review were a smaller 50p, either seven-sided as at present or round, and for a new £2 circulating coin, either nickel-brass or bi-metal, both lighter than the present commemorative coin.

GOLD

4201

4204

4201 Five pounds. As illustration

1980 Proof *FDC* £400	1982 Proof *FDC* £450	1984 Proof *FDC* £400
1981 Proof *FDC* £400		

4202 As 4201 but, 'U' in a circle to left of date

1984 .... *Unc* 350

4203 Two pounds

1980 Proof *FDC* £225	1982 Proof *FDC* £225	1983 Proof *FDC* £175

4204 Sovereign. As illustration

1974 .... *Unc* BV	1980 .... *Unc* BV	— Proof *FDC* £80
1976 .... *Unc* BV	— Proof *FDC* £80	1983 Proof *FDC* £85
1978 .... *Unc* BV	1981 .... *Unc* BV	1984 Proof *FDC* £85
1979 .... *Unc* BV	— Proof *FDC* £80	
— Proof *FDC* £90	1982 .... *Unc* BV	

4205 Half-sovereign

1980 Proof *FDC* £50	— Proof *FDC* £50	1984 Proof *FDC* £55
1982 .... *Unc* BV	1983 Proof *FDC* £55	

(For proof sets which include some or all of the above coins, see the list on pages 356-7.)

SILVER

4211 Maundy Set (4p, 3p, 2p and 1p). Uniform dates. Types as 4131

	FDC £		*FDC* £
1971 *Tewkesbury Abbey*	55	1984 *Southwell Minster*	55
1972 *York Minster*	55	1985 *Ripon Cathedral*	55
1973 *Westminster Abbey*	55	1986 *Chichester Cathedral*	55
1974 *Salisbury Cathedral*	55	1987 *Ely Cathedral*	75
1975 *Peterborough Cathedral*	55	1988 *Lichfield Cathedral*	75
1976 *Hereford Cathedral*	55	1989 *Birmingham Cathedral*	75
1977 *Westminster Abbey*	65	1990 *Newcastle Cathedral*	75
1978 *Carlisle Cathedral*	55	1991 *Westminster Abbey*	75
1979 *Winchester Cathedral*	55	1992 *Chester Cathedral*	85
1980 *Worcester Cathedral*	55	1993 *Wells Cathedral*	85
1981 *Westminster Abbey*	55	1994 *Truro Cathedral*	85
1982 *St. David's Cathedral*	55	1995 *Coventry Cathedral*	85
1983 *Exeter Cathedral*	55		

4212 — fourpence, 1971-95 .... *from* 13
4213 — threepence, 1971-95 .... *from* 13
4214 — twopence, 1971-95 .... *from* 13
4215 — penny, 1971-95 .... *from* 15

The Queen's Maundy are now the only coins struck regularly in .925 silver. The place of distribution is shown after each date.

NICKEL-BRASS

4221

4222

	UNC £
4221 One pound (Royal Arms design). Edge DECUS ET TUTAMEN	
1983	3
— Specimen in presentation folder	3
— Proof *FDC* £5	
— Proof in Æ *FDC* £20	
— Proof piedfort in Æ *FDC* £110	
4222 One pound (Scottish design). Edge NEMO ME IMPUNE LACESSIT	
1984	2
— Specimen in presentation folder	4
— Proof *FDC* £5	
— Proof in Æ *FDC* £18	
— Proof piedfort in Æ *FDC* £50	

CUPRO-NICKEL

4223

4224

4223 Fifty new pence (seven-sided). R. Britannia r.

	UNC £				*UNC* £
1969	2	1976	2	1979	2
1970	4	— — Proof *FDC* £2		— — Proof *FDC* £3	
1971 Proof *FDC* £4		1977	2	1980	2
1972 Proof *FDC* £5		— — Proof *FDC* £2		— — Proof *FDC* £2	
1974 Proof *FDC* £3		1978	2	1981	2
1975 Proof *FDC* £3		— — Proof *FDC* £3		— — Proof *FDC* £2	

4224 Accession to European Economic Community. R. Clasped hands, 1973 .... 1.50

— — Proof in case *FDC* £3

4225

4225 Fifty (50) pence. 'New' omitted. As illustration

1982	2	1983	2	1984*	3
— — Proof *FDC* £2		— — Proof *FDC* £2		— — Proof *FDC* £2	

4226

4226 Twenty-five pence. Silver Wedding Commemorative, 1972 .... 1.00
— Proof (in 1972 Set, See PS22) £4
— Æ proof in case *FDC* £20

4227

UNC
£

4227 Twenty-five pence Silver Jubilee Commemorative, 1977 .... 0.60
— Cu.-ni. Specimen striking. Issued in Royal Mint folder 2
— Proof (in 1977 Set, See PS27) £4
— Æ proof in case *FDC* £15
— Cu.-ni. proof. issued in 1977 Mint set. See PS27 £4

4228

4228 Twenty-Five Pence Queen Mother 80th Birthday Commemorative, 1980 .... 0.75
— Cu.-ni. Specimen striking. Issued in Royal Mint folder 2
— Æ proof in case *FDC* £30

4229

4229 Twenty-five pence. Royal Wedding Commemorative, 1981 .... 1.25
— Cu.-ni. Specimen striking. Issued in Royal Mint folder 2
— Æ proof in case *FDC* £23

4230 4233

	UNC £		UNC £		UNC £
4230 Twenty (20) pence. ℞ crowned rose					
1982	0.40	1983	0.40	1984	0.40
— — Proof *FDC* £2		— — Proof *FDC* £1		— — Proof *FDC* £1	
— — Proof piedfort in Æ *FDC* £36					

4231 4232 4234

4231 Ten new pence. R. Lion passant guardant.

1968 .... 0.30
1969 .... 0.30
1970 .... 0.30
1971 .... 0.40
— — Proof *FDC* £2
1972 Proof *FDC* £3
1973 .... 0.40
— — Proof *FDC* £2
1974 .... 0.40
— — Proof *FDC* £1
1975 .... 0.50
— — Proof *FDC* £1
1976 .... 0.50
— — Proof *FDC* £1
1977 .... 0.50
— — Proof *FDC* £2
1978 Proof *FDC* £4
1979 .... 0.50
— — Proof *FDC* £2
1980 .... 0.75
— — Proof *FDC* £1
1981 .... 0.75
— — Proof *FDC* £1

4232 Ten (10) pence. As illustration

1982* 3
— — Proof *FDC* £1
1983* 3
— — Proof *FDC* £2
1984* 2
— — Proof *FDC* £1

4233 Five new pence. R. Crowned thistle

1968 .... 0.20
1969 .... 0.30
1970 .... 0.30
1971 .... 0.20
— — Proof *FDC* £2
1972 Proof *FDC* £2
1973 Proof *FDC* £2
1974 Proof *FDC* £2
1975 .... 0.20
— — Proof *FDC* £1
1976 Proof *FDC* £2
1977 .... 0.20
— — Proof *FDC* £1
1978 .... 0.20
— — Proof *FDC* £1
1979 .... 0.20
— — Proof *FDC* £1
1980 .... 0.20
— — Proof *FDC* £1
1981 Proof *FDC* £2

4234 Five (5) pence. As illustration

1982* 2
— — Proof *FDC* £2
1983* 2
— — Proof *FDC* £2
1984* 2
— — Proof *FDC* £1

BRONZE

4235 4236

UNC £ *UNC* £ *UNC* £

4235 Two new pence. R. Plumes

1971 .... 0.10
— — Proof *FDC* £1
1972 Proof *FDC* £2
1973 Proof *FDC* £2
1974 Proof *FDC* £2
1975 .... 0.20
— — Proof *FDC* £1
1976 .... 0.20
— — Proof *FDC* £1
1977 .... 0.10
— — Proof *FDC* £1
1978 .... 0.30
— — Proof *FDC* £1
1979 .... 0.15
— — Proof *FDC* £1
1980 .... 0.15
— — Proof *FDC* £1
1981 .... 0.15
— — Proof *FDC* £1

4236 Two (2) pence. As illustration

1982* 1
—— Proof *FDC* £1
1983* 1
—Error. ℞ as 4235...
—— Proof *FDC* £1
1984* 1
—— Proof *FDC* £1

4237 4238 4239 4240

4237 One new penny. ℞. Crowned portcullis

1971 .... 0.10
—— Proof *FDC* £1
1972 Proof *FDC* £2
1973 .... 0.20
—— Proof *FDC* £1
1974 .... 0.20
—— Proof *FDC* £1
1975 .... 0.20
—— Proof *FDC* £1
1976 .... 0.20
—— Proof *FDC* £1
1977 .... 0.10
—— Proof *FDC* £1
1978 .... 0.20
—— Proof *FDC* £1
1979 .... 0.10
—— Proof *FDC* £1
1980 .... 0.10
—— Proof *FDC* £1
1981 .... 0.20
—— Proof *FDC* £1

4238 One (1) penny. As illustration

1982 .... 0.10
—— Proof *FDC* £1
1983 .... 0.20
—— Proof *FDC* £1
1984* 1
—— Proof *FDC* £1

4239 Half new penny. ℞. Crown

1971 .... 0.10
—— Proof *FDC* £1
1972 Proof *FDC* £2
1973 .... 0.20
—— Proof *FDC* £1
1974 .... 0.20
—— Proof *FDC* £1
1975 .... 0.25
—— Proof *FDC* £1
1976 .... 0.20
—— Proof *FDC* £1
1977 .... 0.10
—— Proof *FDC* £1
1978 .... 0.10
—— Proof *FDC* £1
1979 .... 0.10
—— Proof *FDC* £1
1980 .... 0.10
—— Proof *FDC* £1
1981 .... 0.20
—— Proof *FDC* £1

4240 Half (1/2) penny. As illustration

1982 .... 0.10
—— Proof *FDC* £1
1983 .... 0.25
—— Proof *FDC* £1
1984* 2.00
—— Proof *FDC* £2

4250 Decimal specimen folder. Contains 1968 10p and 5p and 1971 2p, 1p and 1/2p 0.50

The new effigy was designed by Raphael David Maklouf, FRSA. It is only the third portrait of the Queen to be used on UK coinage, the previous change of portrait being in 1968 with the introduction of decimal coins. The designer's initials R.D.M. appear on the truncation. There is no portrait change on the Maundy coins.

GOLD

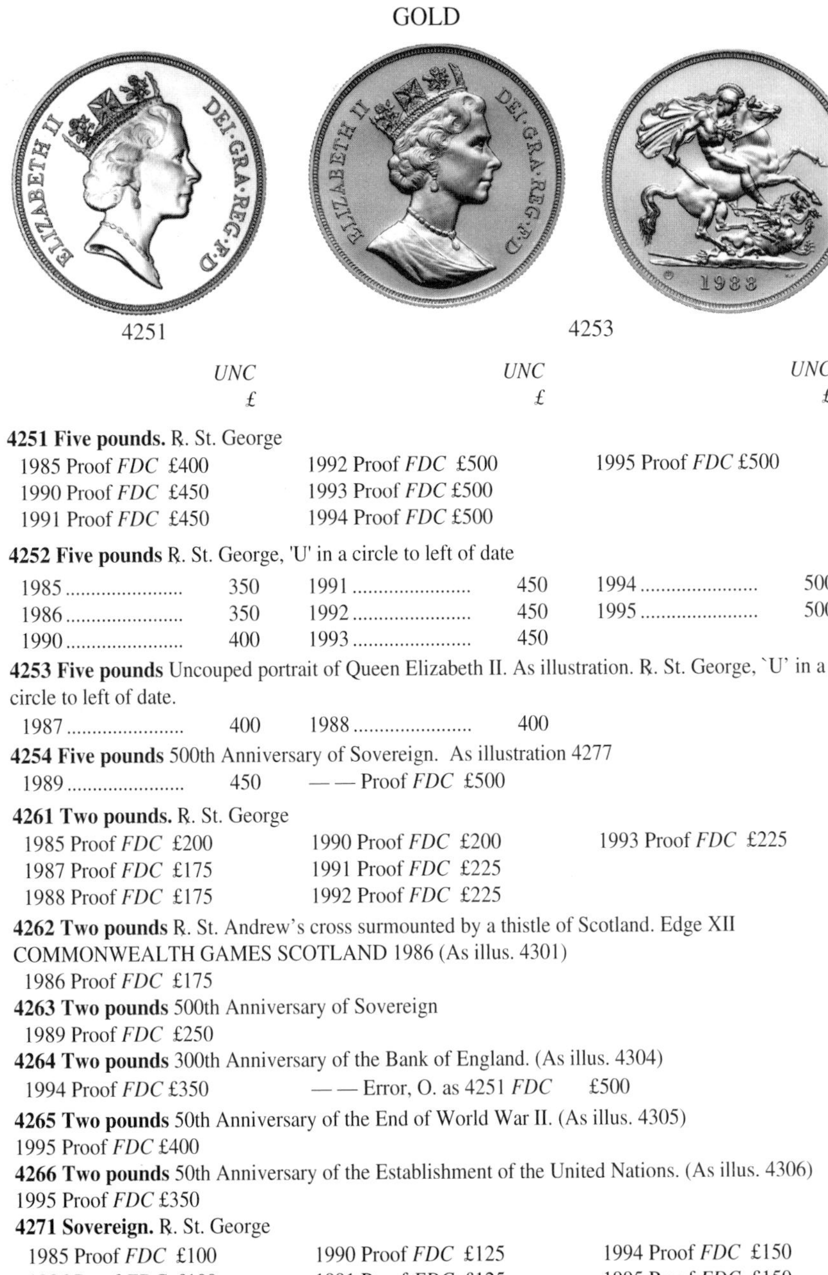

4251 4253

	UNC £		*UNC* £		*UNC* £

4251 Five pounds. R. St. George

1985 Proof *FDC* £400 — 1992 Proof *FDC* £500 — 1995 Proof *FDC* £500
1990 Proof *FDC* £450 — 1993 Proof *FDC* £500
1991 Proof *FDC* £450 — 1994 Proof *FDC* £500

4252 Five pounds R. St. George, 'U' in a circle to left of date

1985	350	1991	450	1994	500
1986	350	1992	450	1995	500
1990	400	1993	450		

4253 Five pounds Uncouped portrait of Queen Elizabeth II. As illustration. R. St. George, `U' in a circle to left of date.

1987	400	1988	400

4254 Five pounds 500th Anniversary of Sovereign. As illustration 4277

1989 .... 450 — — Proof *FDC* £500

4261 Two pounds. R. St. George

1985 Proof *FDC* £200 — 1990 Proof *FDC* £200 — 1993 Proof *FDC* £225
1987 Proof *FDC* £175 — 1991 Proof *FDC* £225
1988 Proof *FDC* £175 — 1992 Proof *FDC* £225

4262 Two pounds R. St. Andrew's cross surmounted by a thistle of Scotland. Edge XII COMMONWEALTH GAMES SCOTLAND 1986 (As illus. 4301)

1986 Proof *FDC* £175

4263 Two pounds 500th Anniversary of Sovereign

1989 Proof *FDC* £250

4264 Two pounds 300th Anniversary of the Bank of England. (As illus. 4304)

1994 Proof *FDC* £350 — — Error, O. as 4251 *FDC* £500

4265 Two pounds 50th Anniversary of the End of World War II. (As illus. 4305)

1995 Proof *FDC* £400

4266 Two pounds 50th Anniversary of the Establishment of the United Nations. (As illus. 4306)

1995 Proof *FDC* £350

4271 Sovereign. R. St. George

1985 Proof *FDC* £100 — 1990 Proof *FDC* £125 — 1994 Proof *FDC* £150
1986 Proof *FDC* £100 — 1991 Proof *FDC* £125 — 1995 Proof *FDC* £150
1987 Proof *FDC* £100 — 1992 Proof *FDC* £150
1988 Proof *FDC* £100 — 1993 Proof *FDC* £150

4272 Sovereign. 500th Anniversary of Sovereign
1989 Proof *FDC* £160

4277

4276 Half-sovereign. ℞. St. George

1985 Proof *FDC* £60	1990 Proof *FDC* £70	1994 Proof *FDC* £75
1986 Proof *FDC* £60	1991 Proof *FDC* £70	1995 Proof *FDC* £75
1987 Proof *FDC* £60	1992 Proof *FDC* £70	
1988 Proof *FDC* £60	1993 Proof *FDC* £70	

4277 Half-sovereign 500th Anniversary of Sovereign
1989 Proof *FDC* £80

4281

UNC
£

4281 Britannia. One hundred pounds. (1oz of fine gold)
℞. Britannia standing.

1987	BV
— Proof *FDC* £300	
1988	BV
— Proof *FDC* £300	
1989	BV
— Proof *FDC* £350	
1990	BV
— Proof *FDC* £350	
1991	BV
— Proof *FDC* £400	
1992	BV
— Proof *FDC* £450	
1993	BV
— Proof *FDC* £450	
1994	BV
— Proof *FDC* £450	
1995	BV
— Proof *FDC* £450	

4286

	UNC £		UNC £
4286 Britannia. Fifty pounds. (1/2oz of fine gold).			
R. Britannia standing.		1991	BV
1987	BV	— Proof *FDC* £200	
— Proof *FDC* £160		1992	BV
1988	BV	— Proof *FDC* £250	
— Proof *FDC* £160		1993	BV
1989	BV	— Proof *FDC* £250	
— Proof *FDC* £175		1994	BV
1990	BV	— Proof *FDC* £250	
— Proof *FDC* £200		1995 Proof *FDC* £250	

4291

4291 Britannia. Twenty five pounds. (1/4oz of fine gold).			
R. Britannia standing.		1991	BV
1987	BV	— Proof *FDC* £120	
— Proof *FDC* £85		1992	BV
1988	BV	— Proof *FDC* £135	
— Proof *FDC* £85		1993	BV
1989	BV	— Proof *FDC* £135	
— Proof *FDC* £100		1994	BV
1990	BV	— Proof *FDC* £135	
— Proof *FDC* £120		1995 Proof *FDC* £135	

4296

4296 Britannia. Ten pounds.(1/10oz of fine gold).			
R Britania standing.		1991	BV
1987	BV	— Proof *FDC* £65	
— Proof *FDC* £50		1992	BV
1988	BV	— Proof *FDC* £65	
— Proof *FDC* £50		1993	BV
1989	BV	— Proof *FDC* £65	
— Proof *FDC* £55		1994	BV
1990	BV	— Proof *FDC* £65	
— Proof *FDC* £65		1995 Proof *FDC* £65	

For proof sets which include some or all of the above see the list on page 368.

NICKEL-BRASS

4301

	UNC £		*UNC* £

4301 Two pounds. ℞. St. Andrew's cross surmounted by a thistle of Scotland. Edge XIII COMMONWEALTH GAMES SCOTLAND 1986

1986	3	— Proof *FDC* £6	
— Specimen in presentation folder	5	— Proof in AR *FDC* £20	
— .500 silver	12	— For specimens struck in AV see 4262	

4302

4303

4302 Two pounds 300th Anniversary of Bill of Rights. ℞ Cypher of William and Mary, House of Commons mace and St. Edward's crown.

1989	3	— Proof AR *FDC* £23	
— Specimen in presentation folder	5	— Proof piedfort in AR *FDC* £45	
— Proof *FDC* £6			

4303 Two pounds 300th Anniversary of Claim of Right (Scotland). ℞. As 4302, but with crown of Scotland.

1989	5	— Proof in AR *FDC* £23	
— Specimen in presentation folder	6	— Proof piedfort in AR *FDC* £45	
— Proof *FDC* £8			

4304

4304 Two pounds 300th Anniversary of the Bank of England. ℞: Bank's original Corporate Seal, with Crown & Cyphers of William III & Mary II. Edge SIC VOC NON VOBIS.

1994	3	— — Proof AR *FDC* £24	
— — Specimen in presentation folder	4	— — Proof piedfort in AR *FDC* £45	
— — Proof *FDC* £6		— — For specimens struck in AV see 4264	

4305

4306

UNC £

4305 Two pounds 50th Anniversary of the End of World War II. R: A Dove of Peace. Edge 1945 IN PEACE GOODWILL

1995 3
— — Specimen in presentation folder 4
— — Proof *FDC* £6
— — Proof AV *FDC* £24
— — Proof piedfort in AV *FDC* £45
— — For specimens struck in AV see 4264

4306 Two pounds 50th Annversary of the Establishment of the United Nations. r: 50th Anniversary symbol and an array of flags. Edge NATIONS UNITED FOR PEACE 1945-1995.

1995 3
— — Specimen in presentation folder 4
— — Proof AR *FDC* £45
— — Proof piedfort in AR *FDC* £45
— — For specimens struck in AV see 4265

4311 4312

UNC £ *UNC* £

4311 One pound (Welsh design). Edge PLEIDIOL WYF I'M GWLAD

1985 2
— Specimen in presentation folder 3
— Proof *FDC* £5
— Proof in AR *FDC* £21
— Proof piedfort in AR *FDC* £45
1990 3
— Proof *FDC* £6
— Proof in AR *FDC* £21

4312 One pound (Northern Ireland design). Edge DECUS ET TUTAMEN

1986 2
— Specimen in presentation folder 3
— Proof *FDC* £4
— Proof in AR *FDC* £18
— Proof piedfort in AR *FDC* £45
1991 3
— Proof *FDC* £6
— Proof in AR *FDC* £20

4313

4314

4313 One pound (English design). Edge DECUS ET TUTAMEN

1987 2
— Specimen in presentation folder 3
— Proof *FDC* £6
— Proof in AR *FDC* £18
— Proof piedfort in AR *FDC* £45
1992 3
— Proof *FDC* £6
— Proof in AR *FDC* £21

4314 One pound (Royal Shield). Edge DECUS ET TUTAMEN

1988 2
— Specimen in presentation folder 3
— Proof *FDC* £8
— Proof in AR *FDC* £25
— Proof piedfort AR *FDC* £45

4315 One pound (Scottish design). Edge NEMO ME IMPUNE LACESSIT (Illus. as 4222)

1989 3
— Proof *FDC* £6
— Proof in AR *FDC* £18
— Proof piedfort in AR *FDC* £60

4316 One pound (Royal Arms design). Edge DECUS ET TUTAMEN (Illus. as 4221)

1993 3
— Proof *FDC* £6
— Proof in AR *FDC* £21
— Proof piedfort in AR *FDC* £45

4317

4317 One pound (Scottish design). R: Lion rampant within a double tressure. Edge NEMO ME IMPUGNE LACESSIT

1994 2
— Specimen in presentation folder 3
— — Proof *FDC* £6
— — Proof AR *FDC* £26
— — Proof piedfort in AR *FDC* £45

4318 One pound (Welsh design). R. Heraldic dragon Edge PLEIDIOL WYF I'M GWLAD

1985 2
— Specimen in presentation folder 3
— Proof *FDC* £5
— Proof in AR *FDC* £21
— Proof piedfort in AR *FDC* £55

CUPRO-NICKEL

4331

UNC
£

4331 Five pounds (crown). Queen Mother 90th birthday commemorative. 1990 7
— Specimen in presentation folder 9
— Proof in AR *FDC* £25
— Proof in AV *FDC* £500

4332

4332 Five Pounds (crown). 40th Anniversary of the Coronation. 1993 7
— Specimen in presentation folder 9
— Proof *FDC* £9
— Proof in Æ *FDC* £25
— Proof in AV *FDC* £650

4341

4341 Fifty pence. ℞. Britannia r.
1985 3
— — Proof *FDC* £3
1986* 3
— — Proof *FDC* £3
1987* 3
— — Proof *FDC* £3
1988* 3
— — Proof *FDC* £4
1989* 4
— — Proof *FDC* £3
1990* 4
— — Proof *FDC* £5
1991* 4
— — Proof *FDC* £5
1992* 4
— — Proof *FDC* £5
1993* 4
— — Proof *FDC* £4
1995* 3
— — Proof *FDC* £4

4342

4342 Fifty pence Presidency of the Council of European Community Ministers and completion of the Single Market. ℞ Conference table top and twelve stars
1992-1993 3
— Proof *FDC* £5
— Proof in Æ in case *FDC* £24
— Proof piedfort in Æ in case *FDC* £45
— Proof in AV in case *FDC* £375

4342A — Specimen in presentation folder with 1992 date 4341 5

4343

4343 Fifty pence 50th Anniversary of the Normandy Landings on D-Day. R: Allied Invasion Force.

1994 1
— — Specimen in presentation folder 2
— — Proof *FDC* £5
— — Proof AR *FDC* £23
— — Proof piedfort in AR *FDC* £45
— — Proof in AV *FDC* £375

4351

4351 Twenty pence. R. Crowned double rose

1985 ....
— — Proof *FDC* £2
1986* 1
— — Proof *FDC* £2
1987 ....
— — Proof *FDC* £2
1988 ....
— — Proof *FDC* £3
1989 ....
— — Proof *FDC* £3
1990 ....
— — Proof *FDC* £3
1991 ....
— — Proof *FDC* £3
1992 ....
— — Proof *FDC* £3
1993 ....
— — Proof *FDC* £3
1994 ....
— — Proof *FDC* £3
1995 ....
— — Proof *FDC* £3

4356

UNC
£

4356 Ten pence. R. Lion passant guardant

1985* 3
— — Proof *FDC* £2
1986* 2
— — Proof *FDC* £2
1987* 3
— — Proof *FDC* £3
1988* 3
— — Proof *FDC* £3
1989* 4
— – Proof *FDC* £3
1990* 4
— — Proof *FDC* £3
1991* 4
— — Proof *FDC* £3
1992* 3
— — Proof *FDC* £4
— — Proof in AR *FDC* £14

4357

4357 Ten pence ℞ Lion passant guardant: diam. 24.5mm

1992 ....
— — Proof *FDC* £3
— — Proof in AR *FDC* £14
— — Proof piedfort in AR *FDC* £30
1993* ....

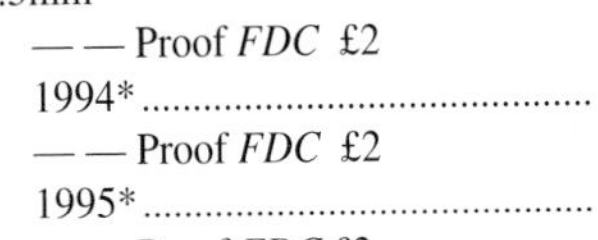

— — Proof *FDC* £2
1994* ....
— — Proof *FDC* £2
1995* ....
— — Proof *FDC* £2

4361

4361 Five pence. ℞. Crowned thistle

1985* 1
— — Proof *FDC* £1
1986* 1
— — Proof *FDC* £1
1987 ....
— — Proof *FDC* £2
1988 ....
— — Proof *FDC* £2
1989 ....
— — Proof *FDC* £2
1990* .... 2 
— — Proof *FDC* £3
— — Proof in AR *FDC* £12

4362

4362 Five pence. ℞. Crowned thistle: diam 18mm

1990 ....
— — Proof *FDC* £2
— — Proof in AR *FDC* £12
— — Proof piedfort in AR *FDC* £25
1991 ....
— — Proof *FDC* £2
1992 ....
— — Proof *FDC* £2
1993* ....
— — Proof *FDC* £2
1994 ....
— — Proof *FDC* £2
1995 ....
— — Proof *FDC* £2

BRONZE

4366

4366 Two pence. ℞. Plumes

1985 ....
— — Proof *FDC* £1
1986 ....
— — Proof *FDC* £1
1987 ....
— — Proof *FDC* £1
1988 ....
— — Proof *FDC* £1
1989 ....
— — Proof *FDC* £1
1990 ....
— — Proof *FDC* £1
1991 ....
— — Proof *FDC* £1
1992* ....
— — Proof FDC £1

4371

4371 One penny. ℞. Portcullis with chains

1985 ....
— — Proof *FDC* £1
1986 ....
— — Proof *FDC* £1
1987 ....
— — Proof *FDC* £1
1988 ....
— — Proof *FDC* £1
1989 ....
— — Proof *FDC* £1
1990 ....
— — Proof *FDC* £1
1991 ....
— — Proof *FDC* £1
1992* ....
— — Proof *FDC* £1

COPPER PLATED STEEL

4376 Two pence ℞. Plumes

1992 ....
1993 ....
— — Proof *FDC* £1
1994 ....
— — Proof *FDC* £1
1995 ....
— — Proof *FDC* £1

4381 One penny ℞. Portcullis with chains

1992 ....
1993 ....
— — Proof *FDC* £1
1994 ....
— — Proof *FDC* £1
1995 ....
— — Proof *FDC* £1

Issued by the Royal Mint in official case from 1887 onwards, but earlier sets were issued privately by the engraver.

All pieces have a finish superior to that of the current coins.

		No. of coins	*FDC £*
PS1	**George IV.** New issue, **1826.** Five pounds to farthing	(11)	18,000
PS2	**William IV.** Coronation, **1831.** Two pounds to farthing	(14)	16,000
PS3	**Victoria,** young head, **1839.** 'Una and the Lion' five pounds, and sovereign to farthing	(15)	27,500
PS4	— **1853.** Sovereign to quarter-farthing, including Gothic type crown	(16)	22,500
PS5	Jubilee head. Golden Jubilee, **1887.** Five pounds to threepence	(11)	5,250
PS6	— — Crown to threepence	(7)	850
PS7	Old head, **1893.** Five pounds to threepence	(10)	5,750
PS8	— — Crown to threepence	(6)	900
PS9	**Edward VII.** Coronation, **1902.** Five pounds to Maundy penny. Matt surface	(13)	1,450
PS10	— — Sovereign to Maundy penny. Matt surface	(11)	375
PS11	**George V.** Coronation, **1911.** Five pounds to Maundy penny	(12)	2,450
PS12	— — Sovereign to Maundy penny	(10)	650
PS13	— — Halfcrown to Maundy penny	(8)	300
PS14	New types, **1927.** Crown to threepence	(6)	200
PS15	**George VI.** Coronation, **1937.** Gold. Five pounds to half-sovereign	(4)	1,450
PS16	— — — Silver, etc. Crown to farthing, including Maundy	(15)	110
PS17	Mid-Century, **1950.** Halfcrown to farthing	(10)	35
PS18	Festival of Britain, **1951.** Crown to farthing	(10)	50
PS19	**Elizabeth II.** Coronation, **1953.** Crown to farthing	(10)	35
PS20	'Last Sterling' set, **1970.** Halfcrown to halfpenny plus medallion	(8)	15
PS21	Decimal coinage set, **1971.** 50 new pence ('Britannia') to 1/2 penny, plus medallion	(6)	10
PS22	— **1972.** As last, but includes the cu.-ni. Silver Wedding crown	(7)	12
PS23	— **1973.** As PS21 but 'EEC' 50p	(6)	10
PS24	— **1974.** As PS21	(6)	8
PS25	— **1975.** As last	(6)	7
PS26	— **1976.** As last	(6)	6
PS27	— **1977.** As PS21 but including the proof Silver Jubilee crown struck in cupro-nickel	(7)	10
PS28	— **1978.** As PS21	(6)	12
PS29	— **1979.** As last	(6)	8
PS30	— **1980.** As last	(6)	7
PS31	— — Five pounds to half-sovereign	(4)	700
PS32	— **1981.** U.K. Proof coin Commemorative collection. (Consists of £5, £1, Royal Wedding crown (25p) in Æ, plus base metal proofs as PS21.)	(9)	500
PS33	— — As PS21	(6)	8
PS34	**Elizabeth II, 1982.** Uncirculated (specimen) set in Royal Mint folder. New reverse types, including 20 pence	(7)	7
PS35	— — As last but proofs in Royal Mint sealed plastic case, plus medallion	(7)	8
PS36	— AV Five pounds to half-sovereign	(4)	750
PS37	— **1983.** As PS34, includes 'U.K.' £1	(8)	12
PS38	— — As PS35, includes 'U.K.' £1	(8)	14
PS39	— — AV £2, £1, £1/2 in case	(3)	300
PS40	— **1984.** As PS37 but with 'Scottish' £1	(8)	11
PS41	— — As PS38 but with 'Scottish' £1	(8)	14
PS42	— — AV £5, £1, £1/2 in case	(3)	525

PS43 — **1985.** As PS37 but with new portrait, also includes 'Welsh' £1. The set does not contain the now discontinued halfpenny .... (7) 8

PS44 — — As last but proofs in Royal Mint sealed plastic case, plus medallion (7) 14

PS45 — — As last but within a deluxe red leather case .... (7) 18

PS46 — — AV £5, £2, £1, £1/2 in case .... (4) 750

PS47 — **1986.** As PS43 but with new two pounds and the 'Northern Ireland' £1 (8) 12

PS48 — — As PS44 but with two pounds and 'Northern Ireland' £1 .... (8) 18

PS49 — — As last but within a deluxe red leather case .... (8) 22

PS50 — — AV £2 (as 4262), £1, £1/2 in a deluxe red leather case .... (3) 300

PS51 — **1987.** As PS43 but with 'English' £1 .... (7) 8

PS52 — — As last but proofs in Royal Mint sealed plastic case, plus medallion (7) 20

PS53 — — As last but within a deluxe red leather case .... (7) 24

PS54 — — AV £2 (as 4261), £1, £1/2 in a deluxe red leather case .... (3) 300

PS55 — — **Britannia AV** proofs. £100, £50, £25, £10 in a deluxe case .... (4) 575

PS56 — — As last but only containing the £25, £10 in a deluxe case .... (2) 125

PS57 — **1988.** As PS43 but with 'Arms' £1 .... (7) 9

PS58 — — As last but proofs in Royal Mint sealed plastic case, plus medallion (7) 25

PS59 — — As last but within a deluxe leather case .... (7) 29

PS60 — — AV £2 (as 4261), £1, £1/2 in a deluxe case .... (3) 325

PS61 — — **Britannia** proofs. As PS55 .... (4) 575

PS62 — — As PS56 .... (2) 125

PS63 — **1989.** As PS43 but with 'Scotland' £1 .... (7) 13

PS64 — — As last but proofs and with 2 x £2 .... (9) 28

PS65 — — As last but within red leather case .... (9) 32

PS66 — — Sovereign Anniversary AV £5, £2, £1, £1/2 .... (4) 900

PS67 — — As last but only containing £2, £1, £1/2 .... (3) 450

PS68 — — 2 x £2 in Royal Mint folder .... (2) 9

PS69 — — As last but silver piedfort proofs .... (2) 85

PS70 — — As last but silver proofs .... (2) 42

PS71 — — **Britannia** proofs. As PS55 .... (4) 675

PS72 — — As PS56 .... (2) 150

PS73 — **1990.** As PS43 but with 'Welsh' £1 and new 5p .... (8) .15

PS74 — — As last but proofs .... (8) 25

PS75 — — As last but within red leather case .... (8) 29

PS76 — — AV £5, £2, £1, £1/2 in case .... (4) 775

PS77 — — AV £2, £1, £1/2 in case .... (3) 375

PS78 — — 2 x 5p AR proofs (as 4361 and 4362) .... (2) 24

PS79 — — **Britannia** proofs. As PS55 .... (4) 725

PS80 — **1991.** As PS43 but with 'Northern Ireland' £1 .... (7) 10

PS81 — — As last but proofs .... (7) 25

PS82 — — As last but within red leather case .... (7) 30

PS83 — — AV £5, £2, £1, £1/2 in case .... (4) 850

PS84 — — AV £2, £1, £1/2 in case .... (3) 400

PS85 — — Britannia proofs. As PS55 .... (4) 775

PS86 — **1992** As PS43 but with 'English £1' and 'European Community' 50p.... (9) 11

PS87 — — As last but proofs .... (9) 28

PS88 — — As last but with red leather case .... (9) 33

PS89 — — AV £5, £2, £1, £1/2 in case .... (4) 875

PS90 — — AV £2, £1, £1/2 in case .... (3) 425

PS91 — — 2 x 10p AR proofs. (As 4356 and 4357.) .... (2) 28

PS92 — — Britannia proofs. As PS55 .... (4) 900

PS93	— **1993.** As PS43 but with 'UK' £1 and 'European Community' 50p	(8)	9
PS49	— — As last but proofs and with Coronation Anniversary £5 but no 'European Community' 50p	(8)	29
PS95	— — As last but with red leather case	(8)	34
PS96	— — AV £5, £2, £1, £½ with silver Pistrucci medal in case	(5)	900
PS97	— — AV £2, £1, £½ in case	(3)	425
PS98	— — **Britannia** proofs. As PS55	(4)	900
PS99	— **1994**. As PS43 but with 'Bank' £2, 'Scotland' £1 and 'D-Day' 50p	(8)	9
PS100	— — As last but proofs	(8)	20
PS101	— — As last but with red leather case	(8)	30
PS102	— — AV £5, £2, £1, £½ in case	(4)	1050
PS103	— — AV £2 (as 4264), £1, £½ in case	(3)	500
PS104	— — **Britannia** proofs. As PS55	(4)	900
PS105	— **1995**. As PS43 but with 'Peace' £2 and 'Wales' £1	(8)	9
PS106	— — As last but proofs	(8)	24
PS107	— — As last but with red leather case	(8)	32
PS108	— — AV £5, £2, £1, £1/2 in case	(4)	1100
PS109	— — AV £2 (as 4265), £1, £1/2 in case	(3)	500
PS110	— — **Britannia** proofs. As PS55	(4)	1000

The prices given are for absolutely perfect sets with uncleaned, brilliant or matt surfaces. Sets are often seen with one or more coins showing imperfections such as scratches,bumps on the edge, etc. Any flaws will substantially affect the value of a set.

APPENDIX I

A SELECT NUMISMATIC BIBLIOGRAPHY

Listed below is a selection of general books on British numismatics and other works that the specialist collector will need to consult.

General Books:

BROOKE, G. C. *English Coins.* (3rd Ed., 1951).
CHALLIS, C. E. (ED.) *A New History of the Royal Mint*
GRUEBER, H. A. *Handbook of the Coins of Great Britain and Ireland.*
KENYON, R. Ll. *Gold Coins of England.*
NORTH, J. J. *English Hammered Coins,* Vol. I, c. 650-1272; Vol. II, 1272-1662.
SEABY, P.J. *The Story of British Coinage*
SUTHERLAND, C. H. V. *English Coinage, 600-1900.*

Specialist Works:

ALLEN, D. *The Origins of Coinage in Britain: A Reappraisal.*
ALLEN, D. F. *English Coins in the British Museum: The Cross-and-Crosslets ('Tealby') type of Henry II.*
BESLY, E. *Coins and Medals of the English Civil War*
BLUNT, C. E. and WHITTON, C. A. *The Coinages of Edward IV and of Henry VI (Restored).*
BROOKE, G. C. *English Coins in the British Museum: The Norman Kings.*
DICKINSON, M. *Seventeenth Century Tokens of the British Isles*
DOLLEY, R. H. M. (ED.). *Anglo-Saxon Coins; studies presented to Sir Frank Stenton.*

KEARY, C. and GREUBER, H. *English Coins in the British Museum: Anglo-Saxon Series.*
LAWRENCE, L. A. *The Coinage of Edward III from 1351.*
LINECAR, H. W. A. *British Coin Designs and Designers.*
MACK, R. P. *The Coinage of Ancient Britain.*
MARSH, M. A. *The Gold Sovereign and The Gold Half Sovereign.*
MORRIESON, LT.-COL. H. W. *The Coinages of Thomas Bushell, 1636-1648.*
NORTH, J. J. and PRESTON-MORLEY, P. J. *The John G. Brooker Collection: Coins of Charles I.*
PECK, C. W. *English Copper, Tin and Bronze Coins in the British Museum, 1558-1958.*
SEABY H.A. and RAYNER, P.A. *The English Silver Coinage from 1649.* 5th ed.
SPINK & SON, LTD. *The Milled Coinage of England, 1662-1946.*
VAN ARSDELL R. *Celtic Coinage of Britain.*
WHITTON, C. A. *The Heavy Coinage of Henry VI.*

Other authoritative papers are published in the *Numismatic Chronicle* and *British Numismatic Journal.* A complete book list is available from Seaby Publications, 4 Fitzhardinge Street, London, W1H 0AH.

APPENDIX II

FOREIGN LEGENDS ON ENGLISH COINS

A DOMINO FACTUM EST ISTUD ET EST MIRABILE IN OCULIS NOSTRIS. (This is the Lord's doing and it is marvellous in our eyes: *Psalm 118.23.*) First used on 'fine' sovereign of Mary.

AMOR POPULI PRAESIDIUM REGIS. (The love of the people is the King's protection.) Reverse legend on angels of Charles I.

ANNO REGNI PRIMO, etc. (In the first year of the reign, etc.) Used around the edge of many of the larger milled denominations.

CHRISTO AUSPICE REGNO. (I reign under the auspice of Christ.) Used extensively in the reign of Charles I.

CIVIUM INDUSTRIA FLORET CIVITAS. (By the industry of its people the State flourishes) On the 1951 Festival crown of George VI.

CULTORES SUI DEUS PROTEGIT. (God protects His worshippers.) On gold double crowns and crowns of Charles I.

DECUS ET TUTAMEN. (An ornament and a safeguard.) This inscription on the edge of all early large milled silver was suggested by Evelyn, he having seen it on the vignette in Card. Richelieu's Greek Testament, and of course refers to the device as a means to prevent clipping. (Virgil, *Aen* v.262.) This legend also appears on the edge of U.K. and Northern Ireland one pound coins.

DIEU ET MON DROIT. (God and my right.) On halfcrowns of George IV and later monarchs

DIRIGE DEUS GRESSUS MEOS. (May the Lord direct my steps.) On the 'Una' 5 pounds of Queen Victoria.

DOMINE NE IN FURORE TUO ARGUAS ME. (O Lord, rebuke me not in Thine anger: *Psalm 6, 1.).* First used on the half-florin of Edward III and then on all half-nobles.

D*omi*N*us Deus Omnipotens* REX. (Lord God, Almighty King.) (Viking coins.)

DUM SPIRO SPERO. (Whilst I live, I hope.) On the coins struck at Pontefract Castle during the Civil War after Charles I had been imprisoned.

EXALTABITUR IN GLORIA. (He shall be exalted in glory.) On all quarter-nobles.

EXURGAT DEUS ET DISSIPENTUR INIMICI EIUS. (Let God arise and let His enemies be scattered: *Psalm* 68, 1.) On the Scottish ducat and early English coins of James I (VI) and was chosen by the King himself. Also on CI, civil war, declaration coins,

FACIAM EOS IN GENTEM UNAM. (I will make them one nation: *Ezek. 37, 22.)* On unites and laurels of James I.

FLORENT CONCORDIA REGNA. (Through concord kingdoms flourish.) On gold unite of Charles I and broad of Charles II.

HANC DEUS DEDIT. (God has given this, i.e. crown .) On siege-pieces of Pontefract struck in the name of Charles II.

HAS NISI PERITURUS MIHI ADIMAT NEMO. (Let no one remove these [letters] from me under penalty of death.) On the edge of crowns and half-crowns of Cromwell.

HENRICUS ROSAS REGNA JACOBUS. (Henry united the roses, James the kingdoms.) On English and Scottish gold coins of James I (VI).

HONI SOIT QUI MAL Y PENSE. (Evil to him who evil thinks.) The Motto of the Order of the Garter, first used on the Hereford (?) halfcrowns of Charles I. It also occurs on the Garter Star in the centre of the reverse of the silver coins of Charles II, but being so small it is usually illegible; it is more prominent on the coinage of George III.

ICH DIEN. (I serve.) Aberystwyth Furnace 2d, and Decimal 2p.

INIMICOS EJUS INDUAM CONFUSIONE. (As for his enemies I shall clothe them with shame: *Psalm* 132, 18.) On shillings of Edward VI struck at Durham House, Strand.

JESUS AUTEM TRANSIENS PER MEDIUM ILLORUM IBAT. (But Jesus, passing through the midst of them, went His way: *Luke iv. 30.)* The usual reverse legend on English nobles, ryals and hammered sovereigns before James I; also on the very rare Scottish noble of David II of Scotland and the unique Anglo-Gallic noble of Edward the Black Prince.

JUSTITIA THRONUM FIRMAT. (Justice strengthens the throne.) On Charles I half-groats and pennies and Scottish twenty-penny pieces.

LUCERNA PEDIBUS MEIS VERBUM EST. (Thy word is a lamp unto my feet: *Psalm 119, 105.)* Obverse legend on a rare half-sovereign of Edward VI struck at Durham House, Strand.

MIRABILIA FECIT. (He made marvellously.) On the Viking coins of (?) York.

NEMO ME IMPUNE LACESSIT. (No-one provokes me with impunity.) On the 1984 Scottish one pound.

NUMMORUM FAMULUS. (The servant of the coinage.) The legend on the edge of the English tin coinage at the end of the seventeenth century.

O CRUX AVE SPES UNICA. (Hail! O Cross, our only hope.) On the reverse of all half-angels.

PAX MISSA PER ORBEM. (Peace sent throughout the world.) The reverse legend of a pattern farthing of Anne.

PAX QUÆRITUR BELLO. (Peace is sought by war.) The reverse legend of the Cromwell broad.

PER CRUCEM TUAM SALVA NOS CHRISTE REDEMPTOR. (By Thy cross, save us, O Christ, our Redeemer.) The normal reverse of English angels.

PLEIDIOL WYF I'M GWLAD. (True am I to my country.) Taken from the Welsh National Anthem. Used on the 1985 Welsh one pound.

POST MORTEM PATRIS PRO FILIO. (For the son after the death of the father.) On siege-pieces struck at Pontefract in 1648 (old style) after the execution of Charles I.

POSUI DEUM ADJUTOREM MEUM. (I have made God my Helper: *comp. Psalm* 54,

4.) Used on many English and Irish silver coins from Edward III until 1603. Altered to POSUIMUS and NOSTRUM on the coins of Philip and Mary.

PROTECTOR LITERIS LITERÆ NUMMIS CORONA ET SALUS. (A protection to the letters [on the face of the coin], the letters [on the edge] are a garland and a safeguard to the coinage.) On the edge of the rare fifty-shilling piece of Cromwell.

QUÆ DEUS CONJUNXIT NEMO SEPARET. (What God hath joined together let no man put asunder: *Matt. 19, 6.)* On the larger silver English and Scottish coins of James I after he succeeded to the English throne.

REDDE CUIQUE QUOD SUUM EST. (Render to each that which is his own.) On a Henry VIII type groat of Edward VI struck by Sir Martin Bowes at Durham House, Strand.

RELIGIO PROTESTANTIVM LEGES ANGLIÆ LIBERTAS PARLIAMENTI. (The religion of the Protestants, the laws of England, the liberty of the Parliament.) This is known as the 'Declaration' and refers to Charles I's declaration to the Privy Council at Wellington, 19th Sept., 1642; it is found on many of his coins struck at the provincial mints during the Civil War. Usually abbreviated to REL:PROT:LEG:ANG:LIB:PAR:

ROSA SINE SPINA. (A rose without a thorn.) Found on some gold and small coins of Henry VIII and later reigns.

RUTILANS ROSA SINE SPINA. (A dazzling rose without a thorn.) As last but on small gold only.

SCUTUM FIDEI PROTEGET EUM or EAM. (The shield of faith shall protect him or her.) On much of the gold of Edward VI and Elizabeth.

SIC VOC NON VOBIS (Thus we labour but not for ourselves). 1994 £2 Bank of England.

TALI DICATA SIGNO MENS FLUCTUARI NEQUIT. (Consecrated by such a sign the mind cannot waver: from a hymn by Prudentius written in the fourth century, entitled 'Hymnus ante Somnum'.) Only on the gold 'George noble' of Henry VIII.

TIMOR DOMINI FONS VITÆ. (The fear of the Lord is a fountain of life: *Prov. 14, 27.)* On many shillings of Edward VI.

TVAETUR UNITA DEUS. (May God guard these united, i.e. kingdoms.) On many English Scottish and Irish coins of James I.

VERITAS TEMPORIS FILIA. (Truth, the daughter of Time.) On English and Irish coins of Mary Tudor.

Some Royal Titles:

REX ANGL*orum*—King of the English.

REX SAXONUM OCCIDENTA LIM —King of the West Saxons.

DEI GRA*tia* ANGL*iae* ET FRANC*iae* D*omi*N*us* HYB*erniae* ET AQVIT*aniae*—*By the Grace of God, King of* England and France, Lord of Ireland and Aquitaine.

D*ei* GRA*tia* M*agnae* B*ritanniae*, FR*anciae* ET H*iberniae* REX F*idei* D*efensor* BR*unsviciensis* ET L*uneburgen-sis* D*ux*, S*acri* R*omani* I*mperii* A*rchi*-TH*esaurarius* ET EL*ector*=By the Grace of God, King of Great Britain, France and Ireland, Defender of the Faith, Duke of Brunswick and Luneburg, High Treasurer and Elector of the Holy Roman Empire.

BRITANNIARUM REX —King of the Britains (i.e. Britain and British territories overseas).

BRITT:OMN:REX:FID:DEF:IND:IMP: —King of all the Britains, Defender of the Faith, Emperor of India.

NUMISMATIC CLUBS AND SOCIETIES

Coins News is the major monthly numismatic magazine. Spink's *Numismatic Circular* is long established, its first edition appeared in December 1892. There are many numismatic magazines which carry articles of interest, such as the *CNG Review* and the *S & B Bulletin*. Many local clubs and societies are affiliated to the British Association of Numismatic Societies, (B.A.N.S) which holds an annual Congress. Details of your nearest numismatic club can be obtained from the Hon. Secretary, Philip Mernick, British Association of Numismatic Societies, c/o Bush, Boake Allen Ltd. Blackhorse Lane, London E17 5QP. The two principal learned societies are the Royal Numismatic Society, c/o Department of Coins and Medals, the British Museum, Great Russell Street, Bloomsbury, London WC1 3DG, and the British Numismatic Society, c/o Graham Dyer, The Royal Mint, Llantrisant, Pontyclun, mid Glamorgan, Wales. Both these societies publish an annual journal.

APPENDIX III

MINTMARKS AND OTHER SYMBOLS ON ENGLISH COINS

A MINTMARK (*mm.),* a term borrowed from Roman and Greek numismatics where it showed the place of mintage, was generally used on English coins to show where the legend began (a religious age preferred a cross for the purpose). Later, this mark, since the dating of coins was not usual, had a periodic significance, changing from time to time. Hence it was of a secret or 'privy' nature; other privy marks on a coin might be the code-mark of a particular workshop or workman. Thus a privy mark (including the *mm.)* might show when a coin was made, or who made it. In the use of precious metals this knowledge was necessary to guard against fraud and counterfeiting.

Mintmarks are sometimes termed 'initial marks' as they are normally placed at the commencement of the inscription. Some of the symbols chosen were personal badges of the ruling monarch, such as the rose and sun of York, the boar's head of Richard III, the dragon of Henry Tudor or the thistle of James I; others are heraldic symbols or may allude to the mint master responsible for the coinage, e.g. the *mm.* bow used on the Durham House coins struck under John Bowes and the WS mark of William Sharrington of Bristol.

A table of mintmarks is given on the next page. Where mintmarks appear in the catalogue they are sometimes referred to only by the reference number, in order to save space, i.e. *mm. 28* (=mintmark Sun), *mm.28/74 (=mm. S*un on obverse, mm. Coronet on reverse), *mm.* 28/- (=*mm.* Sun on obverse only).

MINTMARKS AND OTHER SYMBOLS

1 Edward III, Cross 1 (Class B+C).
2 Edward III, broken Cross 1 (Class D).
3 Edward III, Cross 2 (Class E)
4 Edward III, Cross 3 (Class G)
5 Cross Potent (Edw. III Treaty)
6 Cross Pattee (Edw. III Post Treaty Rich. III).
7 (a) Plain of Greek Cross. (b) Cross Moline.
8 Cross Patonce.
9 Cross Fleuree.
10 Cross Calvary (Cross on steps).
11 Long Cross Fitchee.
12 Short Cross Fitchee.
13 Restoration Cross (Hen. VI).
14 Latin Cross.
15 Voided Cross (Henry VI).
16 Saltire Cross.
17 Cross and 4 pellets.
18 Pierced Cross.
19 Pierced Cross & pellet.
20 Pierced Cross & central pellet.
21 Cross Crosslet.
22 Curved Star (rayant).
23 Star.
24 Spur Rowel.
25 Mullet.
26 Pierced Mullet.
27 Eglantine.
28 Sun (Edw. IV).
29 Mullet (Henry V).
30 Pansy.
31 Heraldic Cinquefoil (Edw. IV).
32 Heraldic Cinquefoil (James I).
33 Rose (Edw. IV).
34 Rosette (Edw. IV).
35 Rose (Chas. I).
36 Catherine Wheel.
37 Cross in circle.
38 Halved Sun (6 rays) & Rose.
39 Halved Sun (4 rays) & Rose.
40 Lis-upon-Half-Rose.
41 Lis-upon-Sun & Rose.
42 Lis-Rose dimidiated.
43 Lis-issuant-from-Rose.
44 Trefoil.
45 Slipped Trefoil, James I (1).
46 Slipped Trefoil, James I (2).
47 Quatrefoil.
48 Saltire.
49 Pinecone.
50 Leaf (-mascle, Hen. VI).
51 Leaf (-trefoil, Hen. VI).
52 Arrow.
53 Pheon.
54 A.
55 Annulet.
56 Annulet-with-pellet.
57 Anchor.
58 Anchor & B.
59 Flower & B.
60 Bell.
61 Book.
62 Boar's Head (early Richard III).
63 Boar's Head (later Richard III).
64 Boar's Head, Charles I.
65 Acorn (a) Hen. VIII (b) Elizabeth.
66 Bow.
67 Br. (Bristol, Chas. I).
68 Cardinal's Hat.
69 Castle (Henry VIII).
70 Castle with H.
71 Castle (Chas. I).
72 Crescent (a) Henry VIII (b) Elizabeth.
73 Pomegranate. (Mary; Henry VIII's is broader).
74 Coronet.
75 Crown.
76 Crozier (a) Edw. III (b) Hen. VIII.
77 Ermine.
78 Escallop (Hen. VII).
79 Escallop (James I).
80 Eye (in legend Edw. IV).
81 Eye (Parliament).
82 Radiate Eye (Hen. VII).
83 Gerb.
84 Grapes.
85 Greyhound's Head.
86 Hand.
87 Harp.
88 Heart.
89 Helmet.
90 Key.
91 Leopard's Head.
91A Crowned Leopard's Head with collar (Edw. VI).
92 Lion.
93 Lion rampant.
94 Martlet.
95 Mascle.
96 Negro's Head.
97 Ostrich's Head.
98 P in brackets.
99 Pall.
100 Pear.
101 Plume.
102 Plume. Aberystwyth and Bristol.
103 Plume. Oxford.
104 Plume. Shrewsbury.
105 Lis.
106 Lis.
107 Portcullis.
108 Portcullis, Crowned.
109 Sceptre.
110 Sunburst.
111 Swan.
112 R in brackets.
113 Sword.
114 T (Henry VIII).
115 TC monogram.
116 WS monogram.
117 y or Y.
118 Dragon (Henry VII).
119 (a) Triangle (b) Triangle in Circle.
120 Sun (Parliament).
121 Uncertain mark.
122 Grapple.
123 Tun.
124 Woolpack.
125 Thistle.
126 Figure 6 (Edw. VI).
127 Floriated cross.
128 Lozenge.
129 Billet.
130 Plume. Bridgenorth or late declaration
131 Two lions.
132 Clasped book.
133 Cross pomee.
134 Bugle.
135 Crowned T (Tournai, Hen VIII)
136 An incurved pierced cross

The reign after a mintmark indicates that from which the drawing is taken. A similar mm. may have been used in another reign and will be found in the chronological list at the beginning of each reign..

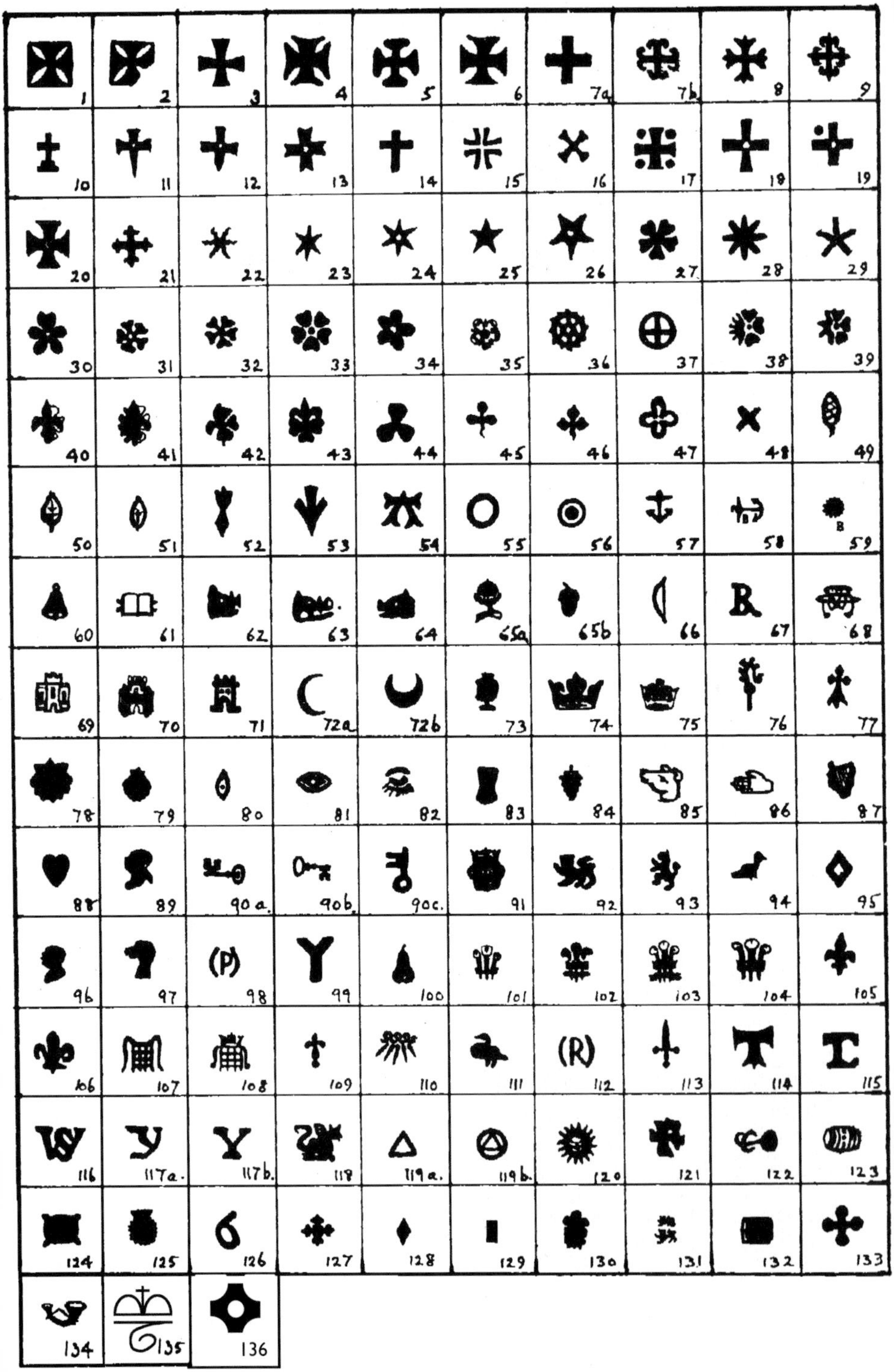

1	2	3	4	5	6	7a	7b	8	9
10	11	12	13	14	15	16	17	18	19
20	21	22	23	24	25	26	27	28	29
30	31	32	33	34	35	36	37	38	39
40	41	42	43	44	45	46	47	48	49
50	51	52	53	54	55	56	57	58	59
60	61	62	63	64	65a	65b	66	67	68
69	70	71	72a	72b	73	74	75	76	77
78	79	80	81	82	83	84	85	86	87
88	89	90a	90b	90c	91	92	93	94	95
96	97	98	99	100	101	102	103	104	105
106	107	108	109	110	111	112	113	114	115
116	117a	117b	118	119a	119b	120	121	122	123
124	125	126	127	128	129	130	131	132	133
134	135	136							

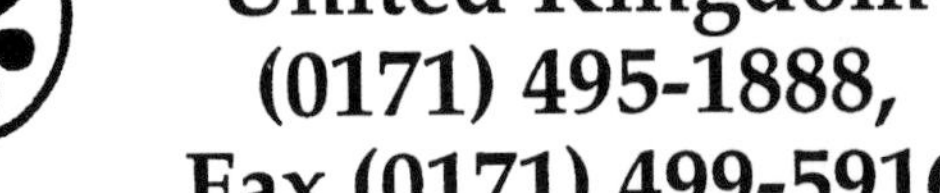

ABOUT THE EDITORS

Stephen Mitchell and Brian Reeds have a combined professional numismatic experience of over 55 years. They both started work at B A Seaby Ltd in the late 1960s having previously been collectors. In the late 1980s, after nearly 20 years with Seaby, they separately established their own independent businesses. During this period they have covered all aspects of British Coins with some specialisation.

Brian and Stephen are well respected within both trade and academic circles, but more importantly by many hundreds of collectors at home and overseas.

They have travelled extensively and as well as at most major auctions can be seen attending all important coin shows. If you would like to contact either of them about this catalogue or as professional dealers, both have regular lists of items for sale and are very keen to purchase single items or collections.

Stephen Mitchell	Brian Reeds
trading as	Grass Walk
Studio Coins	Wood Lane, South Heath
16 Kilham Lane	Great Missenden
Winchester	Buckinghamshire
SO22 5PT	HP16 0RB
Tel: 01962 853156	Tel: 01494 862161
SAE for list.	SAE for list.